ALL·IN·ONE

CCSP®

Certified Cloud Security Professional

EXAM GUIDE

Daniel Carter

New York   Chicago   San Francisco
Athens   London   Madrid   Mexico City
Milan   New Delhi   Singapore   Sydney   Toronto

Library of Congress Cataloging-in-Publication Data

Names: Carter, Daniel, CISSP, author.

Title: CCSP certified cloud security professional all-in-one exam guide /
   Daniel Carter.

Description: 1 | New York : McGraw-Hill Education, [2017]

Identifiers: LCCN 2016048628| ISBN 9781259835438 (book) | ISBN 9781259835445
   (CD) | ISBN 9781259835469 (set)

Subjects: LCSH: Cloud computing—Security measures—Examinations—Study
   guides. | Computer networks—Security measures—Examinations—Study
   guides. | Telecommunications engineers—Certification—Study guides. |
   BISAC: COMPUTERS / Certification Guides / General.

Classification: LCC QA76.585 .C357 2017 | DDC 004.67/82—dc23 LC record available at
https://lccn.loc.gov/2016048628

McGraw-Hill Education books are available at special quantity discounts to use as premiums and sales promotions, or for use in corporate training programs. To contact a representative, please visit the Contact Us pages at www.mhprofessional.com.

CCSP® Certified Cloud Security Professional All-in-One Exam Guide

23456789   LCR   21 20 19 18 17

ISBN: Book p/n 978-1-25-983543-8 and CD p/n 978-1-25-983544-5
of set 978-1-25-983546-9

MHID: Book p/n 1-25-983543-X and CD p/n 1-25-983544-8
of set 1-25-983546-4

Sponsoring Editor	Technical Editor	Production Supervisor
Wendy Rinaldi	Gerry Sneeringer	Lynn M. Messina
Editorial Supervisor	**Copy Editor**	**Composition**
Janet Walden	Bart Reed	Cenveo Publisher Services
Project Manager	**Proofreader**	**Illustration**
Anju Joshi,	Rick Camp	Cenveo Publisher Services
Cenveo® Publisher Services	**Indexer**	**Art Director, Cover**
Acquisitions Coordinator	Jack Lewis	Jeff Weeks
Claire Yee		

This book is dedicated to my children—Zachariah, Malachi, Alannah, and Ezra. I love you all so much, and look forward to seeing how each of you four very unique souls will change the world for the better!

ABOUT THE AUTHOR

Daniel Carter, CISSP, CCSP, CISM, CISA, is currently working as a Systems Security Officer for U.S. Federal Healthcare at Hewlett-Packard Enterprise as well as a project manager for a large-scale Splunk implementation. An IT security and systems professional for almost 20 years, he has worked extensively with web-based applications and infrastructure, as well as LDAP and federated identity systems, PKI, SIEM, and Linux/Unix systems. He is currently working on teams developing cloud computing and security roadmaps for federal government use and healthcare systems, from both a security and cloud computing perspective. Daniel holds a degree in criminology and criminal justice from the University of Maryland and a master's degree in technology management, with a focus on homeland security management, from the University of Maryland, University College.

About the Technical Editor

Gerry Sneeringer, CISSP, has been an IT professional with the University of Maryland for the past 30 years. He has been involved in customer support, systems programming, system administration (including operation of one of the Internet's root domain name servers), and network engineering. For the past 15 years, he has been the head of security in the university's central IT office. Gerry currently serves as the university's Chief Information Security Officer, overseeing the protection of university computing services hosted locally and in the cloud. Gerry holds a bachelor's degree in computer science from the University of Maryland.

CONTENTS AT A GLANCE

CONTENTS

ACKNOWLEDGMENTS

This is my first entry into the world of writing, and I first want to thank Matt Walker for connecting me to this opportunity and encouraging me to take it on. As a new author, I hope that you find this book to be a very informative and comprehensive aid in your own professional development and growth.

I want to thank Gerry Sneeringer for his efforts as technical editor on this project first and foremost, but more importantly for all the knowledge and experience he has bestowed on me for the almost 20 years I have known him. My background and expertise have never been in networking, and the knowledge in that area I do have I owe almost exclusive to Gerry. I also owe him enormous thanks for getting me into IT security from systems administration and working on middleware systems, which was my original background.

I worked with David Henry for many years at the University of Maryland and gained much of my knowledge about middleware and systems architecture from him. I owe much of my philosophy and approach to facing IT challenges today to the things I learned working for and with him. There are so many others from my days at the University of Maryland from whom I learned so much. However, I want to specifically call out John Pfeifer, David Arnold, Spence Spencer, Kevin Hildebrand, Prasad Dharmasena, Fran LoPresti, Eric Sturdivant, Willie Brown, Sonja Kueppers, Ira Gold, and Brian Swartzfager.

From my time at the Centers for Medicare & Medicaid Services, I want to specifically thank Jon Booth and Ketan Patel for giving me the opportunity to move into a formal security position for the first time and trusting me to oversee incredibly public and visible systems. Also, thanks to Zabeen Chong for giving me the opportunity to join CMS and expand beyond my roots in the academic world. Finally, I could never leave out my dear friend Andy Trusz, who from my first day at CMS showed me the ropes of the workplace and became a very close personal friend. Sadly, he lost his battle with cancer the very day I left CMS for Hewlett Packard Enterprise. I will never forget his friendship and all he showed me!

With any project of this scale, one needs enormous support and understanding from bosses and coworkers. Ruth Pine has been an amazing boss and is always supportive, giving me the time and encouragement to work on this project, as well as giving me the opportunity at all times to work on new challenges and expand my areas of expertise, most notably with cloud and SIEM technologies. Thanks also to Brian Moore, Joe Fuhrman, Steve Larson, BJ Kerlavage, David Kohlway, Seref Konur, Jack Schatoff, and the already mentioned Matt Walker for being part of an amazing team at HPE and showing me so many different perspectives and new approaches to challenges! I also have to thank some colleagues from other companies I have worked closely with on projects over the years for all their support and encouragement—specifically, Anna Tant, Jason Ashbaugh, and Richie Frieman.

Thank you to my parents, Richard and Susan, for all of your support and encouragement!

Last and most certainly not least, I want to thank my amazing wife, Robyn, for always being supportive with everything I have done professionally and personally. With four young kids at home, I would have never been able to even consider this project without her help and understanding—and for running interference with all our kids and pets!

INTRODUCTION

Over the last few years, the term *cloud* has become common in the modern lexicon of even lay persons with no connection to, training in, or expertise in the IT industry. It has become common in commercials targeting the public at large, and is often used as a main selling point for various services. Even those who do not understand what cloud computing is or how it works have largely come to understand it as a positive feature for a product or service, feeling it means higher reliability, speed, and an overall more beneficial consumer experience. Many companies are flocking to cloud computing at a rapid pace due to its benefits and features.

With this enormous paradigm shift in the industry, the demand for skilled professionals who understand cloud computing has grown at a similarly rapid pace. This demand applies to professionals in all facets of computing, but the unique aspects and features of cloud computing make the need for skilled security personnel paramount to any organization in order to properly safeguard and protect their systems, applications, and data.

Cloud computing represents a paradigm shift in how IT experts—and certainly IT security experts—look at protecting data and the various techniques and methodologies available to them. Some of you approaching this certification are experienced security professionals and already hold other certifications such as the CISSP. For others, this certification will be your first as a security professional. Some of you have been working with cloud computing from its onset, while others are learning the basics of cloud for the first time. This certification guide aims to fulfill the requirements of anyone approaching this challenging exam, regardless of background or specific experience in security or general computing.

This guide will give you the information you need to pass the CCSP exam, but it will also expand your understanding and knowledge of cloud computing and security beyond just being able to answer specific exam questions. My hope is that you will find this guide to be a comprehensive desktop reference that serves you long past the exam for the core cloud concepts and approaches.

The structure of this *All-in-One* guide is closely aligned with the subjects of the official exam guide from (ISC)² and covers every objective and component of it. Before diving into the six domains of the CCSP exam, this guide provides a general introduction to IT security for those who are approaching the CCSP as their first security certification. Those of you who are experienced and hold other security certifications may find it a useful refresher for basic concepts and terminology.

Regardless of your background, experience, and certifications, I hope you find the world of cloud computing and its unique security challenges to be enlightening and intellectually stimulating. Cloud represents a very dynamic, exciting new direction in computing, and one that seems likely to be a major paradigm for the foreseeable future.

How to Obtain the CCSP and Introduction to Security

This chapter covers the following topics:
- Why the CCSP certification is valuable
- How to obtain the CCSP certification
- An introduction to the six CCSP domains
- An introduction to basic security concepts

As cloud computing has exploded in use and popularity, so has the need for skilled security professionals who have the specific knowledge that cloud computing demands. While many organizations have skilled security professionals and operations staff, much of the knowledge from a traditional data center is not sufficiently applicable to the unique challenges and facets of cloud computing. To bridge this gap, (ISC)² and the Cloud Security Alliance (CSA) collaborated to form the Certified Cloud Security Professional (CCSP) certification as a means of verifying the knowledge and skills of cloud security professionals and providing the education needed to provide adequate security in the cloud environment.

Why Get Certified?

Obtaining an industry standard certification that is widely respected and recognized will serve the career of any IT professional. With cloud computing growing rapidly and more organizations clamoring to leverage its potential, the CCSP will serve as an independent verification of your skills and understanding of these concepts to any employer or regulatory agency. The CCSP can benefit anyone working in IT security at any level, from starting security analysts up to an organization's Chief Information Security Officer (CISO). While the CCSP will in many cases complement other security certifications such as the CISSP, it can also serve as a first or stand-alone certification as well.

How to Get Certified

The following steps and requirements for the CCSP were valid at the time of writing, but as with anything in the IT industry and its rapidly changing landscape, you should always verify directly with (ISC)² as to the most current requirements. The website for the CCSP can be found at https://www.isc2.org/ccsp.

The requirements to obtain the CCSP certification are as follows:

- **Experience**   A candidate must have five years of fulltime IT work experience. Within this five-year period, they must have three years minimum experience in IT security, and at least one year minimum in at least one of the CCSP domains. If a candidate has the CCSK certificate from the CSA, it can be substituted for the CCSP domain experience requirement, and the CISSP from (ISC)² can be used solely to fulfill the entire experience requirement for the CCSP.

- **Exam**   The candidate must register for and pass the CCSP certification exam. Information about registration and the required fees can be found on the CCSP website. The exam is four hours in duration with 125 questions. A candidate can successfully pass the exam with a scaled score of 700 out of 1000 points.

- **Endorsement**   Upon meeting the experience requirements and successfully passing the exam, a candidate must have their application endorsed by a current (ISC)² certification holder. This endorsement must be done by someone who knows the candidate and can attest to the validity of their experience and professional credentials.

- **Maintenance**   After being awarded the CCSP, a certification holder must complete specific continuing professional education (CPE) requirements and pay annual maintenance fees (AMF). Refer to the official (ISC)² site for current information about both requirements.

CCSP Domains

The CCSP exam content is structured into six distinct but interrelated domains that cover the wide range of cloud-related security and operational concerns and issues. The six domains, as well as an introduction to the material in each, follow.

Domain 1: Architectural Concepts and Design Requirements

The Architectural Concepts and Design Requirements domain lays the foundation for a strong understanding of the basics of cloud computing. These building blocks are based on the ISO/IEC 17788 standard. The domain defines the different and crucial roles that individuals and other entities play within a cloud implementation, from the perspective of both the cloud service provider and the cloud service customer. It outlines the key characteristics of cloud computing, including on-demand self-service, broad network access, multitenancy, rapid elasticity and scalability, resource pooling, and measured service.

It also introduces the key building blocks for a cloud environment, such as virtualization, storage, networks, and the underlying infrastructures that host and control them.

The domain covers the Cloud Reference Architecture, introducing cloud computing activities, cloud service capabilities, cloud service categories, cloud deployment models, and cross-cutting aspects of cloud computing that impact all areas of cloud implementations and deployments. The cloud computing activities are based on the ISO/IEC 17789 standard and include the key roles of the cloud service provider, cloud service customer, and cloud service partner, as well as the wide range of sub-roles encapsulated under each. The main cloud service capabilities, including the application, infrastructure, and platform service capabilities, are introduced and defined, as they form the basis of many of the cloud structures and models that are commonly used and understood. Following the cloud service capabilities, the major cloud service categories are introduced, including Infrastructure as a Service (IaaS), Platform as a Service (PaaS), and Software as a Service (SaaS). The cloud service categories can exist within different cloud deployment models as well, including public, private, hybrid, and community clouds. The last component of the Cloud Reference Architecture is a collection of cross-cutting aspects of cloud computing that are applicable to all cloud environments, regardless of the service category or deployment model. These cross-cutting aspects include interoperability, portability, reversibility, availability, security, privacy, resiliency, performance, governance, maintenance and versioning, service levels and service level agreements (SLAs), auditability, and regulation.

While security concepts are important and central to any hosting environment, there are special considerations that make them applicable to cloud computing. What's more, some security concepts are unique to cloud computing. As with any data center environment, security is vital in regard to network security, access control, data and media sanitation, cryptography, and virtualization. All of these are very similar to a traditional data center model, but the importance of cryptography is significantly higher in a cloud environment with multitenancy, as multiple customers are residing within the same pool of resources, as opposed to the isolation of a traditional data center. This also applies to the unique challenges with data and media sanitation, where access to and disposal of physical media are not feasible or practical in a cloud environment. The common security threats facing cloud computing are introduced, as published by the Open Web Application Security Project (OWASP), along with a discussion about how security challenges apply to the different cloud categories (IaaS, PaaS, SaaS) and any unique security challenges of each.

There are specific design requirements for secure cloud computing. While there is overlap with a traditional data center, certain aspects of a cloud environment require special considerations or methodologies. This applies to the cloud secure data lifecycle as well as the different approaches for business continuity and disaster recovery in a cloud environment. With these differing approaches and considerations, an organization must undertake a cost–benefit analysis that includes the operational changes, policy changes, regulatory challenges, and any configuration changes that would be necessary to move to a cloud environment—even whether they should consider moving to a cloud environment. The functional security requirements of cloud computing, including interoperability, portability, and vendor lock-in, are introduced.

Lastly, Domain 1 delves into certifications as a way of instilling trust in cloud systems. Because they do not host and control the entire environment, cloud customers are left looking for other means of verifying the security posture and operations of a cloud provider, and an easy and trustworthy means to do so is to look at independently tested and verified certifications. These certifications are based on published and well-understood standards and requirements; they serve as a means for trusting the security posture and controls of a cloud provider, as well as provide a common means for comparing different providers. Certifications can be done for entire environments and applications, or they can be focused on specific components and services. The Common Criteria is an international security standard that has been adopted with widespread use, whereas other certifications and standards such as FIPS 140-2 are focused on specific cryptographic modules, their security, and validations.

Domain 2: Cloud Data Security

The Cloud Data Security domain delves into the design, principles, and best practices for systems and applications to protect data, taking into account all types of systems, services, virtual machines, networks, and storage technologies within the hosting environment. Domain 2 begins with a discussion of the cloud data lifecycle, which shows how data flows from its creation through its disposal, and how it is handled through varied uses and activities while it remains within a system or application.

Each of the cloud categories (IaaS, PaaS, and SaaS) has different types and methodologies of storage associated with and used by it. Domain 2 explains the volume and object storage types of IaaS, the structured and unstructured data types of PaaS, and the information and storage management as well as the content and file storage possibilities of SaaS. With each type of storage come unique and applicable security challenges, but strategies to address them are often similar and uniform. This includes strategies such as encryption and data loss prevention (DLP).

The technologies employed in a cloud environment to ensure data security are similar to those of a traditional data center; they just take on increased importance within a cloud due to multitenancy and virtualization technologies. The main data security approaches used are encryption, including the importance of key management, along with masking, obfuscation, and tokenization. The exact use of specific technologies, including how they are used and to what extent, will be dependent on the type of data being processed or stored, along with its data classification and any regulatory or legal requirements for specific security controls or policies. Domain 2 also touches on some new and emerging technologies, such as homomorphic encryption, and the likely and important role they will play in the future of data security in general, and specifically within a cloud environment.

With any type of data security, the processes of data discovery and data classification are important. Data discovery involves finding and making value out of data that exists within a system or application, as well as ensuring that all data is known and has the proper security controls attached. Within a cloud environment, data discovery is even more complex and important because data is housed over disparate and diverse systems, where data owners and cloud customer may not even have a good understanding of where exactly it resides. Once data is known, data classification is the process of determining the appropriate security controls and policies needed based on attributes of that data. The data classification rules can originate from corporate policy or from legal or regulatory requirements. Within a cloud environment, this is increasingly important due to possible exposure through multitenancy to unauthorized entities.

Many data classifications, especially those dealing with personally identifiable information (PII), are driven by appropriate jurisdictional requirements and controls. These originate from various privacy acts, which then dictate the necessary data discovery and classification processes required. The appropriate controls can then be mapped and applied to meet jurisdictional requirements.

Two of the main approaches for protecting data are through data rights management (DRM) and information rights management (IRM). DRM applies to the protection of consumer media, whereas IRM applies on the system side to protecting information. These concepts and the specific tools that implement them can be used to set policy for auditing, expiration of access, policy control, protection, and support for many different applications and formats of data. Both allow for a much great level of granularity and control than typical system or application data controls allow.

With any data policy, the concepts of retention, deletion, and archiving are extremely important. Many regulatory and legal requirements set explicit retention policies for data and especially for logs, and it is up to the organization and data owner to determine what policies and technologies are necessary for compliance. With any archiving system, it is crucial to ensure that archives are properly created and secured, and can be accessed and read for the duration of any retention policies or regulations. Clearing data for removal from a system must be done in a comprehensive and secure manner to ensure that it cannot be recovered and accessed later by unauthorized parties.

Lastly, a key component to data security is the logging of appropriate and detailed events from systems and applications. This includes both system- and application-level events and logs, and should be scoped to the specific type of data or application as to what kind of events and to what detail. Regulatory and legal requirements are also key factors in determining the types of events and detail required. This collection of events can be utilized for regulatory compliance, security oversight, and also for business intelligence and system resource utilization. Most organizations use a centralized collection and aggregation implementation for logs and analysis. As with any type of digital evidence and data, the proper mechanisms to preserve chain of custody and nonrepudiation are crucial for event logs and the systems that store and preserve them.

Domain 3: Cloud Platform and Infrastructure Security

A cloud environment consists of a physical infrastructure and a virtual infrastructure, and both carry with them unique security concerns and requirements. While cloud systems are built on virtualization and virtual components, underneath those virtualization layers is physical hardware and its security requirements, the same as with a traditional data center. This includes access to physical systems, such as the BIOS and hardware layers, as well as the software that hosts and maintains the virtualized environments on top of them. Any breach of security or controls on the physical layer could put all virtual hosts managed within it at risk as well. Security controls within a cloud environment apply to the standard set of resources: network and communications, storage, and computing. However, the use of virtualization also requires the consideration of security in regard to the management plane used to control the virtual machines. Domain 3 delves into the cloud-specific risks, the risks associated with virtualization, and the specific countermeasure strategies that can be employed.

With cloud computing used extensively to bridge organizations and provide services to large numbers and groups of users, identity and access management is a crucial concept for the Cloud Security Professional to be well versed in. Topics covered included the proper identification of users and the security mechanisms commonly employed to authenticate them and prove their identity to the satisfaction of either policy or regulatory requirements. Once identity has been proven, tight authorization controls are necessary to ensure users only access information for which they are authorized, and through the means they are authorized to do so. A commonly used approach with many cloud-based systems is federated identity, where users can authenticate through their own organization's identity provider and then have a service provider accept those authentication tokens for access, rather than the users needing an account on the specific system.

Lastly, Domain 3 covers the concepts of business continuity and disaster recovery (BCDR). Although a cloud platform and its inherent redundancy can mitigate many typical outages that might impact a traditional data center, proper planning and analysis are still crucial. For applications that are completely within a cloud environment, interoperability and portability enable organizations to utilize other cloud providers or other offerings within the same cloud provider for BCDR strategies. Even applications still hosted in traditional data centers can use cloud offerings for BCDR, especially considering cloud services only incur costs when they are used, thus alleviating the need for standby hardware. For proper BCDR strategies to be implemented, the planning stages are crucial, but it is also imperative to conduct regular tests to ensure all components are still appropriate and feasible.

Domain 4: Cloud Application Security

Using cloud environments and cloud technologies is quickly gaining in popularity for their cost and flexibility. Cloud environments offer incredible efficiencies and ease in bringing online environments and virtual machines quickly for developers, and costs are only incurred while they are live and operating; the lead time and costs associated with procuring environments or test servers in a traditional data center are largely mitigated in a cloud environment. In order for optimal cloud development to be leveraged, especially with security in mind, the Cloud Security Professional and developers need a solid understanding of the realities of cloud environments, what is required to secure them, as well as the common threats and vulnerabilities facing a cloud.

While not unique to cloud hosting or development, several different types of application testing and scanning are discussed in Domain 4. These types consist of different approaches and views, and used in combination they allow for exhaustive and comprehensive testing of systems and applications. Dynamic application security testing (DAST) is considered "black-box" testing, which is done against live systems with no special or inside knowledge of them, whereas static application security testing (SAST) is done with full knowledge of system configurations, as well as access to source code, and is done against non-live systems. Penetration testing is done with the same approach and toolsets that attackers would use against systems to determine vulnerabilities, whereas runtime application self-protection (RASP) focuses on the capabilities of some systems and applications to self-protect and block or mitigate attacks as they occur.

Because most modern applications, especially those typically found in cloud environments, are built on components, services, and APIs that consume other services and data, the selection and verification of appropriate pieces that meet security requirements is essential. The old adage about the weakest link is certainly valid within this context, as any weakness of a single component could expose an entire application or system to threats and exploits. The same verification process and selection applies regardless of the source of the components, including commercial, open source, and community-sourced applications.

Domain 4 covers the software development lifecycle (SDLC) as it relates to a cloud environment, including an in-depth walk through of each phase, what it entails, and the key components to be addressed before moving to the next stage, as well as the cyclical nature of SDLC. The main threats and vulnerability concepts from the STRIDE and DREAD models are introduced, including their applicability to cloud environments.

On top of secure development concepts and methodologies, other commonly used technologies and paradigms within cloud computing are introduced. These include XML appliances, web application firewalls (WAFs), and systematic approaches such as sandboxing and application virtualization. Their importance in regard to cloud computing as well as their essential use and reliance on cryptography are also discussed. Lastly, Domain 4 covers the strategic approaches to identity and access management and building them into applications during development, including multifactor authentication technologies.

Domain 5: Operations

The operations domain begins with a discussion of planning for data centers, including both the physical and logical layers and technologies employed. This also incorporates how environmental concerns and needs are addressed along with physical requirements, including reliable and redundant access to cooling and electrical resources, as well as adequate protection from natural disasters and environmental issues.

Although cloud environments are mostly virtualized in the manner that most think, they still have the underlying physical environment and concerns of a traditional data center, even if those burdens are being handled and maintained by the cloud provider and are largely abstracted from view and concern of the users and cloud customers. The physical layer consists of the servers that are hosting the virtualized environment, as well as storage and network components. From the network perspective, all the concerns of a traditional data center are still present, such as firewalls, routing, and network-based intrusion protection and detection systems. Physical devices can be operated in a stand-alone or clustered configuration as well, depending on specific concerns for the environment or specific requirements and expectations. The physical environment also carries many of the same requirements in a cloud environment as servers would in a traditional data center, including patch management and versioning, access control, log collection and preservation, and auditing requirements. The physical environment, because it has a direct impact on the virtualized environment, requires extensive planning and scheduling for maintenance and management activities.

The logical environment carries the same burdens and requirements as the physical environment for the most part, but with a different focus on the systems and applications of the cloud customer, such as the actual virtual machines and network appliances used within cloud environments. These systems also require patch management and versioning strategies, but, depending on the cloud model used, the approach can differ widely from that of a traditional data center model. The logical environment will necessitate robust performance monitoring because it ties into the performance of the physical environment as well as how systems are dynamically balanced and how resources are allocated across physical systems to maintain optimal performance, because loads and demands constantly shift. Backup and recovery of logical systems is also covered.

Domain 5 covers extensively the components and concepts from ITIL, a set of best practices for IT service management used widely throughout the IT industry, as they form a comprehensive approach to operations management that can be applied to any system or application. Ten main components are addressed, including ones very familiar to all that work in IT systems and services, such as change management, configuration management, and information security management.

As part of operations management, the conducting of risk assessments with logical components is very important to the cloud customer, and will be a large task of the Cloud Security Professional. This risk assessment process follows through four stages: framing, assessing, responding, and monitoring. Each stage builds in sequence, starting with defining the process and risk categories, undertaking the assessment, determining appropriate responses or accepting any risks identified, and then monitoring those risks for future evolution or change in response strategies. Overall, risk can be accepted, avoided, transferred, mitigated, or a combination of approaches.

Another important part of operations is the collection and preservation of electronic records for use as digital evidence. These systems and programs need to be an integral part of an operational plan, and not something that's only addressed when the need arises. Domain 5 covers these topics from an introductory operational standpoint, which are expanded more from a regulatory standpoint in Domain 6.

Lastly, Domain 5 covers as an important aspect of operations the appropriate communication with relevant stakeholders. The stakeholders include those at all levels of an engagement or contract, including venders, customers, partners, regulators, and any other potential stakeholders based on the particulars of the data, application, or system. Proper and efficient communication is important for fostering and maintaining strong relationships, and may be required specifically in regard to both frequency and level of detail, as required by contracts, SLAs, or regulations.

Domain 6: Legal and Compliance

Domain 6 is focused on the legal and regulatory compliance requirements for IT systems, including how they are specifically related to cloud computing and its many unique facets. Cloud computing presents many unique risks and challenges because it often spans different regulatory or national borders. As such, it is subjected to many different requirements, which are sometimes in conflict with each other. This domain explores legally mandated controls from the perspective of multiple jurisdictions, as well as legal risks that are specific to cloud computing. The specific definitions and legal requirements for personal information and privacy as they relate to jurisdictional controls are covered, as well as the differences between contractual and regulated personal data protections.

Some of the most common legal impacts on any IT system or application are e-discovery orders and requirements to produce records or data in response to a formal court order or request. The domain explores the overall concept of e-discovery and digital forensics, especially as they relate to cloud computing and the specific challenges a cloud implementation represents. Many of the tools and processes for both areas that people are familiar with are not directly feasible in a cloud environment, because the cloud customer will not have the type of access required to perform data collection, so such requests must be addressed through contracts and other formal processes.

One of the most important aspects to IT security and compliance is the auditing process. Domain 6 delves into the various types of audits, their purposes, and the requirements from a regulatory perspective, as well as their specific impact on cloud computing. A major challenge with cloud computing is visibility and access into the underlying infrastructure on behalf of the cloud customer, and how cloud providers use audits and auditing reports to ensure confidence in security programs for multiple customers, without giving each customer access or having to do multiple infrastructure audits. Domain 6 covers extensively the standards surrounding auditing and certification, the commonly used auditing paradigms and reports, the applicable use and audience for each, and the proper identification of relevant stakeholders.

Risk management is also explored in depth in Domain 6, as well as its specific applications and concerns with regard to cloud computing. The introduction of cloud computing and the loss of direct control can become major facets of risk management within an organization and require special evaluation and understanding. The various processes and procedures for risk management, as well as different risk frameworks and assessment methodologies, are covered.

Lastly, Domain 6 covers the various concerns and requirements for managing and scoping contracts for cloud hosting engagements. This includes guidance for selecting a cloud provider as well as the key components and issues that need to be addressed in the contract that are specific to cloud hosting and the concerns a cloud customer will have.

Introduction to IT Security

Although many candidates pursuing the CCSP certification will already hold other major security certifications such as the CISSP, this is not a requirement. What follows is a brief introduction to some basic security concepts that are integral to all security professionals. Also included are brief introductions to the concepts of risk management and business continuity and disaster recovery (BCDR). If you have extensive experience in IT security or hold another major certification, feel free to skip this section and dive right into the next chapter, which covers the first domain for the exam. However, even if you are an experienced professional, you may find this information of value, especially if you are pursuing your first security certification.

Basic Security Concepts

The following are basic concepts of security that apply to all systems and applications, regardless of the purpose or technological details.

Least Privilege

The main driving principle in the world of IT security is that of "least privilege." The foundation of the least privilege principle is that all access to systems, applications, or data should be granted to users in a manner that allows only the access that is explicitly required for their purposes and authorization. For example, users who have administrative privileges on a system should only use that level of access when it is absolutely necessary, and only for the specific functions and duration required. These users should operate with normal user access, and elevate to administrative-level access only when necessary. They should then return to user status immediately after performing the necessary functions.

Adhering to this best practice has multiple security and operational implications and benefits for an organization. First, it prevents a user operating for long durations of time with administrative access, where the likeliness of error or a mistaken command could have wide-reaching ramifications for a system. It also prevents the compromise of an account leading to extensive access to systems in instances where the elevation to administrative access is done without other independent verifications or requirements. In many instances, administrative access will be restricted to certain means of access, such as a requirement that users be on their corporate network, where other defensive security measures are in place to mitigate risk. It is also very common to require either multifactor authentication or separate and distinct credentials to elevate to administrative privileges. With additional credentials required, even if a user's password were to be compromised, achieving administrative level access would necessitate further compromise, where the likeliness of detection or prevention would be higher.

The same concept also applies to the service or system accounts utilized within an environment or application. Components such as web servers, application servers, databases, and so on, all run on the system as a specific account. Much like with user accounts, these system accounts should also run where only the minimal level of permissions required are assigned to them. This serves to separate and isolate processes on a system, and prevent them from accessing other data or processes without an explicit need to do so. For example, rather than processes being run as the "root" or "admin" account on a system, separate accounts specific to those applications or processes should be created and utilized. When processes are run under such accounts with wide access and privileges, if they were to be compromised, the malicious actor would automatically gain wide access to the system and any data or other processes contained or running on it.

While most associate privileges with the ability to read data, it also applies to the ability to update files on a system. Unless explicitly needed, services and processes should not be able to write or modify files on the file system. If this functionality is needed, then steps must be taken to limit where writing and updating can occur, and these actions should be as isolated and restricted as possible. No service should have the ability to update binaries or application configurations on a system to prevent Trojans or malware from being introduced and executed. An obvious and common exception is enabling a process to write log files to the system, but this also should be restricted to specific locations or files, and access should be enforced by file system permissions or other security settings specific to the environment.

The actual implementation of least privilege can be tricky in any environment. It is not possible to get to a point where a process has only the exact level of access needed because a system is built on common libraries and configurations that all processes on the system will need to access or execute. The key is ensuring that sensitive data and functions are not exposed, as well as ensuring that a process cannot update or delete data or configurations without an explicit need and authorization. All access needs to be evaluated within an organization's risk management processes, with specific access documented and approved before being granted.

Defense in Depth

The premise behind defense in depth is the use of multiple layers and different types of technologies and strategies to provide security. With multiple layers, a failure or vulnerability at any single point can possibly be mitigated or minimized through other security mechanisms and systems in place. While multiple layers of security will not totally eliminate any potential attacks or successful exploits, they can dramatically increase the difficulty of success, or make it far more likely for an attack to be discovered and prevented before it can be successful.

Many common strategies can be used together to constitute a defense-in-depth approach for a system or application. The obvious starting point is the security on the actual system or application itself. In front of the end point are other technologies such as firewalls, virtual private networks (VPNs), intrusion detection or prevention systems (IDSs/IPSs), vulnerability scans, physical security, logging and monitoring, and many other approaches and strategies. Based on scans and audits of the actual systems or applications, the selection of specific other strategies and technologies can be done with an eye toward specific mitigations and weaknesses, as well as the standard depth approach that data centers already employ.

Using multiple and independent devices and technologies for security also removes the interdependence of specific defenses and makes their successful exploit or bypassing far more difficult. For example, if an application uses a variety of software on a server for security, such as firewalls and virus scans, if the server itself has an administrative compromise, those processes could be disabled, stopped, or have configurations altered to make them useless, many times in a manner where detection of such changes is very difficult because the attacker will have full control over the server. By using appliances and components that are not running on the same server, as well as hardware-based implementations, the possibility of concurrent compromise is effectively eliminated. While this largely mitigates successful exploit from the outside, having separate devices or appliances that are managed by different teams and policies also mitigates prospects of insider threats.

Confidentiality, Integrity, Availability

The concepts of confidentiality, integrity, and availability are considered the base of IT security and the foundation of pretty much everything after that. While all three concepts work together, different types of data will have greater or lesser importance in each of the three areas depending on specific needs and regulatory requirements.

- **Confidentiality**   The prevention of sensitive data from being accessed or viewed by any party other than those authorized. The level and degree of protection is typically based on the damage or consequences of the data being disclosed, either in regard to an organization's reputation or possible regulatory or legal consequences from data disclosure to unauthorized parties. Security controls to promote or enforce confidentiality can be technological in nature, but also typically involve user training on policies, best practices, and safe handling.

- **Integrity**   Maintaining the consistency and validity of data at all times within a system or application. Integrity ensures that the data has not been altered by any unauthorized parties, and that it has not been altered during transit. While access controls will be the main tactic used to prevent unauthorized modification, other technologies such as checksums are commonly used to verify that a file or data is still in its intended form and can immediately detect if any changes at all have been made to it.

- **Availability**   Although availability may seem like an operational issue rather than a security issue, many aspects of security play a crucial role in availability. While ensuring that data is protected and valid is crucial in regard to confidentiality and integrity, respectively, if systems aren't available to those authorized users who are dependent on them, they are of no organizational use. Security practices such as firewalls, intrusion protection systems, and the prevention of denial-of-service attacks are all key components of a security program. This also extends to the prevention of data loss and business loss through backup and recovery, business continuity, and disaster recovery.

Cryptography

Cryptography is the process of making information unreadable by unauthorized entities, while keeping it easily readable to those who are authorized to access it. Cryptography essentially takes data and makes it appear as completely random gibberish by using mathematical formulas and complex algorithms. The process of encrypting and decrypting data is based on the use of keys. Someone in possession of the keys can easily decrypt data, which can be virtually impossible to do without them. For the most part, all encryption can be broken with the appropriate amount of time and computational resources. The level of strength of the encryption is based on the time required to break it with available resources, technology, and knowledge. For example, although modern encryption systems are possible to break, doing so could take hundreds, if not thousands, of years, even with the required computing resources. Of course technology, computing power, and mathematical breakthroughs are always occurring, so what is considered secure today could be vulnerable tomorrow. Cryptography and the use of keys falls into two categories: symmetric and asymmetric.

With a symmetric key implementation, the same key is used to encrypt and decrypt the data, so the key must be known and available on both sides from the onset. However, the use of a shared key also makes the processing of the encryption much faster than the asymmetric method. The use of symmetric encryption is typically confined to communications that are ongoing and established between two trusted parties, such as server-to-server communications and tunneling implementations that are used regularly or continuously.

With asymmetric (or public-key) encryption, different keys are used to encrypt and decrypt communications. While this is slower than symmetric encryption, it is the most commonly used method because parties are typically not known ahead of usage, such as when a user communicates with a secure website. Public-key encryption relies on the use of a pair of keys from each party, which are commonly known as the public key and the private key. The public key is exactly what it sounds like: publicly available and distributed or published by the user. The associated private key of the pair is always held securely and never distributed. When a secure communication is needed, the sending party can encrypt the data or communication using the public key of the recipient. Because the key is public, the initial communication channel does not need to be secure, which is not true with symmetric encryption. This is another major benefit of asymmetric encryption, which is commonly used with web and mobile applications. The receiving party then decrypts that data or communications channel using their private key, which is known only to them. The same method can be used to digitally sign data to authenticate the sender or originator, and to ensure that it has not been modified during transport. Public-key encryption systems form the basis for common security protocols such as TLS and SSL.

Certificates

A certificate forms the basis for proving identity and authenticating ownership of a public key to a specific user. The certificate contains information about the user, their organization, locality, and so on, and will be visible to the requesting party. To ensure validity and trust, certificates are digitally signed and issued commonly by a certificate authority (CA). In most instances, this will be a commercial vendor that is trusted by users and applications. For example, web browsers contain a number of "root" certificates of CAs that are considered trusted. These organizations have established and rigorous processes in place to ensure the identity and standards required to issue a trusted certificate. This third-party trust relationship is what allows communications to be secured and trusted between two parties that otherwise have no prior relationship or established credential exchanges. With both parties trusting the CA, they can be assured of the validity of each other.

While the use of prominent CAs is very common, within specific applications and uses, a smaller community may establish their own CA for their own purposes and users. For example, a university may establish their own CA for issuing certificates to all students and the systems that only their population of users access, alleviating the costs associated with procuring commercially verified certificates for their community. In these types of scenarios, rather than having to accept individually each certificate for a person or system, the user can choose to trust the root certificate of the CA, Thus, it works the same as those root certificates and all certificates signed under the CA's authority that are commonly loaded in a browser.

If a user attempts to communicate with an entity that does not present a trusted certificate, the user will receive a warning in their browser or client that they are being presented with an untrusted certificate, or that the root authority is not a trusted issuer. Although the user has the option to override and accept the certificate, this should only ever be done when the user has very specific knowledge about why this warning has appeared, and they know themselves that the source can be trusted. This should never be done with systems that are used by the larger public community or with commercial sites.

Physical Security

While most security discussions in regard to IT systems are based on the protection of data through hardware and software solutions, the protection of physical assets and access is also paramount to IT security. Physical security is related to the actual defense of the building and location where IT resources and data are housed, as well as the physical equipment on which the data resides. The same defense-in-depth principles that are used with IT security also apply to physical security. With a physical structure, layered security such as fencing, surveillance, security guards, locked doors, hardened structures, and many other concepts all play a central role.

A breakdown of physical security or having insufficient physical security can lead to many problems with the loss of data or services for an organization. The most obvious is a loss of services due to the destruction of physical assets such as servers, storage systems, or network connectivity. A breach of physical security can also lead to someone using physical access to break into systems as they are running. However, even when systems have robust security for perimeter attacks and access, in many situations they are still susceptible to someone with physical access to the consoles and hardware, and thus to the systems themselves. Lastly, a lack of physical security can lead to theft of physical assets. While countermeasures can be employed to prevent a malicious actor from accessing systems over a network, if someone manages to steal hardware or storage systems with sensitive data on them, they would have access to extensive tools and methods for accessing the data to them, without the constraint of time or other mechanisms for disabling their access.

Risk Management

Risk management is the process of determining through analysis and testing the specific weakness, vulnerabilities, and risks associated with the data and systems in place for an organization. This also includes determining the appropriate mitigation efforts or accepting specific risks. Risks can come in many different forms, including physical threats, natural or environmental threats, software weaknesses and exploits, as well as malicious insider threats. All organizations must constantly evaluate risks to all systems, applications, and data, coupled with management's appetite for risk and the level of risk they are willing to accept. Although it is not possible to totally eliminate all risks, a sound approach is to mitigate those risks that you can, and to minimize the likeliness of occurrence of the rest and any potential damage they could cause. Many decisions in risk management are also guided by specific requirements from regulatory or legal systems, as well as potential and specific penalties for data access or exposure as a result of a successful exploit.

Business Continuity and Disaster Recovery

BCDR is the planning for handling the sudden, unexpected, or catastrophic loss of systems or data for an organization. It encompasses several different aspects of IT operations, including the incorporation of resiliency within IT systems, the ability to recover from any loss, and the contingencies for handling major incidents or disasters that have a long recovery time.

The first major concept of BCDR is resiliency. Systems and processes should be implemented with sufficient redundancy and capacity to mitigate most types of threats or issues from the onset, preferably without noticeably affecting the users of the systems. This can be accomplished through having redundant systems and resources at all levels, ranging from power and cooling, through system availability and personnel.

The second major concept of BCDR is the ability to recover from outages or system corruption. Within this context, recovery refers to outages where physical resources are likely still available and the loss comes from corruption or physical failure of portions of a system or environment. In this case, backups can be used to restore systems to a recent point. This will be defined by management as to what level of data loss they are willing to assume in the case of a failure or outage, and in most instances services can be restored quickly and within the same environment.

The last major concept is disaster recovery, where a catastrophic loss from a natural disaster, terrorist attack, fire, or other such major incident occurs. In this case, recovering from the widespread loss within an acceptable time is not feasible. In such instances, planning and preparation are required for moving to another hosting arrangement, where data and services can be recovered and returned to operational status within an acceptable timeframe. These efforts are to be considered a last resort to be used for a catastrophic outage, because the time, money, and resources required to make such a switch, and to return to normal services down the road, can be very substantial.

Chapter Review

This first chapter covered the requirements for obtaining the CCSP, as well as provided an overview of the domains that comprise the content for the examination. It also provided a brief introduction to some basic security concepts that will serve as the basis for the more in-depth and comprehensive discussions that follow.

Architectural Concepts and Design Requirements

This chapter covers the following topics in Domain 1:

- Cloud computing players and terms
- Cloud computing essential characteristics
- Cloud service categories
- Cloud deployment models
- Security concepts relevant to cloud computing
- Certifications
- Cloud cost–benefit analysis
- Cloud architecture models

For the past few years the term "cloud" has been heard almost everywhere in advertising and popular culture. From the television commercials proclaiming "take it to the cloud" to the ubiquitous presence of products such as Apple's iCloud, the term is one that even the most novice technology consumers know, even if they have scant knowledge or understanding of what a cloud is or does.

As security professionals working in a cloud environment, much of our knowledge and best practices from traditional data center models still apply, but a thorough understanding of cloud computing concepts and the different types of clouds and cloud services is paramount to successfully implementing and overseeing a security policy and compliance.

The National Institute of Standards and Technology (NIST) of the United States has published Special Publication (SP) 800-145, "The NIST Definition of Cloud Computing," which gives their official definition of cloud:

> Cloud computing is a model for enabling ubiquitous, convenient, on-demand network access to a shared pool of configurable computer resources (e.g., networks, servers, storage, applications, and services) that can be rapidly provisioned and released with minimal management effort or service provider interaction. This cloud model is composed of five essential characteristics, three service models, and four deployment models.

Rather than the classic data center model with server hardware, network appliances, cabling, power units, and environmental controls, cloud computing is predicated on the concept of purchasing "services" to comprise various levels of automation and support based on the needs of the customer at any point in time. This is in contrast to the classical data center model, which requires a customer to purchase and configure systems for their maximum capacity at all times, regardless of need, due to business cycles and changing demands.

Cloud Computing Concepts

Before we dive into more thorough discussions of cloud concepts and capabilities, it is important to lay a strong foundation of cloud computing definitions first via a general overview of the technologies involved. This will form the basis for the rest of this chapter as well as the book as a whole.

Cloud Computing Definitions

The following list presents some introductory definitions for this chapter, based on ISO/IEC 17788, "Cloud Computing—Overview and Vocabulary." Many more definitions will be given later to build on this definitions primer (see also the glossary in this book).

- **Cloud application** An application that does not reside or run on a user's device but rather is accessible via a network.
- **Cloud application portability** The ability to migrate a cloud application from one cloud provider to another.
- **Cloud computing** Network-accessible platform that delivers services from a large and scalable pool of systems, rather than dedicated physical hardware and more static configurations.
- **Cloud data portability** The ability to move data between cloud providers.
- **Cloud deployment model** How cloud computing is delivered through a set of particular configurations and features of virtual resources. The cloud deployment models are public, private, hybrid, and community.
- **Cloud service** Capabilities offered via a cloud provider and accessible via a client.
- **Cloud service category** A group of cloud services that have a common set of features or qualities.
- **Community cloud** A cloud services model where the tenants are limited to those that have a relationship together with shared requirements, and are maintained or controlled by at least one member of the community.
- **Data portability** The ability to move data from one system or another without having to re-enter it.

- **Hybrid cloud**   A cloud services model that combines two other types of cloud deployment models.
- **Infrastructure as a Service (IaaS)**   A cloud service category where infrastructure-level services are provided by a cloud service provider.
- **Measured service**   Cloud services are delivered and billed for in a metered way.
- **Multitenancy**   Having multiple customers and applications running within the same environment but in a way that they are isolated from each other and not visible to each other, but share the same resources.
- **On-demand self-service**   A cloud customer can provision services in an automatic manner, when needed, with minimal involvement from the cloud provider.
- **Platform as a Service (PaaS)**   A cloud service category where platform services are provided to the cloud customer, and the cloud provider is responsible for the system up to the level of the actual application.
- **Private cloud**   Cloud services model where the cloud is owned and controlled by a single entity for their own purposes.
- **Public cloud**   Cloud services model where the cloud is maintained and controlled by the cloud provider, but the services are available to any potential cloud customers.
- **Resource pooling**   The aggregation of resources allocated to cloud customers by the cloud provider.
- **Reversibility**   The ability of a cloud customer to remove all data and applications from a cloud provider and completely remove all data from their environment.
- **Software as a Service (SaaS)**   Cloud service category in which a full application is provided to the cloud customer, and the cloud provider maintains responsibility for the entire infrastructure, platform, and application.
- **Tenant**   One or more cloud customers sharing access to a pool of resources.

Cloud Computing Roles

These definitions represent the basic and most important roles within a cloud system and the relationships between them, based on ISO/IEC 17788:

- **Cloud auditor**   An auditor that is specifically responsible for conducting audits of cloud systems and cloud applications
- **Cloud service broker**   A partner that servers as an intermediary between a cloud service customer and cloud service provider
- **Cloud service customer**   One that holds a business relationship for services with a cloud service provider

- **Cloud service partner** One that holds a relationship with either a cloud service provider or a cloud service customer to assist with cloud services and their delivery
- **Cloud service provider** One that offers cloud services to cloud service customers
- **Cloud service user** One that interacts with and consumes services offered by a cloud services customer

Key Cloud Computing Characteristics

Cloud computing has five essential characteristics. In order for an implementation to be considered a cloud in a true sense, each of these five characteristics must be present and operational:

- On-demand self-service
- Broad network access
- Resource pooling
- Rapid elasticity
- Measured service
- Multitenancy

Each of these characteristics is discussed in more detail in the following sections.

On-Demand Self-Service

Cloud services can be requested, provisioned, and put into use by the customer through automated means without the need to interact with a person. This is typically offered by the cloud provider through a web portal, but can also be provided in some cases through web API calls or other programmatic means. As services are expanded or contracted, billing is adjusted through automatic means.

In the sense of billing, this does not just apply to large companies or firms that have contractual agreements with cloud providers for services and open lines of credit or financing agreements. Even small businesses and individuals can take advantage of the same services through such simple arrangements as having a credit card on file and an awareness of the cloud provider's terms and charges, and many systems will tell the user at the time of request what the additional and immediate costs will be.

Broad Network Access

All cloud services and components are accessible over the network and accessible in most cases through many different vectors. This ability for heterogeneous access through a variety of clients is a hallmark of cloud computing, where services are provided while staying agnostic to the access methods of the consumers. In the case of cloud computing, services can be accessed typically from either web browsers or thick or thin clients, regardless of whether the consumer is using a mobile device, laptop, or desktop, and either from a corporate network or from a personal device on an open network.

The cloud revolution in computing has occurred concurrently with the mobile computing revolution, making the importance being agnostic concerning the means of access a top priority. Because many companies have begun allowing bring-your-own-device (BYOD) access to their corporate IT systems, it is imperative that any environments they operate within be able to support a wide variety of platforms and software clients.

CAUTION BYOD can be a major headache for IT security professionals. It is often seen by management as a cost-cutting method or a way to appease employees regarding their personal access, but it adds a host of additional concerns to any network or application regarding secure access methods. In a cloud environment, BYOD can potentially be less of an issue, depending on the type of cloud model employed, but it always must be safely monitored. Cloud storage also alleviates the need for users to store their data on their devices and instead access it via the network, thus increasing security by removing data storage physically from the device.

Resource Pooling

One of the most important concepts in cloud computer is resource pooling, or multi-tenancy. In a cloud environment, regardless of the type of cloud offering, you always will have a mix of applications and systems that coexist within the same set of physical and virtual resources. As cloud customers add to and expand their usage within the cloud, the new resources are dynamically allocated within the cloud, and the customer has no control over (and, really, no need to know) where the actual services are deployed. This aspect of cloud can apply to any type of service deployed within the environment, including processing, memory, network utilization and devices, as well as storage. At the time of provisioning, services can and will be automatically deployed throughout the cloud infrastructure, and mechanisms are in place for locality and other requirements based on the particular needs of the customer and any regulatory or legal requirements that they be physically housed in a particular country or data center. However, these will have been configured within the provisioning system via contract requirements before they are actually requested by the customer, and then they are provisioned within those rules by the system without the customer needing to specify them at that time.

Many corporations have computing needs that are cyclical in nature. With resource pooling and a large sample of different systems that are utilized within the same cloud infrastructure, companies can have the resources they need on their own cycles without having to build out systems to handle the maximum projected load, which means these resources won't sit unused and idle at other nonpeak times. Significant cost savings can be realized for all customers of the cloud through resource pooling and the economies of scale that it affords.

TIP From my own experience working for an academic institution and in healthcare, the cyclical nature of computing needs is a huge benefit of cloud computing. In both environments, you have defined periods of the year with greatly increased loads and slow periods for most of the rest of the year. Having resources pooled and available when needed is a huge benefit.

Rapid Elasticity

With cloud computing being decoupled from hardware and with the programmatic provisioning capabilities, services can be rapidly expanded at any time additional resources are needed. This capability can be provided through the web portal or initiated on behalf of the customer, either in response to an expected or projected increase in demand of services or during such an increase in demand; the decision to change scale is balanced against the funding and capabilities of the customer. If the applications and systems are built in a way where they can be supported, elasticity can be automatically implemented such that the cloud provider through programmatic means and based on predetermined metrics can automatically scale the system by adding additional resources and can bill the customer accordingly.

In a classic data center model, a customer needs to have ready and configured enough computing resources at all times to handle any potential and projected load on their systems. Along with what was previously mentioned under "Resource Pooling," many companies that have cyclical and defined periods of heavy load can run leaner systems during off-peak times and then scale up, either manually or automatically as the need arises. A prime example of this would be applications that handle healthcare enrollment or university class registrations. In both cases, the systems have very heavy peak use periods and largely sit idle the remainder of the year.

Measured Service

Depending on the type of service and cloud implementation, resources are metered and logged for billing and utilization reporting. This metering can be done in a variety of ways and using different aspects of the system, or even multiple methods. This can include storage, network, memory, processing, the number of nodes or virtual machines, and the number of users. Within the terms of the contract and agreements, these metrics can be used for a variety of uses, such as monitoring and reporting, placing limitations on resource utilization, and setting thresholds for automatic elasticity. These metrics also will be used to some degree in determining the provider's adherence to the requirements set forth in the service level agreement (SLA).

Many large companies as a typical practice use internal billing of individual systems based on the usage of their data centers and resources. This is especially true with companies that contract IT services to other companies or government agencies. In a classic data center model with physical hardware, this was much more difficult to achieve in a meaningful way. With the metering and reporting metrics that cloud providers are able to offer, this becomes much more simplistic for companies and offers a significantly greater degree of flexibility, with granularity of systems and expansion.

Multitenancy

A traditional data center model typically has physical separation between different customers. In most cases, this is done through cages and completely separate network gear. However, a cloud environment can have many different customers running resources and applications within the same physical hardware devices and rely on virtual and logical segregation within the hosting model instead.

Building-Block Technologies

Regardless of the service category or deployment model used for a cloud implementation, the core components and building blocks are the same. Any cloud implementation at a fundamental level is composed of processor or CPU, memory/RAM, networking, and storage solutions. Depending on the cloud service category, the cloud customer will have varying degrees of control over or responsibility for those building blocks. The next section introduces the three main cloud service categories and goes into detail about what the cloud customer has access to or responsibility for.

Cloud Reference Architecture

A few major components fit together to form the full picture of a cloud architecture and implementation. These components include the activities, roles, and capabilities that go into managing and operating a cloud environment, as well as the actual cloud service categories and cloud deployment models that serve as the basis for delivery of cloud hosting and services. This includes numerous features and components common to all cloud environments, regardless of the service category or deployment model.

Cloud Computing Activities

Different sets of cloud computing activities are performed by the cloud service customer, the cloud service provider, and the cloud service partner, as outlined in ISO/IEC 17789, "ISO/IEC 17789:2014 : Information technology—Cloud computing—Reference architecture." To keep things simple, we will keep our discussion to a high-level overview and sampling of the activities, all of which we will go into greater detail throughout the book.

Cloud Service Customer

The following roles are performed by the cloud service customer:

- **Cloud service user**   Uses the cloud services
- **Cloud service administrator**   Tests cloud services, monitor services, administers security of services, provides usage reports on cloud services, and addresses problem reports
- **Cloud service business manager**   Oversees business and billing administration, purchases the cloud services, requests audit reports as necessary
- **Cloud service integrator**   Connects and integrates existing systems and services to the cloud

Cloud Service Provider

The following roles are performed by the cloud service provider:

- **Cloud service operations manager**   Prepares systems for the cloud, administers services, monitors services, provides audit data when requested or required, manages inventory and assets

- **Cloud service deployment manager**   Gathers metrics on cloud services, manages deployment steps and processes, defines the environment and processes
- **Cloud service manager**   Delivers, provisions, and manages the cloud services
- **Cloud service business manager**   Oversees business plans and customer relationships as well as processes financial transactions
- **Customer support and care representative**   Provides customer service and responds to customer requests
- **Inter-cloud provider**   Responsible for peering with other cloud services and providers as well as overseeing and managing federations and federated services
- **Cloud service security and risk manager**   Manages security and risks and oversees security compliance
- **Network provider**   Responsible for network connectivity, network services delivery, management of network services

Cloud Service Partner

The following roles are performed by the cloud service partner:

- **Cloud service developer**   Develops cloud components and services and the testing and validation of services
- **Cloud auditor**   Performs audits as well as prepares and authors audit reports
- **Cloud service broker**   Obtains new customers, analyzes the marketplace, secures contracts and agreements

Cloud Service Capabilities

In a discussion of cloud service delivery, three main cloud service capabilities form the basis for the cloud service categories:

- **Infrastructure service capability**   The cloud customer can provision and have substantial configuration control over processing, storage, and network resources.
- **Platform service capability**   The cloud customer can deploy code and applications using programming languages and libraries that are maintained and controlled by the cloud provider.
- **Software service capability**   The cloud customer uses a fully established application provided by the cloud provider, with minimal user configuration options allowed.

Cloud Service Categories

Although many different terms are used for the specific types of cloud service models and offerings, only three main models are universally accepted:

- Infrastructure as a Service (IaaS)
- Platform as a Service (PaaS)
- Software as a Service (SaaS)

A brief overview of these models is given in Figure 2-1, with more information on each model provided in the following sections.

Infrastructure as a Service (IaaS)

IaaS is the most basic cloud service and the one where the most customization and control is available for the customer. The following is from the NIST SP 800-145 definition for IaaS:

> The capability provided to the consumer is to provision processing, storage, networks, and other fundamental computing resources where the consumer is able to deploy and run arbitrary software, which can include operating systems and applications. The consumer does not manage or control the underlying cloud infrastructure but has control over operating systems, storage, and deployed applications; and possibly limited control of selected networking components (e.g., host firewalls).

IaaS	PaaS	SaaS
• Cloud provider maintains and controls the underlying architecture • Customer controls services deployed within the cloud: operating systems, storage, deployed applications • Limited control over network components for the customer • Customer can deploy and run arbitrary software and systems • Rapid provisioning and scalability • High availability	• Cloud provider is responsible for the operating system and hosting environment, including libraries, services, and tools • Customer is responsible for deploying their applications within the provided platform infrastructure • Cloud provider is responsible for patching and deploying systems • Auto-scaling • Flexibility and choice of hosting environments	• Cloud provider supplies a full cloud platform and software application to the customer • Provider is responsible for maintaining entire system and all underlying infrastructure • Customer provisions user access and permissions to data for their requirements • Lowest support requirements for the customer • Customer has limited configuration options

Figure 2-1   An overview of cloud service categories

Key Features and Benefits of IaaS   The following are the key features and benefits of IaaS. Some key features overlap with other cloud service models, but others are unique to IaaS.

- **Scalability**   Within an IaaS framework, the system can be rapidly provisioned and expanded as needed, either for predictable events or in response to unexpected demand.

- **Cost of ownership of physical hardware**   Within IaaS, the customer does not need to procure any hardware either for the initial launch and implementation or for future expansion.

- **High availability**   The cloud infrastructure, by definition, meets high availability and redundancy requirements, which would result in additional costs for a customer to meet within their own data center.

- **Physical security requirements**   Because you're in a cloud environment and don't have your own data centers, the cloud provider assumes the cost and oversight of the physical security of its data centers.

- **Location and access independence**   The cloud-based infrastructure has no dependence on the physical location of the customer or users of the system, as well as no dependence on specific network locations or applications or clients to access the system. The only dependency is on the security requirements of the cloud itself and the applications settings used.

- **Metered usage**   The customer only pays for the resources they are using and only during the durations of use. There is no need to have large data centers with idle resources for large chunks of time just to cover heavy-load periods.

- **Potential for "green" data centers**   Many customers and companies are interested in having more environmentally friendly data centers that are high efficiency in terms of both power consumption and cooling. Within cloud environments, many providers have implemented "green" data centers that are more cost effective with the economies of scale that would prohibit many customers from having on their own. Although this is not a requirement for a cloud provider, many major providers do market this as a feature, which is of interest to many customers.

Platform as a Service (PaaS)

PaaS allows a customer to fully focus on their core business functions from the software and application levels, either in development or production environments, without having to worry about the resources at the typical data center operations level. The following is from the NIST SP 800-145 definition of PaaS:

> The capability provided to the customer is to deploy onto the cloud infrastructure consumer-created or acquired applications created using programming languages, libraries, services, and tools supported by the provider. The customer does not manage or control the underlying cloud infrastructure including network, servers, operating systems, or storage, but has control over the deployed applications and possibly configuration settings for the application-hosting environment.

Key Features and Benefits of PaaS   The following are the key features of the PaaS cloud service model. Although there is some overlap with IaaS and SaaS, each model has its own unique set of features and details.

- **Auto-scaling**   As resources are needed (or not needed), the system can automatically adjust the sizing of the environment to meet demand without interaction from the customer. This is especially important for those systems whose load is cyclical in nature, and it allows an organization to only configure and use what is actually needed so as to minimize idle resources.

- **Multiple host environments**   With the cloud provider responsible for the actual platform, the customer has a wide choice of operating systems and environments. This feature allows software and application developers to test or migrate their systems between different environments to determine the most suitable and efficient platform for their applications to be hosted under without having to spend time configuring and building new systems on physical servers. Because the customer only pays for the resources they are using in the cloud, different platforms can be built and tested without a long-term or expensive commitment by the customer. This also allows a customer evaluating different applications to be more open to underlying operating system requirements.

- **Choice of environments**   Most organizations have a set standards for what their operations teams will support and offer as far as operating systems and platforms are concerned. This limits the options for application environments and operating system platforms that a customer can consider, both for homegrown and commercial products. The choice of environments not only extends to actual operating systems, but it also allows enormous flexibility as to specific versions and flavors of operating systems, contingent on what the cloud provider offers and supports.

- **Flexibility**   In a traditional data center setting, application developers are constrained by the offerings of the data center and are locked into proprietary systems that make relocation or expansion difficult and expensive. With those layers abstracted in a PaaS model, the developers have enormous flexibility to move between providers and platforms with ease. With many software applications and environments now open source or built by commercial companies to run on a variety of platforms, PaaS offers development teams enormous ease in testing and moving between platforms or even cloud providers.

- **Ease of upgrades**   With the underlying operating systems and platforms being offered by the cloud provider, upgrades and changes are more simple and efficient than in a traditional data center model, where system administrators need to perform actual upgrades on physical servers, which also means downtime and loss of productivity during upgrades.

- **Cost effective**   Like with other cloud categories, PaaS offers significant cost savings for development teams because only systems that are actively and currently used incur costs. Additional resources can be added or scaled back as needed during development cycles in a quick and efficient manner.

- **Ease of access**   With cloud services being accessible from the Internet and regardless of access clients, development teams can easily collaborate across national and international boundaries without needing to obtain accounts or access into propriety corporate data centers. The location and access methods of development teams become irrelevant from a technological perspective, but the Cloud Security Professional needs to be cognizant of any potential contractual or regulatory requirements. For example, with many government contracts, there may be requirements that development teams or hosting of systems and data be constrained within certain geographic or political boarders.

 EXAM TIP   Although the exam focuses on broad applications and shies away from specific governments and their requirements, it is important to be aware of this potential extra issue because it definitely comes up with United States government and European Union privacy requirements.

- **Licensing**   In a PaaS environment, the cloud provider is responsible for handling proper licensing of operating systems and platforms, which would normally be incumbent on an organization to ensure compliance. Within a PaaS cloud model, those costs are assumed as part of the metered costs for services and incumbent on the cloud provider to track and coordinate with the vendors.

Software as a Service (SaaS)

SaaS is a fully functioning software application for a customer to use in a turnkey operation, where all the underlying responsibilities and operations for maintaining systems, patches, and operations are abstracted from the customer and are the responsibility of the cloud services provider. The following is from the NIST SP 800-145 definition of SaaS:

> The capability provided to the customer is to use the provider's applications running on a cloud infrastructure. The applications are accessible from various client devices through either a thin client interface, such as a web browser (e.g., web-based email), or a program interface. The consumer does not manage or control the underlying cloud infrastructure including network, servers, operating systems, storage, or even individual application capabilities, with the possible exception of limited user-specific application settings.

Key Features and Benefits of SaaS   The following are the key features and benefits of the SaaS cloud service model. Some are similar to those of IaaS and PaaS, but due to the nature of SaaS being a fully built software platform, certain aspects are unique to SaaS.

- **Support costs and efforts**   In the SaaS service category, the cloud services are solely the responsibility of the cloud provider. Because the customer only licenses access to the software platform and capabilities, the entire underlying system, from network to storage and operating systems, as well as the software and application platforms themselves, is entirely removed from the responsibility of the consumer. Only the availability of the software application is important to the customer, and any responsibility for upgrades, patching, high availability, and operations solely reside with the cloud provider. This enables the customer to focus solely on productivity and business operations instead of IT operations.

- **Reduced overall costs** The customer in a SaaS environment is only licensing use of the software. The customer does not need to have systems administrators or security staff on hand, nor do they need to purchase hardware and software, plan for redundancy and disaster recovery, perform security audits on infrastructure, or deal with utility and environmental costs. Apart from licensing access for appropriate resources, features, and user counts from the cloud provider, the only cost concern for the customer is training in the use of the application platform and the device or computer access that their employees or users need to use the system.

- **Licensing** Similar to PaaS, within a SaaS model the licensing costs are the responsibility of the cloud provider. Whereas PaaS offers the licensing of the operating system and platforms to the cloud provider, SaaS takes it a step further with the software and everything included, leaving the customer to just "lease" licenses as they consume resources within the provided application. This removes both the bookkeeping and individual costs of licenses from the customer's perspective and instead rolls everything into the single cost of utilization of the actual software platform. This model allows the cloud provider, based on the scale of their implementations, to also negotiate far more beneficial bulk licensing savings than a single company or user would ever be able to do on their own, and thus drive lower total costs to their customers as well.

- **Ease of use and administration** With SaaS implementations being a fully featured software installation and product, the cost and efforts of administration are substantially lowered as compared to a PaaS or IaaS model. The customer only bears responsibility for configuring user access and access controls within the system, as well as minimal configurations. The configurations typically allowed within a SaaS system are usually very restricted and may only allow slight tweaks to the user experience, such as default settings or possibly some degree of branding; otherwise, all overhead and operations are held by the cloud provider exclusively.

- **Standardization** Because SaaS is a fully featured software application, all users will by definition be running the exact same version of the software at all times. A major challenge that many development and implementation teams face relates to patching and versioning, as well as configuration baselines and requirements. Within a SaaS model, because this is all handled by the cloud provider, it is achieved automatically.

Cloud Deployment Models

As shown in Figure 2-2, four main types of cloud deployment and hosting models are in common use, each of which can host any of the three main cloud service models.

	Public	Private	
• Available to the general public • Located on the premises of the cloud provider • May be owned by a private company, organization, academic institution, or a combination of owners • Easy setup and inexpensive to the customer • Pay only for services consumed			• Owned and controlled by a single entity • Primarily used by that entity for their own purposes, but may be opened to collaborating organizations • May be operated by the organization or a third party • Can be located on or off premises • Can be used by different departments with internal billing
• Composed of two or more different cloud models (public, private, community) • Standardized or proprietary technologies that enable portability between models • Typically leveraged for load balancing, high availability, or disaster recovery	Hybrid	Community	• Owned by a group of similar organizations for use within the group • Models and features similar to a private cloud • Managed and controlled by the member organizations • May exist on or off premises of the ownership organization

Figure 2-2 Cloud deployment models

Public Cloud

A public cloud is just what it sounds like. It is a model that provides cloud services to the general public or any company or organization at large without restriction beyond finances and planning. The following is the NIST SP 800-145 definition:

> The cloud infrastructure is provisioned for open use by the general public. It may be owned, managed, and operated by a business, academic, or government organization, or some combination of them. It exists on the premises of the cloud provider.

Key Benefits and Features of the Public Cloud Model   The following are key and unique benefits and features of the public cloud model:

- **Setup**   Setup is very easy and inexpensive for the customer. All aspects of infrastructure, including hardware, network, licensing, bandwidth, and operational costs, are controlled and assumed by the provider.

- **Scalability**   Even though scalability is a common feature of all cloud implementations, most public clouds are offered from very large corporations that have very broad and extensive resources and infrastructures. This allows even large implementations the freedom to scale as needed and as budgets allow, without worry of hitting capacity or interfering with other hosted implementations on the same cloud.

- **Right-sizing resources**   Customers only pay for what they use and need at any given point in time. Their sole investment is scoped to their exact needs and can be completely fluid and agile over time based on either expected demand or unplanned demand at any given point in time.

Private Cloud

A private cloud differs from a public cloud in that it is run by and restricted to the organization that it serves. A private cloud model may also be opened up to other entities, expanding outward for developers, employees, contractors, and subcontractors, as well as potential collaborators and other firms that may offer complementary services or subcomponents. The following is the NIST SP 800-145 definition:

> The cloud infrastructure is provisioned for exclusive use by a single organization comprising multiple consumers (e.g., business units). It may be owned, managed, and operated by the organization, a third party, or some combination of them, and it may exist on or off premises.

Key Benefits and Features of the Private Cloud Model   The following are key benefits and features of the private cloud model and how it differs from a public cloud:

- **Ownership retention**   Because the organization that utilizes the cloud also owns and operates it and controls who has access to it, that organization retains full control over it. This includes control of the underlying hardware and software infrastructures, as well as control throughout the cloud in regard to data policies, access polices, encryptions methods, versioning, change control, and governance as a whole. For any organization that has strict policies or regulatory controls and requirements, this model would facilitate easier compliance and verification for auditing purposes versus the more limited controls and views offered via a public cloud. In cases where contracts or regulations stipulate locality and limitations as to where data and systems may reside and operate, a private cloud ensures compliance with requirements beyond just the contractual controls that a public cloud might offer, which also would require extensive reporting and auditing to validate compliance.

- **Control over systems**   With a private cloud, the operations and system parameters of the cloud are solely at the discretion of the controlling organization. Whereas in a public cloud model an organization would be limited to the specific offerings for software and operating system versions, as well as patch and upgrade cycles, a private cloud allows the organization to determine what versions and timelines are offered without the need for contractual negotiations or potentially increased costs if specific versions need to be retained and supported beyond the time horizon that a public cloud is willing to offer.

- **Proprietary data and software control**   Whereas a public cloud requires extensive software and contractual requirements to ensure the segregation and security of hosted systems, a private cloud offers absolute assurance that no other hosted environments can somehow gain access or insight into another hosted environment.

Community Cloud

A community cloud is a collaboration between similar organizations that combine resources to offer a private cloud. It is comparable to a private cloud with the exception of multiple ownership and/or control versus singular ownership of a private cloud. The following is the NIST SP 800-145 definition:

> The cloud infrastructure is provisioned for exclusive use by a specific community of consumers from organizations that have shared concerns (e.g., mission, security requirements, policy, and compliance considerations). It may be owned, managed, and operated by one or more of the organizations in the community, a third party, or some combination of them, and may exist on or off premises.

Hybrid Cloud

As the name implies, a hybrid cloud combines the use of both private and public cloud models to fully meet an organization's needs. The following is the NIST SP 800-145 definition:

> The cloud infrastructure is a composition of two or more distinct cloud infrastructures (private, community, or public) that remain unique entities, but are bound together by standardized or proprietary technology that enables data and application portability (e.g., cloud busting for load balancing between clouds).

Key Benefits and Features of the Hybrid Cloud Model   Building upon key features and benefits of the public and private cloud models, these are the key features of the hybrid model:

- **Split systems for optimization**   With a hybrid model, a customer has the opportunity and benefit of splitting out their operations between public and private clouds for optimal scaling and cost effectiveness. If desired by the organization, some parts of systems can be maintained internally while leveraging the expansive offerings of public clouds for other systems. This can be done for cost reasons, security concerns, regulatory requirements, or to leverage toolsets and offerings that a public cloud may provide that their private cloud does not.

- **Retain critical systems internally**   When a company has the option to leverage a public cloud and its services, critical data systems can be maintained internally with private data controls and access controls.

- **Disaster recovery**   An organization can leverage a hybrid cloud as a way to maintain systems within its own private cloud, but utilize and have at its disposal the resources and options of a public cloud for disaster recovery and redundancy purposes. This would allow an organization to utilize its own private resources but have the ability to migrate systems to a public cloud when needed, without having to incur the costs of a failover site that sits idle except when an emergency arises.

Because public cloud systems are only used in the event a disaster, no costs would be incurred by the organization until such an event occurs. Also, with the organization building and maintaining its own images on its private cloud, these same images could be loaded into the provisioning system of a public cloud and be ready to use if and when required.

- **Scalability**   Along the same lines as disaster recovery usage, an organization can have at the ready a contract with a public cloud provider to handle periods of burst traffic, either forecasted or in reaction to unexpected demand. In this scenario, an organization can keep its systems internal with its private cloud but have the option to scale out to a public cloud on short notice, only incurring costs should the need arise.

Cloud Cross-Cutting Aspects

Several aspects of cloud computing are universal, regardless of the particular service category or deployment model.

Interoperability

Interoperability is the ease at which one can move or reuse components of an application or service. The underlying platform, operating system, location, API structure, or cloud provider should not be an impediment to moving services easily and efficiently to an alternative solution. An organization that has a high degree of interoperability with its systems is not bound to one cloud provider and can easily move to another if the level of service or price is not suitable. This keeps pressure on cloud providers to offer a high level of services and be competitive with pricing or risk losing customers to other cloud providers at any time. With services only incurring costs as they are used, it is even easier to change providers with a high degree of interoperability because long-term contracts are not set. Further, an organization also maintains flexibility to move between different cloud hosting models, such as moving from public to private clouds, and vice versa, as its internal needs or requirements change over time. With an interoperability mandate, an organization can seamlessly move between cloud providers, underlying technologies, and hosting environments, or it can split components apart and host them in different environments without impacting the flow of data or services.

Performance, Availability, and Resiliency

The concepts of performance, availability, and resiliency should be considered de facto aspects of any cloud environment due to the nature of cloud infrastructures and models. Given the size and scale of most cloud implementations, performance should always be second nature to a cloud unless it is incorrectly planned or managed. Resiliency and high availability are also hallmarks of a cloud environment. If any of these areas fall short, then customers will not stay long with a cloud provider and will quickly move to other providers. With proper provisioning and scaling by the cloud provider, performance should always be a top concern and focus. In a virtualized environment, it is easy for a cloud provider with proper management to move virtual machines and services around within its environment to maintain performance and even load. This capability is also what allows a cloud provider to maintain high availability and resiliency within its environment. As with many other key aspects of cloud computing, SLAs will determine and test the desired performance, availability, and resiliency of the cloud services.

Portability

Portability is the key feature that allows systems to easily and seamlessly move between different cloud providers. An organization that has its systems optimized for portability opens up enormous flexibility to move between different providers and hosting models, and can be leveraged in a variety of ways. From a cost perspective, portability allows an organization to continually shop for cloud hosting services. Although cost can be a dominant driving factor, an organization may change providers for improved customer service, better feature sets and offerings, or SLA compliance issues. Apart from reasons to shop around for a cloud provider, portability also enables an organization to span their systems across multiple cloud hosting arrangements. This can be for disaster recovery reasons, locality diversity, or high availability, for example.

Service Level Agreements (SLAs)

Whereas a contract will spell out the general terms and costs for services, the SLA is where the real meat of the business relationship and concrete requirements come into play. The SLA spells out in clear terms the minimum requirements for uptime, availability, processes, customer service and support, security controls and requirements, auditing and reporting, and potentially many other areas that will define the business relationship and the success of it. Failure to meet the SLA requirements will give the customer either financial benefits or credits, or form the basis for contract termination if acceptable performance cannot be rectified on behalf of the cloud provider.

Regulatory Requirements

Regulatory requirements are those imposed upon a business and its operations either by law, regulation, policy, or standards and guidelines. These requirements are specific to the locality in which the company or application is based or specific to the nature of the data and transactions conducted. These requirements can carry financial, legal, or even criminal penalties for failure to comply, either willfully or accidently. Sanctions and penalties can apply to the company itself or even in some cases the individuals working for the company and on its behalf, depending on the locality and the nature of the violation. Specific industries often have their own regulations and laws governing them above and beyond general regulations, such as the Health Insurance Portability and Accountability Act (HIPAA) in the healthcare sector, the Federal Information Security Management Act (FISMA) for U.S. federal agencies and contractors, and the Payment Card Industry Data Security Standard (PCI DSS) for the financial/retail sectors. These are just a few examples of specific regulations that go above and beyond general regulations that apply to all businesses, such as the Sarbanes–Oxley (SOX) Act. The Cloud Security Professional needs to be aware of any and all regulations in which his or her systems and applications are required to comply; in most cases, failure to understand the requirements or ignorance of the requirements will not shield a company from investigations or penalties, nor potential damage to its reputation.

TIP Both the United States and European Union have especially strong and defined policy and security requirements for applications. Being familiar with the EU regulations on data governance and applicable requirements is very important for any professional operating within either jurisdiction.

Security

Security is of course always a paramount concern for any system or application. Within a cloud environment, there can be a lot of management and stakeholder unease with using a newer technology, and many will be uncomfortable with the idea of having corporate and sensitive data not under direct control of internal IT staff and hardware, housed in proprietary data centers. Depending on company policy and any regulatory or contractual requirements, different applications and systems will have their own specific security requirements and controls. Within a cloud environment, this becomes of particular interests because many customers are tenants within the same framework, and the cloud provider needs to ensure each customer that their controls are being met, and done so in a way that the cloud provider can support, with varying requirements. Another challenge exists with large cloud environments that likely have very strong security controls but will not publicly document what these controls are so as not to expose themselves to attacks. This is often mitigated within contract negotiations through nondisclosure agreements and privacy requirements, although this is still not the same level of understanding and information as an organization would have with its own internal and proprietary data centers.

The main way a cloud provider implements security is by setting baselines and minimum standards, while offering a suite of add-ons or extensions to security that typically come with an additional cost. This allows the cloud provider to support a common baseline and offer additional controls on a per-customer basis to those that require or desire them. On the other hand, for many smaller companies and organizations, which would not typically have extensive financial assets and expertise, moving to a major cloud provider may very well offer significantly enhanced security for their applications at a much lower cost than they could get on their own. In effect, they are realizing the economies of scale, and the demands of larger corporations and systems will benefit their own systems for a cheaper cost.

Privacy

Privacy in the cloud environment requires particular care due to the large number of regulatory and legal requirements that can differ greatly by use and location. Adding additional complexity is the fact that laws and regulations may differ based on where the data is stored (data at rest) and where the data is exposed and consumed (data in transit). In cloud environments, especially large public cloud systems, data has the inherent ability to be stored and moved between different locations, from within a country, between countries, and even across continents.

Cloud providers will very often have in place mechanisms to keep systems housed in geographic locations based on a customer's requirements and regulations, but it is incumbent on the Cloud Security Professional to verify and ensure that these mechanisms are functioning properly. Contractual requirements need to be clearly spelled out between the customer and cloud provider, but strict SLAs and the ability to audit compliance are also important. In particular, European countries have strict privacy regulations that a company must always be cognizant of or else face enormous penalties that many other countries do not have; the ability of the cloud provider to properly enforce location and security requirements will not protect a company from sanctions and penalties for compliance failure because the burden resides fully on the owner of the application and the data held within.

Auditability

Most leading cloud providers supply their customers with a good deal of auditing, including reports and evidence that show user activity, compliance with controls and regulations, systems and processes that run and an explanation of what they do, as well as information, data access, and modification records. Auditability of a cloud environment is an area where the Cloud Security Professional needs to pay particular attention because the customer does not have full control over the environment like they would in a proprietary and traditional data center model. It is up to the cloud provider to expose auditing, logs, and reports to the customer and show diligence and evidence that they are capturing all events within their environment and properly reporting them.

Governance

Governance at its core involves assigning jobs, tasks, roles, and responsibilities and ensuring they are satisfactory performed. Whether in a traditional data center or a cloud model, governance is mostly the same and undertaken by the same approach, with a bit of added complexity in a cloud environment due to data protection requirements and the role of the cloud provider. Although the cloud environment adds complexity to governance and oversight, it also brings some benefits as well. Most cloud providers offer extensive and regular reporting and metrics, either in real time from their web portals or in the form of regular reporting. These metrics can be tuned to the cloud environment and configured in such as way so as to give an organization greater ease in verifying compliance as opposed to a traditional data center, where reporting and collection mechanisms have to be established and maintained. However, care also needs to be taken with portability and migration between different cloud providers or hosting models to ensure that metrics are equivalent or comparable to be able to maintain a consistent and ongoing governance process.

Maintenance and Versioning

With the different types of cloud service categories, it is important for the contract and SLA to clearly spell out maintenance responsibilities. With a SaaS implementation, the cloud provider is basically responsible for all upgrades, patching, and maintenance, whereas with PaaS and certainly IaaS, some duties belong to the cloud customer while the rest are retained by the cloud provider. Outlining maintenance and testing practices and timelines with the SLA is particularly important for applications that may not always work correctly because of new versions or changes to the underlying system. This requires the cloud provider and cloud customer to work out a balance between the needs of the cloud provider to maintain a uniform environment and the needs of the cloud customer to ensure continuity of operations and system stability. Whenever a system upgrade or maintenance is performed, it is crucial to establish version numbers for platforms and software. With versioning, changes can be tracked and tested, with known versions available to fall back to if necessary due to problems with new versions. There should be an overlap period where a previous version (or versions) is available, which should be spelled out in the SLA.

Reversibility

Reversibility is the ability of a cloud customer to take all their systems and data out of a cloud provider and have assurances from the cloud provider that all the data has been securely and completely removed within an agreed-upon timeline. In most cases this will be done by the cloud customer by first retrieving all their data and processes from the cloud provider, serving notice that all active and available files and systems should be deleted, and then removing all traces from long-term archives or storage at an agreed upon point in time.

Security Concepts Relevant to Cloud Computing

Most security concepts for any system or data center are the same for cloud computing:

- Cryptography
- Access control
- Data and media sanitation
- Network security
- Virtualization security
- Common threats

However, due to the unique nature of the cloud, specific considerations are needed for each concept.

Cryptography

In any environment, data encryption is incredibly important to prevent unauthorized exposure of data, either internally or externally. If a system is compromised by an attack, having the data encrypted on the system will prevent its unauthorized exposure or export, even with the system itself being exposed. This is especially important where there are strict regulations for data security and privacy, such as healthcare, education, tax payment, and financial information.

Encryption

There are many different types and levels of encryption. Within a cloud environment, it is the duty of the Cloud Security Professional to evaluate the needs of the application, the technologies it employs, the types of data it contains, and the regulatory or contractual requirements for its protection and use. Encryption is important for many aspects of a cloud implementation. This includes the storage of data on a system, both when it is being accessed and while it is at rest, as well as the actual transmission of data and transactions between systems or between the system and a consumer. The Cloud Security Professional must ensure that appropriate encryption is selected that will be strong enough to meet regulatory and system requirements, but also efficient and accessible enough for operations to seamlessly work within the application.

Data in Transit

Data in transit is the state of data when it is actually being used by an application and is traversing systems internally or going between the client and the actual application. Whether the data is being transmitted between systems within the cloud or going out to a user's client, data in transit is when data is most vulnerable to exposure of unauthorized capture. Within a cloud hosting model, the transmission between systems is even more important than with a traditional data center due to multitenancy; the other systems within the same cloud are potential security risks and vulnerable points where data capture could happen successfully.

In order to maintain portability and interoperability, the Cloud Security Professional should make the processes for the encryption of data in transit vendor-neutral in regard to the capabilities or limitations of a specific cloud provider. The Cloud Security Professional should be involved in the planning and design of the system or application from the earliest stages to ensure that everything is built properly from the ground up, and not retrofitted after design or implementation has been completed. Whereas the use of encryption with the operations of the system is crucial during the design phase, the proper management of keys, protocols, and testing/auditing are crucial once a system has been implemented and deployed.

The most common method for data-in-transit encryption is to use the well-known SSL and TLS technologies under HTTPS. With many modern applications utilizing web services as the framework for communications, this has become the prevailing method, which is the same method used by clients and browsers to communicate with servers over the Internet. This method is now being used within cloud environments for server-to-server internal communication as well. Beyond using HTTPS, other common encryption methods for data in transit are VPNs (virtual private networks) and IPsec. These methods can be used by themselves but are most commonly used in parallel to provide the highest level of protection possible.

 NOTE Over time, many versions of SSL and TLS have been declared unsafe or compromised. This also applies to specific encryption ciphers used by SSL and TLS. As a Cloud Security Professional, it is very important to stay on top of this matter, especially if SSL and TLS are provided on behalf of the cloud provider. Regulatory bodies as well as industry certification groups will often dictate the disabling of ciphers that are no longer considered safe or sufficient, so this one area to always stay abreast of developments and news.

Data at Rest

Data at rest refers to information stored on a system or device (versus data that is actively being transmitted across a network or between systems). The data can be stored in many different forms to fit within this category. Some examples include databases, file sets, spreadsheets, documents, tapes, archives, and even mobile devices.

Data residing on a system is potentially exposed and vulnerable far longer than short transmission and transaction operations would be, so special care is needed to ensure its protection from unauthorized access. With transaction systems and data in transit, usually a small subset of records or even a single record is transmitted at any time, versus the comprehensive record sets maintained in databases and other file systems.

While encrypting data is central to the confidentiality of any system, the availability and performance of data are equally as important. The Cloud Security Professional must ensure that encryption methods provide high levels of security and protection and do so in a manner that facilitates high performance and system speed. Any use of encryption will cause higher load and processing times, so proper scaling and evaluation of systems are critical when testing deployments and design criteria.

With portability and vendor lock-in considerations, it is important for a Cloud Security Professional to ensure that encryption systems do not effectively cause a system to be bound to a proprietary cloud offering. If a system or application ends up using a proprietary encryption system from a cloud provider, portability will likely be far more difficult and thus tie that customer to that particular cloud provider. With many cloud implementations spanning multiple cloud providers and infrastructures for disaster recovery and continuity planning, having encryption systems that can maintain consistency and performance is important.

Key Management

With any encryption system, a method is needed to properly issue, maintain, and organize keys. If a customer has their own key management systems and procedures, they can better ensure their own data security, as well as prevent being "locked in" with a cloud provider and the systems they provide, which may be proprietary in nature. Beyond the vendor lock-in that can occur with using a key management system from the cloud provider, your keys are also being managed within a system that contains similar keys for other systems. A customer that maintains control of their own key management systems ensures a higher degree of portability and segregation of systems for security reasons.

Two main key management services (KMSs) are commonly used within cloud computing systems: remote and client-side.

Remote Key Management Service   A remote key management service is maintained and controlled by the customer at their own location. This offers the highest degree of security for the customer because the keys will be contained under their sole control and outside of the boundaries of the cloud provider. This implementation allows the customer to fully configure and implement their own keys and fully control who can access and generate key pairs. The main drawback to a remote KMS is that connectivity will have to be open and always maintained in order for the systems and applications hosted by the cloud provider to function properly. This introduces the potential for network connectivity latency or periods of downtime, either accidental or by design, which eliminates the high-availability features of a cloud provider and is dependent on the availability of the KMS.

Client-Side Key Management Service   Most common with SaaS implementations, client-side KMS is provided by the cloud provider but is hosted and controlled by the customer. This allows for seamless integration with the cloud environment, but also allows complete control to still reside with the customer. The customer is fully responsible for all key generation and maintenance activities.

Access Control

Access control combines the two main concepts of authentication and authorization, but adds a crucial third concept of accounting as well. With authentication, a person or system verifies who they are, and with authorization they acquire the appropriate minimum system access rights that they should have based on their role to use the system and consume data. Accounting involves maintaining the logs and records of authentication and authorization activities, and for both, operational and regulatory needs are absolutely crucial.

Access control systems can have a variety of different types of authentication mechanisms that provide increasing levels of security based on the type of data sensitivity. On the low end, this can involve the use of a user ID and password, which everyone is familiar with in regard to typical system access. For higher levels of security, systems can and should use multiple factors of authentication in combination. This will typically be a combination of the classic user ID and password with an additional requirement such as a physical possession. Types of secondary factors typically include biometric tests (fingerprints and retina scans), a physical token device that is plugged into a computer and read by the system, and the use of a mobile device or callback feature, where the user is provided with a code to input in addition to their password for access. There are many other types of potential secondary authentication methods, but the ones just mentioned are the most common. Physical secondary types of authentication can also be layered in combination; for example, the user could have to provide a retina scan as well as a physical token device.

The four main areas of access management concerns are described in the following sections.

Account Provisioning

Before any system access can be granted and roles determined, accounts must be created on the system that will form the basis of access. At this stage, the most crucial aspect for an organization is the validation of users and verification of their credentials to be allowed to acquire accounts for the system. It is incumbent on an organization and their security policies and practices to determine the appropriate level of proof required to verify a new user and issue credentials. This can be based solely on the policies of the organization, or it can include extensive additional processes based on contractual, legal, or regulatory requirements. A prime example would be government contracts, where specific documentation for verification must be submitted to approve authorities outside of the organization, or even to obtain security clearance through separate vetting processes as an additional requirement before account access can be provisioned. The big key for any organization is making a process that is efficient and consistent across the user base so that the account provisioning process can be audited and trusted. While most of the discussion so far has been based on granting and verifying access, it is equally important for an organization to have a well-defined and efficient procedure for removing accounts from the systems at the appropriate time, either for security incident responses purposes, job role changes, or the termination or resignation of employees.

 NOTE   Some industries, and particularly the academic world, employ federated identity systems to allow people from different organizations to use tokenized credentials to access collaborative systems without needing an actual account on those systems. Depending on the industry you work in (or intend to work in), explorations of open source systems such as Shibboleth would be very valuable.

Directory Services

The backbone of any access management system is the directory server that contains all of the information that applications need to make proper authentication and authorization decisions. Although various solutions for directory services are offered by many different vendors, the core of virtually all of them is the Lightweight Directory Access Protocol (LDAP). LDAP is a highly optimized system of representing data as objects with associated attributes, which can be single- or multi-valued in nature. The data is stored in a hierarchical representation where a DN (distinguished name) acts as the primary key for an object. When users log into a system, LDAP can provide authentication. Then, depending on the application and its needs, it can provide a variety of information about that user from the attributes associated with their object. This information can be anything, such as the department of an organization they are part of, job titles or codes, flags to determine managers and other special designations, specific system information and roles the user is allowed to access, and essentially any other type of information an organization has determined to be part of their user object. LDAP systems are highly optimized to handle very large numbers of queries of a read-only nature and are able to scale out quickly and efficiently with a model of data replication to servers that can be placed behind load balancers or geographically distributed, depending on the needs and designs of the system implementation.

Administrative and Privileged Access

Although managing all accounts and access is essential to any application and system environment, the management of administrative and privileged accounts is especially important. In this sense, administrative and privileged accounts are those accounts that have access above and beyond what users of the systems would have. These are permissions that allow control and configuration of the software, control over access roles, and control over the underlying operating systems and environments that make up the system. They have the ability to do the greatest damage to the system and expose private data, which could lead to loss of reputation on behalf of the organization or expose the organization to potential regulatory or legal issues.

For the most part, the requirements for account provisioning are the same for this class of users, though certainly it will be a much smaller part of the overall population, typically restricted to very specific groups within the organization where higher scrutiny during the hiring process would have already been undertaken. The crucial part that comes into play with this class of users and elevated privileges is the ability to track and audit what the users are doing with the access. Although many systems come by default with administrative accounts built in that could be used, it is a best practice to disable those accounts and ensure that everyone within this class is using their own personal accounts, and that activities done with those accounts can be logged and tracked. The best way to do this, depending on the capabilities of the system and applications, is to have regular accounts that have the ability to elevate privileges for specific tasks. This must be done in such a way that the elevation and tasks undertaken are logged, preferably in a manner that the user cannot edit or destroy. This can be accomplished through systems that automatically store the logs somewhere that is not accessible by the users of the system. However, with some operating systems and environments, it can be very difficult to keep the separation of logging capabilities and privileged users because the granularity of access and the method for administrative elevation may not be cleanly distinct.

Authorization

So far we have focused on getting users their accounts and the ability to access the system, but the most important aspect beyond just being able to access the system is ensuring that the users have the appropriate roles and privileges within the system. Whereas administrative users will gain access to an entire system, the vast majority of users fall into specific roles that are given access to specific functions or sections within the application or system.

The directory system can and usually does provide the application with the information it needs to determine what features and sections the given user should be granted access to. Whereas authentication is typically a one-time event per session, authorization is an ongoing function that is repeatedly performed within the session. As the user performs transactions and traverses the system, the authorization mechanisms need to continually evaluate their access and determine if they are performing appropriate actions each step of the way. Note that this does not necessarily mean a callback operation to the directory for information about the user because the initial block of attributes could be maintained in state and used throughout the session. The main drawback to doing it this way, though, would be if the permissions of a user were to change during the session, although this could be mitigated by a system that makes the user log back in when changes occur and begin a new session.

Data and Media Sanitation

In a cloud environment, two main issues present themselves when it comes to data and media sanitation. The first is the ability to easily and efficiently move data from one cloud provider to another, to maintain interoperability and reduce vendor lock-in.

The other is the ability to ensure that all data has been removed and sanitized when leaving a cloud provider or environment. This involves cleaning and erasing any data in the environment as well as ensuring that if any data is missed or left behind in some capacity, it is not accessible or readable by anyone.

Vendor Lock-in for Data

Vendor lock-in from a general perspective refers to a customer being bound to a particular provider, either based on systems, security requirements, data storage systems, application environments, versions, or any other aspect that limits the customer's ability to easily change providers. When it comes to data systems, this lock-in can occur in a wide range of ways, either with underlying file or database systems, data structures, encryption systems, or even size and scale of data that another provider may not be able to easily accommodate. A cloud provider may have proprietary systems that scale well and work efficiently, but if they are implemented in a way that makes it difficult for a customer to export data, then portability becomes a major concern and limiting factor.

Apart from just the ability to export data, there is a big concern with the ability to sanitize the data from the cloud provider once it has been exported. With virtual machines, there is the ability to destroy images and sanitize from that perspective, but with data storage systems, if they are implemented in a manner where multiple customers are using them, the data sanitation can become more challenging. Regulatory requirements based on the type and content of data must be consulted to ensure the cloud provider can meet the minimum requirements for sanitation as well as provide ample auditing and evidence of proper sanitation being performed. Because degaussing or destruction of physical media is not possible or practical within a cloud framework, the Cloud Security Professional needs to be aware of what a cloud provider offers before any data is introduced into the provider's environment. A full understanding of the cloud provider's capabilities prior to introducing any data, combined with having appropriate SLAs in place to ensure the needs of the customer will be addressed and verified when and if needed, will ensure a sound security policy and confidence among management and auditors.

Data Sanitation

When moving from one system to another—or on a bigger scale, moving from one data center to another (cloud providers included)—it is always imperative that data be properly and completely cleansed from any storage system. In a cloud environment, many of these issues related to data sanitation become even more pressing because the customer does not have access to or control of the physical storage media. In a traditional data center, where the customer owns and possesses the actual hard drives and storage systems, sanitation can be a bit easier because there are more methods available, such as shredding, degaussing, and incineration, methods not available within a cloud environment, so other means must be the focus.

Overwriting   Data overwriting (also known as the "zeroing" of data) is perhaps the most common method used for data sanitation. When files are deleted from a system, the data really remains on the system, even though it is no longer visible to users. Through the use of common and widely available tools, even someone without a huge amount of technical knowledge can recover portions or all of the data that has been erased in this manner, and those highly skilled with these tools can often recover almost anything that is on the media. With data overwriting, the common practice is to write over erased data with either arbitrary data or zero values. This is done multiple times so as to ensure that the data has been overwritten and is no longer available. However, highly sophisticated tools and techniques are sometimes able to recover even data that has gone through multiple steps of overwriting, so this method of data sanitation is not typically used for data that is highly sensitive or classified in nature.

 CAUTION Many regulatory requirements stipulate the specific software, overwriting scheme, and the number of times an overwrite must be performed until a system can be considered sanitized. Make sure to verify with any regulatory agencies that you operate within as to their specific requirements, which may go above and beyond company policy. It is imperative to ensure that the cloud provider's sanitation practices and policies meet the regulatory requirements.

Cryptographic Erasing   One very common method for data sanitation is to leverage encryption and the destruction of the keys as a way to ensure data destruction. With systems that have large volumes of data, it can be a time-consuming process to both delete and overwrite data on a system. This is further complicated in a cloud environment with data that can be written over large systems, making it difficult to ensure that all copies have been safely removed and overwritten.

Network Security

Within a cloud environment network, security is essential, as with any system, but due to multitenancy and loss of control of the underlying hardware infrastructure, it is much more crucial in a cloud environment than in a traditional data center. Because the main access point for cloud environments, regardless of the cloud architecture model (IaaS, PaaS, or SaaS), is via the Internet versus any physically connected methods, network security is crucial.

There are two avenues to consider with a cloud environment from a network standpoint. The first is the actual physical layer to the environment. Because the customer is dependent on the cloud provider to ensure the security of the underlying physical network within their environment, the cloud provider needs to impart to the customer through a degree of transparency and contractual assurances that proper security controls are being implemented and audited. The cloud provider, due to portability aspects of cloud computing, has strong motivation to implement meaningful security controls and assurances to the customer, or risk losing business to a competitor quickly. From a logical perspective, network services are a top concern considering all the network traffic from various customers, the protocols being used, and the endpoints of data traversing the network.

Because cloud environments are typically large and have a high number of hosted customers, some aspects of networking become crucial more so than in a traditional data center model. With a traditional data center, the outside border coming in represents the logical segmentation point where the network changes from public to private. Because the cloud has many customers, although the outside border is still a logical segmentation point, there is the added complexity of numerous private networks within the cloud to separate customers from each other. This adds a layer of complexity, both with load and configuration within the cloud, for which the provider must be able to maintain appropriate controls and monitoring to handle. Because any customer can consume enormous resources based on load or attacks, the network segmentation and any limiting factors can shield customers from the predicaments of other customers to maintain the high degree of availability and scalability. When systems grow and scale, especially through automatic means, it is imperative that the virtual network controls and segmentation automatically scale to continually encompass the systems.

Virtualization Security

Virtualization forms the backbone of a cloud infrastructure as well as the basis of scalability, portability, multitenancy, and resource pooling. With the central role virtualization plays in a cloud environment, the security of the underlying hypervisor and virtualization infrastructure is absolutely essential for any Cloud Security Professional. Attacks and vulnerabilities at the hypervisor layer, if successfully exploited by an attacker, expose the entire cloud environment to attacks and threats.

The two types of hypervisors have different security concerns, as detailed next.

Type 1 Hypervisors

A Type 1 hypervisor is tied to the underlying hardware and hosts virtual machines on top of it, and it operates as the sole layer between the hardware (bare metal) and host (virtual servers) layer. A common example would be VMware ESXI.

Due to the proprietary nature of Type 1 hypervisor software and the close intrinsic tie that it has to the underlying hardware, security can be maintained with a very high degree of confidence. Because the vendor controls both the hardware and software, the hypervisor implementation is tightly controlled as to its features and capabilities, making a much leaner and tighter software platform that is more difficult to exploit. With the vendors having full proprietary control of the software, they also control upgrades and patches without extending that capability to anyone else. The tight control and proprietary knowledge make it much more difficult for someone to inject malicious code to gain access and run exploits.

Type 2 Hypervisors

A Type 2 hypervisor is software based. It resides on the host system itself and then orchestrates the hosts under its purview. In this case, the hypervisor is not tied directly to the bare-metal infrastructure and instead runs within an operating system as software. A common example would be VMware Workstation.

With software-based hypervisors, you are dependent on an operating system that is independent of the hardware and virtualization system to operate. The hypervisor must interact with the operating system and rely on it for access to the underlying hardware and system processes. With this dependency, the hypervisor is then vulnerable (to an extent) to any potential flaws and software exploits that can strike the underlying operating system, which could then be used to launch attacks against the hypervisor. When you add in the large degree of flexibility that operating systems offer as a platform, as well as the many flavors of operating systems themselves, the security with Type 2 hypervisors is not as tight and dependable as the native solution that Type 1 provides. Tight control, patching, and vigilance of the underlying operating system platform can go a long way toward a much more security platform.

Common Threats

In 2016, the Cloud Security Alliance published "The Treacherous 12: Cloud Computing Top Threats in 2016" (https://cloudsecurityalliance.org/group/top-threats/). The well-known threats identified are the top issues the Cloud Security Professional faces:

- Data breaches
- Insufficient identity, credential, and access management
- Insecure interfaces and APIs
- System vulnerabilities
- Account hijacking
- Malicious insiders
- Advanced persistent threats
- Data loss
- Insufficient due diligence
- Abuse and nefarious use of cloud services
- Denial of service
- Shared technology issues

Data Breaches

A data breach is the unauthorized exposure of sensitive and private data to a party that is not entitled to have it. This is often a top worry of management and security professionals, and can occur either by accidental exposure or from a direct attack by someone looking to steal data. With a cloud environment and multitenancy, the threat carries more particular risks because accidental exposure to someone completely external to the company is significantly more possible than in a private data center, although this threat is also magnified more in a public cloud than it would be in a private cloud.

Through the use of technologies such as data encryption, a company can significantly reduce the likeliness of a successful data breach, but this also introduces problems with data loss (for example, if the keys are lost). The data breach threat applies to IaaS, PaaS, and SaaS models.

Insufficient Identity, Credential, and Access Management

The probability of a data or system breach increases dramatically for an environment where there are not sufficient controls over the identity and credential systems used for access. This can be in the form of passwords that are not of sufficient strength or are not changed regularly, as well as certificates and other access tokens that are not rotated on a regular schedule. Any systems that use passwords should always employ multifactor authentication, unless a system cannot support it, in which case more stringent password change and quality requirements should be in place. Whether passwords or certificate mechanisms are used, it is imperative to not have them embedded in source code or configuration objects. Any systems within an environment that are a central store of authentication credentials are of extremely high value to an attacker and must be hardened and monitored with more diligence than any other systems. The insufficient identity, credential, and access management threat applies to IaaS, PaaS, and SaaS models.

Insecure Interfaces and APIs

Insecure interfaces or APIs are a particular threat in cloud environments because cloud services—from the underlying infrastructure and administration, up to the functioning of most cloud applications and their design—heavily use APIs and web services to function and operate. These interfaces form the backbone of a cloud environment and deployment. Without them, functions such as auto-scaling and provisioning will not work from the cloud infrastructure aspect, and functions such as authentication, authorization, and the actual operations of the cloud application will not work. Many cloud applications also offer APIs that are exposed for public use or use by other applications in a dependency model, which can be broken and cause reputation harm. To mitigate this threat, both the cloud provider and the application owner need to ensure that tight and strong security controls are in place, including the use of strong encryption and authorization access to APIs and connectivity. The threat of insecure interfaces and APIs applies to the IaaS, PaaS, and SaaS models.

System Vulnerabilities

System vulnerabilities are not new or unique to cloud computing in any way. They are vulnerabilities present in the underlying system or operating system that expose it to compromise and put all services on it at risk. System vulnerabilities are obviously a big concern, but there are also established and mature processes for mitigating and minimizing them. With well-developed patching procedures, system monitoring, and regular scanning and testing, system vulnerabilities can be well minimized within the environment. The system vulnerabilities threat applies to the IaaS, PaaS, and SaaS models.

Account Hijacking

Account hijacking is not unique to cloud environments, nor new, but the threat in a cloud environment is often more significant than in a traditional data center model. Within a cloud with many hosted environments and customers, and given the large scale and visible nature of many cloud environments, especially public clouds, systems are a particularly ripe target for attackers. If an attacker is able to gain access through either exploiting your own system or another system in the same cloud environment, they can use that exploit to eavesdrop or capture your traffic or use it to attack others in the cloud or the underlying cloud infrastructure. Either occurrence could harm the reputation of the owner of the exploited system. Multifactor authentication methods and strong account provisioning controls and access requirements can minimize the risk. The account hijacking threat applies to IaaS, PaaS, and SaaS models.

Malicious Insiders

The malicious insider threat is centered on an individual who has (or had) appropriate access and uses it for unauthorized purposes to exploit systems or data. This can be related to the confidentiality, integrity, or availability of the systems. Within a cloud environment, the malicious insider threat is further compounded by the employees who works for the cloud provider itself. In a cloud infrastructure, the administrators of the system have access to the hypervisor, web portals, deployment and provision systems, as well as the actual virtual images themselves. This is above and beyond what the customer has access to through their own employees, and it is dependent on the security policies and practices of the cloud provider to mitigate the risk of its own staff. The malicious insider threat applies to the IaaS, PaaS, and SaaS models.

Advanced Persistent Threats

Advanced persistent threats are those where attackers target systems with the intent of establishing themselves and stealing data over the long term. Social engineering tactics are often employed by attackers to gain access to a system and establish themselves. They then use methods to blend in with normal traffic and traverse systems. These types of attacks can be very difficult to detect and eliminate, so both advanced technology solutions to detect these attacks as well as a focus on training to minimize problems such as social engineering are common methods used in their prevention and elimination. Advanced persistent threats can be used against the IaaS, PaaS, and SaaS models.

Data Loss

Data loss occurs when the data that an organization relies on becomes lost, unavailable, or destroyed when it should not have been. This can happen through lost encryption keys, accidental deletion, or corruption of data. The threat of data loss can be largely mitigated by a robust and regular backup design and schedule, and should always include having the data backed up off-premises from the cloud environment for the most protection. Of course with any backup system, especially an offsite one, the possibility of a data breach increases because a lot more possible points are exposed for one to occur. The use of encryption and security safeguards for offsite backups will greatly minimize the chances of a data breach happening, though. The data loss threat applies to IaaS, PaaS, and SaaS models.

 EXAM TIP Make sure you understand the differences between data breach and data loss, and also know that data loss can happen due to negligence, carelessness, or be caused by the intentional acts of an attacker.

Insufficient Due Diligence

When an organization is considering moving their systems and applications from a traditional data center model to a cloud environment, they must evaluate a lot of variables and factors to determine if the move to a cloud system is appropriate or feasible. Without proper and thorough evaluation of their systems, designs, and controls, an organization may unintentionally expose themselves to more security risk and vulnerabilities by moving to a cloud environment. For example, if an application or system has been secured using a high degree of reliance on internal network designs or controls within a data center, then moving that application or system to a cloud environment should not be considered until an exhaustive study is conducted of what can be done in the cloud environment to either change the design of the system or put in place similar mitigating controls within the cloud. Moving in a rush to a cloud environment will likely expose a system or application to security threats and vulnerabilities that are new and mitigated against in the current environment. The insufficient due diligence threat applies to IaaS, PaaS, and SaaS models.

Abuse and Nefarious Use of Cloud Services

Cloud environments have vast and enormous resources as their disposal to be able to handle the load and systems of the large number of customers that host applications and systems within their infrastructure. Although this threat isn't a particular concern to cloud customers other than a possible degradation of services, it is a very valid concern and threat to cloud providers. Using a small or single system as a launching pad for other attacks only provides limited resources to an attacker, but gaining access to a cloud environment and its enormous pool of resources is a much more attractive, and as such the cloud environment will be the target of far more sophisticated and coordinate attempts to compromise it. It is incumbent on the cloud provider to ensure this threat is mitigated and to perform active monitoring to detect any instances of it. The abuse of cloud services threat applies to the IaaS and PaaS models.

Denial of Service

Denial-of-service (DoS) attacks can come in a variety of forms and methods and are meant to disrupt the normal access and use of an application or system. Typically a denial-of-service attack will render an application or system inaccessible or significantly degrade service, but in a cloud environment the consumption of a high degree of system or network resources can cause problems for all tenants of the cloud. Although a cloud provider typically has a very high level of resources, especially with the large public cloud systems, most also do billing based on the amount of resources a customer consumes. Even if the cloud provider has sufficient resources to handle the DoS attack without catastrophic degradation of services to their customers, it could cause a customer to rack up an enormous bill due to the resources the attack used, and thus cause significant financial impact to a customer. The denial-of-service threat applies to the IaaS, PaaS, and SaaS models.

Shared Technologies Issues

The shared technologies vulnerability relates to the way cloud providers can accommodate large numbers of customers by leveraging platforms that are consistent and repeatable. This feature drives down costs and enables such attributes as auto-scaling with the cloud environment. However, this also magnifies risk within the environment and requires a very high level of diligence with configuration management, patching, and auditing. Because the entire cloud platform will use a similar or identical set of base images and configurations, a vulnerability due to a misconfiguration or mistake can put the entire environment at risk for all customers hosted within it. Integral parts of the cloud that can affect the entire environment are of particular concern, especially technologies such as the hypervisor. The shared technologies vulnerability applies to IaaS, PaaS, and SaaS.

Security Considerations for the Different Cloud Categories

Each cloud category will carry some similar as well as some different security considerations due to the differing responsibilities on behalf of the cloud customer and key features of a typical deployment.

Security Concerns for IaaS

IaaS security involves several key and unique security concerns, as detailed in this section.

Multitenancy   In the traditional data center model, there is a physical and real separation of an organization's IT resources from those of any other organization or network. In a cloud environment, resources are hosted within a cloud system that contains multiple other systems, and for very large cloud providers this could be thousands of other systems. Extra consideration and care must be given to a cloud environment because the burden of trust for separation of systems falls on the cloud provider through software controls and contractual requirements. This is true even within a private cloud that only a single corporation has access to, because different departments have systems that require higher security and would not want their systems to be exposed to other departments. For example, the accounting department and software development department should not be able to see the HR systems and data. The use of tools such as encryption becomes far more important than in a physical data center due to this reality; more indepth analysis of this and other technologies is provided in later sections.

Co-Location   With multiple virtual machines hosted by the same physical hardware, the cloud environment introduces attacks between virtual machines as well as attacks from virtual machines to the hypervisor. Of particular concern within a virtual environment is the state of image files for virtual hosts. In a physical environment, if a server is powered off or disabled, it is completely isolated from attacks. However, within a virtual environment, because the images must exist in storage, if the hypervisor is compromised, the images are always open to attacks from malware, corruption, and patching, even when turned off or disabled.

Hypervisor Security and Attacks   With traditional data center models, individual servers are utilized that have a close relationship between the hardware and operating system. In a cloud environment, where virtualization is used, the hypervisor layer is introduced between physical hardware and member servers. This also introduces another level of security that cannot be overlooked beyond the physical security and operating system security. If the hypervisor is compromised, all hosted virtual servers are now susceptible and vulnerable as well. This type of access by an attacker would make all hosts under that hypervisor vulnerable, spanning across multiple systems and likely multiple customers.

Network Security   With a traditional data center, an organization has the option to deploy extensive tools throughout their network for security monitoring and auditing. This included IDS/IPS systems, packet captures, application firewalls, and the ability to physically separate network switches and firewalls in order to segregate networks. There could be a physical separation between development and production systems, or between zones in the architecture, such as presentation, application, and data. Within a cloud environment, both types of issues require special consideration. Most cloud providers offer a selection of networking tools for their hosted customers, but even the most liberal cloud environment won't allow network access and monitoring that even come close to approaching what a customer could do in their own data center. With multitenancy and other customers, a cloud provider simply cannot give broad access and insight into a network. Even in a private cloud with different departments, cloud administrators have to limit how much each system can see into the network layer and the level of abstraction that is required for the cloud system. Without a physical separation between systems and zones, software separation and access controls are utilized within a cloud, and it is incumbent on the cloud provider to ensure they are properly configured and tested.

Virtual Machine Attacks   Virtual machines are susceptible to all the same traditional security attacks as a physical server. However, if a virtual machine has been compromised, because it is sharing a host with multiple other virtual machines, this raises the possibility of attacks across the virtual machines. It is quite possible that the other virtual machines sharing the same host are from a different company or service, so this adds a layer of abstraction where a customer is solely reliant on the cloud provider to detect and mitigate any such attacks, because each customer will only have insight into their own services within the cloud and will be completely unaware of another compromised host within the cloud.

Virtual Switch Attacks   Virtual switches are susceptible to the same degree of attacks, especially on Layer 2, as physical switches. In a cloud environment, because virtual switches are part of the same hosting environment as the other services and virtual machines, they are also susceptible to attacks and vectors if one of those other hosts were to be compromised.

Denial-of-Service Attacks (DoS) Any environment is open to potential DoS attacks, but this also bring some unique challenges and issues in a cloud environment. With multitenancy, a host is open to problems that originate from or target another host on the same cloud host. If a host is suffering a DoS attack externally, it is possible that the resources being consumed by the attack will negatively impact the remaining hosts on the hypervisor, by consuming processor, memory, or network resources. Although hypervisors have the capability to ensure that no single host can consume 100 percent of the resources and thus make the others inaccessible, even without hitting 100 percent, enough resources will be consumed to negatively impact performance and resources. Another potential issue are DoS attacks that originate within the cloud from other hosts as internal attacks.

 NOTE Many large applications in a cloud environment use a front-end caching service to increase performance and security. A prime example of this is Akamai. The use of a service like this can mostly eliminate denial-of-service attacks to the actual application from the outside because the traffic would be handled at that layer before it hits the application.

Security Concerns for PaaS

With PaaS being a platform-based rather than infrastructure-based model, there are slightly different security concerns than with IaaS.

System Isolation In a typical PaaS environment, the customer will have very little and highly constrained system-level access, if they have any access at all. If system-level or shell access is granted, it is almost always done without administrative privileges on the virtual machines so as to prevent the customer from making any platform- or infrastructure-level changes. This allows the cloud provider to maintain the level of consistency within their platform necessary for a PaaS implementation as well as to tightly control the security of the environment. If customers are able to change the underlying configurations of the platform, it is significantly more difficult for the cloud provider to perform proper patching and security controls. Allowing customers to change configurations leads to increased support costs as well as the possibility that security incidents from one customer can cross over and impact other customers within the cloud.

User Permissions Any application and system, regardless of hosting model, requires particular and careful attention to user access permissions and proper establishment of roles and groups. The cloud environment is no different from a traditional data center model, but it also adds some additional complexities within a PaaS implementation. As systems are provisioned and expanded, it is crucial for the Cloud Security Professional to ensure that roles and access are properly provisioned at the same time. It is imperative to not only ensure that developers and users have the correct permissions but also that permissions do not expand in scope over time or that inheritance gets muddied. However, when properly configured and monitored, auto-scaling is very possible, and the full benefits of PaaS can be realized in an efficient manner.

User Access Within any application, user access is of utmost importance to business operations and security alike. Users need to be able to gain proper and quick access to systems that they need for work productivity and development, and having a model in place to quickly and correctly provision this access within a very fluid cloud environment is essential. As a first step, the Cloud Security Professional needs to analyze the business requirements for proper user access and develop a model that will work within the cloud environment. In this case, it is not too dissimilar from a traditional data center model, just with the added complexity of how rapidly systems may be created, disabled, or discarded.

Once the business requirements have been completed satisfactorily, the importance shifts to proper implementation of authentication and authorization mechanisms. With the elasticity and auto-scaling features of a cloud environment, proper automation of provisioning of user access management is crucial. However, if the user access models are properly designed and implemented within the cloud environment, this will allow an organization to properly harness all the benefits of the cloud and enable their users to get and use the proper access very quickly as systems are expanded and added.

Malware, Trojans, Backdoors, and Administration Nightmares Apart from the threat of typical malicious Trojans and malware, many developers often embed backdoors into their systems for easy access for either administrative reasons or as a fail-safe to use at times when normal access methods are unavailable or failing. Within a PaaS model, these backdoors can pose special risks because they can expose all systems within the cloud to potential attacks and can also be used to gain access to a virtual machine and use it as a platform to attack the hypervisor layer. As systems expand and auto-scale, the number of places where a potential backdoor can be discovered and exploited expands commensurately with the expansion of the system. Because the auto-scaling process is automated and not actively overseen by security personnel, the number of potential vectors is constantly fluid without the necessary oversight.

Security Concerns for SaaS

Most of the security solutions and problems for SaaS, with it being a fully featured software application platform, fall on the side of the cloud provider, but still very much are issues that the Cloud Security Professional needs to be aware of.

Web Application Security Applications that are hosted within a SaaS model are expected to have high availability and to be "always on." Because the applications are exposed to the Internet and expected to have broadly available access, this also means they are constantly exposed to attacks and potential exploits. With the expected high availability, any disruption, even a slight one, due to security vulnerabilities and exploits can cause major problems both for the customer, who is dependent on the SaaS application for security, and for the cloud provider, who needs to meet contractual and SLA requirements.

Although all public-facing and Internet-facing applications are exposed to constant scanning and hacking attempts, many SaaS implementations are big, well-known applications that have a visible and large footprint, which makes them lucrative, obvious, and tempting targets for exploit—not to mention the potential data exposure that having a large customer base brings. Within a SaaS implementation, the customer is reliant on the cloud provider for code scanning, security procedures, and maintaining an active security program to catch and block attacks in real time. Because SaaS systems are unique, once a customer decides to use one, they are substantially locked in to that system with productivity dependency and they lose a large degree of flexibility to move to a different cloud provider like someone using IaaS or even PaaS would have in the event of security problems or exploits. SaaS implementations, being in a cloud environment, also might not be watched successfully with the major IDS/IPS systems and scanning tools that do work in a traditional data center model, so extra care in a cloud environment is necessary.

Data Policies   A cloud provider that offers a SaaS solution must carefully balance data polices and access that takes into account the needs of individual customers but is stringent enough that it does not impede the cloud provider's ability to offer a broad solution that many customers can leverage. It is essential for the Cloud Security Professional to be able to review existing policies on data access and mesh them with the degree of customizable flexibility that is afforded by the cloud provider. In some instances, the customer policies may need to be altered to some degree to fit within the paradigm of flexibility that is offered by the cloud provider. When an organization is evaluating a SaaS solution, existing policies and any flexibility they may be afforded need to be weighed against what the SaaS provider can support. With multiple customers (and quite possibly a large number of customers) using a SaaS solution, some degree of data-access customization is likely to be permitted, but certainly not to the degree that an organization hosting their own solution would be able to accomplish. It is crucial not only to ensure that customer data will be protected from other customers within the same SaaS implementation but also that a single customer can offer granularity of access within their own organization so that the various departments or audiences of users (for example, HR vs. developers, managers vs. staff) are able to see only the data appropriate for their job role and duties.

Data Protection and Confidentiality   With multiple customers in the same SaaS environment, it is incredibly important to keep data segregated and protected, as mentioned previously about data policies. With all data being in one application and one data store, the urgency to protect against SQL injection attacks and cross-site scripting (XSS) becomes even more paramount. If either of these types of vulnerabilities exist within a SaaS implementation, then potentially every customer's data within the system is exposed and vulnerable. The SaaS provider should build their data models in a way so that the data for each customer is segregated as much as possible, including the use of different data stores for each customer, and very tight access controls are provided. Code scanning and penetration testing to make sure accidental exposure and vulnerabilities do not exist for XSS and SQL injection, as well as other standard attacks to exploit code and expose vulnerabilities, become essential. The Cloud Security Professional must extensively evaluate the security policies and data policies of any SaaS implementation, as well as have tight contractual requirements for application audits and penetration testing, as well as ways for the customer to verify their compliance with the contractual requirements. Regardless of the cloud provider, the customer will ultimately be held responsible for any data breaches or exposure and the resulting negative impact on their reputation or possible legal consequences.

Design Principles of Secure Cloud Computing

Many of the same principles of security from a traditional data center model apply, with some additional considerations and features provided by the cloud. Cloud computing carries with it unique challenges and benefits in the areas data security and management, business continuity, and disaster recovery planning and strategies. Also, a different approach and considerations are required when undertaking a cost–benefit analysis to determine if the cloud is an appropriate platform for a system or application.

Cloud Secure Data Lifecycle

Data is always a top concern for protection, as previously discussed. It is imperative to have a strong understanding of the data lifecycle in order to properly build and adhere to a security policy, and the proper sequence of steps is also needed.

The data lifecycle is listed next and shown in Figure 2-3.

1. **Create**   Data is either created from scratch, generated, inputted, or modified into a new form and value.

2. **Store**   Data is placed into a storage system. This includes but is not limited to databases, files, and spreadsheets. This is typically done as part of the previous operation or immediately thereafter.

3. **Use**   Data is used by the application or users in some way or modified from its original state.

4. **Share**   Data is used in an application where it is viewable to users, customers, administrators, and so on.

5. **Archive**   Data is removed from active access and use and is placed into a static state where it is preserved longer term.

6. **Destroy**   Data is permanently removed and sanitized through processes previously discussed and is no long accessible or useable.

Although this represents the sequence of events in the data lifecycle, it is purely a representation of a process and is not indicative of security requirements or polices

Figure 2-3
Cloud secure
data lifecycle

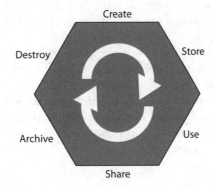

that are needed at each step of the process, depending on the nature and regulatory requirements of the specific data.

The data lifecycle is covered in much more depth in Chapter 3.

 TIP It may seem with modern web applications especially that some of the initial phases can occur simultaneously, but make sure you understand the distinct differences, even if they do seem to be concurrent operations.

Cloud-Based Business Continuity/Disaster Recovery Planning

Business continuity and disaster recovery are similar in nature but also have some distinct differences. Business continuity encompasses the full range of possible service disruptions and how a company can minimize, mitigate, and respond to them and keep business operations running, available, and secure. On a similar note, disaster recovery is also concerned with the continuity of business operations but is focused on events arising from natural disasters or other events that cause an immediate and catastrophic loss of business operations. It involves how to get critical operations back up and running as quickly as possible, either in whole or in part, based on the priorities and expectations of management.

Many customers move to a cloud environment with high availability and redundancy of services in mind, and this plays right into their expectations and plans for business continuity and disaster recovery. Many cloud environments, especially large public clouds, are built and designed to incorporate geographic diversity, and high availability offerings as a main selling point. While these aspects might make planning a bit easier for the Cloud Security Professional, the same level of diligence and responsibilities exists as with a traditional data center.

With cloud computing and the stress on portability, proper planning and testing of continuity and disaster recovery plans can become more complex. As cloud services move between platforms and cloud providers, keeping up-to-date and valid plans becomes increasingly difficult. What's more, the responsibility for ensuring availability falls on the cloud provider and their infrastructure.

The main difference with a cloud environment when it comes to continuity and disaster planning is having a full understanding of the roles and responsibilities for the cloud provider and customer. In a multitenancy situation, each customer needs to understand how recovery will proceed in the event of a major situation and how priorities are established for systems. The customer will need to have a full understanding of the cloud provider's recovery plans and will need to perform regular audits and verifications that the plans are current, acceptable, and realistic for their needs. The customer will have to ensure that the communications plan for the cloud provider in the event of a disaster is responsive and comprehensive. Thus, the customer will need to make an informed decision, based on their business needs and expectations, as to whether they need to make arrangements with another cloud provider for either off-site backups and redundancy or for disaster recovery operations.

The plans for continuity and disaster recovery should be clearly defined and articulated in the SLA between the cloud provider and customer as another facet for performance and acceptable minimum criteria. The SLA should fully document to requirements for redundancy, including the elimination of any single points of failure within the cloud environment. The requirements for backups and the ability to move to another cloud provider if SLA requirements for uptime and disaster recovery are not met should be a key aspect as well. Regular auditing and reporting on adherence to SLA requirements in this area should be clearly defined and timetables established for regular review.

While planning for all events in any hosting environment is not possible, the key features of a cloud environment can make it very amenable to quick recovery and minimization of disaster scenarios from the onset. With proper auditing, SLAs, and communication plans, management can be assured that recovery will be quick and efficient. With all the other customers also depending on the cloud provider for service, the pressure is on cloud providers with strong industry competition to build very robust and sound systems.

Cost–Benefit Analysis

This chapter has provided a broad overview of cloud computing and the various forms it can take and has introduced the topic of cloud security, which we will discuss in greater depth in the remaining chapters. Any organization considering a move to a cloud environment should undertake a rigorous cost–benefit analysis to determine whether it is appropriate for their specific systems or applications, weighed against what a cloud can and cannot provide. In the following sections, we discuss several factors that figure prominently into any cost–benefit analysis.

Resource Pooling and Cyclical Demands

As previously mentioned, many organizations have a cyclical nature to their system demands to some extent or another. With a traditional data center, an organization has to maintain sufficient resources to handle their highest load peaks, which demands much larger upfront hardware and ongoing support costs. A move to a cloud environment would in this case be a benefit to a company in that they would only incur costs as needed, and the initial upfront costs would be far lower without having to build up massive infrastructure from the onset. However, if a company has steady load throughout the year and is not susceptible to large bursts or cycles, then a move to a cloud environment may not yield the same level of benefits.

Data Center Costs vs. Operational Expense Costs

A typical data center setup for an organization carries expenses for facilities, utilities, systems staff, networking, storage, and all the components needed to run an operation from the ground up. In a cloud environment, with those components being largely or wholly the responsibility of the cloud provider, the focus is then shifted to management and oversight, as well as requirements building and auditing. While the higher costs for data centers will be mitigated by a cloud, the customer will spend a far larger amount on operations and oversight in a cloud environment. It is important for any organization thinking about moving to a cloud environment to fully assess the staff and talents they already have and whether they can adapt to the new demands and changing roles in a cloud environment and whether they are willing and able to make those changes, either through training or staff changes.

Focus Change

Moving to a cloud environment brings a large degree of change in focus to an organization. Many organizations are structured in a manner that contains both operations and development staff. With a move to a cloud, the operations side will fundamentally change away from running systems to overseeing them, as discussed previously. An organization will need to evaluate whether they are ready and able to make such a focus shift, as much of their upper management, policies, and organizational structure may well be built around functional focuses. A rush to a cloud environment could disrupt productivity, cause internal fighting, or even result in a significant loss of staff, talent, and corporate knowledge.

Ownership and Control

When an organization owns their data centers and all the hardware, they get to set all the rules and have full control over everything. In a move to a cloud environment, the organization gives up direct control over operational procedures, system management and maintenance, as well as upgrade plans and environment changes. While an organization can put in place strong contracts and SLA requirements, they still will not have the degree of flexibility and control that they would have in a proprietary data center. The organization will have to gauge the temperament and expectations of their management to determine whether this change is something that will be manageable over time or will cause bigger issues and tension.

Cost Structure

Costs are very predictable in a traditional data center. An organization can appropriate funds for capital expenditures for hardware and infrastructure and then allocate appropriate staffing and resources to maintain the hardware and infrastructure over time. In a cloud environment with metered pricing, costs are realized as resources are added and changed over time. This can cause an unpredictable schedule of costs that may or may not work for a company and the way it handles finances internally. It is an aspect that will have to be carefully evaluated and understood by management. Different billing structures are available, or a middle contractor can be used to provide services that are priced on a longer term basis, but that will vary greatly based on the needs and expectations of the organization.

Identify Trusted Cloud Services

As with any computing platform and infrastructure, there are certification criteria and guidelines that an organization can follow to develop an acceptable level of trust and confidence in the security of a cloud implementation and in the cloud services provider.

Certification Against Criteria

A key aspect of any security program is the ability to audit and verify compliance with security standards, guidelines, and best practices. With cloud computing being so new, even after growing substantially the past few years, there is yet to be an agreed-upon standard for cloud security, so there is a reliance on multiple standards, listed here, that adhere to the applications and systems hosted within a cloud environment rather than to cloud technologies specifically:

- ISO/IEC 27001 and 27001:2013
- NIST SP 800-53
- Payment Card Industry Data Security Standard (PCI DSS)
- SOC 1, SOC 2, and SOC 3
- Common Criteria
- FIPS 140-2

System/Subsystem Product Certifications

The following is an in-depth discussion of those certifications that are common and prevalent with cloud customers and cloud security.

ISO/IEC 27001 and 27001:2013

ISO 27001 and its more recent update 27001:2013 are widely considered the be the gold standard when it comes to the security of information systems and their data. It is designed to be platform and vendor neutral and focuses purely on methods and practices for IT security. While it is not focused on or designed toward cloud specifically, its open and flexible nature makes it easy to apply to cloud platforms and a good framework for security compliance and standards.

The latest 2013 revision contains a group of 114 controls organized under the following 14 control domains:

- Information security policies
- Organization of information security
- Human resource security
- Asset management
- Access control
- Cryptography
- Physical and environmental security
- Operations security
- Communications security

- System acquisition, development, and maintenance
- Supplier relationships
- Information security incident management
- Information security aspects of business continuity management
- Compliance

The one main drawback to 27001—and most other security standards, since they were not designed for cloud environments—is that they fall short on being able to confidently span multiple environments and compensate for portability issues and requirements. The frameworks can be very valuable and applicable within a cloud environment of a single provider, but once systems adopt hybrid models or span multiple providers, it gets far trickier when accounting for the differences in providers and their security policies, even if they are similar.

NIST SP 800-53

NIST, as part of the United States government, puts out security standards for systems that are used by the federal government and its contractors, specifically for systems that are not classified under national security. Although NIST Special Publication (SP) 800-53 is written exclusively for those doing business with the U.S. federal government and agencies of the government, it provides a strong security baseline and certification that have value for private corporations as well. The one drawback is that because it is focused exclusively on the U.S. federal government, it is not a document that cloud providers are required to follow and may contain elements that would be difficult for a private organization to comply with.

The latest revision of SP 800-53, Revision 4, was initially released in draft form in 2012. It brought many modern elements and updates into the fold that are pertinent to cloud environments and provide overlap with concepts we previously discussed. Although this is not an exhaustive list of revisions, it highlights those most important to a Cloud Security Professional:

- Insider threats and malicious activity
- Software application security, including web-based applications and APIs
- Social networking
- Mobiles devices
- Cloud computing
- Persistent threats
- Privacy

Also contained in Revision 4 is a matrix mapping similarities and areas of overlap with ISO 27001, which we previously discussed.

Payment Card Industry Data Security Standard (PCI DSS)

The PCI DSS standard was developed by the major credit card labels, and all merchants that accept credit cards under those labels are required to comply with it. PCI DSS applies to the major labels—Visa, MasterCard, Discover, American Express, and JCB—and does not apply to private label and store-brand cards. It is a tiered system of technical and nontechnical requirements based on the number of transactions a vendor processes per year.

The PCI DSS standard is found in a series of 12 compliance requirements:

- Install and maintain a firewall configuration to protect cardholder data.
- Do not use vender-supplied defaults for system passwords and other security parameters.
- Protect stored cardholder data.
- Encrypt transmission of cardholder data across open, public networks.
- Use and regularly update antivirus software on all systems commonly affected by malware.
- Develop and maintain secure systems and applications.
- Restrict access to cardholder data by business need-to-know.
- Assign a unique ID to each person with computer access.
- Restrict physical access to cardholder data.
- Track and monitor all access to network resources and cardholder data.
- Regularly test security systems and processes.
- Maintain a policy that addresses information security.

The vendors strongly enforce PCI DSS compliance, and failure to maintain its controls and standards can lead to penalties for merchants. This can include financial penalties, more stringent requirements for higher tiers, more regular and invasive auditing, or even being denied the ability to take cards under the major label brands and being blocked from their networks.

Although PCI DSS is a proprietary requirement of the card labels, it is often used by many other industries and organizations as a security standard.

SOC 1, SOC 2, and SOC 3

SOC, or Service Organization Control, comprises a series of standards that evaluate and audit the use and control of financial information that companies in the services sector use. SOC was developed and published under the professional standards from SSAE 16 and ISAE 3402.

The SOC 1 reports are done in accordance with the standards set forth in SSAE (Statements on Standards for Attestation Engagements) 16. The SOC 1 report focuses on the kinds of information that would be relevant and pertinent to a financial audit of an organization and their financial statements. It includes information about the management structure of the organization, the targeted client and customer base, as well as information about the regulations the organization is subjected to and the auditors that verify compliance.

SOC 2 reports expand beyond basic financial audit primers to include five areas. The one most important to the Cloud Security Professional is the security principle (the others are availability, processing integrity, confidentiality, and privacy). The security principle includes seven categories:

- Organization and management
- Communications
- Risk management and design implementation of controls
- Monitoring of controls
- Logical and physical access controls
- System operations
- Change management

Under the published guidelines, any evaluation that is not on the privacy principle must include the security principle as part of the report. Therefore, if the evaluation is on confidentiality, processing integrity, or confidentiality, security must be included.

Common Criteria

Common Criteria is an ISO/IEC international standard for computer security certification. It carries the designation of ISO/IEC 15408. Common Criteria is designed to allow an organization to make substantive claims as to their security practices and results, which are then evaluated for validity to provide assurances to agencies, users, or their customers as to their security practices.

The way that Common Criteria works is that an organization can put forth their security functional requirements (SFRs) and their security assurance requirements (SARs) via a mechanism that they have employed called a protection profile (PP). Once the PP has been established, vendors can make claims against their products and services that are then tested to see if they meet the claims, thus providing validity and external concurrence to security claims. If the claims are verified, it gives reputation and evidence to their security strength and claims from an independent perspective.

Once an evaluation has been completed, it receives an evaluation assurance level (EAL), which is a numeric score based on the depth and validity of testing against the claims. The possible EAL scores are as follows:

- **EAL1** Functionally tested
- **EAL2** Structurally tested
- **EAL3** Methodically tested and checked

- **EAL4**   Methodically designed, tested, and reviewed
- **EAL5**   Semi-formally designed and tested
- **EAL6**   Semi-formally verified design and tested
- **EAL7**   Formally verified design and tested

For more in-depth information on Common Criteria, see https://www.commoncriteriaportal.org/.

FIPS 140-2

FIPS (Federal Information Processing Standard) 140-2 is a criterion also put out by NIST of the United States federal government that pertains to accreditation of cryptographic modules. Although this standard was last revised in 2002, before cloud computing technologies came into existence, because it pertains to cryptographic standards and implementations, it is a relevant standard to apply to cloud communications and systems.

The FIPS 140-2 standard defines four levels of security. They are aptly called Levels 1–4, with increasing levels of requirements and scrutiny:

- **Level 1**   Provides the lowest level of security. The only requirements are based on the cryptographic modules being used, and at least one on the approved list must be present. There are no physical security requirements at Level 1.
- **Level 2**   Requires role-based authentication where a cryptographic module is used for actual authentication processes. The module must also have mechanisms that show evidence of any attempts to tamper with it.
- **Level 3**   Requires physical protection methods to ensure a high degree of confidence that any attempts to tamper are evident and detectable. It requires the cryptographic module to not only authenticate the user to the system but also to verify authorization.
- **Level 4**   Provides the highest level of security and tamper detection. The criteria at Level 4 is that any attempts to tamper will be detected and prevented, any data that is clear text will be zeroed should a tamper be successful. Level 4–certified modules are very useful in systems that lack physical security protections and need to rely more on data protections.

The FIPS 140-2 standard is divided into 11 sections that define security requirements:

- Cryptographic Module Specification
- Cryptographic Module Ports and Interfaces
- Roles, Services, Authentication
- Finite State Model
- Physical Security

- Operational Environment
- Cryptographic Key Management
- Electromagnetic Interference/Electromagnetic Compatibility (EMI/EMC)
- Self-Tests
- Design Assurance
- Mitigation of Other Attacks

More information about FIPS 140-2 specifications and requirements can be found at http://csrc.nist.gov/publications/fips/fips140-2/fips1402.pdf.

Cloud Architecture Models

 NOTE Although this material is not part of the official exam guide, it is very valuable information for any security professional to know and understand, and some superficial material from it may appear on the exam. For a professional education, it would be very beneficial to explore these models in more depth because they are commonly used throughout industry and often referenced. In some cases, these models offer their own certifications.

The Cloud Security Alliance (CSA) is the leading professional organization devoted to promoting cloud security best practices and organizing cloud security professionals. The CSA has put out a general cloud enterprise architecture model to help professionals conceptualize the components of a successful cloud implementation. The CSA mission, programs, information, and generalized enterprise architecture can be found at https://cloudsecurityalliance.org.

The four main components to the CSA architecture are discussed next. The Cloud Security Professional should have a good understanding of them from a framework standpoint. We will briefly go over their main points here because they are not an in-depth aspect of the exam. However, future exploration of each component's website would provide good reference information for any Cloud Security Professional.

Sherwood Applied Business Security Architecture (SABSA)

The SABSA official website can be found at www.sabsa.org. SABSA provides a group of components, listed next, that can be used in part or in whole as an approach to security architecture for any system:

- Business Requirements Engineering Framework (known as Attributes Profiling)
- Risk and Opportunity Management Framework
- Policy Architecture Framework

- Security Services-Oriented Architecture Framework
- Governance Framework
- Security Domain Framework
- Through-Life Security Service Management & Performance Management Framework

IT Infrastructure Library (ITIL)

The ITIL is a collection of papers and concepts that lay out a vision for IT Service Management (ITSM). It is essentially a collection of best practices to give companies of all sizes (but more targeted toward large companies) a framework for providing IT services and user support. ITIL can be found at https://www.axelos.com/best-practice-solutions/itil. Five main publications form the core of ITIL:

- ITIL Service Strategy
- ITIL Service Design
- ITIL Service Transition
- ITIL Service Operation
- ITIL Continual Service Improvement

NOTE   Apart from ITIL's use within the Cloud Security realm, learning ITIL or even getting ITIL certification would be a smart consideration for any security professional. Many organizations in all sectors use its principles heavily, and it would add a lot to the overall resume of a security professional.

The Open Group Architecture Framework (TOGAF)

TOGAF is meant to be an open enterprise architecture model that offers a high-level design approach. It is intended to provide a common framework for architecture design that teams can leverage for a standardized approach. It helps teams avoid common pitfalls, proprietary lock-in, and communication problems during design and implementation phases as well as throughout the lifecycle of a system. TOGAF, which can be found at www.opengroup.org/subjectareas/enterprise/togaf, addresses the following four critical areas:

- Common language and communications
- Standardizing on open methods and technologies to avoid proprietary lock-in
- Utilizing resources more effectively and efficiently to save money
- Demonstrating return on investment

NIST Cloud Technology Roadmap

The NIST Cloud Technology Roadmap, put out by NIST of the United States federal government in SP 500-293, is a comprehensive guide for U.S. government agencies concerning their use of and migration to cloud computing platforms. It is not a rigid set of requirements for federal agencies or contractors but rather a solid framework to guide IT departments across the government in evaluating cloud technologies, the suitability of these technologies for their IT operations, and security models within a cloud framework to meet federal IT security standards. The roadmap spells out ten steps for the government and contractors to follow in moving resources to cloud platforms. Although the steps are specific to the federal government and its IT requirements, components of these steps and common themes are very important to all Cloud Security Professionals.

Exercise

You have just been hired into the security team for a major corporation and your role is specifically focused on cloud security. Your company is just beginning the evaluation of public cloud platforms to determine the feasibility of moving some major production systems under a cloud environment. You have been asked to develop a plan to evaluate these systems from a security perspective.

1. Based on all you have learned in this chapter, what are the initial steps you will take in this evaluation?

2. How will you advise both management and the operations teams as to what they need to consider and analyze?

3. What will you advise your legal, compliance, and privacy teams on?

Chapter Review

This chapter provided a broad overview of cloud computing, its major aspects and components, as well as the major security issues facing the technology. A Cloud Security Professional needs to have a strong grasp of all these concepts in order to properly advise management on the cost–benefit analysis when considering a move to a cloud platform, and then be able to build a strong and sound security program that is adapted to the cloud platform and chosen provider if the decision to move is made. With a strong grasp of cloud basics, a Cloud Security Professional can provide a sound risk management assessment of an organization's systems and applications and their appropriateness for the cloud, as well as advise on any shortcomings in their security model or reliance on their current data center for security prior to migrating to the cloud.

Questions

1. Which of the following are common threats facing cloud computing platforms? (Choose two.)
   A. Denial of service
   B. Cryptographic hashing
   C. Data breaches
   D. Phishing attacks

2. Which of the following standards is commonly applied to cloud computing security?
   A. ISO/IEC 27001:2010
   B. ISO/IEC 27003:2013
   C. ISO/IEC 27013:2000
   D. ISO/IEC 27001:2013

3. Which of the following methods is commonly used to ensure that data removed from a cloud system is not recoverable?
   A. Deletion
   B. Degaussing
   C. Overwriting
   D. Shredding

4. Which type of hypervisor is a software implementation that runs on top of an operating system rather than tied to the hardware?
   A. Type 1
   B. Type 2
   C. Type 3
   D. Type 4

5. Which component of the NIST Cloud Technology Roadmap pertains to the minimum requirements between the cloud provider and cloud customer to meet contractual satisfaction?
   A. SLAs
   B. Regulatory requirements
   C. Governance
   D. Auditability

6. Which of the following is a unique benefit of a private cloud versus other models?

   A. Scalability

   B. Right-sizing resources

   C. Disaster recovery

   D. Ownership retention

7. Which of the following characteristics of cloud computing would be *most* attractive to management when looking to save money?

   A. On-demand self-service

   B. Measured service

   C. Resource pooling

   D. Rapid elasticity

8. What feature of IaaS would be most beneficial to a new company starting up with more limited capital?

   A. Scalability

   B. Physical hardware costs

   C. Physical security requirements

   D. High availability

9. Which common threat, which a customer could be totally unaware of at the time, could lead to a direct financial cost without loss of reputation or privacy exposure?

   A. Data breaches

   B. Malicious insiders

   C. Denial of service

   D. Insufficient due diligence

10. What certification would be most appropriate to use for financial statement auditing?

    A. NIST SP 800-53

    B. FIPS 140-2

    C. ISO/IEC 27001

    D. SOC 1, SOC 2, and SOC 3

11. Which component of the NIST Cloud Computing Roadmap pertains to the ability to split up applications and reuse components?

    A. Portability

    B. Interoperability

    C. Auditability

    D. Availability

12. Which problem would make it least likely for an application or system to be able to easily move to another cloud provider?

    A. Data lock-in

    B. Operating systems

    C. Patching cycles

    D. Insecure APIs

13. Which cloud hosting model would be the most appropriate for a company looking to leverage multiple cloud providers for disaster recovery or load bursts?

    A. Public cloud

    B. Community cloud

    C. Private cloud

    D. Hybrid cloud

14. Which concept would be most important to consider for data security while it is being used by an application?

    A. Malicious insiders

    B. Data in transit

    C. Data at rest

    D. Denial of service

15. Which phase of the cloud data lifecycle typically occurs immediately after or simultaneous with the Create phase?

    A. Use

    B. Share

    C. Store

    D. Consume

Questions and Answers

1. Which of the following are common threats facing cloud computing platforms? (Choose two.)

    A. Denial of service

    B. Cryptographic hashing

    C. Data breaches

    D. Phishing attacks

    A, C. Denial-of-service attacks are used to overwhelm system resources with traffic or malformed requests with the intent to block legitimate and authorized users from the application or data and legitimate business access. Data breaches involve a malicious actor accessing, viewing, copying, or transferring data that they do not have an authorization or legitimate business use to do so. Cryptographic hashing involves the protection of data and is not a threat facing cloud computing platforms, and phishing attacks can target any application regardless of hosting configurations or technologies used, and is not cloud-specific attack either.

2. Which of the following standards is commonly applied to cloud computing security?

   A. ISO/IEC 27001:2010

   B. ISO/IEC 27003:2013

   C. ISO/IEC 27013:2000

   D. ISO/IEC 27001:2013

   D. ISO/IEC 27001:2013 is commonly applied to cloud computing security as a standard and certification system for promoting and continually improving upon the security applied to a system or application. The other certifications listed are not relevant or fabricated numbers for example purposes only.

3. Which of the following methods is commonly used to ensure that data removed from a cloud system is not recoverable?

   A. Deletion

   B. Degaussing

   C. Overwriting

   D. Shredding

   C. Overwriting is a common method used for ensuring removed data is no longer accessible in a cloud environment by replacing valid and sensitive data with random data, null values, or repeating data so that it cannot be read. Simple deleting only removes pointers to data and not the data itself, and degaussing and shredding are physical media destruction techniques that would not be available within a cloud environment.

4. Which type of hypervisor is a software implementation that runs on top of an operating system rather than tied to the hardware?

   A. Type 1

   B. Type 2

   C. Type 3

   D. Type 4

B. Type 2 is the type of hypervisor that is hosted on top of an operating system as a software package, rather than connected directly to the underlying physical hardware like a Type 1 hypervisor would be. Type 3 and 4 hypervisors do not exist and were simply included for example purposes.

5. Which component of the NIST Cloud Technology Roadmap pertains to the minimum requirements between the cloud provider and cloud customer to meet contractual satisfaction?

   A. SLAs

   B. Regulatory requirements

   C. Governance

   D. Auditability

   A. SLAs are the criteria to meet minimum requirements for contractual satisfaction between the cloud provider and cloud customer. They document specific requirements and metrics that are required and how they will be measured, as well as specific methods for remedy should they not be met. Regulatory requirements do not dictate specific performance metrics in most cases, and even if they do, the SLA would be the vehicle that would document and establish their performance requirements within the business relationship. Auditability refers to a system or application and the aspects of it that make it subjected to audits and the ease at which they can be done, and is not a framework for specifying contractual performance requirements.

6. Which of the following is a unique benefit of a private cloud versus other models?

   A. Scalability

   B. Right-sizing resources

   C. Disaster recovery

   D. Ownership retention

   D. Ownership retention is a unique benefit of the private cloud model, where the cloud customer will have significantly more input and control over how the cloud is deployed and managed, versus a public cloud model, where specific customers have very little input or leverage. Scalability is a feature of all cloud models and is not specific to the private cloud model. Right-sizing resources is synonymous with what scalability and elasticity provide and are also not specific to private cloud models. Disaster recovery is a larger concept that applies to any type of hosting, including both traditional data centers and cloud environments, and is not specific to any one model or implementation.

7. Which of the following characteristics of cloud computing would be *MOST* attractive to management when looking to save money?

   A. On-demand self-service

   B. Measured service

   C. Resource pooling

   D. Rapid elasticity

   B. While all aspects could potentially save an organization money, measured service and only paying for what you consume—when you consume it—would be the most attractive option. With a traditional data center, a system must essentially be built to handle peak load, leaving a lot of excess resources at most times. With a cloud environment, resources can be scaled up and added when needed for peak times or cycles, and only incur those costs to the customer while they are actually being used. On-demand self-service refers to the mechanism for scaling a system and provisioning resources, and itself is not a specific way to save money. Resource pooling refers to the overall aggregation of resources between all tenants of a cloud environment and the allocation between them to meet demand. Rapid elasticity is the concept that enables a cloud customer to add resources when needed, but is not the specific cost-saving mechanism that is represented with measured service.

8. What feature of IaaS would be most beneficial to a new company starting up with more limited capital?

   A. Scalability

   B. Physical hardware costs

   C. Physical security requirements

   D. High availability

   B. Physical hardware costs would be most beneficial to a new company starting out with limited capital because IaaS would remove the need for a large upfront investment in data center expenses. A startup would only need to pay for the specific resources that they need and when they need them, and not the full data center and all the components that are necessary for it. Physical security requirements are also a component that would make IaaS attractive to a customer, but it would be the same for PaaS and SaaS as well; the physical hardware costs are more directly related to the specific question. Scalability and high-availability are not appropriate answers as they may not be specific requirements of an individual customer and would not necessarily factor into the hosting decisions and costs.

9. Which common threat, which a customer could be totally unaware of at the time, could lead to a direct financial cost without loss of reputation or privacy exposure?

   A. Data breaches

   B. Malicious insiders

   C. Denial of service

   D. Insufficient due diligence

   C. A denial-of-service attack could lead to direct financial costs for a customer without data exposure due to the pricing model of cloud computing measured against consumed resources. With elasticity and auto-scaling, and cloud environments capable of handling very high loads, especially public clouds, a cloud customer may not even be immediately aware of the resources their systems are utilizing at the moment.

10. What certification would be most appropriate to use for financial statement auditing?

    A. NIST SP 800-53

    B. FIPS 140-2

    C. ISO/IEC 27001

    D. SOC 1, SOC 2, and SOC 3

    D. SOC 1, SOC 2, and SOC 3 pertain to financial statements and auditing, and also extend past that with the latter two for more broad auditing of systems and practices. The NIST SP 800-53 publication pertains to security and privacy controls for federal government IT systems within the United States, and is not an auditing framework. FIPS 140-2, also from the United States federal government, is a set of standards and accreditation for cryptographic modules, and ISO/IEC 27001 is a general certification and standards publication for IT security.

11. Which component of the NIST Cloud Computing Roadmap pertains to the ability to split up applications and reuse components?

    A. Portability

    B. Interoperability

    C. Auditability

    D. Availability

    B. Interoperability is the ability to split up and reuse components throughout systems and applications. Portability refers to the ability to move systems and applications easily between different cloud providers. Auditability refers to the ability to audit the controls and practices of a system or application, and availability refers to one of the main three security principles, focused on data and systems being available to authorized users when needed.

12. Which problem would make it least likely for an application or system to be able to easily move to another cloud provider?

    A. Data lock-in

    B. Operating systems

    C. Patching cycles

    D. Insecure APIs

    A. Data lock-in would make it very difficult for a customer to easily move to another cloud provider, as they would be dependent on proprietary offerings from the cloud provider. Operating systems would not be an impediment as any cloud provider could offer the same operating systems, and patching cycles would fall into the same type of universal offerings. Insecure APIs are a major security risk and, if anything, would be a primary reason for a cloud customer to leave for a different cloud provider.

13. Which cloud hosting model would be the most appropriate for a company looking to leverage multiple cloud providers for disaster recovery or load bursts?

    A. Public cloud

    B. Community cloud

    C. Private cloud

    D. Hybrid cloud

    D. A hybrid cloud would give the most flexibility for moving between different clouds and hosting models, as well as incorporating disaster recovery options. A public cloud and a private cloud are both single models that would not span between multiple cloud providers, and while a community cloud incorporates similar and aligned organizations together, it is likely also a single cloud model. Only a hybrid cloud spans multiple different cloud providers.

14. Which concept would be most important to consider for data security while it is being used by an application?

    A. Malicious insiders

    B. Data in transit

    C. Data at rest

    D. Denial of service

B. Data in transit concerns data while it is being used and exchanged during processing. Malicious insiders are not a unique risk to data only while it is being used or transmitted, and denial of service is also not a unique risk to data in any state, but is instead focused on availability. Data at rest would not be dependent on the data actually being used or transmitted, and refers to data that is in archived or storage states.

15. Which phase of the cloud data lifecycle typically occurs immediately after or simultaneous with the Create phase?

    A. Use

    B. Share

    C. Store

    D. Consume

C. The Store phase typically occurs as part of the Create phase or immediately thereafter. The Use and Share phases of data occur after the data has been created and stored in some manner, and there is no dependency or immediate connection between the creating and storing of data to the actual use or sharing of it. Consuming of data is not an actual phase of the data lifecycle and would be synonymous with the Use or Share phase.

Cloud Data Security

This chapter covers the following topics in Domain 2:

- The cloud data lifecycle
- How storage systems are different between cloud hosting models
- How to design security strategies for data protection within a cloud environment
- The process of data discovery and how it relates to data classification
- Privacy acts and how they relate to cloud environments
- The concepts of Data Rights Management and Information Rights Management
- The identification and collection of event data within a cloud environment, and how to leverage and analyze it for business value and regulatory compliance

The most important aspect of any application or system is the data contained within it; the data holds the most value for any company or organization. Although many of the principles of data security and protection are the same within a cloud environment as in a traditional data center, there are some differences and challenges unique to the cloud environment.

Understanding the Cloud Data Lifecycle

The cloud data lifecycle plays a crucial role throughout this domain, and all aspects of data management and security apply to some or all of the various phases.

Phases

The phases of the data lifecycle were covered at a cursory level in Chapter 2. However, a more thorough understanding of the various aspects, risks, and technologies at play in each phase is needed. For a quick review, the phases of the lifecycle are shown in Figure 3-1. Note that although the lifecycle is shown as a series of distinct steps, there is no requirement that data actually go through each step in the process; some steps in the lifecycle may be skipped altogether, repeated, or taken out of order.

Figure 3-1
The data lifecycle

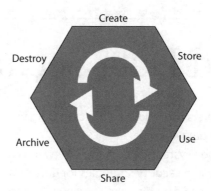

Create

Although this initial phase is called "Create," it can also be thought of as modification. In essence, any time data is considered "new," it is in the Create phase. This can be data that is newly created, data that is imported into a system and new to that system, or data that is already present and modified into a new form or value. It is also the most appropriate time to determine the data is classified as secure. When data is created, its value and sensitivity are known and can be handled properly from the onset, as all additional phases build off this phase. It also is the most appropriate time to deal with data modification. The classification of data after modification should always be done as a new process, taking into account the state of the data after modification, not before modification, because the level of sensitivity may very well have changed during the modification process. Decisions made during the creation process as far as classification will impact all additional phases, beginning immediately with how the data is stored and protected. Security controls be initially implemented at the Create phase as well, specifically in the form of technologies such as SSL/TLS with data that is inputted or imported.

Store

Immediately after the data is created, it must be stored in a way that is useable to the system or application (in many cases, this is an almost simultaneous and complimentary process). Data can be stored in numerous ways. Storage methods include files on a file system, remote object storage in a cloud, and data written to a database. All storage of data must be done in accordance with the data classification determined during the Create phase. The Store phase is the first place where security controls can be implemented to protect the data at rest, and the Cloud Security Professional must ensure that all storage methods employ whatever technologies are necessary for its data classification level, including the use of access controls, encryption, and auditing. The use of appropriate redundancy and backup methods also comes into play immediately at the Store phase to protect the data on top of the security controls.

Use

The Use phase is where the data is actually consumed and processed by an application or user. At this point, because the data is being used, viewed, or processed, it is more exposed and faces increased chance of compromise or leak. At this time, the data will transition from data at rest to data in use, as it is being displayed in a web browser or other client, moving between the data and application layers or the presentation layer of an application, or just traversing through a network. Since the data is being viewed or processed, it also must be exposed in an unencrypted state, as opposed to sitting static in an encrypted database or data set somewhere in the Store phase. Allowing the data to be unencrypted also puts expectations on the client side for protection, both from being viewed and stored, once it has been released from its official storage system and exposed. We cover other data protection methods later in this chapter, but the exposing of data requires auditing and logging mechanisms to be in place as it is accessed for the first time. The Use phase is considered to be purely in a read-only mode because this phase does not cover modification in this sense; modification is covered in the Create phase of the lifecycle.

Share

In the Share phase, data is made available for use outside the system it was explicitly created on or for. This presents a big challenge for a system to ensure proper protections are in place once the data leaves the system and is shared externally. Unlike the Use phase, with the Share phase the data is being enabled for use by customers, partners, contractors, and other associated groups, and once the data leaves the main system, it is no longer under the security control mechanisms employed there. That being said, all is not lost as far as securing data once it leaves the environment. Technologies such as DLP (data loss prevention) and various rights management packages can be utilized to either detect additional sharing or attempt to prevent modification. However, neither method is completely secure or complete.

Archive

Archiving simply involves moving data to long-term storage, thus removing it from being active or "hot" within a system. The archiving process can range from moving data to a lower storage tier that is slower and not as redundant but still accessible from the system, all the way up to removing it from the active system entirely and placing it on different media all together. In the latter instance, the data can be recovered and read by the system again, but typically will involve substantially more time, effort, or cost to do so. In many instances where the data is completely removed from the active system, it is stored offsite for disaster recovery reasons as well—sometimes even being hundreds or thousands of miles away. One of the more overlooked aspects of archiving data is the ability to retrieve and recover it as well.

CAUTION Depending on company policies or legal and regulatory requirements, some data may have a requirement to be archived and maintained for several years. As technologies change over time, so will backup and recovery systems. For example, if you have a requirement to keep data for seven years and you change backup systems after four years, you must maintain the ability to recover the older data from the previous system as well. Many times an organization will move onto the new system and decommission the old one, not realizing they are losing the ability to recover historical data. Although it may be possible to find a third party to do the recovery if needed, the costs can be significant, both in money and staff time. A strategy that many firms employ is to determine if the data can be exported from proprietary formats into a more flexible and interoperable format. However, that strategy also carries an inherent risk in protecting the integrity of data under regulatory rules, so special care must be taken and a full understanding of the requirements is essential.

Destroy

The Destroy phase of the lifecycle is where the data is either made inaccessible or permanently erased and protected, with the method and approach being based on the classification and sensitivity of the data. Many would not consider the simple deletion of data to actually be part of this phase, because this merely erases pointers but leaves the data very vulnerable to recovery. Using methods such as overwriting and cryptographic erasure is far more prevalent in a cloud environment, and is required by many regulations and laws, especially considering that physically destructive methods such as degaussing and shredding are not available within a cloud environment. The same requirements and methods apply to any long-term archiving solution as well. Special care also is required to oversee data sanitation requirements based on the type of cloud system involved. Whereas IaaS and PaaS tend to have storage dedicated more to a single customer in the case of volume storage, SaaS tends to be far more interconnected with data from across the entire platform. The Cloud Security Professional needs to pay particular attention to contractual and SLA terms within any type of cloud platform, but in particularly in SaaS.

Design and Implement Cloud Data Storage Architectures

Each of the three hosting models with a cloud environment—IaaS, PaaS, and SaaS—uses its own unique storage methods, as shown in Figure 3-2. Each model also has its own unique challenges and threats.

Storage Types

Different storage types are typically used and offered based on the type of cloud platform being used and the special considerations and support models that each entails.

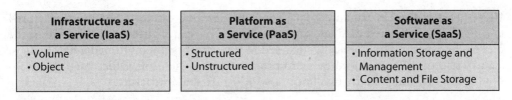

Infrastructure as a Service (IaaS)	Platform as a Service (PaaS)	Software as a Service (SaaS)
• Volume • Object	• Structured • Unstructured	• Information Storage and Management • Content and File Storage

Figure 3-2   Cloud storage types by hosting model

IaaS

Although IaaS has the most freedom and support requirements for the customer, the same basic tenants of measured service and virtualization come into play pertaining to storage. Storage is allocated and maintained by the cloud provider based on the specific needs and requirements of the customer. With IaaS, storage falls into two basic categories: volume and object.

Volume   Volume storage is a virtual hard drive that is allocated by the cloud provider and attached to the virtual host. The operating system sees the drive the same way it would in the traditional server model and can interact with the drive in the same way. The drive can be formatted and maintained as a file system in the traditional sense and utilized as such. Most cloud providers allocate and maintain storage using the volume method for IaaS.

Object   Object storage is file storage that operates as an API or a web service call. Rather than being located in a file tree structure and accessible as a traditional hard drive, files are stored as objects in an independent system and given a key value for reference and retrieval. Many cloud systems use object storage for virtual host images and large files.

PaaS

The storage design for PaaS is quite a bit different from IaaS because the cloud provider is responsible for the entire platform and the customer is responsible for the application itself. This puts responsibility for the storage systems under the cloud provider as well. With PaaS, storage falls into the categories of structured and unstructured.

Structured   Structured data is organized and categorized data that can easily be placed within a database or other storage system that is created with rule sets and a normalized design. This data construct allows the application developers to easily import data from other data sources or nonproduction environments and have it ready to use for the production systems. The data is typically organized and optimized for searching technologies to use without the need for customization or tweaking. This allows the cloud customer to fully realize the power and potential of cloud hosting for their applications. However, special attention is required on the part of the application developers and Cloud Security Professional to avoid vendor lock-in.

Unstructured   Unstructured data is information that cannot be used or easily used in a rigid and formatted database data structure. This can be because of the size of the files or the types of files. Typically included in this category are multimedia files (videos, audio), photos, files produced by word processing and Microsoft Office products, website files, or anything else that will not fit within a database structure.

 EXAM TIP   There will almost certainly be questions pertaining to which storage types are part of which service type, either with direct identification and matching, or asking the differences within the service model (e.g., the difference between volume and object with IaaS, or asking which service model structured/unstructured pertains too). Make sure you know each type and how they relate to each service model.

SaaS

With a SaaS offering, the cloud provider is solely responsible for the entire infrastructure and application as well. As such, the customer has very little control over storage in any way other than placing data into it. The two most common storage types for SaaS are information storage and management as well as content and file storage.

Information Storage and Management   This is the classic form of storing data within databases that the application uses and maintains. Data is either generated by the application or imported via the application through interfaces and loaded into the database.

Content and File Storage   Content and file storage is where the SaaS application allows for the uploading of data that is not part of the underlying database. The files and content are held by the application in another means of storage to be accessible to the users.

Threats to Storage Types

The most common and well understood threat to storage is the unauthorized access or use of the data itself. This can be an external threat or a compromise of a system, or it can be in the form of a malicious insider who possesses the credentials to access the data but uses them for unauthorized purposes. Although this threat tends to be focused on the confidentiality principle of security, it most certainly applies to the integrity of the data as well. An attack that is able to modify or destroy data within an application poses a central threat to the business processes of the organization, even if it might not face the same liability from a regulatory standpoint that the unauthorized disclosure of confidential data would.

The nature of a cloud environment and how storage is spread across large systems, often with geographic diversity, leads to an increase in the possibility of data leakage or exposure. This is further complicated in a cloud environment because you also have to compensate for the personnel of the cloud provider having administrative and privileged access to systems within that environment.

Storage systems within a cloud also face threats from the network and physical perspectives. From a network perspective, storage systems are also susceptible to DoS attacks, which goes to the core of the availability principle that is a major feature of cloud computing. Although cloud environments have very redundant systems, they still face the same threats from data corruption or physical destruction and failure as well.

When data is slated for destruction, the main challenge is ensuring that it is completely sanitized to meet policy and regulatory guidelines. In a cloud environment, the physical destruction of media is not possible as compared to a traditional server model, so software mechanisms for overwriting or cryptographic erasure will need to be relied upon instead.

Technologies Available to Address Threats

A major concept and approach employed in a cloud environment to protect data is known as *data loss prevention* (DLP), or sometimes as *data leakage prevention.* (Later in this chapter we discuss in depth encryption and other data-masking approaches.) DLP is a set of controls and practices put in place to ensure that data is only accessible and exposed to those users and systems authorized to have it. The goals of a DLP strategy for an organization are to manage and minimize risk, maintain compliance with regulatory requirements, and show due diligence on the part of the application and data owner. However, it is vital for any organization to take a holistic view of DLP and not focus on individual systems or hosting environments. The DLP strategy should involve their entire enterprise, particularly with hybrid cloud environments, or those where there is a combination of cloud and traditional data center installations.

DLP Components

Any DLP implementation is composed of three common components: discovery and classification, monitoring, and enforcement.

The discovery and classification stage is the first stage of the DLP implementation; it is focused on the actual finding of data that is pertinent to the DLP strategy, ensuring that all instances of it are known and able to be exposed to the DLP solution, and determining the security classification and requirements of the data once it has been found. This also allows the matching of data within the environment to any regulatory requirements for its protection and assurance.

Once data has been discovered and classified, it can then be monitored with DLP implementations. The monitoring stage encompasses the core function and purpose of a DLP strategy. It involves the actual process of watching data as it moves through the various states of usage to ensure it is being used in appropriate and controlled ways. It also ensures that those who access and use the data are authorized to do so and are using it in an appropriate manner.

The final stage of a DLP implementation is the actual enforcement of policies and any potential violations caught as part of the monitoring stage. If any potential violations are detected by the DLP implementation, a variety of measures can be automatically taken, depending on the policies set forth by management. This can range from simply logging and alerting of a potential violation to actually blocking and stopping the potential violation when it is first detected.

DLP Data States

With data at rest (DAR), the DLP solution is installed on the systems holding the data, which can be servers, desktops, workstations, or mobile devices. In many instances, this will involve archived data and long-term storage data. This is the simplest DLP solution to deploy throughout the enterprise overall but might also require network integration to be the most effective.

With data in transit (DIT), the DLP solution is deployed near the network perimeter to capture traffic as it leaves the network through various protocols, such as HTTP/HTTPS and SMTP. It looks for data that is leaving or attempting to leave the area that does not conform to security policies, either in subject or in format. One thing to note: if the traffic leaving the environment is encrypted, the DLP solution will need to be able to read and process the encrypted traffic in order to function, which might require key management and encryption aspects coming into play.

Lastly, with data in use (DIU), the DLP solution is deployed on the users' workstations or devices in order to monitor the data access and use from the endpoint. The biggest challenges with this type of implementation are reach and the complexity of having all access points covered. This can be especially true within a cloud environment where users are geographically dispersed and use a large variety of clients to access the systems and applications.

 CAUTION DLP on end-user devices can be a particular challenge for any cloud application. Because it requires the end user to install an application or plug-in to work, you will need to make sure you fully understand the types of devices your users will be utilizing, as well as any costs and requirements associated with the use of the technology. The growth of "bring your own device" (BYOD) within many organizations will also have a profound impact on any DLP strategies and should be reflected in policies.

DLP Cloud Implementations and Practices

The cloud environment brings additional challenges to DLP, much like any other type of implementation or policy, when compared to those challenges in a traditional data center. The biggest difference/challenge is in the way cloud environments store data. Data in a cloud is spread across large storage systems, with varying degrees of replication and redundancy, and oftentimes where the data will be stored and accessed is unpredictable. For a DLP strategy, this can pose a particular challenge because it makes properly discovering and monitoring all data used by a system or application more difficult, especially because the data can change locations over time, effectively becoming a moving target. With a cloud system using metered resource cost models and DLP adding additional load and resource consumption to the system, the potential for higher costs, above and beyond the costs of the DLP solution, is a real concern.

Design and Apply Data Security Strategies

Several toolsets and technologies are commonly used as data security strategies:

- Encryption
- Key management
- Masking
- Obfuscation
- Anonymization
- Tokenization

These range from the encryption of data to prevent unauthorized access, to the masking and tokenization of data to render it protected in the event that it is leaked or accessed.

Encryption

With the concepts of multitenancy and resource pooling being central to any cloud environment, the use of encryption to protect data is essential and required, as the typical protections of physical separation and segregation found in a traditional data center model are not available or applicable to a cloud environment. The architecture of an encryption system has three basic components: the data itself, the encryption engine that handles all the encryption activities, and the encryption keys used in the actual encryption and use of the data.

Encryption with Data States

Encryption is used in various manners and through different technology approaches, depending on the state of the data at the time—in use, at rest, or in motion. With data in use, the data is being actively accessed and processed. Because this process is the most removed from and independent of the host system, technologies such as data rights management (DRM) and information rights management (IRM) are the most capable and mature approaches that can be taken at this time (both are discussed in depth later in this chapter). Data in transit pertains to the active transmission of data across the network, and as such, the typical security protocols and technologies employed are available within a cloud environment (for example, TLS/SSL, VPN, IPsec, and HTTPS). With data at rest, where the data is sitting idle within the environment and storage systems, file-level and storage-level encryption mechanisms will be employed, depending on the location and state of the data; files sitting on a file system versus in a database or other storage architecture will likely require different types of encryption engines and technologies to secure them based on the particular needs and requirements of the system employed. The Cloud Security Professional must pay particular attention to any specific regulatory requirements for the classification of the data under consideration and ensure that the encryption methods chosen satisfy the minimums of all applicable standards and laws.

Challenges with Encryption

There is a myriad of challenges with implementing encryption. Some are applicable no matter where the data is housed, and others are specific issues to cloud environments. A central challenge to encryption implementations is the dependence on key sets to handle the actual encryption and decryption processes. Without the proper security of encryption keys, or exposure to external parties such as the cloud provider itself, the entire encryption scheme could be rendered vulnerable and insecure. (More on the specific issues with key management will follow in the next section.) With any software-based encryption scheme, core computing components such as processor and memory are vital, and within a cloud environment specifically, these components are shared across all the hosted customers. This can make systems such as memory vulnerable to exposure and could thus compromise the implementation of the encryption operations. It can also be a challenge implementing encryption throughout applications that are moving into a cloud hosting environment that were not designed initially to engage with encryption systems, from both a technical and performance capacity, because code changes or unacceptable levels of performance degradation may become apparent with the integration of encryption. As a last major concern, encryption does not ensure data integrity, only confidentiality within an environment. Additional steps will need to be integrated for those environments where integrity is a pressing concern.

 EXAM TIP   Make sure you understand and remember that encryption will not do anything to ensure integrity, only confidentiality. Other methods such as checksums, covered elsewhere in this text, will need to be used where integrity is important or crucial.

Encryption Implementations

The actual implementation of encryption and how it is applied will depend largely on the type of storage being used within the cloud environment.

With database storage systems, two layers of encryption are typically applied and available. First, database systems will reside on volume storage systems, resembling a typical file system of a server model. The actual database files can be protected through encryption methods at the file system level; this also serves to protect the data at rest. Within the database system itself are encryption methods that can be applied to the data set, either wholesale or on a granular level, by encrypting specific tables or columns of data. This type of encryption can be handled by the database application itself or by the actual software application that handles the encryption and stores the data in that state.

For object storage, apart from the encryption at the actual file level, which is handled by the cloud provider, encryption can be used within the application itself. The most prevalent means for this is through IRM technologies or via encryption within the applicant itself. With IRM, which will be covered later in this chapter, encryption can be applied to the objects to control their usage after they have left the system. With application-level encryption, the application effectively acts as a proxy between the user and the object storage and ensures encryption during the transaction. However, once the object has left the application framework, no protection is provided.

Lastly, with volume storage, many of the typical encryption systems used on a traditional server model can be employed within a cloud framework. This encryption is most useful with DAR-type scenarios. Due to the application itself being able to read the encrypted data on the volume, any compromise of the application will render the file system encryption ineffective when it comes to protecting the data.

Key Management

Key management is the safeguarding of encryption keys and the access to them. Within a cloud environment, key management is an essential and highly important task, while also being very complex. It is one of the most important facets of cloud hosting for the Cloud Security Professional to focus on at all times.

One of the most important security considerations with key management is the access to the keys and the storage of them. Access to keys in any environment is extremely important and critical to security, but in a cloud environment, where you have multitenancy and the cloud provider personnel having broad administrative access to systems, there are more considerations than in a traditional data center concerning the segregation and control of the staff of the customer. Of course, there can also be a big difference in key management between IaaS and PaaS implementations, as well as the level of involvement and access that the cloud provider's staff will need to have. Where the keys are stored is also an important consideration within a cloud environment. In a traditional data center configuration, the key management system will typically be on dedicated hardware and systems, segregated from the rest of the environment. Conversely, within a cloud environment, the key management system can be put on its own virtual machine, but this does nothing to alleviate concerns regarding multitenancy and access by the staff of the cloud provider. The Cloud Security Professional will always need to consult with applicable regulatory concerns for any key management, access, and storage requirements, and determine whether a cloud provider can meet those requirements.

No matter what hosting model is used by an organization, a few principles of key management are important. Key management should always be performed only on trusted systems and by trusted processes, whether in a traditional data center or a cloud environment. In a cloud environment, careful consideration must be given to the level of trust that can be established within the environment of the cloud provider, and whether that will meet management and regulatory requirements. Although confidentiality and security are always the top concerns with key management, in a cloud environment, where heavy use of encryption throughout the entire system is paramount, the issue of the availability of the key management system is also of central importance. If the key management system were to become unavailable, essentially the entire system and applications would also become unavailable for the duration of the outage. One way to mitigate the possibility of cloud provider staff having access to the keys used within the environment is to host the key management system outside of the cloud provider. Although this will certainly attain the segregation of duties and provide higher security in regard to that one specific area, it also increases the complexity of the system overall and introduces the same availability concerns. In other words, if the externally hosted key management system becomes unavailable or inaccessible, even if caused by something as mundane as an inadvertent firewall or ACL change, the entire system will be inaccessible.

Key storage can be implemented in a cloud environment in three ways. The first is internal storage, where the keys are stored and accessed within the same virtual machine as the encryption service or engine. Internal storage is the simplest implementation, it keeps the entire process together, and it is appropriate for some storage types such as database and backup system encryption. However, it also ties the system and keys closely together, and compromise of the system overall can lead to potential key compromise—although it does alleviate the external availability and connection problems. The second method is external storage, where the keys are maintained separately from the systems and security processes (such as encryption). The external hosting can be anywhere so long as it is not on the same system performing the encryption functions, so typically this would be a dedicated host within the same environment, but it could be completely external. In this type of implementation, the availability aspect is important. The third method involves having an external and independent service or system host the key storage. This will typically increase security precautions and safeguards in a widely accepted manner because the key storage is handled by an organization dedicated to that specific task that maintains systems specifically scoped for that function, with well-documented security configurations, policies, and operations.

Masking/Obfuscation/Anonymization

The theory behind masking or obfuscation is to replace, hide, or remove sensitive data from data sets. The most common use for masking is making available test data sets for nonproduction and development environments. By replacing sensitive data fields with random or substituted data, these nonproduction environments can quickly utilize data sets that are similar to production for testing and development, without exposing sensitive information to systems with fewer security controls and less oversight. Many regulatory systems and industry certification programs have requirements to not use sensitive or real data in nonproduction environments, and masking is often the easiest and best way to meet such a requirement.

Typically masking is accomplished either by entirely replacing the value with a new one or by adding additional characters to a data field. This can be done wholesale on the entire field or just portions of it. For example, many times with credit card fields, as most who have ever purchased anything online can attest, the entire credit card number will be masked with a character such as an asterisk, but the last four digits visible will be left visible for identification and confirmation. Another common method is to shift values, either with the entire data set or with specific values within a field based on an algorithm, which can be done from a random or predetermined perspective. The last major method is to delete the data wholesale or just parts of the data from a field, or to replace the data with overwritten null pointers or values.

The two primary strategies or methods for masking are static masking and dynamic masking. With static masking, a separate and distinct copy of the data set is created with masking in place. This is typically done through a script or other process that will take a standard data set, process it to mask the appropriate and predefined fields, and then output the data set as a new one with the completed masking done. The static method is most appropriate for data sets that are created for nonproduction environments, where testing is necessary or desired and having a data set very similar in size and structure to production is paramount. This allows testing to be done without exposing sensitive data to these environments or to developers. With dynamic masking, production environments are protected by the masking process being implemented between the application and data layers of the application. This allows for a masking translation to take place live in the system and during normal application processing of data.

 NOTE Dynamic masking is usually done where a system needs to have full and unmasked data but certain users should not have the same level of access. An example from my own personal experience is healthcare data, where the back-end system needs to have the full data, but users such as enrollment assistants and customer service representatives only need a subset of the data, or just enough of a data field to be able to verify codes or personal information without seeing the entire field of data.

With data anonymization, data is manipulated in a way to prevent the identification of an individual through various data objects. It's often used in conjunction with other concepts such as masking. Data generally has direct and indirect identifiers, with direct identifiers being the actual personal and private data, and indirect identifiers being attributes such as demographic and location data that, when used together, could lead to the identity of the individual. Data anonymization is the process of removing the indirect identifiers to prevent such an identification from taking place.

Tokenization

Tokenization is the practice of utilizing a random and opaque "token" value in data to replace what otherwise would be a sensitive or protected data object. The token value is usually generated by the application with a means to map it back to the actual real value, and then the token value is placed in the data set with the same formatting and requirements of the actual real value, so that the application can continue to function without different modifications or code changes. Tokenization represents a way for an organization to remove sensitive data from an application without having to introduce more intensive processes such as encryption to meet regulatory or policy requirements. As with any technology used to complement an application, especially in regard to data security, the system and processes used for tokenization will need to be properly secured. Failure to implement proper controls with the tokenization process will lead to the same vulnerabilities and problems as insecure key management with encryption or other data safeguard failures. The tokenization process provided on behalf of the cloud provider should be carefully vetted, both to ensure the security and governance of it and to limit any possibility of vendor lock-in.

Application of Technologies

When choosing which technologies will be used within any environment for data protection, the Cloud Security Professional must properly evaluate both the system and application frameworks, along with the data used in them and the regulatory frameworks they are subjected to. Within a cloud environment, some additional needs must be evaluated beyond those of a traditional data center model.

The first step is to understand the data that is to be protected. This will encompass any regulatory requirements if the data is personal information, health data, financial transaction data, and so on. This step also includes understanding the structure of the data and how it is represented within the application, such as database system, object storage, volume storage, or structured or unstructured storage.

The next step is to understand the nature and details of the hosting environment. For a cloud environment, this involves determining whether the model used is IaaS, PaaS, or SaaS, and then using that knowledge to understand the types of storage systems currently in use and those offered by the cloud provider. Each type of hosting model uses different storage types, and a thorough understanding of how the particular cloud provider has architected them will be essential to planning any security technologies. The Cloud Security Professional will also need to determine what types of technologies are supported or allowed within the cloud environment. An assumption should not be made that all technologies and software packages will automatically work in all environments; even from one cloud provider to another, there may be differences in policies and controls that make some technologies infeasible.

With an understanding of the data and the hosting environment, the Cloud Security Professional must next determine the data ownership and classification requirements. This will largely drive the implementation of technologies and ensure they meet all policy and regulatory requirements, as well as give a picture of the access and use requirements for the data. The regulatory requirements will likely set minimum encryption levels and retention timelines that will form a strong basis for comparing possible technologies and whether they meet the current needs (and likely future needs) of the organization and anticipate future regulatory requirement changes or enhancements.

Lastly, as with any implementation of a technology, appropriate monitoring and auditing need to be planned and tested before production rollout. This includes the backup and retention models for the data. All systems and processes should be actively monitored to ensure they are functioning as intended or required, with more extensive periodic reviews and audits to fully test the implementations. Tests of restorations should also be performed as part of periodic reviews to ensure regulatory requirement compliance as well as instill management confidence in the use of the specific technologies and their success in managing or mitigating risk.

Emerging Technologies

As with any area of technology, changes and advancements with data security are rapid and continual. For a Cloud Security Professional, it is vital to stay on top of these rapid changes and advancements to evaluate the appropriateness for inclusion within their systems. Many advancements are also drivers for regulatory changes or in reaction to regulatory requirement changes.

Leading cloud service providers have very prolific and innovative development teams that are constantly adding and expanding on new technology and feature enhancements. These can range from new APIs that add expanded features and management capabilities, to new methods for auto-scaling and rapid provisioning, to new service offerings for storage methods and virtual image security and hosting. It is a rapidly changing environment on the feature and security fronts—and something to always ensure you are on top of.

Encryption technologies in particular continue to rapidly evolve and improve, both in the strength of encryption and in the speed and efficiency of utilizing encryption within an application. Although still in the early stages of development and testing, technologies such as homomorphic encryption, which allows the manipulation of encrypted data without actually unencrypting it, could provide enormous benefits within a cloud environment once they are more mature and widely available.

There are, of course, many other emerging and rapidly developing technologies. Therefore, make sure you stay on top of new technologies and read from many different IT Security publications and websites to learn about them as they emerge and evolve.

 EXAM TIP   As new technologies emerge and become commonly used with cloud environments, exam questions may appear specifically geared toward them. This will be especially true with encryption, the continued widespread adoption of collaboration tools and code-repositories, and widespread utilities for monitoring, scanning, and data analytics. You should be cognizant of this possibility and make sure to have a broad understanding of these emerging trends and technologies, so as to not be surprised if exam questions do materialize.

Data Discovery and Classification Techniques

Data discovery and classification techniques are very important concepts for both utilizing data and protecting it. Through data discovery, an organization can fully utilize their data in new and creative ways, while data classification is centered on using the proper security controls.

Data Discovery

Data discovery is a business intelligence operation and a user-driven process where data is visually represented and analyzed to look for patterns or specific attributes. This is a bit different from many data analysis operations because it heavily relies upon a user's expertise and experience to interpret and develop meaningful inferences from it. Data discovery is an iterative process, where initial findings lead to a refinement of parameters and representation in order to dive deeper into the data and continue to scope it toward to the objective desired.

Organizations can use a few main toolsets and approaches to leverage data discovery that are also especially pertinent to a cloud environment. Big Data implementations are becoming very common, especially within large public cloud environments, and with them come the enormous volume of data and the ability to do extensive data discovery. These implementations are not without their own issues, though, as the volume of data requires efficient tools to process and can become very burdensome. Any organization that intends to perform successful data discovery within a Big Data implementation will need to ensure that they have very clearly defined scopes and objectives, combined with the appropriate tools and applications to assist with the process. As with many cloud environments and modern application frameworks, real-time analytics are powerful toolsets, and many applications exist and continue to be developed to aide in their implementation. These types of approaches can be used with data discovery but will need to be done in a manner that is optimized for their specific approach and application; otherwise, potentially slow response times and ineffective results will be the ultimate fate of such an approach.

With any volume of data, it is crucial to know the ways in which it is organized and accessible in order to perform any sort of analysis or discovery with it. Data discovery tools typically scan databases and data sets, looking for information of value or pertinent to the exact discovery effort the user is undertaking. When scanning these data sources, discovery tools can use a handful of useful attributes that offer various degrees of efficiency for processing large volumes of data. One efficient approach is the use of metadata. In short, metadata is data about data. It contains information about the type of data, how it is stored and organized, or information about its creation and use. For example, this could include filenames or headers and column names in a database or spreadsheet, which, if named and labeled properly and in a meaningful way, could allow for a quick analysis of the type of data present in that set or field and its applicability to the data discovery process undertaken.

Similar to metadata are labels, which can be used to group data elements together and provide some information about them. Whereas metadata is a formal part of the data, because it is used in the official data repositories to categorize and organize the data, labels are more informal and created by users or processes to show data categories based on subjective and qualitative analysis. Unlike metadata, though, the usefulness of labels is entirely dependent on the way they are applied and how consistently and widespread they are used within a data set. If they are only used in certain areas but not others, even though the data should contain the same labels, their effectiveness and usefulness will be greatly diminished.

The last method is to analyze the exact content of the data, which is typically considered to be content analysis. This involves looking at the exact data itself and employing various checksum, heuristics, statistical, or other types of analysis to determine what it is and its applicability to data discovery. As tools and processes become more advanced and sophisticated, content analysis will continue to expand in usefulness and efficiency to become a predominant method.

Although the tools and processes for data discovery have become more advanced and efficient, there are still challenges that apply to virtually all environments. The main problem when it comes to data discovery is the quality of the data that analysis is being performed against. Data that is malformed, incorrectly stored or labeled, or incomplete makes it very difficult to use analytical tools against. This can largely be mitigated by having strong internal policies and controls for how data is created, structured, and stored. If data is flawed and incomplete, it also will lead to the same results for any reports, alerts, and dashboards that are created from the data. This can lead to management being fed inaccurate or incorrect data, and even possibly lead to the wrong decisions being made based off of it, causing potential loss of customers, money, or even the jobs of developers or staff responsible for the flawed data. Another huge challenge with data discovery is dealing with the volume of data and the system resources needed to read and process all of it. An organization will need robust platforms with enormous resources to process the data volume in a quick and efficient manner, leading to substantial costs and investment.

Another major benefit of a robust data discovery program and strategy is the visibility into and the discovery of data that requires the application of security controls. While data classifications and controls would typically be applied in the early phases of the data lifecycle, an ongoing discovery and review process will ensure that data is properly classified and maintained over its lifespan.

Being in a cloud environment presents some particular challenges to data discovery as well. The foremost challenge is knowing exactly where all the data is located and being used. With cloud infrastructures spread across wide resources and even geographic locations, combined with high availability and processing power, data is constantly in motion and being stored and used in many places simultaneously. The Cloud Security Professional will need to pay particular attention to this aspect in many possible scenarios, and data discovery is certainly a big part of it. Depending on the cloud model used, data may be accessible in multiple ways. In a traditional data center, staff will have full access to and knowledge of data and data storage mechanisms. Within a cloud environment, the storage systems may be sufficiently abstracted from the cloud customer so that knowing all data locations and even having sufficient access to them can be a very real challenge and concern. A final major concern is data preservation and retention. Within a cloud environment, it is crucial to have appropriate SLA and contractual requirements in place for data retention, making sure they adhere to the organization's policies or regulatory requirements at a minimum. This particular problem with retention can apply to the actual data itself, but also to metadata and labels.

Classification

Classification is the process of analyzing data for certain attributes, and then using that to determine the appropriate policies and controls to apply to ensure its security. These attributes can include the creator of the data, the type of data, where it is stored and how it is accessed, security controls already applied to it, and any regulatory requirements for its protection. Most major regulatory and certifications bodies have their own classification requirements or guidelines for member organizations to follow, and many legal requirements also are attached to how data is classified and handled. The most prominent industry certifications, including PCI DSS and ISO 27001, hold data classification as one of their core concepts and requirements.

Based on the attributes of the data and the classification derived from them, an organization can then map that data classification to security controls and policies, typically through automated means. This can mean data is automatically subjected to specific security controls, storage mechanisms, encryption, access controls, as well as specific regulatory requirements such as retention periods and destruction methods. Although the ideal is to have data classified and labeled in an automatic way, in some instances this is left as a manual process. This is typically done through creation procedures, where a data custodian or content developer must make decisions at the time as to what the classification should be. Many times, when data sets are created for special purposes or to meet specific finite requests that are outside of normal operating procedures and practices, manual classification will need to be performed.

Within a cloud environment, proper data classification is even more crucial than in a traditional data center. Because many customers and hosts are located within the same multitenant environment, improper data classification or controls can lead to a much higher and more immediate unacceptable level of risk. Data classification needs to be ensured by the Cloud Security Professional to happen immediately upon data creation or modification, with the proper security controls attached immediately as well. Many times this can be performed via the metadata attached to a file or information based on where it was created, which process or user created it, or the department or unit that owns the data. Once the classification is determined, the data can immediately be placed under the proper encryption or other data protection methods within the cloud environment.

Relevant Jurisdictional Data Protections for Personally Identifiable Information

Depending on the jurisdiction involved, data protections can vary widely in regulatory requirements for storage and access, data destruction techniques, and certainly in regard to what data can be collected and stored as well as what level of notice is required to be given to or the consent needed from the end user. Although many types of data have specific regulatory requirements attached to them, personally identifiable information (PII) has some of the most stringent and clearly defined consequences for failure to properly protect it; the only data that carries more consequences from the privacy standpoint under regulations is protected health information (PHI).

Data Privacy Acts

Many nations and groups of nations have established their own rules and policies regarding the handling of PII. One important concept to understand is jurisdiction. In a cloud environment, where data can be easily moved and located in geographically diverse locations, the concept of which applicable laws and policies are pertinent to the data at any time and for any use are extremely important to understand.

United States

Unlike other bodies such as the European Union, the United States does not have a comprehensive data privacy law, but rather has a variety of laws and regulatory agencies and policies that combined form a rudimentary basis for privacy. Most laws in the United States are based on specific types of personal information rather than an overall approach to privacy at a holistic level. For example, in regard to healthcare data and financial data, stringent requirements are set forth in laws such as HIPAA (Health Insurance Portability and Accountability Act) that control how information can be used, who owns the data, the user's right to the data, as well as retention requirements. With financial information, established and constantly refined laws and policies are set forth that require transparency to the users of data that is kept on them within certain parameters, such as credit history, as well as requirements for the timely notification of users for any potential exposure or leakage of their financial information. Beyond those types of cases, there is ongoing debate about the future of privacy and likely additional laws and regulations, but the most public and known current ones are put forth in narrow areas rather than in a comprehensive way.

European Union

The European Union (EU) has a series of directives and policies that forms a very strong user privacy base, and many other areas around the world base their privacy requirements on those from the EU. The biggest impact policy is found in Directive 95/46/EC, which is titled "On the protection of individuals with regard to the processing of personal data and on the free movement of such data." This directive is far more expansive than any privacy laws in the United States, as it covers all sectors of the economy and all users of data, not just specific subsets such as healthcare and financial data. This was then expanded and refined under Directive 2002/58/EC, regarding data breaches and the use of cookies in tracking users. This directive is titled "Concerning the processing of personal data and the protection of privacy in the electronic communications sector." At the time of writing, the EU is working toward more formal and structured policy regulations and enforcement that are expected to be implemented in 2017. The European Union has also been a big champion of laws concerning the "right to be forgotten," which encompass an individual's right to have their presence removed from search engine indexes and results.

Other Jurisdictions

Apart from the United States and the European Union, the other big body that has established privacy protections and regulations is APEC, the Asian-Pacific Economic Cooperation. APEC has put forth the APEC Privacy Framework, which focuses on the protection of individual privacy, but with the needs of commerce and information flow also recognized and attempts to drive policies that can meet the needs of both.

Privacy Roles and Responsibilities

Within a cloud environment there are different roles and responsibilities between the cloud provider and the cloud customer in regard to data privacy, and those roles differ depending on where the IaaS, PaaS, or SaaS hosting model is employed.

- **Physical environment**   Sole responsibility of the cloud provider for all cloud models

- **Infrastructure**   Sole responsibility of the cloud provider for PaaS and SaaS, with shared responsibility for IaaS between the cloud provider and cloud customer

- **Platform**   Sole responsibility of the cloud provider for SaaS, shared responsibility for PaaS, and responsibility of the cloud customer for IaaS

- **Application**   Shared responsibility for SaaS, and sole responsibility of the cloud customer for both IaaS and PaaS
- **Data**   Sole responsibility for the cloud customer for all models
- **Governance**   Sole responsibility of the cloud customer for all models

Implementation of Data Discovery

Data discovery is a prime method for an application or system owner to show and ensure compliance with data privacy regulations. With the application owner being responsible for compliance with regulatory requirements and privacy acts, having a strong data discovery process in place will serve as a due diligence metric to provide to auditors or oversight reviews as far as compliance is concerned. From the side of the cloud provider, supporting and assisting the cloud customer with the implementation of data discovery processes also serves to show due diligence on the part of the provider for their role in compliance with data privacy regulations and laws.

One aspect of data privacy laws is the requirement to report any data leakages or breaches to those individuals who may have had their data compromised, and to do so in a timely manner. There also may be requirements with certain types of data to serve notice to regulatory bodies as well. With the implementation of data discovery, combined with DLP strategies and implementations, the detection and discovery of potential leakages can happen in near real time, and either serve notice or stop the actual breach in progress before it can be exposed. The discovery process within a cloud environment is also of particular importance because it exposes the locations of data throughout the environment. This can serve to ensure the jurisdictional coverage of privacy requirements as well as assist in reporting or discovery requirements that involve the knowledge of all applicable data sources and repositories.

Classification of Discovered Sensitive Data

We previously discussed data discovery and the applicability of data classification as it pertains to organizational policies for security controls. Within the realm of data privacy acts, this same process can be augmented to also ensure compliance with regulatory controls from the legal realm.

Taking the requirements of data protection from privacy acts, the additional classes or categories of protected and sensitive information can expand upon those already part of the classification program. While many regulatory requirements may focus on specific types of data such as with healthcare and financial data, privacy acts may add additional concerns and requirements. For example, certain demographic data may be collected as part of an application about a user, such as race, religion, sexual orientation, political leanings, or any other similar type of information. Although these data points may not be of any concern to a regulation such as PCI DSS, they may be core and important parts of a privacy act that is focused solely on the protection of an individual's data. With the integration of privacy act requirements onto the classification system, these important private data points can be more efficiently protected, monitored, and reported on.

A Cloud Security Professional must be able to fully understand whether the privacy acts have particular requirements for these points as far as retention and secure destruction are concerned.

Mapping and Definition of Controls

With the various requirements mapped out in privacy acts, a central role of the Cloud Security Professional is the mapping of those requirements to the actual security controls and processes in place with both the application and the cloud environment under the responsibility of the cloud provider. For large applications that may span multiple jurisdictions and privacy acts, this will be of particular importance. The cloud customer and cloud provider will need to work together through appropriate contractual or SLA requirements to ensure compliance for both parties in regard to the requirements for regulatory bodies or applicable privacy acts.

Application of Defined Controls

With the complexity of large cloud environments, it can sometimes be difficult to ensure that all applicable privacy act requirements can and are being met by both the cloud customer and cloud provider. It is imperative from the onset that both the contract and SLAs clearly define the roles for both cloud provider and cloud customer, and that the requirements and responsibilities for each aspect of the privacy acts are addressed. With large cloud environments that span multiple jurisdictions, it is likely that multiple agreements and frameworks will need to be implemented to ensure compliance with all applicable requirements.

The Cloud Security Alliance Cloud Controls Matrix (CCM) provides a strong framework and applicable security control domains within a cloud environment that encapsulate the various requirements set for with privacy acts, as well as various industry certification and regulatory bodies. These domains can be used by the Cloud Security Professional as the basis for implementing the overall control definitions to ensure that all areas are covered and addressed. The CCM can be found at https://cloudsecurityalliance .org/group/cloud-controls-matrix/.

Here are the security domains presented and outlined by the CCM:

- Application and Interface Security
- Audit Assurance and Compliance
- Business Continuity Management and Operational Resilience
- Change Control and Configuration Management
- Data Security and Information Lifecycle Management
- Data Center Security
- Encryption and Key Management
- Governance and Risk Management
- Human Resources

- Identity and Access Management
- Infrastructure and Virtualization Security
- Interoperability and Portability
- Mobile Security
- Security Incident Management, eDiscovery, and Cloud
- Supply Chain Management, Transparency, and Accountability
- Threat and Vulnerability Management

NOTE Not all controls will be applicable to all regulatory or privacy act requirements, but the overall CCM serves as a holistic approach to controls and serves a broader purpose. Nonetheless, the requirements for privacy acts will fit within its framework in the appropriate places.

Data Rights Management

Data rights management is an extension of normal data protection, where additional controls and ACLs are placed onto data sets that require additional permissions or conditions to access and use beyond just simple and traditional security controls. This is encapsulated within the concept of information rights management (IRM).

NOTE Many are familiar with the common meaning of data rights management (DRM). DRM applies to the protection of consumer media, such as music, publications, video, movies, and so on. In this context, IRM applies to the organizational side to protect information and privacy, whereas DRM applies to the distribution side to protect intellectual property rights and control the extent of distribution.

Data Rights Objectives

With IRM, a few main concepts are important to the Cloud Security Professional. In a typical environment, access controls are placed on a data object, such as a file, that determine who on the system can read or modify that object (file). In such instances, there will be sets of users that have administrative rights on the server or application that can read the file as well. Also, providing read permissions to a file allows a user to inherently perform other operations such as copying, renaming, printing, sending, and more. With IRM, additional control layers are applied to a file that allow for much more granular and powerful control over what can be done with it. With IRM, all the functions mentioned can be further controlled and restricted, providing additional layers of security and control over documents beyond what can be achieved from normal file system permissions. This also serves to make data storage more removed from data consumption and allows for more flexibility in choosing hosting platforms and providers.

IRM can also be used as a means for data classification and control. IRM controls and ACLs can be placed immediately upon data at the time of creation. This can be based on virtually any attributes concerning the creation process or even the user, including where the data is created, when it is created, and who created it. This allows for granularity from the very initial stages of the data lifecycle and enables an organization to maintain very stringent data control. This can effectively be maintained as a security baseline for organizational policies and work toward satisfying some aspect of regulatory requirements, and it can be provided as part of the auditing and compliance process.

Tools

Rather than focusing on specific software technologies or implementations for IRM, we will instead focus on the typical attributes and features of those tool sets and what they can provide for IRM and security:

- **Auditing**   IRM technologies allow for robust auditing of who has viewed information, as well as provide proof as to when and where they accessed the data. This can aid greatly with compliance requirements where an organization needs to ensure that an appropriate audience has read a new policy or document, or where there is a need to provide solid evidence that only those who are entitled to access the data are the ones that have.

- **Expiration**   IRM technologies allow for the expiration of access to data. This gives an organization the ability to set a lifetime for the data and enforce policy controls that disallow it to be accessible forever, as is the case in most systems once data has been presented to users or is allowed to leave its host system and controls.

- **Policy control**   IRM technologies allow an organization to have very granular and detailed control over how their data is access and used. The ability to control, even with different audiences, who can copy, save, print, forward, or access any data is far more powerful than what is afforded by traditional data security mechanisms. An IRM implementation also gives an organization the ability to change policy at any time, revoking or expiring data down the road if necessary. This gives the organization the ability to ensure that users are always viewing the most current copy of data or policies as well as to expire the old ones once new ones are available.

- **Protection**   With the implementation of IRM technologies and controls, any information under their protection is secure at all times. Unlike many systems, which require separate practices and technologies for data at rest versus data in transit, IRM provides persistent protection at all times that is integrated with the data regardless of its current access state.

- **Support for applications and formats**   Most IRM technologies support a range of data formats and integration with application packages commonly used within organizations, such as e-mail and various office suites. This enables the integration of IRM systems and processes without the organization needing to make major changes to their current operational practices.

Data Retention, Deletion, and Archiving Policies

For any data policy to be effective and ensure compliance with regulatory or corporate compliance requirements, the concepts of retention, deletion, and archiving are of the utmost importance. Whereas other data policies and practices are focused on the security and production usage of data, these three concepts are typical of those that fulfill regulatory obligations, which can come in the form of legal requirements or mandates from certification or industry oversight bodies.

Data Retention

Data retention involves the keeping and maintaining of data for a period of time as well as the methods used to accomplish these tasks. Typically, the retention requirements are to meet regulatory demands and have set periods of time mandated as the minimums for them. Corporate policies for data retention can and sometimes do require longer periods of time, but the regulatory requirements will serve as the minimum basis for retention. The data retention policy also addresses the means of storage and the ability to access the data when required for a variety of reasons, including regulatory requirements, corporate history or processing, and legal discovery requirements. A data retention policy that does not also address the access of data and the availability of it will miss the main focus and points of data preservation because the data will effectively be useless or cost prohibitive to access.

The data retention policy goes beyond just time requirements and access. As part of the policy, it is also imperative to address the formats and storage methods, as well as the security that will be utilized along with the preservation decisions. The decisions for all aspects of the data retention policy will be driven by regulatory requirements first and foremost because they represent the base minimum of obligations an organization must fulfill. These requirements will always outline the time of retention, but may also mandate particular methods and security minimums that must be applied as well. This enables an organization to determine the data classification for the retained data and use that to map to security requirements and methods. The classification will be based on the entirety of the data required for retention and the sensitivity levels of the overall data set. If more secure and valuable data is included with less sensitive data, the higher and stricter classification requirements will always prevail and apply to the entire data set.

 CAUTION While regulations and policies determine the length of time for which data must be preserved, some caution is also warranted for data that may end up being kept past the stated policies. This can come into play particularly with eDiscovery requirements for evidence preservation and searching. Many organizations will make declared statements that they retain data for a set period of time and use that to define their scope of eDiscovery compliance. If proper systems are not in place to securely remove data once it has reached the policy requirements, it could lead to a failure to disclose and consequences with an eDiscovery order, where search parameters are limited to policy requirements.

Data Deletion

While data deletion may seem like a final step in the data lifecycle, it is one that carries with it as much importance from a security standpoint as any other phase in regard to data protection. When data is no longer needed in a system, it must be removed in a secure way that guarantees it is no longer accessible or recoverable in the future. In many instances, regulatory and industry requirements dictate methods for how data deletion must be performed to ensure true data destruction to meet standards.

There are multiple methods available in a traditional data center environment that are not transferable to a cloud environment due to the technical realities of how cloud infrastructures are designed and implemented. Within a traditional data center and server model, methods such as degaussing and physical destruction of media are feasible if requirements dictate them or the company desires to use them. However, within a cloud environment with shared infrastructure and multitenancy, these methods are not available to the cloud customer. In large public cloud infrastructures, the data is typically also written across large data storage systems, and the ability to isolate where data exists or ever has existed is almost impossible, thus making physical destruction of media or degaussing impossible, as it would likely impact the entire environment to ensure an acceptable degree of confidence in deletion.

Within a cloud environment, the main methods available for the customer are overwriting and cryptographic erasure (also known as *cryptographic shredding*). Overwriting is the process of using random data or null pointers to write over the data sectors that previously contained sensitive or proprietary information. Most regulatory and industry standard requirements will dictate the exact methods of overwriting that are acceptable, as well as how many times an overwriting process must be completed before an acceptable confidence degree of deletion is obtained. However, due to the previously mentioned aspect of cloud computing writing data across large expanses of storage with no real way to track or locate it all, overwriting is not a method that can be used with a high degree of confidence within a cloud because it is unlikely for the customer to be able to ensure they know all locations of the data to overwrite.

For proper destruction of data within a cloud environment, the most important and useful method is cryptographic shredding or erasure. With this method, the data is destroyed via encryption, with the resulting keys being permanently destroyed to ensure that the data can never be recovered.

Regardless of the particular method or approach being used for data deletion and sanitation, the roles, responsibilities, and procedures should be clearly defined and outlined within the contract between the cloud customer and cloud provider. These would typically be located within a data destruction clause of the contract.

Data Archiving

Although the process of data archiving removes the data from production or easily accessible systems, that does not mean that there are any less strict or comprehensive security requirements for it. Archiving typically involves removing data from production systems and placing it onto other systems that are usually cheaper storage options, scaled and configured for long-term storage (oftentimes offsite and removed from the

How is the data represented and stored?	**Format**	**Technologies**	What specific software applications are used to create and maintain the archives?
How long must data be retained and other requirements for its preservation?	**Regulatory Requirements**	**Testing**	Ensuring that backups can and will work when needed

Figure 3-3 Data archiving concepts and requirements

regular systems). This not only provides cheaper and more specialized storage for the data, but also allows the production systems to be more optimized and contain less data in their data sets, allowing for quicker searches and access times.

In order to properly implement a data archiving and retention policy, the key concepts outlined in Figure 3-3 are all crucial.

Format

For any archiving policy, a decision must be made as to the format of the archived data. With the long-term nature of archiving, data format is very important. As platforms, software, and technologies change over the years, a company may end up left with data that is archived in a state where it is not easily retrievable, or perhaps an outside vendor must be used to access the data at a much higher cost. With archived data being stored in a lot of cases for many years, the ability to recover it if necessary becomes a very real consideration and concern. The company must ensure that data in long-term storage has a means of recovery, which could be complicated over time with changing technologies and vendors going out of business or dropping product lines.

Technology

The archiving of data, beyond policy and the decision on the format of the data, will rely on specific technologies or standards to maintain and store the data. This will typically be in some sort of backup system, often involving tape systems and offsite storage. In most cases, automated functions will regularly run to transfer data that has reached either a size or time requirement, based on the company's policy, and rotate that data from the production systems into the archiving system. This may or may not include other operations such as encryption and the compression of the data sets, or performed on a holistic level with the media itself rather than with specific data sets and files. As mentioned previously with formats, the most important aspect with the actual archiving technology is the maintenance of the system over the years. Many vendors change products regularly, or even phase out systems or software packages over time. It is imperative for the Cloud Security Professional to ensure that the company maintains the capability to restore data for as long as company policy or regulatory requirements dictate is necessary. This can be through maintaining the software or systems internally to read the media for as long as is required, or the company can negotiate an agreement or contract with an outside firm to perform restores if necessary. Without maintaining the ability to restore and read the archives should the need arise, a company potentially faces regulatory sanctions, loss of reputation, or extra costs associated with obtaining services in a short period of time under contract to recover the data.

 NOTE   Ensuring the technology required to read archived data is available is extremely important. As technology changes over the years, organizations often overlook the need to keep systems in place to read archived data, and only realize the problem once it is too late. When this happens, an external firm must be contracted to read old data after systems have been inadvertently disposed of, and the cost typically comes at an extreme premium.

Regulatory Requirements

Most regulatory requirements, whether from a legal entity or an industry certification, will specify the minimum duration for data archiving as well as the procedures and reasons why retrieval is required or could be requested. These requirements often also specify the minimum encryption levels or technologies needed, or even the particular formats, standards, or technologies to be used. With legal requirements, the concept of eDiscovery comes into play, where data retrieval can be required to fulfill obligations for assistance with criminal or civil legal proceedings. The Cloud Security Professional will need to pay particular attention to legal and regulatory requirements for eDiscovery because they often proscribe time periods for retrieval and presentation. Therefore, the technology and facilities used for data archiving need to be chosen in a manner that management is confident will meet any of these requirements; otherwise, the company could potentially be exposed to penalties or fines.

Testing

Although data formats, technologies, and regulatory requirements form the core of a data archiving program, without proper testing to validate and audit the policies and procedures, there is no way for a company to ensure that their program is valid and usable in the event it is needed. A company should perform periodic and regular restore processes from archived data to test both the procedures and technologies used. This will ensure that data formats can still be read and processed, as well as verify that the encryption used can be deciphered and that the key management policies are sound. The testing procedure should ensure the entire process works from beginning to end, starting with the retrieval of storage sources from the remote site, all the way up to and including reading and verifying the actual data after the restoration.

Auditability, Traceability, and Accountability of Data Events

With a solid understanding of the types of data and policies for handling and preserving them, the Cloud Security Professional identifies collects, and analyzes the actual data events in order to make valuable use of them. The Open Web Application Security Project (OWASP) provides a sound and comprehensive set of definitions and guidelines for identifying, labeling, and collecting data events that are useful and pertinent to applications and security, whether in a cloud or traditional data center. The OWASP information can be found at https://www.owasp.org/index.php/Main_Page and will be used extensively in this section, with appropriate and direct links provided for each reference.

Definition of Event Sources

Which events are important and available for capture will vary and depend on the particular cloud service model employed.

IaaS Event Sources

With an IaaS environment, the cloud customer has the most access and visibility into the system and infrastructure logs of any of the cloud service models. Because the cloud customer has full control over their entire environment, including system and network capabilities, virtually all logs and data events should be exposed and available for capture. However, some logs outside of the typical purview of the cloud customer might also be of high value, and access to those logs should be clearly articulated in the contract and SLA between the cloud provider and the cloud customer. These logs include hypervisor logs, DNS logs, portal logs, network perimeter logs outside the scope of the cloud customer's view, and also the logs from the management and self-service portal that the cloud customer uses to provision and manage their services and billing records.

PaaS Event Sources

A PaaS environment does not offer or expose the same level of customer access to infrastructure and system logs as the IaaS environment, but the same detail of logs and events is available at the application level. In most cases, the exposure of events from the application is a combination of standard logging, based on the technology and platform employed, and specific and custom logs made available by the application developers. The following OWASP guidelines can be followed as to which kinds of events to log and process (https://www.owasp.org/index.php/Logging_Cheat_Sheet#Which_events_to_log):

- Input validation failures (for example, protocol violations, unacceptable encodings, invalid parameter names, and values)
- Output validation failures (for example, database record set mismatch and invalid data encoding)
- Authentication successes and failures

- Authorization (access control) failures
- Session management failures (for example, cookie session identification value modification)
- Application errors and system events (for example, syntax and run-time errors, connectivity problems, performance issues, third-party service error messages, file system errors, file upload virus detection, and configuration changes)
- Application and related systems' startups and shutdowns as well as logging initialization (starting, stopping, or pausing)
- Use of higher-risk functionality (for example, network connections, addition or deletion of users, changes to privileges, assigning users to tokens, adding or deleting tokens, use of systems administrative privileges, access by application administrators, all actions by users with administrative privileges, access to payment cardholder data, use of data encrypting keys, key changes, creation and deletion of system-level objects, data import and export, including screen-based reports, and submission of user-generated content, especially file uploads)
- Legal and other opt-ins (for example, permissions for mobile phone capabilities, terms of use, terms and conditions, personal data usage consent, and permission to receive marketing communications)

The same model also extends to some events that may be available or necessary under certain circumstances and may be of value to the application or security teams:

- Sequencing failure
- Excessive use
- Data changes
- Fraud and other criminal activities
- Suspicious, unacceptable, or unexpected behavior
- Modifications to the configuration
- Application code file and/or memory changes

SaaS Event Sources

Given the nature of a SaaS environment and the cloud provider being responsible for the entire infrastructure and application, the amount of log data that is typically available to the cloud customer is minimal and highly restricted. Any access to log data, either in raw format or through a cloud provider tool, will need to be clearly articulated in the contract and SLA requirements between the provider and customer. Typically, the log data provided by the cloud provider is explicitly scoped to just what the cloud customer needs and tailored to fit their aspects of the application usage. The most important logs for a cloud customer in a SaaS environment are typically application logs (web, application, and database), usage logs, access logs, and billing records.

Identity Attribution Requirements

OWASP also puts out the following robust and detailed model for which event attributes to capture and log (https://www.owasp.org/index.php/Logging_Cheat_Sheet#Event_attributes):

When:

- Log date and time (international format)
- Event date and time—the event timestamp may be different from the time of logging (for example, server logging where the client application is hosted on a remote device that is only periodically or intermittently online)
- Interaction identifier

Where:

- Application identifier (for example, name and version)
- Application address (for example, cluster/host name or server IPv4 or IPv6 address and port number, workstation identity, or local device identifier)
- Service (for example, name and protocol)
- Geolocation
- Window/form/page (for example, entry point URL and HTTP method for a web application or dialog box name)
- Code location (for example, script name or module name)

Who (human or machine user):

- Source address (for example, the user's device/machine identifier, the user's IP address, cell/RF tower ID, or mobile telephone number)
- User identity, if authenticated or otherwise known (for example, user database table's primary key value, user name, or license number)

What:

- Type of event
- Severity of event (for example, {0=emergency, 1=alert, ..., 7=debug} or {fatal, error, warning, info, debug, trace})
- Security-relevant event flag (if the logs contain non-security event data too)
- Description

OWASP also lists the following event attributes that should strongly be considered for logging:

- Secondary time source (for example, GPS) event date and time
- Action—the original intended purpose of the request (for example, log in, refresh session ID, log out, or update profile

- Object—the affected component or other object, such as the user account, data resource, or file (for example, URL, session ID, user account, of file)
- Result status—whether the action aimed at the object was successful (for example, Success, Fail, or Defer)
- Reason—why the status occurred (for example, user not authenticated in database check... or incorrect credentials)
- HTTP status code (web applications only)—the status code returned to the user (often 200 or 301)
- Request HTTP headers or HTTP User Agent (web applications only)
- User type classification (for example, public, authenticated user, CMS user, search engine, authorized penetration tester, or uptime monitor)
- Analytical confidence in the event detection (for example, low, medium, high, or a numeric value
- Responses seen by the user and/or taken by the application (for example, status code, custom text messages, session termination, and administrator alerts)
- Extended details (for example, stack trace, system error messages, debug information, HTTP request body, and HTTP response headers and body)
- Internal classifications (for example, responsibility and compliance references)
- External classifications (for example, NIST's Security Content Automation Protocol [SCAP] or Mitre's Common Attack Pattern Enumeration and Classification [CAPEC])

However, although robust and detailed logging is very important for proper application security and monitoring, some data should never be saved or recorded. OWASP provides the following guidelines for which data to exclude (https://www.owasp.org/index.php/Logging_Cheat_Sheet#Data_to_exclude):

- Application source code
- Session identification values (consider replacing with a hashed value if needed to track session specific events)
- Access tokens
- Sensitive personal data and some forms of personally identifiable information (for example, health, government identifiers, vulnerable people)
- Authentication passwords
- Database connection strings
- Encryption keys and other master secrets
- Bank account or payment card holder data
- Data of a higher security classification than the logging system is allowed to store

- Commercially sensitive information
- Information that is illegal to collect in the relevant jurisdictions
- Information a user has opted out of for collection or has not consented to (for example, use of Do Not Track or where consent to collect has expired)

Data Event Logging

Once attributes and event types have been determined and categorized by management, security staff, and application teams, the next step in the process is to collect and verify the actual event data and logging capabilities. OWASP gives the following robust framework for event collection (https://www.owasp.org/index.php/Logging_Cheat_Sheet#Event_collection):

- Perform input validation on event data from other trust zones to ensure it is in the correct format (and consider alerting and not logging if there is an input validation failure).
- Perform sanitization on all event data to prevent log injection attacks—for example, carriage return (CR), line feed (LF), and delimiter characters (and optionally to remove sensitive data).
- Encode data correctly for the output (logged) format.
- If writing to databases, read, understand, and apply the SQL injection cheat sheet.
- Ensure failures in the logging processes/systems do not prevent the application from otherwise running or do not allow information leakage.
- Synchronize time across all servers and devices.

Of course, an integral part of data collection, especially when it pertains to regulatory requirements for archiving and record preservation, is the verification that data and data events are actually being collected in the intended manner, and that the full data set is present. The following verification framework (from OWASP) provides a robust method and guidelines to follow for data event collection verification (https://www.owasp.org/index.php/Logging_Cheat_Sheet#Verification):

- Ensure the logging is working correctly and as specified.
- Check that events are being classified consistently and that the field names, types, and lengths are correctly defined to an agreed standard.
- Ensure logging is implemented and enabled during application security, fuzz, penetration, and performance testing.
- Test that the mechanisms are not susceptible to injection attacks.
- Ensure there are no unwanted side effects when logging occurs.

- Check the effect on the logging mechanisms when external network connectivity is lost (if this is usually required).

- Ensure logging cannot be used to deplete system resources (for example, by filling up disk space or exceeding database transaction log space, thus leading to denial of service).

- Test the effect on the application of logging failures such as simulated database connectivity loss, lack of file system space, missing write permissions to the file system, and run-time errors in the logging module itself.

- Verify access controls on the event log data.

- If log data is utilized in any action against users (for example, blocking access or account lockout), ensure this cannot be used to cause denial of service (DoS) of other users.

Storage and Analysis of Data Events

With the volume of logs created and collected for any system or application, there is a need for a method or technology to catalogue and make those events searchable and reportable. Without having a system in place to synthesize and process the event data, there would basically be a huge pool of data collected that doesn't serve any useful or meaningful purpose and that's not accessible for the fulfillment of auditing and regulatory requirements.

The main technology used for this type of operation is known as a security and information event management (SIEM) system. SIEM systems collect and index logs from almost any source within an environment, and they make those sources searchable and reportable to the organization and its users. Some examples of prominent SIEM solutions in the industry are Splunk, HPE Arcsight, and LogRhythm. Depending on the SIEM solution, it can be installed within the data center or cloud environment and maintained by the customer, or it can be run as a SaaS cloud implementation from the vendor, with log data forwarded to it from the environment and applications.

Many organizations use SIEM solutions in a variety of ways and for a variety of functions and goals, including the following:

- Aggregation
- Correlation
- Alerting
- Reporting
- Compliance
- Dashboards
- Retention

Aggregation and Correlation

SIEM solutions aggregate data from a large number of sources into a single indexed system. This brings about the obvious benefits of being able to search from a single location rather than logging into individual servers. In large application deployments, there could be dozens or hundreds of servers in the environment, so having a single place to search allows developers or security staff to perform searches in a much quicker and more responsive manner than would ever have been available by going server to server. SIEM solutions also tend to offer far more robust searching tools than are available through native tool sets built into operating systems, and they typically use syntax much more aligned with prominent search engines than with command-line or built-in tool sets.

Along with the aggregation of log data to a single location, not only is application data available and indexed, but data from throughout the environment is available as well. This will typically include operating system data, network data, security scanning and intrusion system data, DNS data, and authentication and authorization system data. With all of this data in one location, it becomes a very powerful tool to correlate events and data throughout an environment. For example, if there is a suspected malicious IP address sending data toward an application, not only can the security team see those log entries from the application level, but the team also can see any logs from the network and intrusion systems pertaining to the same IP address, both in real time and however long historical data is maintained within the SIEM solution. This gives the immediate and efficient capability to the security team to search data, which, had it been done at the individual server and appliance level, would have taken substantially longer and likely would have involved a large number of staff from all the various teams responsible for each piece of technology. This has the added bonus of allowing the security teams to have access to log data from the entire environment, without having to give them access to the actual servers and appliances and thus maintain separation of duties. Once the logs have been sent to the SIEM solution, it also provides a safeguard against a malicious attack being able to alter the logs on a compromised host, because the logs would have already been sent external to the system.

Alerting

With all the log data indexed within the SIEM solution, alerting can be implemented on any type of event that is searchable and defined. These types of alerts can range from searching for specific error codes, watching for specific IP addresses or users, and even watching for slow response times or error rates within an application. Alerts typically run at all times and catch occurrences quickly and report to those defined to receive them.

CAUTION One thing that a Cloud Security Professional will need to be aware of and monitor is the number and complexity of alerts used within the SIEM solution. Because alerts run more or less in a "live" manner, any additional alerts added to a system will consume a certain amount of resources at all times, depending on the complexity and volume of log data they are watching and alerting against. A Cloud Security Professional will need to ensure that the system is properly sized to handle the load for alerts, combined with the other reporting and searching needs and the indexing overhead of the system itself.

Reporting and Compliance

SIEM solutions make it very easy for a company to set up extensive reporting that can be used for both internal purposes and compliance purposes. Reporting can be anything from usage reports to user logins, errors, and configuration change reports. These reports can also be used as a way to summarize log data for long-term retention, without having to keep in place the raw log files and the volume of storage they require over time. On the compliance side, many regulatory bodies require the periodic review of logs for failed logins, user account creations and modifications, configuration changes, and so on. Having an SIEM solution provides an easy and efficient way to capture these reports from an entire application environment, and once the reporting syntax is written, changing the frequency of the reports or running ad hoc reports is very trivial.

Dashboards

A dashboard is typically a single screen that shows various reports and alerts to a user. This allows a user or monitoring group to keep one screen up that gives them an instant view into a variety of items without having to click around an application in multiple places to find the information. Using a dashboard can also be an easy and effective way for developers and security professionals to enable the management of a live view of a system and various aspects of it while keeping the underlying mechanics and details hidden. With a variety of alerts and reports written within a SIEM solution, most systems offer an easy-to-use (and oftentimes drag-and-drop) capability to build a dashboard. Many also offer customizations on top of the already-built reports and alerts to make them more appropriate for a dashboard or to limit or sort the data in the way it is presented.

Retention and Compliance

With logs aggregated in an SIEM solution, many organizations opt to use their SIEM solution for long-term log retention and regulatory compliance. Many organizations put in place pretty aggressive log rotation and cleanup mechanisms on servers once an SIEM solution is implemented, and then use the SIEM solution as a single repository for log retention and compliance. SIEM solutions have various tiers of data within them—from the tier that is the most active and searchable, down to the tiers designed to be placed on cheaper storage and optimized for long-term retention based on their lower incidence of access and need for availability. Using the SIEM solution for long-term retention enables an organization to focus on a singular solution and removes the need to ensure log retentions and backups from the large number of systems they control.

Continuous Optimizations

In order for any events collection and analysis implementation to be successful, it must be continuously optimized and tuned over time. Applications and systems are in a constant state of flux and change, and without a flexible and responsive program in place, events will start to be missed, leading to inaccurate reporting and security monitoring, as well as potentially failing to meet regulatory requirements.

The most important aspect of log and event collection is audit logging. This analysis looks for events that have occurred that could be indicative of threats and vulnerabilities, thus providing an organization with the ability to take corrective action to further harden their systems for the future. In the case of a possible compromise, the company can begin an immediate investigation to determine the extent of the compromise and then start the mitigation and remediation process.

In order for a company to make audit logging work successfully over the long term, systems and processes need to be in place to ensure that new event types are discovered. Applications are in a continual state of flux, and additional features and updates over time will introduce new types of events and logging. With a static program in place that is unable to detect new event types, a system is open to attacks and compromises that will go undetected, both before and after the attack has occurred. Combined with the ability to understand and detect new events is the need to update rules to look for those new events. Rules in any logging and alerting scheme will need continual tweaking and updating with the current operational status of any system or application. This should be an integral part of the release and change management processes for any application changes, especially any major platform or design changes. This constant rule tweaking also reduces false positive reporting and alerting. If false positives are not properly tuned out, in a best case scenario this means wasted time for security and operations staff chasing down phantom problems, but in a worst case scenario the staff will being ignoring alerts and missing legitimate ones.

The Cloud Security Professional also needs to be aware of changes in regulatory requirements, both from legal sources and from changes to industry certifications and specifications. Often this involves guidelines that change due to shifts in technology, new threats, and new legislation, and typically involve changes to the auditing and collection of events data from within a system or application. These requirements can be changes in secure data destruction requirements or changes in discovery and retention policies. In most cases, an organization will be given a specified timeframe in which changes must be implemented to maintain compliance. This is something the Cloud Security Professional will need to ensure is discussed with management and developers in order for the necessary changes to be incorporated within their design lifecycles at the appropriate times for their own internal timelines, as well as to meet those timelines required by the regulatory changes.

Chain of Custody and Nonrepudiation

Chain of custody at its core is the documented possession and preservation of data and evidence from the time it was created until the time it is preserved or entered into official record, often in a court proceeding. Chain of custody is very important when it comes to any evidence—without it, the evidence will typically not be admissible in court because neither the validity nor the integrity can be confirmed. The chain-of-custody records comprise a comprehensive history of data from creation until disposal or final form, with records of all manipulations, possession changes, alterations, locations, formats, storage technologies, and access.

In a traditional data center hosting model, it is typically straightforward to maintain a proper chain of custody because the company or organization will have full control over their resources, servers, storage systems, and backup systems. However, in a cloud environment, with the way most clouds (especially large public clouds) scatter data and hosting resources over enormous pools of resources, the chain of custody can be far more complicated to maintain. In most instances, the way this process is ensured with compliance to the highest degree possible is through contracts and SLAs between the cloud provider and cloud customer that put the requirements on the cloud provider to do their best effort to main chain of custody and to ensure that all data points are known and preserved when necessary. Many large public cloud providers have established mechanisms in place for data assurance; whether they are part of the default offerings or are acquired through additional costs and contracts can and will vary from provider to provider.

Nonrepudiation is the ability to confirm the origin or authenticity of data to a high degree of certainty. This typically is done through digital signatures and hashing, to ensure that data has not been modified from its original form. This concept plays directly into and complements chain of custody for ensuring the validity and integrity of data.

Exercise

You have been hired by a company that does business under the jurisdiction of the European Union. You are tasked with providing data protection within a cloud environment for an application handling online financial transactions.

1. What privacy acts and regulatory requirements are you subjected to?

2. What tool sets and technologies can you use to meet those requirements and ensure compliance?

3. What challenges will you face if your company decides to go with an IaaS implementation versus a PaaS implementation?

Chapter Review

In this chapter, we covered the different types of storage available in a cloud environment, depending on the hosting model chosen. We then covered the various technologies available to protect data and privacy within a cloud environment, as well as the regulatory bodies that govern policies and how those requirements relate to cloud environments. Lastly, we discussed collecting, auditing, and reporting on events within a cloud environment, and how these events can be leveraged through business intelligence to gain insight into the usage and optimization of a cloud system.

Questions

1. Which of the following is *NOT* a type of storage used within a cloud environment?

   A. Structured

   B. Volume

   C. Container

   D. Object

2. Which of the following is *NOT* part of the CCM domains?

   A. Environmental

   B. Human resources

   C. Threat and vulnerability management

   D. Mobile security

3. Which of the following logs could be exposed to a cloud customer in a Software as a Service environment, if the contract allows it?

   A. Billing records

   B. Management plane logs

   C. Network captures

   D. Operating system logs

4. Which of the following storage types are used in a Platform as a Service model?

   A. Volume and object

   B. Structured and unstructured

   C. Content and database

   D. Volume and labeled

5. Where would the DLP solution be located for data-in-use monitoring?

   A. On the application server

   B. On the user's device

   C. On the network boundary

   D. Integrated with the database server

6. Which of the following data destruction methods would be available in a public cloud model?

   A. Degaussing

   B. Shredding

   C. Encryption

   D. Recycling

7. Which of the following is *NOT* a feature of an SIEM solution?

    A. Monitoring

    B. Aggregation

    C. Alerting

    D. Dashboards

8. Which of the following is *NOT* a key component of a data archiving strategy?

    A. Format

    B. Technologies

    C. Testing

    D. Size

9. Which of the following laws in the United States governs the protection of health data?

    A. SOX

    B. HIPAA

    C. Dodd–Frank

    D. ACA

10. Which of the following is the sole responsibility of the cloud customer in a PaaS environment?

    A. Physical security

    B. Data

    C. Infrastructure

    D. Platform

11. Which of the following is *NOT* a key feature of an IRM solution?

    A. Expiration

    B. Policy control

    C. Chain of custody

    D. Auditing

12. Encryption that is part of a database and not noticeable by the user is called what?

    A. Transparent

    B. Embedded

    C. Passive

    D. Active

13. What are the three methods of data discovery?

    A. Metadata, labels, content analysis

    B. Metadata, categories, content analysis

    C. Categories, labels, structure

    D. Volumes, labels, metadata

14. Which cloud model gives responsibility for the physical environment to the cloud customer?

    A. IaaS

    B. PaaS

    C. SaaS

    D. None of the above

15. Which of the following involves replacing data in a data set with random values that can then be mapped back to the actual data via a separate index?

    A. Anonymization

    B. Tokenization

    C. Encryption

    D. Obfuscation

Questions and Answers

1. Which of the following is *NOT* a type of storage used within a cloud environment?

    A. Structured

    B. Volume

    C. Container

    D. Object

    C. Container is not a storage type used in a cloud environment. Both the volume and object storage types are used within Infrastructure as a Service, and the structured storage type is used as part of a Platform as a Service offering.

2. Which of the following is *NOT* part of the CCM domains?

    A. Environmental

    B. Human resources

    C. Threat and vulnerability management

    D. Mobile security

A. Environmental is not an explicit domain under the CCM. The other three options, human resources, threat and vulnerability management, and mobile security are all actual domains explicitly named in the CCM.

3. Which of the following logs could be exposed to a cloud customer in a Software as a Service environment, if the contract allows it?

    A. Billing records

    B. Management plane logs

    C. Network captures

    D. Operating system logs

    A. Billing records would most likely be available in a Software as a Service environment if allowed or required by the contract. The other choices, management plane logs, network captures, and operating system logs would all be solely accessible and used by the cloud provider in an SaaS environment, as none of the systems that generate those logs falls under the responsibility or access allowed to the cloud customer.

4. Which of the following storage types are used in a Platform as a Service model?

    A. Volume and object

    B. Structured and unstructured

    C. Content and database

    D. Volume and labeled

    B. Structured and unstructured storage types are used in the Platform as a Service model. The volume and object storage types are used within the Infrastructure as a Service model. The other two options, content and database, as well as volume and labeled, are not used as a pair with any cloud service category, although volume is part of Infrastructure as a Service, and the use of databases would be a major component of the structured storage type offered under Platform as a Service.

5. Where would the DLP solution be located for data-in-use monitoring?

    A. On the application server

    B. On the user's device

    C. On the network boundary

    D. Integrated with the database server

    B. On the user's device is the correct choice of data-in-use monitoring. Integrated with the database server would provide coverage for data at rest, while on the network boundary would provide coverage for data in transit. On the application server is also not appropriate as the actual use and viewing of data would occur through the client, as well as being outside the immediate security enclave of the application.

6. Which of the following data destruction methods would be available in a public cloud model?

   A. Degaussing

   B. Shredding

   C. Encryption

   D. Recycling

   C. Encryption is a data destruction method available in a public cloud model. Cryptographic erasure, in which the encryption keys are deleted as a means to protect and destroy data, is a software process that is always available in any environment. Degaussing, shredding, and recycling are all physically destructive methods that would not be available with a cloud hosting arrangement, and most certainly not with a public cloud environment.

7. Which of the following is *NOT* a feature of an SIEM solution?

   A. Monitoring

   B. Aggregation

   C. Alerting

   D. Dashboards

   A. Monitoring is not a feature of an SIEM solution. SIEM solutions work by aggregating data, which can then be used for alerting on specific conditions, but not used in the sense of system monitoring. Dashboards are also a common feature of SIEM solutions to present reporting and alerting outputs to users or management.

8. Which of the following is *NOT* a key component of a data archiving strategy?

   A. Format

   B. Technologies

   C. Testing

   D. Size

   D. The size of archives is not a key component of a data archiving strategy. The main driving components of a data archiving strategy deal with the format of the archives, the technologies used with the archiving, and the ongoing and successful testing of restoration abilities.

9. Which of the following laws in the United States governs the protection of health data?

A. SOX

B. HIPAA

C. Dodd–Frank

D. ACA

B. HIPAA governs the protection of healthcare-related data. While the ACA is related to healthcare as well, it is focused on the delivery of healthcare and health insurance coverage, and not the specific security and privacy concerns with the data. SOX is focused on financial systems and the security controls and reporting necessary for them, while Dodd–Frank is focused on corporate reforms and consumer protection.

10. Which of the following is the sole responsibility of the cloud customer in a PaaS environment?

A. Physical security

B. Data

C. Infrastructure

D. Platform

B. Data is the sole responsibility of the cloud customer in all environments. Physical security is always the responsibility of the cloud provider. With PaaS, the cloud provider is also responsible for both the infrastructure and platform aspects of the environment.

11. Which of the following is *NOT* a key feature of an IRM solution?

A. Expiration

B. Policy control

C. Chain of custody

D. Auditing

C. Chain of custody is not part of an IRM solution, as it is central to eDiscovery and other legal mechanisms. With an IRM solution, and the protection of data assets, the concepts of expiration, policy control, and the auditing of acceptable and authorized use are all key components.

12. Encryption that is part of a database and not noticeable by the user is called what?

    A. Transparent

    B. Embedded

    C. Passive

    D. Active

    A. Transparent encryption is part of the database and not known to the user; it is integrated with the actual database processes and works as part of the ongoing workflow. The other choices, embedded, passive, and active, are general IT terms that are not applicable to this specific question.

13. What are the three methods of data discovery?

    A. Metadata, labels, content analysis

    B. Metadata, categories, content analysis

    C. Categories, labels, structure

    D. Volumes, labels, metadata

    A. Metadata, labels, and content analysis are the three methods of data discovery. Metadata is looking at the "data on data" aspects, such as the creator, timestamps, software used, column headers, field names, etc. Labels are subjective and applied to the data by systems or actual staff members, and are only as good as they are consistently and correctly applied. Content analysis involves making subjective determinations about the data from the actual content of, either through technological or personnel efforts. The other terms used with the other responses are not parts of data discovery or are not applicable here.

14. Which cloud model gives responsibility for the physical environment to the cloud customer?

    A. IaaS

    B. PaaS

    C. SaaS

    D. None of the above

    D. None of the environments gives responsibility for physical security to the cloud customer. In all cloud hosting environments, the cloud provider has sole responsibility for the physical infrastructure and the security of it.

15. Which of the following involves replacing data in a data set with random values that can then be mapped back to the actual data via a separate index?

   A. Anonymization

   B. Tokenization

   C. Encryption

   D. Obfuscation

   B. Tokenization is the mapping of random values to the actual data via a separate index. Anonymization and obfuscation also involve replacing sensitive data fields with random or opaque data, but the replacing of data is not done in a way that it can be mapped back to the actual data fields as with tokenization. Encryption is the protection of the confidentiality of sensitive data by altering the actual contents of the data.

Cloud Platform and Infrastructure Security

This chapter covers the following topics in Domain 3:
- Physical aspects of a cloud environment
- Key components that make up a cloud environment
- Risks associated with cloud computing
- Designing and planning for cloud-based security controls
- Auditing in a cloud environment
- Disaster recovery and business continuity in a cloud environment

Cloud platforms bring unique benefits to an organization and have many attractive capabilities, including performance and scalability, removal of focus on hardware and instead a focus on business requirements, and measured service—all for a possible lower total cost and investment than running their own data center. However, these platforms also bring unique challenges and risks because of the very same factors, and cost savings are not always what they may appear to be at the onset, or not on the scale often presumed. This chapter goes over those risks and challenges, how to address and mitigate them, as well as disaster recovery and business continuity requirements and benefits in a cloud environment.

Cloud Infrastructure Components

The cloud infrastructure is made up of many of the same components that a traditional data center has, just applied from the perspective of a cloud environment. The cloud infrastructure also adds some unique components, as shown by Figure 4-1.

Physical Environment

While the model of cloud computing has been a revolutionary technological approach that organizations take for hosting systems and applications, the underlying architecture and requirements of the data center are no different from the traditional model; the cloud environment simply abstracts that level of concern and detail from the cloud customer.

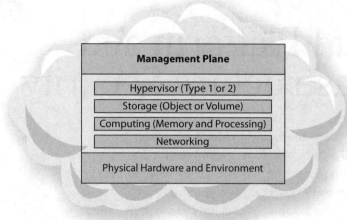

Figure 4-1 Cloud infrastructure components

However, especially with the large public cloud systems, the scale and coordination required in a cloud environment can be far more intricate and complex.

A traditional corporate data center, especially for a large company, will have thousands of computers and incredible cooling and utility needs. With a major cloud environment, you are typically looking at tens of thousands or hundreds of thousands of servers, spread across multiple (sometimes dozens of) physical locations.

Having such large-scale data centers requires enormous power and cooling resources. With the expectations in a cloud environment of high availability and resiliency, all systems must absolutely be redundant and allow maintenance to be performed in a way that does not cause any downtime or create single points of failure during any maintenance periods. With most cloud environments hosting a significant number of customers, any downtime will have enormous impact and be very visible to the customers and to the cloud provider. On the positive side, with so many customers pooling resources and the cloud provider focusing on an infrastructure specifically built for their cloud offerings and not for hosting numerous different types of systems with different needs, economies of scale can be leveraged in a way that an organization hosting their own data center would not be able to do.

Internally, a data center needs redundant power and cooling, and the actual physical grounds have additional redundancy concerns. A cloud provider needs multiple and independent power feeds, on top of typically having generator power and battery backups to serve in the interim or in the event that the power feeds become unavailable. Key needs for cloud redundancy are shown in Figure 4-2.

To minimize risk from environmental and natural disaster concerns, a cloud provider should seek out the best possible locations for their data centers, without being bound geographically to a headquarters location or office locations like a typical organization would have to contend with. Because cloud access by definition occurs via networks (and not physical access), as long as a cloud provider has significant and sufficient network

Figure 4-2
Areas of focus
for cloud
redundancy

External Redundancy	Internal Redundancy
• Power feeds/lines • Power substations • Generators • Generator fuel tanks • Network circuits • Building access points • Cooling/chilling infrastructure	• Power distribution units • Power feeds to racks • Cooling chillers and units • Networking • Storage units • Physical access points

bandwidth, the location of a cloud environment can be anywhere in the country or the world to take advantage of cheaper facilities, land, and utilities. Another enormous physical security benefit of a cloud environment comes in the economies of scale with large data centers and the number of customers that leverage them. Sophisticated and redundant levels of security can be very expensive for a data center, but when the costs can be spread among all customers, each customer benefits from far greater and more technologically advanced security than they would be able to afford on their own.

Networking

Networking is essential to a cloud environment because it provides the only way for customers and users to access their systems, applications, and software tools. In the sense of cloud offerings, the network is fully the responsibility of the cloud provider and something that the cloud customer and users will just expect to always work and never have issues.

Networking Hardware

When it comes to building out a network, multiple layers come into play and that have their own issues and challenges, even if the customer and users do not really see these aspects. At the basic level are the physical network components such as the actual wiring and cabling. Especially in large data centers, the volume of wiring is extremely high and often teams are dedicated just to organizing the physical wiring.

Once the physical wiring is in place, it has to be hooked into devices and machines. This forms the next layer of the network in a data center. A large network of switches, routers, and network security devices make up this next level. These are typically constructed in a layered or tiered system that physically segments networks for isolation and security in layers. Segmenting a network physically offers additional security by separating different tiers of servers or restricting traffic within certain sectors. If a successful attack manages to penetrate a data center to the network layer, this physical separation can minimize the extent of vulnerabilities and access.

Beyond the physical segmenting of a network, software and virtual separation is obtained through such mechanisms as virtual local area networks (VLANs). VLANs allow dedicated IP address spacing for servers that are in the same class or belong to the same application or customer, giving enhanced security and isolation from other systems at the network level. VLANs are not dependent on physical network devices and as such can span across data centers regardless of where hardware is physically located; servers do not need to be in the same racks or even connected to the same switches or routers.

Software-Defined Networking

An important aspect of cloud computing is the use of software-defined networking (SDN). With SDN, the decisions concerning where traffic is filtered or sent and the actual forwarding of traffic are completely separate from each other. With cloud computing, this separation is important because it allows the administrators of the cloud network to quickly and dynamically adjust network flows and resources based on the current needs and demands of the cloud customers. With the separation from the actual network components, a cloud provider can build management tools that allow staffers using web portals or cloud administrative interfaces to make changes to the network without having to log into the actual network components or have the command knowledge of a network administrator to make changes. With the level of access provided and the types of resources available to control, a high level of security needs to be attached to any SDN implementation, with access tightly controlled and monitored regularly.

Computing

As with a traditional data center model, cloud computing is built around processing capabilities. Simply put, computing and processing capabilities are defined as the CPU and memory (RAM) of the system and environment. In a traditional server setup using physical servers, it is easy to define and manage both resources because each server represents a finite and unique unit, both in configuration and in the ability to run metrics and observe trends. Within a cloud environment, considering resource pooling and multitenancy, the computing capabilities become far more complex in both planning and management. With large virtual environments, it becomes imperative for the cloud provider to build out enormous resources that can be shared between all the systems, applications, and customers, and done in such a way that each has the resources it requires at any given point in time to meet high availability, performance, and scalability demands.

Reservations

A reservation is a minimum resource that is guaranteed to a customer within a cloud environment. A reservation can pertain to the two main aspects of computing: memory and processing. With a reservation in place, a cloud customer is guaranteed by the cloud provider to always have at minimum the necessary resources available to power on and operate any of their services. In large cloud environments with a large number of customers, this feature can be of particular importance in the case of denial-of-service attacks or high-utilization services from other hosts and systems that may use considerable cloud resources because it offers a minimum level of operating guarantee to all customers.

Limits

As opposed to reservations, limits are put in place to enforce maximum utilization of memory or processing by a cloud customer. These limits can either be done at a virtual machine level or a comprehensive level for a customer. They are meant to ensure that enormous cloud resources cannot be allocated or consumed by a single host or customer to the detriment of other hosts and customers. Along with cloud computing features such as auto-scaling and on-demand self-service, limits can be either "hard" or "fixed," but can also be flexible and allowed to change dynamically. Typically, when limits are allowed to change dynamically based on current conditions and consumption, it is done by "borrowing" additional resources rather than making an actual change in the limits themselves.

Shares

The concept of shares within a cloud environment is used to mitigate and control customer requests for resource allocations in case the environment does not have the current capability to provide these resources. Shares work by prioritizing hosts within a cloud environment through a weighting system that is defined by the cloud provider. When periods of high utilization and allocation are reached, the system automatically uses the scoring of each host based on its share value to determine which hosts get access to the limited resources still available. The higher the value a particular host has, the more resources it will be allowed to utilize.

Virtualization

As previously discussed, virtualization forms the backbone of a cloud environment and all its hosting models. Virtualization is what allows a cloud environment to offer most of its top benefits to its customers, especially resource pooling, on-demand self-service, and scalability. The use of virtualization breaks free from the old paradigms and limitations of single servers where the host is tied to the server. Instead, virtualization allows very large pools of resources to be leveraged across many hosts and applications. Virtualization also allows the abstraction from the hardware via the use of a hypervisor.

Hypervisors

As discussed in Chapter 2 as part of the Architectural Concepts and Design Requirements domain, there are two types of hypervisors within virtualization: Type 1 and Type 2. An overview of both hypervisor types is shown in Figure 4-3.

Type 1 Hypervisors   As covered in Chapter 2, a Type 1 hypervisor is a native implementation that runs tied directly into the underlying hardware. In other words, it runs natively and directly on top of the hardware with direct access to its components and resources. The Type 1 hypervisor is specifically written and tuned to run on top of bare metal and provide the hosting environment; because of this, it has very tightly written code and is lean overall because it does not have to fulfill any additional requirements.

Figure 4-3
Type 1 and Type 2
hypervisors

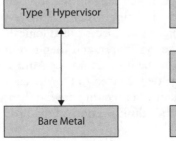
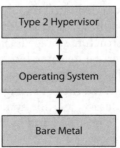

As such, it also allows for much tighter security and controls because there are no additional applications or utilities running within the hypervisor other than those to fulfill its intended mission. Therefore, there are far fewer potential attack vectors and vulnerabilities than a traditional operating system that is designed to be highly flexible would contain.

Type 2 Hypervisors From Chapter 2, you know that a Type 2 hypervisor differs from a Type 1 hypervisor in that it runs under a host operating system rather than directly tied into the underlying hardware of the virtual host servers. With this type of implementation, additional security and architecture concerns come into play as the interaction between the operating system and the hypervisor becomes a critical link. The hypervisor no longer has direct interaction and control over the underlying hardware, which means that some performance will be lost due to the operating system in the middle needing its own resources, patching requirements, and operational oversight. It also means that any security concerns within the underlying operating system can impact the hypervisor as well.

 TIP Due to the nature of Type 2 hypervisors and their reliance on the underlying operating system, the Cloud Security Professional needs to be extra vigilant in securing both the hypervisor and the host because of the added complexity. If a cloud provider has robust hypervisor security but is lacking in host security, the entire platform becomes vulnerable and exposed. However, most large and/or public cloud implementations do not use Type 2 hypervisors, so exposure to this type may be well limited. However, care should be taken to know what type is being used.

Storage

Mass storage in a cloud environment from the hardware perspective is not much different than in a traditional data center or server model. Storage typically consists of RAID (redundant array of inexpensive disks) implementations or SANs (storage area networks), which are then connected to the virtualized server infrastructure.

Volume Storage

As covered in Chapter 3, volume storage is where storage is allocated to a virtual machine and configured as a typical hard drive and file system on that server. Although the storage is from a centralized storage system and/or is connected to the network, it will appear to the server as a dedicated resource, much the same as other computing and infrastructure services appear to a virtualized operating system. With a volume storage system, the main infrastructure storage is sliced into pieces called logical units (LUNs), assigned to a particular virtual machine by the hypervisor, and then mounted via a particular method based on the operating system of the host. From the storage allocation perspective, this is only a reserved slice of storage that is given to the virtual machine. All configurations, formatting, usage, and file-system-level security are handled by the particular operating system of the host VM and by the administrators of the host.

Object Storage

As you learned from Chapter 3, object storage is where data is stored on a system separate from the application and access occurs via APIs, network requests, or a web interface. Oftentimes object storage is implemented as an additional step of redundancy and as a performance measure. By removing the storage from the actual host instances, a cloud provider can focus dedicated resources on managing an object storage system in a way that is specific to optimizing storage performance and security. Object storage also has its own redundancy and scaling systems that are separate from the host and can also be optimized for a particular function or mission.

Rather than a traditional file system with a directory and tree structure, object storage utilizes a flat system and assigns files and objects a key value that is then used to access them. Different implementations of object storage may call this value different names, but in the end it is the same concept—a unique value, oftentimes completely opaque, is used to access data versus using the traditional filename nomenclature. Many cloud providers use object storage for central pieces of infrastructure such as their library of virtual host images.

 EXAM TIP Make sure you understand the differences between object and volume storage types that are used with IaaS. There will likely be questions relating to how and when both are used. One item to make sure you remember is that object storage within a cloud will be used for the storage of virtual machine images.

Management Plane

The concept of a management plane within the context of cloud computing is a bit different from the traditional definition of a network management plane, though the overall concept is very similar. Within a cloud environment, the management plane is focused on the management of the environment and all the hosts within it. By utilizing the management plane, the cloud provider can manage all the hosts within the environment from a centralized location, without the need to go to each individual server to perform certain tasks. The management plane is typically run from dedicated servers, and it has its own physical connections to the underlying hardware so as to separate out its functions and dependencies from any other aspects of the environment, including the hypervisor.

The management plane can be used to do the bulk of the tasks that enable cloud computing to be the unique technology that it is. From the management plane, virtual servers can be provisioned with the appropriate resources allocated to them, such as network configurations, processing, memory, and storage. Apart from provisioning and allocating resources, the management plane can also start and stop virtual hosts and services.

The functions of the management plane are typically exposed as a series of remote calls and function executions or exposed as a set of APIs. Those APIs are typical leveraged either through a client or more commonly via a web portal The web portal is typically proprietary within each cloud implementation, with the appropriate underlying scripts and functions for that environment and the level of exposure that the cloud provider wants to make accessible with the management plane.

Given the access and privileges with which the management plane operates, concerns over security are of the highest level. A compromise of the management plane would give an attacker complete control of the entire environment and make the entire cloud vulnerable, which is well above the risk and threat a compromised hypervisor would provide because the management plane controls multiple hypervisors. Only the most highly vetted and limited set of administrative staff should have access to the management plane, and all access and functions should be tightly audited and reviewed on a regular basis.

Risks Associated with Cloud Infrastructure

Cloud-based systems have the same level of risk as other hosting models, but with the addition of risks specific to cloud hosting. A cloud-based system should be approached and managed as any other outsourced platform, with the same types of concerns, risks, and audit/governance requirements as an external hosting environment.

Risk Assessment and Analysis

A cloud hosting environment has the same areas of risk as all systems and applications, with cloud-specific risks on top of those risks or as key aspects expanding upon them.

From an organizational and regulatory perspective, there are risks related to lock-in, governance, data security and privacy, and any legal and regulatory controls and reporting required for a system or application. One of the biggest benefits of the cloud hosting model is portability and the ability move between providers at will. If an organization chooses a particular cloud provider that has a lot of propriety requirements, they may get locked into that provider and incur substantial costs later if they decide to switch.

With any external hosting arrangement, a company loses substantial control over their systems and their governance. Even with strong contractual requirements and SLAs in place, their level of control and access will be less than what it would be in their own proprietary data centers. Depending on the regulatory requirements for the type of application and data to be hosted, the choice of cloud provider may be limited, or even non-existent. Cloud providers have to serve a large number of customers with their business model, which makes complying with several types of certifications and requirements difficult. A primary concern for any company is where their data will be stored and whether sufficient protections are in place to ensure its confidentiality and integrity. A cloud environment presents many challenges for appropriate governance, made even more complicated by possible eDiscovery requirements, depending on the nature and type of the data, that many cloud providers might be unable or unwilling to meet. All these aspects need to be carefully evaluated and weighed prior to making a cloud hosting decision.

NOTE eDiscovery is the process through which electronic data is requested or required by a legal entity for use in a criminal or civil legal proceeding. It is the responsibility of the application or system owner to thoroughly analyze and search for all data that is within scope and pertinent to the official request, and then provide it to the legal entity with a certification that it is complete and secured.

Apart from the risk factors that play into any hosting environment, a cloud environment has additional factors that are unique in nature. A major risk in a cloud environment is ensuring that data can be completely removed from the system when necessary or required. As covered in Chapter 2, in a traditional data center, physical media can be destroyed to ensure data destruction, which is not possible in a cloud environment, so concepts such as cryptographic erasure and overwriting are prominently used. Along the same lines of data protection is the security of system images within a cloud environment. Because the images themselves are just files on a file system without any physical separation of servers, combined with the possibility of malware being injecting into an image even when it is not running, their security becomes important in a cloud environment, where the cloud provider bears sole responsibility for assurance.

With the self-service aspects of cloud computing, an enormous amount of software is involved in running a cloud environment—everything from image creation and deployment, to auditing and reporting tools, to user management and key management. Every piece of software throughout the environment—from full application suites down to small utility scripts—carries with it an inherent risk of compromise and vulnerabilities. This software is also removed from the customer's visibility and inspection, and it's solely the responsibility of the cloud provider to ensure its security. Because this is outside the run-time environment of the cloud system in general, in many instances this software will go overlooked in audits and monitoring, and the Cloud Security Professional should apply due diligence when selecting a cloud provider to ensure that they are aware of the risks associated with these tools and have strong auditing and monitoring policies and systems in place. The underlying software running the actual virtual hosts is also certainly susceptible to risk of compromise and vulnerabilities, which will we cover in the following section on virtualization risks. However, the key points include the hypervisor being compromised as well as the potential for guests to break out and access other systems and data in the cloud if security controls are not properly implemented and monitored.

Virtualization Risks

With the added layers and complexities of virtualization also come additional risks not found in a traditional server model.

If a hypervisor were to be compromised in any way, the underlying virtual machines that are hosted by it are also vulnerable. Because the hypervisor has control over the hosts and their access to computing resources, the possibility of malware injections and open attack vectors become pronounced for any virtual machines hosted under or controlled by the hypervisor.

Beyond just the virtual machines connected to the hypervisor, because it does play a central role within the cloud infrastructure, a compromised hypervisor can also be used to attack other hypervisors or components within the same cloud environment. A compromised hypervisor can also be used as a launching pad to compromise virtual machines hosted by other hypervisors that are accessible within the cloud.

Another big risk with virtualization involves how network traffic is handled, monitored, and logged. With a traditional network in a data center with physical servers, communication between the servers has to pass through a physical network appliance such as a switch, even for servers within the same physical rack space. During this transmission, it is possible to log and analyze the network traffic, use intrusion detection systems (IDSs) if desired, and have more control over the actual network flow and security measures. In a virtualized environment, between virtual hosts under the same hypervisor there will not necessarily be this type of transmission where such analysis is possible or logging is implemented. If this is the case within the virtualized environment, either it will have to become an accepted risk or other methods will need to be designed and implemented to maintain the same level of analysis and security monitoring. As cloud and virtualized environments have gained in popularity and use, especially with large and visible production systems, most major vendors now offer virtualized versions of traditional physical network gear, such as switches, firewalls, and IDSs.

A significant difference and potential drawback with a virtualized environment versus a traditional server model is the reality of how images and virtual machines are stored and operate. With a traditional server model, the operating system is deployed on top of the underlying hardware and interacts directly with it. However, in a virtualized environment, a "server" is nothing more than a disk image that resides on an actual file system in some manner or another. While a virtual host is up and running, it is susceptible to all the same types of attacks and vulnerabilities that a physical host would be, based on its operating system and compensating security controls. However, due to the nature of a disk image existing in the environment, there is an extra vulnerability should the disk image itself be attacked from the hypervisor and file system side. From this attack vector, no compensating security controls or monitoring would be effective at mitigating the attack, especially because this method is not dependent on the image even being live or running at the time.

TIP As a Cloud Security Professional, much of your attention should be paid to the actual run-time environment and the protection of data. However, do not overlook due diligence in ensuring that the cloud provider takes substantial steps toward securing the virtualized environment and protecting the hypervisor layer as well as has in place strong security controls and monitoring to ensure that virtual images cannot be modified while in a live or inactive state from the file system level.

Countermeasure Strategies

While the unique challenges and additional risks of cloud computing are well known, so too are the many mitigation strategies that have become commonplace and best practices.

The same high degree of automation that a cloud platform provides between provisioning and reporting can be applied to the implementation of security controls. As systems auto-scale and expand, by using base images for virtual hosts that already have been hardened and scanned, you can ensure that new hosts, as they are brought online, are already secured in the exact same manner as the baseline. The same methodology can be applied within a cloud framework for patching and updating. Rather than performing upgrades and large-scale automated patching, which then requires scanning and auditing to ensure everything was applied correctly and comprehensively, a cloud provider can instead opt to reimage the hosts using a new baseline image that has been patched and tested. Instead of thousands of hosts being patched and tested, efforts can be focused on one host and then deployed across the cloud to all others.

Cloud environments are designed to be high availability by nature with redundancy, auto-scaling, and rapid elasticity. This architectural design makes the patching, maintenance, and isolation of hosts in the event of a possible security breach much easier because they can be removed from production pools. It also allows for updating, scanning, and making configuration changes without impacting the customer and users of a system or application, thus reducing the risk to availability.

Design and Plan Security Controls

In order to ensure a sound security policy and overall governance, the Cloud Security Professional should concentrate on several different area, as detailed in this section.

Physical and Environmental Protection

Physical and environmental protection relates to any and all physical devices and infrastructure components. While the access and technologies used with a cloud infrastructure offer a unique set of services to customers, underneath it is all is a classic data center model, albeit in most cases on a much larger scale. However, because a cloud by definition is a system that is accessible over broad networking, such as the public Internet, physical protections must also extend to those systems that are used to access the cloud.

The physical assets in the actual data center include servers, cooling units, power distribution units, networking gear, physical racks, and miles of cabling, as well as the actual physical facilities and the auxiliary systems located on the premises, such as battery backups, power conduits, generators, fuel tanks, and the surrounding periphery. Outside the data center property there are still more physical devices and infrastructure that are important to the Cloud Security Professional. These include the power and network conduits that the data center relies on, as well as the endpoints of access for the users and customer, such as mobile devices, workstations, laptops, tablets, and any other client systems.

From a physical perspective, the approach to security is no different than in any other system, with defense in layers being the guiding principle. From the outside of a data center building, you will have typical security measures such as fences, cameras, lights, vehicle access control and barriers, as well as personnel stationed at various locations. Access to the interior of the buildings should be tightly controlled by personnel, doors, key card access, identity proofing, and other various aspects that are similar to how you would gain access to an IT system, including multifactor authentication, in the form of badges, codes, biometrics, and so on. Once inside, access to the actual floor space where the systems reside should be further controlled and restricted by the use of cages and sectioning, as well as employing different levels of access control and monitoring. In some cases, there may be contractual or regulatory requirements to have different types of systems segmented off from others in physical cages, depending on the type of system, the jurisdictions that have authority over it, and the type of data that it stores and consumes.

Any utilities and facilities that the data center depends on, especially in regard to power and cooling, should be redundant both inside and outside the data center. From the outside there should be multiple independent power supplies coming into the data center. Inside the data center, the power distribution units that send power to the racks and servers should also be redundant. This way, whether there is a power failure internally or externally, there are independent redundant power supplies. The same applies to the network, with independent network feeds and redundancy both internally and externally.

Extensive and rigorous background checks should be employed for any personnel allowed access to the center in any capacity. Along the same lines of system security, personnel should be granted physical access based on the least privilege principle. Even with personnel, it is crucial to have proper monitoring and reviews in place, as well as continual training to remind them of policies, procedures, and proper safeguards.

System and Communication Protection

Although the cloud infrastructure is presented to the customer via virtualization, underneath is the same real hardware and systems that would be present in a traditional data center. Depending on the type of cloud hosting model employed, there are varying degrees of customer exposure and responsibilities.

While the cloud provider is responsible for the underlying hardware and network regardless of cloud service model, the remaining services and security responsibilities either lie with the customer or are split between the customer and cloud provider. It is incumbent on the Cloud Security Professional to clearly know the demarcation lines between the customer's and cloud provider's responsibilities, which should be clearly articulated and documented in the contracts and SLAs.

As with any application, the protection of data is a primary concern, and different methods are needed for different states of data:

- **Data at rest** The main protection point for data at rest is the through the use of encryption technologies.

- **Data in transit** With data in transit, the main methods of protection are network isolation and the use of encrypted transport mechanisms such as TLS.

- **Data in use** Data in use is protected through secure API calls and web services via the use of encryption, digital signatures, or dedicated network pathways.

Virtualization Systems Protection

As previously discussed, virtualization forms the backbone of any cloud infrastructure and allows for many of the features that make a cloud environment a unique and popular technology and platform. Given the visible and important role that virtualization plays, the components and systems that make up the virtualized infrastructure are the most obvious and attractive targets for attackers.

The management plane, with full control over the environment and exposed APIs for allowing administrative tasks, is the most visible and important aspect to fully protect.

The management plane is made up of a series of APIs, exposed function calls and services, as well as web portals or other client access to allow its use. Any and all of these points are potential vulnerabilities. The Cloud Security Professional needs to develop a holistic picture of threats and vulnerabilities at each level and for each component of the management plane. If the Cloud Security Professional does not break down each component to realize its particular vulnerabilities and threats and then form them together into a comprehensive view, the entire system could be impacted due to the possibility of a missed weakness.

As with any system, role-based access controls are extremely important with the management plane and virtualization infrastructure. All administrative access must be tightly controlled as well as regularly and comprehensively audited. Very detailed logging should take place not only at the level of each piece of the virtualization infrastructure, but also at the level of the web portal or wherever the client accesses the management plane. All logs should be captured in a way where they are removed, indexed, and evaluated away from the actual system itself. This allows log preservation if the actual component is compromised, with sufficient administrative access to modify or delete the logs that are local in nature.

Apart from maintaining cloud features such as auto-scaling and resiliency, a major function of the virtualization environment and infrastructure is to promote and maintain multitenancy. Allowing for multitenancy is not a major challenge from a creation and implementation standpoint because, at its root, multitenancy is a management task versus a technological task. From a virtualization standpoint, virtual machines are just hosts; there is no dependency on what kind of customer or contractual requirements they contain. Where the importance of controls comes into play with multitenancy is the requirement to keep tenants separate and protected from each other. This includes both keeping system interaction and security isolated between tenants, but also resources and utilization to ensure that all tenants have what their particular systems and applications need to meet contractual and SLA requirements.

While logging and auditing are certainly important to security, these are reactionary mechanisms and do not prevent an actual vulnerability from being exploited initially. Many of the same approaches and strategies that are used at the system level in a traditional data center also are adapted for a virtualization infrastructure in a cloud environment. A prime example is the establishment of trust zones, in the same manner a network separation between servers and systems would be implemented as a defensive layering strategy. Trust zones can be segmented in a variety of ways, depending on the particular needs of the environment or customer contracts. Before implementing trust zones, the cloud provider should undertake a rigorous threat and vulnerability assessment to determine where weaknesses are in their infrastructure and where trust zones could be beneficial. You do not want to take an approach based on practices from other cloud providers without knowing and understanding your own cloud environment first. Going down that path may lead to a false sense of security, to additional complexity added where it's not needed, and even to risks and vulnerabilities that we were not present before due to the addition of unnecessary points and mechanisms.

Trust zones can be established and segmented using many different strategies. The most common way involves separating out the different tiers of the system architecture (for example, you could separate the web/presentation, application, and data zones of the infrastructure). This allows each zone to have its own protections and monitoring using tools and strategies that are pertinent and specific to its actual needs and functions. It allows the application and data zones to be isolated from external network access and traffic, thus further adding security controls and enhancements.

With this isolation and segmentation, those responsible for managing the systems will need access beyond just what the applications need to operate. Although communications channels will be open internally for the applications to function, that does not facilitate what an administrator needs to gain access, and under no circumstances from a security perspective would you want to open external connectivity for administrative access. The most common ways to allow administrator access in such a configuration is through the use of virtual private networks (VPNs) or jump servers. With a VPN connection, administrators can use most native methods and protocols to access their hosts because they will be secured from their device up to the inside of the cloud environment, and thus not exposed to the public Internet. The VPN connection will have its own authentication and authorization mechanisms, and it will use encrypted communications tunneling, thus adding additional layers of security. With jump servers, the concept is to have a server in the environment that is open and exposed to the public Internet to which administrators can connect and have access internally to the appropriate resources. This method allows security to be focused on the jump server rather than all servers, and it allows the appropriate access controls, monitoring, and logging to be put in place on a much smaller and more specialized scale. The security of the jump server becomes imperative, but it does remove the security concerns directly on the hosts themselves, and it allows the administrators to connect without the need for VPN software and profiles. Another concept that is often used is that of a bastion host. A bastion host is a server that is fully exposed to the public Internet; it is extremely hardened to prevent attacks and is usually focused for a specific application or usage only. This singular focus allows for much more stringent security hardening and monitoring. However, these implementations can, and often are, used together for additional security.

Management of Identification, Authentication, and Authorization

Like applications, cloud systems require identification, authentication, and authorization. However, this need is also extended to include nonperson entities such as devices, clients, and other applications. Federation is another important aspect of cloud computing, especially with public clouds that have a large number of customers and users. It allows the use of "home" or "native" systems to provide identification and authentication, without needing a user base to establish credentials with the cloud provider(s).

Federation

Federation is where a standard base of policies and technologies is employed by different organizations so that they can join their identity systems and allow applications to accept their credentials while still maintain their autonomy. By establishing policies and guidelines that each member organization must adhere to, trust is established with identities

Figure 4-4
The relationship
flow within a
federated system

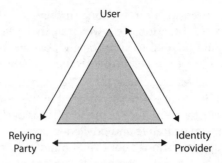

User

Relying
Party

Identity
Provider

provided by each member organization, and each application that accepts them has the understanding that the sufficient level of background checks and proofing has already been followed and approved under each identity provider. When a system or user who is part of a federation needs to access an application that accepts credentials from that federation, that system or person must obtain local tokens through their own authentication process, which are then passed to the application for acceptance and access. The members that participate run their own "identity providers," and the systems that accept them are known as the "relying party." The typical relationship flow between the user, identity provider, and relying party is shown in Figure 4-4.

Identification

As covered briefly in Chapter 2, identification is the process of singling out an entity—either a person or system/application—in a manner that makes them unique from any other identity. In pretty much all organizations there is already an established identity system, usually based on some form of LDAP. Many organizations, such as academic institutions, small businesses, and nonprofits, tend use open source or other similar identity systems, versus the corporate world where proprietary and commercially supported systems such as Active Directory tend to be the dominant players. With the emergence of large public cloud systems, many organizations and cloud providers have moved toward the OpenID and OAuth standards. Regardless of which particular flavor of identity provider is used by an organization and consumed by the relying party, the vast majority employ the SAML (Security Assertion Markup Language) and WS-Federation standards for passing identity information.

NOTE Because many large companies and prominent cloud providers have moved toward OpenID, it would be well worth your time doing some additional exploration on the subject so that you have a good understanding of how it works. More information can be found at http://openid.net/.

Authentication

Whereas identification establishes a unique presence of an entity or person, authentication is the process by which one can be certain that the identification presented is true. By policy, this is done to an extent that a system can properly trust the access request.

As previously discussed, this can be done through a variety of methods—from the basic user ID/password combination for lower security levels, to strong multifactor authentication, which should be used in all instances possible, but always for administrative and privileged access. The process of authentication is handled by the identity provider.

 EXAM TIP Make sure you remember the use of multifactor authentication in all instances where authentication is performed, but especially crucial with administrative and privileged account users. You are very likely to see multiple questions about what multifactor authentication is, where it is used, and why it is essential to promoting security best practices.

Authorization

Once an identity has been established and authentication satisfied to the extent required, authorization grants of the actual roles and entitlements appropriate for the user or system process to gain access to data and applications. During the authentication process, the identity provider sends certain predetermined attributes about the user to the relying party. The relying party then uses this information (name, location, job title, and so on) to determine the appropriate level and type of access to grant, or whether to grant access at all. The relying party, even in a federated system, makes this determination because it is tied to the actual application, and it makes the decisions based on the policies, requirements, or regulations of the data being accessed.

In making a determination as to whether to grant access and what level of access, the application can take from the identity provider any number of attributes about the entity. The determination can be based on a single attribute, all the way up to complicated conditionals and combinations of attributes.

As an example, take the case of a library system with online journals at a university. In most cases, the sole requirement for access based on the licensing agreements is that the individual be affiliated with the university, and the exact type of affiliation is not important. In this instance, the mere acknowledgement from the identity provider that the person is in fact a valid affiliate of the university satisfies the licensing requirements of the relying party, so access is granted.

On the opposite end of the spectrum, some systems and applications use very complex decision-making algorithms to determine what level of access to grant. For example, an application that a corporation runs may allow immediate access for those on the corporate network, but require more extensive validation for those not on the corporate network. As a first conditional step, the relying party can check where the user is connecting from. If the user is on the corporate network, access may be granted immediately. If the user is not on the corporate network, the relying party may require the user to authenticate through the identity provider. Upon successful authentication, the identity provider will provide the relying party with more information about the user to determine access.

No matter which route an entity attempts for access, the principles of least privilege and risk assessment must be adhered to through policy and auditing. Every access to a system is based on a risk assessment for data security, which is established by company policy and the manner in which access is attempted. If the party presents credentials and attributes that align with what has been determined as an acceptable risk to the data, then access may proceed.

Auditing

Auditing in the traditional sense involves the ensuring of compliance with policy, guidelines, and regulations. Audits are performed from a security perspective to measure effectiveness at meeting security controls from a variety of sources that together form the entirety of the security requirements for a system or application. In many instances this will include internal security policy requirements, contractual requirements, regulatory requirements from the local, state, or federal government, as well as any industry or organizational requirements such as PCI DSS. Auditing is performed by analyzing security control requirements, meshing those with configurations and internal policies, and then collecting logs, screenshots, data sets, or anything else to prove and show compliance to the satisfaction of management, customers, or independent/government auditors.

In today's IT climate, auditing is also employed for an ever-growing list of reasons beyond the traditional requirements. Audits are used for ongoing security compliance and testing from an internal perspective, and are also increasingly used to provide evidence of value and performance to customers and clients. They can be used far beyond security compliance to show system performance, uptime, user access and load, and virtually any other metric that can be collected and quantified.

Within a cloud environment, auditing presents additional challenges and complexities over a traditional data center and hosting model. Cloud environments are large and distributed hosting platforms, in many instances spanning multiple data centers and even multiple countries and jurisdictions. Many systems are also hosted in a hybrid cloud setup where they span multiple cloud providers and/or hosting models, or are even a combination of cloud and traditional data center hosting configurations. Depending on the cloud model used (IaaS, PaaS, or SaaS), the audit scope will be defined based on the level of access a customer has and the level of information that will be supplied contractually by the cloud provider. The contract and SLAs between the cloud provider and cloud customer should clearly spell out the requirements for auditing and the delineation of responsibilities between both sides, as well as the frequency for any audit testing and reporting. Because a cloud is a multitenant environment, in almost all cases any penetration testing or audit testing must be coordinated between the cloud provider and the cloud customer to ensure that the tests do not conflict with or harm the needs of any other cloud customers hosted in the same environment.

Because the underlying cloud systems and architecture are controlled by and are the responsibility of the cloud provider, any audit requirements will have to be clearly spelled out in the contract and with support and assistance provided by the cloud provider. With large public clouds especially, hosting hundreds or even thousands of different customers, there is no way for each customer to do their own exhaustive audits in any appreciable sense. The cloud customer will need to rely on audits commissioned on behalf of the cloud provider and have contractual language in place requiring them to be done. Typically, a cloud provider will have the cloud environment audited by a large reputable firm that meets the requirements of the cloud provider's individual tenants and customers, and will provide reports of sufficient detail to meet those audit expectations. A prominent method a cloud provider can use is to have their cloud environment certified under rigorous standards, such as those discussed in Chapter 2. If well-known and established standards are used, the cloud customer can accept the certification as evidence of security control implementations, policies, and ongoing audit requirements being met by the cloud provider.

An advantage a cloud provider has is to leverage their self-service capabilities to provide a set of auditing tools and reports to their customers. Through their self-service portal, they can enable customers to access a suite of prebuilt reports, log-collection capabilities, and scripts that provide metrics for a large collection of control testing and data points. This enables the customer to collect audit reports and evidence from these tools whenever needed, without having to engage the cloud provider or auditors to do so.

Another big advantage for audit compliance that a cloud environment enjoys is the use of virtualization and server images. The cloud provider or cloud customer has the ability to construct a base image with all the security controls already implemented and tested, and then use that image to deploy any other hosts within the environment. This drastically cuts down on the time and effort a traditional data center would require for each server to be built and the need to have the baselines applied and tested before the server is deemed ready for use. In a cloud environment using the same identical image, the customer knows that each host instance from the onset is fully compliant and configured correctly to meet their security baseline requirements. The image can also be built to contain monitoring tools or data collection tools as well, so that as hosts are brought online, especially through auto-scaling, these capabilities are already established and running from the start. Having these hooks established on each server plays a big part in having self-service auditing capabilities and continual monitoring capabilities as well, without having to take the time to ensure they are installed, configured, and running properly in each instance.

Disaster Recovery and Business Continuity Management Planning

A cloud environment represents a natural opportunity for a robust business continuity and disaster recovery (BCDR) program for any organization due to its constructs around resiliency, portability, interoperability, and elasticity. However, the cloud environment also presents its own unique challenges, as we will discuss next.

Understanding the Cloud Environment

A cloud environment can be used for BCDR in a few different types of scenarios, such as hosting for either the primary or the BCDR site as a traditional data center or a cloud environment, or both environments being hosted in cloud environments.

The first scenario is where an organization has their primary computing and hosting capabilities in a traditional data center and uses the cloud to host their BCDR environment.

This type of plan would typically revolve around already existing BCDR plans the organization has in place, where the cloud environment takes the place of the failover site should the need arise, versus having a BCDR site at another data center. This scenario leverages the on-demand and metered service aspects of a cloud platform, which makes it a very cost-effective method. With a traditional BCDR plan and a secondary data center, hardware must be procured and available for use, usually in a dedicated fashion, making costs significantly higher and requiring far more substantial prep time. Of course, as we discussed previously, extra care is required in going from a data center model to a cloud model to ensure that all security controls and requirements are being met, and there is no reliance on local security controls and configurations that cannot be easily duplicated or duplicated at all in a cloud environment.

NOTE Apart from the cost benefits of not having hardware standing by and ready at a BCDR site is the benefit of being able to test and configure without having staff onsite. Traditionally, BCDR tests involve staff traveling to the location to configure equipment, but in a cloud environment everything is done via network access. However, do not overlook the fact that in a real emergency, unless staff is geographically dispersed already, some travel may be required if network access is not available at the primary location.

A second scenario is where a system or application is already hosted in a cloud environment, and a separate additional cloud provider is used for the BCDR solution. This would be used in the case of a catastrophic failure at the primary cloud provider causing the migration of all servers to the secondary cloud provider. This requires the Cloud Security Professional to fully analyze the secondary cloud environment to ensure it has the same or similar security capabilities to satisfy the risk tolerance of the company. Although the system and applications may be portable enough that they do not suffer from vendor lock-in and can easily move between different cloud environments, the secondary cloud environment may offer completely different security settings and controls from the primary environment. There is also the need to ensure that images from one cloud provider can be used by the other cloud provider, or there is additional complexity in preparing and maintaining two sets of images should a sudden disaster occur. As with any BCDR approach, there is the need to have data replicated between the two cloud providers so that the necessary pieces are ready in the event of a sudden disaster. Many times this can be implemented by using the secondary site to back up the primary site.

A third scenario is where an application is hosted in a cloud provider and another hosting model is used within the same cloud provider for BCDR. This is more prevalent with large public clouds that are often divided geographically because it provides resiliency from an outage at one data center of the cloud provider. This setup certainly streamlines configuration and minimizes configuration difficulties for the customer, because both locations within the same cloud provider will have identical configurations, offerings, options, and requirements. This differs in regard to having a BCDR configuration between different cloud providers or data centers in that vendor lock-in is not a prevailing concern.

Understanding Business Requirements

Three big concepts are crucial to determining the business requirements for BCDR, whether implemented with a traditional data center model or a cloud hosting model:

- **Recovery point objective (RPO)**   The RPO is defined as the amount of data a company would need to maintain and recover in order to function at a level acceptable to management. This may or may not be a restoration to full operating capacity, depending on what management deems as crucial and essential.

- **Recovery time objective (RTO)**   The RTO is a measurement of the amount of time it would take to recover operations in the event of a disaster to the point where management's objectives for BCDR are met.

- **Recovery service level (RSL)**   The RSL measures the percentage of the total, typical production service level that needs to be restored to meet BCDR objectives in the case of a failure.

 EXAM TIP   Be sure to know the difference between these three concepts and to recognize them by their acronyms.

These three measures are all crucial in making a decision as to what needs to be covered under the BCDR strategy, as well as the approach to take when considering possible BCDR solutions. The prevailing strategy for any company will constitute a cost–benefit analysis between the impact of downtime on business operations or reputation versus the costs of implementing a BCDR solution and to what extent it is done.

Management first needs to determine the appropriate values for RPO and RTO. This step serves as the framework and guidelines for the IT staff and security staff to begin forming a BCDR implementation strategy. These calculations and determinations are completely removed from the possible BCDR solutions and are made strictly from the business requirement and risk tolerance perspectives.

Once management has analyzed and assigned requirements for the RPO and RTO, the organization can set about determining which BCDR solutions are appropriate to meet their needs, weighed against cost and feasibility. While this entire analysis is agnostic of the actual solution, there are some key aspects of cloud computing, spanning multiple areas of concern, that need to be addressed.

A primary concern when it comes to BCDR solutions in the cloud goes back to two main regulatory concerns with cloud hosting in general—where the data is housed and the local laws and jurisdictions that apply to it. This can be a particular concern for those opting for a model with a traditional data center and then using a cloud provider for their BCDR solution, where they are moving into an entirely different paradigm than their production configurations and expectations. However, it also plays prominently in the other two scenarios as well, because even within the same cloud provider, the other data centers will be in different geographic locations and possibly susceptible to different jurisdictions and regulations, and the same holds true for using a different cloud provider.

Understanding Risks

With any BCDR plan, there are two sets of risks—those that require the execution of the plan in the first place, and those that are realized as a result of the plan itself.

Many risks could require the execution of the BCDR plan, regardless of the particular solution the company has opted to take. These risks include the following:

- Natural disasters (earthquakes, hurricanes, tornadoes, floods, and so on)
- Terrorists attacks, acts of war, or purposeful damage
- Equipment failures
- Utility disruptions and failures
- Data center or service provider failures or neglect

Apart from the risks than can lead to the initiation of a BCDR plan, there are also risks associated with the plan that need to be considered and understood:

- **Change in location** Although cloud services are normally accessed over broad networking, a change in geographic hosting location in a BCDR situation can cause network latency or other performance issues. This can impact both the user and customer perspectives when it comes to the system or application, as well as the business owner's ability to update and maintain data, especially if large data updates or transfers are required. Latency can also implement timing issues between servers and clients, especially with many security and encryption systems that rely heavily on time syncing to ensure validity or timeout processes.

- **Maintaining redundancy** With any BCDR plan, a second location will need to be maintained to some extent, depending on the model used and the status and design of the failover site. Both sites will need additional staffing and oversight to ensure they are compatible and maintained to the same level in the event an unforeseen emergency happens without notice.

- **Failover mechanism** In order for a seamless transition to occur between the primary and failover sites, there must be a mechanism in place to facilitate the transfer of services and connectivity to the failover site. This can be done through networking changes, DNS changes, global load balancers, and a variety of other approaches. The mechanism used can involve caching and timeouts that impact the transition period between sites.

- **Bringing services online** Whenever a BCDR situation is declared, a primary issue or concern is the speed at which services can be brought online and made ready at the failover site. With a cloud solution, this typically will be quicker than in a traditional failover site because a cloud provider can take advantage of rapid elasticity and self-service models. If the images and data are properly maintained at the failover site, services online can brought quickly.

CAUTION A common practice is to leave images offline at the BCDR site when not in use. This can cause major problems in the event of a BCDR situation if the system images are not patched and up to date with configurations and baselines for the production systems. If the images are to remain largely offline, the Cloud Security Professional will need to ensure that appropriate processes and verifications are in place with images at the BCDR site.

- **Functionality with external services** Many modern web applications rely on extensive web service calls out to other applications and services. With a BCDR situation, a crucial concern is ensuring that all hooks and APIs are accessible from the failover site in the same manner and at the same speed as they are with the primary location. If there are keys and licensing requirements to access services from the application, those also must be replicated and made ready at the failover site. If the service has checks in place for the origination of IP addresses or some other tie into actual hosts and locations, the company will need to ensure that the same service can be accessed from the failover site with whatever information necessary already available and configured. Although the failover cloud site may have on-demand and self-service capabilities, it is likely that any external tie-ins will not have the same capabilities and will cause complications while the staff is trying to get their own services up and running.

Disaster Recovery/Business Continuity Strategy

Once management has determined the requirements for the BCDR plan, weighed the appropriate risks and issues, and made the necessary decisions, it is time to create the BCDR plan, the implementation steps and processes for it, and the ongoing testing and validation plan. The continual process of the BCDR strategy is shown in Figure 4-5.

In order to create a BCDR plan for a system, we must take into account all previous material we have covered in this section. The steps for the actual formulation of the plan from the perspective of the Cloud Security Professional are discussed next.

Figure 4-5
The BCDR
continual process

Define Scope
The first step in plan formulation is to ensure that security concerns are an intrinsic part of the plan from the start, rather than trying to retrofit them into the plan after it is developed. This allows security to clearly define the roles and areas of concern during the planning and design phase and to ensure that proper risk assessments are conducted and accepted by management along the way.

Gather Requirements
Requirements gathering takes into account the RPO and RTO objectives we previously discussed. This determines what needs to be included in the plan as well as gives a sense of what types and models of solutions are necessary to meet those objectives. From the perspective of the Cloud Security Professional, the determination of critical systems and the time necessary to establish operations in the event of a BCDR situation requires the analysis and application of threats and vulnerabilities that pose a risk to the data and systems. Regulations, laws, policies, customer expectations, and public relations will all play a role in this determination for possible solutions.

Analyze
This step is where the requirements and scope are combined to form the objectives and roadmap for the actual plan design. This step involves a thorough analysis of the current production hosting location for the system or application, a determination of components that need to be replicated for a BCDR situation, and the areas of risk associated with that. With moving to a new environment, new risks are inevitable due to differences in configurations and support models, as well as new hosting staff who do not have a history or familiarity with the application or system. A primary concern with moving to a secondary host provider for BCDR reasons is whether they can handle the load and expectations for the system or application like the primary production hosting arrangement does.

Assess Risk
In any IT system, regardless of hosting circumstances or providers, risk assessments are an ongoing and continual process to ensure security compliance and regulatory requirements. Here's a list of the main risks that are assessed:

- **Load capacity at the BCDR site**   Can the site handle the needed load to run the application or system, and is that capacity readily and easily available? Can the BCDR site handle the level of network bandwidth required for the production services and the user community accessing them?

- **Migration of services**   Can the BCDR site handle the bandwidth and requirements to get the production services mirrored and configured in a timely manner? If there are huge data sets, will incremental copies be performed regularly versus having to do a single large transfer at the time when services are down? How many services will be on standby and can be rapidly deployed and expanded when needed?

- **Legal and contractual issues**   Are appropriate SLAs and contracts in place with the BCDR provider, and do they meet all the requirements the application or system owner must comply with for legal or regulatory reasons? Is all appropriate licensing in place—either system and software licensing or licensing to access external web services or data sources?

Design

The design phase is where the actual technical evaluation of BCDR solutions is considered and matched to the company's requirements and policies. In many aspects, the requirements are the same as what procuring a primary production hosting arrangement would entail. Both the technical and support requirements need to be firmly established and articulated in contracts, SLAs, and policies. This includes identifying the owners of each aspect of the system and process, the technical contacts, and the required turnaround times for service expectations. The plan must include the specific requirements that define when the BCDR situation would be declared and the plan put into motion so that the business owner and the hosting environments understand their requirements and what preparations are necessary. Other absolutely crucial parts of the plan are how the testing of the plan will be conducted and how the restoration of services back to the steady production state will be handled once the appropriate time arrives.

Implement the Plan

Once the plan and design have been fully vetted and filled in, the actual implementation of the plan will likely require changes from both technical and policy standpoints.

The actual production applications and hosting may need to be augmented or modified to provide additional hooks or capabilities to enable the BCDR plan to work. This can include system configuration modifications to bring the two hosting environments more in synergy, or providing data replication and configuration replication services to the BCDR host for continual updating and maintaining consistency. From this point forward, the BCDR planning and strategy should be integrated as a key component of ongoing management of IT services and all change and configuration management activities.

 NOTE   The idea of having to make modifications to existing production platforms in order to implement a BCDR solution is one that is often dismissed outright by management. Often, very good and sound solutions may get overlooked because management is set on finding a solution that can simply be dropped into place without incurring additional costs or modifications to existing systems. As a Cloud Security Professional, be sure to perform a cost–benefit analysis as to the extent of modifications required and the benefits that even minor modifications may bring to the overall organization.

Test the Plan

Once a BCDR plan is established, designed, and implemented, it can only really be considered sound and valid once testing has been performed to ensure its accuracy and feasibility. Also, testing should not be considered a one-time activity. As systems change, new versions of code and configurations are rolled out, new data is added, and any other typical activities are done that denote change over time within a system or application, testing is required as an ongoing activity to ensure the plans are still valid and accurate. Testing essentially turns the plans and designs from theory into reality should a real event occur. It not only confirms planning and expectations, but also serves to provide the staff with experience and familiarity with the overall steps before they are executed in a real emergency situation.

With any test, the primary goal is to ensure that the RPO and RTO goals are achievable with the plans that have been designed and implemented. The testing plan should clearly define the scope of the tests, the applications involved, and the steps taken to replicate or simulate an actual BCDR situation. The tests should involve well-defined and plausible situations that simulate real disaster situations of varying degrees and with multiple variables at play. Tests should be conducted at least once a year, and more frequently if required by any certifications, laws, regulations, or policies. Tests should also be conducted whenever major system or configuration changes are made to ensure their continued validity. It is also crucial to ensure that BCDR validation tests do not impact current production capabilities or services. These tests should be done in a way to minimize any disruption to business operations and staffing.

When developing the test plan, staff should closely follow the objectives and decisions made as part of the RPO and RTO analysis and the steps designed to satisfy them. The test should evaluate each component of the plan to ensure that it is necessary, feasible, and accurate for a real-world situation. Starting at the beginning of the plan and going through each step in sequence, the tests can show any deficiencies or incorrect assumptions, thus providing feedback for augmenting the plan with the discovered issues. Once corrected, the test plans should be run again to test the changes within the scope of how an actual event would unfold.

It is imperative that testing not just be done in a one-way manner. Although testing to ensure that failover to a BCDR site is well documented, planned, and validated is important, it is equally important to fully test the recovery path and restoration of original production services as well. Without the restoration testing, a company could find themselves running an alternate hosting arrangement and unsure of how to get back to normal operations, thus further impacting their business operations or data protection and security, as well as incurring potentially substantial additional costs and overhead of both staff and money.

Report and Revise

Once the testing has been completed, a full and comprehensive report detailing all activities, shortcomings, changes made during the course of testing, and the results of the effectiveness of the overall BCDR strategy and plan should be presented to management for review. Management will evaluate the effectiveness of the plan, coupled with the goals and metrics deemed suitable and the costs associated with obtaining such goals. Once management has had a full briefing and the time to evaluate the testing reports, the iterative process can begin anew with changes and modifications to the BCDR plan.

Exercise

As a senior security officer within your company, you have been tapped to be part of a technical review committee to evaluate new disaster recovery solutions. You currently host your systems in a traditional data center that your company runs, but the committee has been told that system availability and reputation are the top priorities right now, and all options are on the table. Many committee members seem eager to jump to a cloud solution based on what they have heard about the financial benefits alone.

1. From a security perspective, what are the first steps you should advise the committee to consider?

2. Because all options are on the table, how do you formulate a plan to consider cloud for a BCDR solution, and what impacts might this have on the current hosting model being employed?

3. How do you plan to drive and articulate concerns that must be considered with any cloud solution, weighed against the enthusiasm of others to push toward it based solely on costs?

Chapter Review

In this chapter, we covered the major pieces of the cloud infrastructure and the risks associated with them specifically, and with a cloud environment in general. We explored the various types of security designs and controls that are implemented to counter these risks, as well as the mechanisms and approaches available within a cloud environment to audit them for effectiveness and compliance. Lastly, we covered the very important topic of disaster recovery and business continuity planning, how it is similar and different with a cloud hosting configuration, and how a cloud environment can be used as a core component to a company's BCDR strategy.

Questions

1. Which of the following is the correct order for some of the steps of a BCDR strategy?

   A. Define, Analyze, Design, Assess Risk, Test, Implement

   B. Define, Assess Risk, Analyze, Design, Implement, Test

    C. Define, Design, Analyze, Assess Risk, Test, Implement

    D. Define, Analyze, Assess Risk, Design, Implement, Test

2. What is the entity called that takes the response from the identity provider to allow access to an application?

    A. Relaying party

    B. Relying party

    C. Relaying system

    D. Relying system

3. Which of the following storage methods provides a key value to call a file from rather than a directory tree structure?

    A. Volume

    B. Structured

    C. Object

    D. Unstructured

4. Which of the following concepts provides evidence that an entity is in fact who they claim to be?

    A. Authentication

    B. Authorization

    C. Federation

    D. Identification

5. Which of the following would be the *LEAST* beneficial reason to consider a cloud platform as a BCDR solution?

    A. Metered service costs

    B. Hardware ownership

    C. Broad network access

    D. Virtual host replication

6. Which concept involves the prioritization of virtual hosts getting system resources when a cloud is experiencing high utilization and might not be able to serve all hosts?

    A. Reservations

    B. Limits

    C. Shares

    D. Quotas

7. Which of the following is the *MOST* important factor in defining the controls used to test an audit?

   A. Regulations

   B. Policies

   C. Laws

   D. All of the above

8. What do reservations define within a cloud environment?

   A. Maximum level of resources available for allocation

   B. Guaranteed minimum level of resources available for allocation

   C. Maximum resources available for allocation to all customers

   D. A reserved pool of resources held for emergency load spikes

9. What is the *MAIN* objective of software-defined networking (SDN)?

   A. Make networking dependent on the operating system of the host and leverage its utilities.

   B. Separate the filtering of network traffic and administration from the actual transport of network traffic.

   C. Allow different operating systems to seamlessly communicate with each other.

   D. Use software to create virtual networks instead of relying on physical network cabling.

10. What is a major security risk with Type 2 hypervisors that does not exist with Type 1 hypervisors?

    A. Slower release of security patches

    B. Proprietary platform controlled by a single vendor

    C. Reliance on a small number of coding platforms

    D. Runs on top of another operating system

11. What is the main method for doing patching in a cloud environment?

    A. Scripts

    B. Host management software

    C. Reimaging

    D. Customers applying patches on affected hosts

12. Apart from annual testing, when would it be *MOST* crucial for a BCDR plan to undergo additional testing?

    A. During a change in senior management

    B. During major configuration changes to an application

    C. When new staff is hired

    D. During a change in encryption keys

13. What type of storage is the *MOST* likely to be used for virtual images?

    A. Structured

    B. Unstructured

    C. Volume

    D. Object

14. Which of the following issues would be the *GREATEST* concern from a regulatory standpoint of using a cloud provider for a BCDR solution?

    A. Location of stored data

    B. Scalability

    C. Self-service

    D. Interoperability

15. Which of the following relates to the acceptable duration of recovery to a BCDR location?

    A. RPO

    B. RSL

    C. RDO

    D. RTO

Questions and Answers

1. Which of the following is the correct order for some of the steps of a BCDR strategy?

    A. Define, Analyze, Design, Assess Risk, Test, Implement

    B. Define, Assess Risk, Analyze, Design, Implement, Test

    C. Define, Design, Analyze, Assess Risk, Test, Implement

    D. Define, Analyze, Assess Risk, Design, Implement, Test

    D. Define, Analyze, Assess Risk, Design, Implement, Test are in the correct order; the other options are all incorrect.

2. What is the entity called that takes the response from the identity provider to allow access to an application?

   A. Relaying party

   B. Relying party

   C. Relaying system

   D. Relying system

   B. The relying party takes the authentication tokens from the identity provider and then grants access and authorization based on its own business rules. The other terms and entities listed are not applicable or correct in this instance.

3. Which of the following storage methods provides a key value to call a file from rather than a directory tree structure?

   A. Volume

   B. Structured

   C. Object

   D. Unstructured

   C. Object storage is a flat storage system that resides on external services, and references storage items based on a key value rather than a traditional file system and organizational structure. Volume storage is a traditional type file system that contains directory structures and hierarchical organization, and uses paths and filenames for access within an Infrastructure as a Service deployment. Structured storage is used with Platform as a Service and is typically a system like a database, which has a predefined structure and organization methodology. Unstructured storage is also used with Platform as a Service and relates to data that does not fit within a predefined structure, such as web files or media objects.

4. Which of the following concepts provides evidence that an entity is in fact who they claim to be?

   A. Authentication

   B. Authorization

   C. Federation

   D. Identification

   A. Authentication provides proof of the identification of an entity to an acceptable degree of certainty based on policy or regulation. Authorization, done after successful authentication, is the process of granting a user access to data or functions within an application and is based on the role or approved needs of the user. Federation is an authentication system that uses external identity providers that will accept authentication tokens for users, without requiring the user to create an account with the actual application. Identification is part of the authentication process.

5. Which of the following would be the *LEAST* beneficial reason to consider a cloud platform as a BCDR solution?

   A. Metered service costs

   B. Hardware ownership

   C. Broad network access

   D. Virtual host replication

   B. Hardware ownership would be the least beneficial reason because a cloud customer does not own the hardware; the cloud provider does. Metered service costs are a major benefit of using a cloud provider for BCDR, as the cloud customer would only pay for services when they are needed, unlike BCDR that typically involves idle hardware sitting in a secondary data center that will likely never be used. Virtual host replication is also a major benefit for a cloud platform and BCDR as it enables production systems to be regularly mirrored to a secondary location and instantly used, unlike traditional backups that would have to be recovered on top of another configured system before they can be used. Broad network access would also be highly beneficial for BCDR, as network availability would not be a concern and the ability to access the environment from anywhere on the Internet in case of a disaster would be a major factor.

6. Which concept involves the prioritization of virtual hosts getting system resources when a cloud is experiencing high utilization and might not be able to serve all hosts?

   A. Reservations

   B. Limits

   C. Shares

   D. Quotas

   C. Shares is a prioritization and weighting system within a cloud environment that sets that order of specific applications or customers to receive additional resources when requested. Those with the higher prioritization number will receive resources first, and those with lower numbers will receive resources later, or not at all. Reservations is the setting aside of resources so that cloud customers will be guaranteed a minimum level of resources to start and use their services, even if they cannot obtain additional ones. Limits are the upper bounds that are set on any level (host, application, customer) that constrain the amount of resources that can be allocated and consumed, in order to protect the overall environment from any entity from consuming enough resources to impact other customers. Quotas are used by some to mean the same thing as a limit, but "limit" is the preferred terminology.

7. Which of the following is the *MOST* important factor in defining the controls used to test an audit?

   A. Regulations

   B. Policies

   C. Laws

   D. All of the above

   D. All of the above are crucial to a security audit. Regulations, policies, and laws are going to be absolutes and require specific testing and validation, and none can be bypassed during a security controls audit.

8. What do reservations define within a cloud environment?

   A. Maximum level of resources available for allocation

   B. Guaranteed minimum level of resources available for allocation

   C. Maximum resources available for allocation to all customers

   D. A reserved pool of resources held for emergency load spikes

   B. Reservations are a guaranteed minimum level of resources available to allocate to a host to power on and perform tasks. The maximum level of resources available for allocation would refer to limits, and the maximum resources available for allocation to all customers for the entire cloud environment would be the concern of the cloud provider and play into their overall resource pooling model.

9. What is the *MAIN* objective of software-defined networking (SDN)?

   A. Make networking dependent on the operating system of the host and leverage its utilities.

   B. Separate the filtering of network traffic and administration from the actual transport of network traffic.

   C. Allow different operating systems to seamlessly communicate with each other.

   D. Use software to create virtual networks instead of relying on physical network cabling.

   B. The main objective of SDN is to separate the filtering of network traffic and administration from the actual transport of network traffic. This allows management to be performed from portals and API calls, rather than by networking specialists. Toolsets and provisioning systems can access and modify network capabilities that are specific to customer needs, without impacting the underlying actual routing and network transport of packets.

10. What is a major security risk with Type 2 hypervisors that does not exist with Type 1 hypervisors?

    A. Slower release of security patches

    B. Proprietary platform controlled by a single vendor

    C. Reliance on a small number of coding platforms

    D. Runs on top of another operating system

    D. Running on top of another operating system versus being tied directly to the hardware is a major security risk with Type 2 hypervisors. This makes the hypervisor potentially subjected to any security exploits or issues the underlying operating system may have, as opposed to Type 1 hypervisors which are tied directly to the hardware and do not rely on security patching and configurations of an external software package.

11. What is the main method for doing patching in a cloud environment?

    A. Scripts

    B. Host management software

    C. Reimaging

    D. Customers applying patches on affected hosts

    C. Patching in a cloud environment is typically performed by reimaging hosts from the new, fully patched baseline image, rather than deploying patches and doing validations across all the various virtual machines. This allows for consistent and uniform management of patches against a tested and validated image, rather than having to validate on a host-by-host basis to ensure patches are properly received and applied.

12. Apart from annual testing, when would it be *MOST* crucial for a BCDR plan to undergo additional testing?

    A. During a change in senior management

    B. During major configuration changes to an application

    C. When new staff is hired

    D. During a change in encryption keys

    B. Major configuration changes with an application should entail new BCDR testing. Any major configuration change or update represents a significant shift in an environment, and, as such, proper testing is needed to ensure that all BCDR implementations and procedures are both still valid and still work as intended. The changes mentioned in the other answer choices are either minor or personnel changes that would not require new comprehensive testing.

13. What type of storage is the *MOST* likely to be used for virtual images?

   A. Structured

   B. Unstructured

   C. Volume

   D. Object

   D. Object storage is the most likely type of storage used for virtual images. Object storage resides externally from specific systems and references each storage object through a key value, which is ideal for system images. System images also do not need any organization structure to them, such as what volume storage would offer. Structured and unstructured would not be appropriate choices as they are geared toward Platform as a Service and are not appropriate for storing system images.

14. Which of the following issues would be the *GREATEST* concern from a regulatory standpoint of using a cloud provider for a BCDR solution?

   A. Location of stored data

   B. Scalability

   C. Self-service

   D. Interoperability

   A. Location of stored data would be the most important concern from a regulatory standpoint due to different jurisdictions and requirements. The other choices are all technological or cloud concepts that would not have any bearing on specific regulatory requirements.

15. Which of the following relates to the acceptable duration of recovery to a BCDR location?

   A. RPO

   B. RSL

   C. RDO

   D. RTO

   D. RTO, or recovery time objective, relates to the acceptable time for restoration of services. The other choices offered are random acronyms that are not applicable here.

Cloud Application Security

This chapter covers the following topics in Domain 4:

- The knowledge needed when considering application deployment in a cloud environment
- Common pitfalls with a cloud environment
- Security and functional testing of applications within a cloud
- The software development lifecycle and how it relates to a cloud project
- Cloud-specific risks and threat models
- Supplemental security devices
- Federated identity systems
- Single sign-on and multifactor authentication

Cloud application development is rapidly increasing in popularity and prevalence. In order for an organization to make informed choices in regard to cloud computing and their specific needs and requirements, they need a well-educated Cloud Security Professional who understands the most common challenges and issues with cloud development. Many of the methodologies and approaches for security scanning and testing are similar between a cloud environment and a traditional data center, but due to levels of access and the controls in place by cloud providers, these methodologies and approaches are not always feasible to the level required and expected.

Training and Awareness in Application Security

Before we get into cloud software and application development and implementation, it is important for you to understand some basics about how cloud applications operate, as well as some common pitfalls of getting into cloud development or migrating to a cloud environment from a traditional data center. The Cloud Security Professional needs a strong understanding of the common vulnerabilities facing cloud applications in order to properly advise on and enforce security policies and best practices throughout the software development lifecycle.

Cloud Development Basics

A major difference between cloud systems and their operations versus a traditional data center is that cloud systems are heavily reliant on—or in many cases, even solely reliant on—APIs (application programming interfaces) for access and functions. Two main types of APIs are commonly used: Representational State Transfer (REST) and Simple Object Access Protocol (SOAP).

REST is a software architectural scheme that applies to the components, connectors, and data conduits for many web applications used on the Internet. It uses and relies on the HTTP protocol and supports a variety of data formats, with JSON and XML being the most widely used, and it allows for caching for performance increases and scalability.

SOAP is a protocol and standard for exchanging information between web services in a structured format. SOAP encapsulates its information in what is known as a *SOAP envelope,* and then leverages common communications protocols for transmission. The most common and prevalent protocol used is HTTP, but others such as FTP are also possible. Unlike REST, SOAP only allows for the use of XML-formatted data, and it also does not allow for caching, leading to lower performance and less scalability when compared to REST. SOAP is most commonly used where design or technical limitations make the use of REST impossible.

Common Pitfalls

Developers, management, and Cloud Security Professionals need to be aware of and understand several issues and pitfalls when contemplating cloud development or moving software to a cloud environment. These issues could cause security or operations problems within the cloud environment if not properly accounted for and understood from the onset of any project plan.

Portability Issues

There is a common misconception that moving services from a traditional data center to a cloud environment is a seamless or transparent process. In many instances, systems and applications have been designed around the security controls and infrastructure for a data center. Many security controls are either supplemented or complemented by the data center infrastructure and setup, and in some cases the actual data center controls may be a significant part of how the overall security for the system or application is implemented. With a move to a cloud environment, some or all of these controls and configurations might not work or require significant reengineering to get to a comparable level.

When an analysis is undertaken to determine the possibility of moving to a cloud environment, the Cloud Security Professional should approach it with an overall mindset that an application hosted in a traditional data center was not designed with a cloud environment in mind, so it may have many features that are not transferable to a cloud environment. Cloud environments use much newer technologies, and these technologies are rapidly changing and evolving. Many legacy systems from a traditional data center are unlikely to be properly programmed or configured to work within the flexible nature and rapidly changing reality of a cloud environment. It is also unlikely that an application from a traditional data center model can simply be "forklifted" to a cloud environment, which in this case means a move with very few, if any, code changes. A forklift process may be appropriate and feasible in some cases, but one can never assume that it is or that all configurations and security controls are possible in a cloud environment.

Cloud Appropriateness

With any application security model, the underlying hosting environment is a significant portion of securing the application and plays a crucial role in the auditing and compliance of an application. Many regulatory requirements involve the underlying infrastructure and hosting environment being certified to an appropriate security level before the actual application that resides therein can be certified. With a cloud environment, such a certification may not be practical or even possible. Especially within a public cloud, the cloud provider is unlikely to be able to meet strict security requirements of many regulatory schemes, or might be unwilling to allow auditors the type and level of access that would need to be granted in order to properly certify the environment. One approach that many cloud providers may opt to take is to undergo a SOC 2 audit and make the report available to cloud customers and potential cloud customers as a way of providing security confidence without having to open their systems or sensitive information to the masses. Cloud environments are also typically focused on web-based applications that are built on modern web service frameworks and cutting-edge programming languages and platforms, and are unlikely to adequately support many legacy systems or programming languages.

Integration Challenges

In a traditional data center, the developers and administrators will have full access to all components, servers, and networking equipment to make integration of services and systems seamless and feasible. With a cloud environment (and even with IaaS), access to these types of systems and services will be severely limited, if even available at all. When attempting to do system integrations, without having full access to both systems and logs, it can be very difficult to troubleshoot or properly engineer the system designs and communications channels. The cloud customer would have to rely heavily on the cloud provider for assistance, and depending on the cloud service model and the demands of the other tenants, it might not be something the cloud provider is willing or able to do. In all likeliness, the cloud customer would have to adopt the APIs and other particular offerings and services from the cloud provider to get the most access and visibility possible, which could also lead to vendor lock-in and a decrease in portability.

Cloud Environment Challenges

With cloud environments involving newer and a rapidly evolving technologies, the focus tends to be on newer application environments and the more modern programming languages and development methodologies. When undertaking cloud development, it is imperative for an organization to ensure that has developers and project managers who are familiar with cloud, its particular issues and challenges, as well as the technologies and systems prevalent in a cloud environment versus traditional data centers.

Cloud Development Challenges

Typical software development lifecycle (SDLC) processes and methodologies revolve around well-documented and well-established practices and procedures. A typical organization will have its own practices that it follows and will have its internal policies and dependent processes integrated with them. With development in a new and different environment such as a cloud, those established process and procedures will likely need to be tweaked or even undergo significant overhaul to meet the unique challenges and demands of a cloud environment. The organization's SDLC process will need to be adapted to be made "cloud aware" and integrate those additional concerns and challenges, from the perspective of systems engineering and architecture, and most certainly additional and differing security controls and practices will need to be taken for a cloud environment.

Another big concern is making sure that the cloud environment used for development matches the intended production environment. Many organizations will use a different cloud hosting model or cloud provider for development, and those cloud environments may not offer the same toolsets and APIs as the intended production environment.

Common Vulnerabilities

In 2013, the Open Web Application Security Project (OWASP) put out its Top 10 Project, which identifies the most critical web application security risks. This project can be found at https://www.owasp.org/index.php/Top_10_2013-Top_10. At the time of this writing, the 2013 version is the latest version. OWASP has put out an open data call for updates, with expected publication in late 2016 or early 2017. The OWASP 2013 Top 10 list is shown in Figure 5-1 and described next:

- **A1: Injection** An injection attack is where a malicious actor sends commands or other arbitrary data through input and data fields with the intent of having the application or system execute the code as part of its normal processing and queries. This can trick an application into exposing data that is not intended or authorized, or potentially allow an attacker to gain insight into configurations or security controls. For example, if an application does not properly sanitize and validate data submitted through an input field, a malicious actor could include a properly formatted SQL SELECT statement in an attempt to get the application to return more data from the database, or even to dump entire schemas or columns of data. The same types of attempts can be made with fields that perform LDAP queries or any other type of lookup with the use of formatted queries appropriate to that technology. The Cloud Security Professional will need to ensure that all data input fields are being properly validated and sanitized by the application before any data is processed through the data stores.

- **A2: Broken Authentication and Session Management** Many applications do not properly secure authentication and session tokens and other mechanisms. Failure to do so leaves open the possibility for a malicious attacker to compromise sessions and assume the identity of a valid user, and thus inherit their access and system functions ability. For example, if an application utilizes a cookie or browser token to maintain state, but does not have any validation processes in place to verify that the token is being submitted by the original and valid obtainer of it, then another user could potentially hijack it and use it for their own purposes. This is especially a risk for mobile applications that people often

A1	Injection	A6	Sensitive Data Exposure
A2	Broken Authentication and Session Management	A7	Missing Function Level Access Control
A3	Cross-Site Scripting (XSS)	A8	Cross-Site Request Forgery (CSRF)
A4	Insecure Direct Object References	A9	Using Components with Known Vulnerabilities
A5	Security Misconfiguration	A10	Unvalidated Redirects and Forwards

Figure 5-1   OWASP Top 10 list

access from public Wi-Fi locations, where the risk is a lot higher that someone could be snooping on network traffic. If an attacker were able to obtain the session token, and it was not properly validated back to the original obtainer, the attacker could construct their own sessions using that same token. The same possibility exists for applications that use browser cookies for sessions and state that are not properly destroyed when the user log out or application times out, and another entity has access to the same browser after the original authorized user has left it.

- **A3: Cross-Site Scripting (XSS)**   XSS is an attack where a malicious actor is able to send untrusted data to a user's browser without going through any validation or sanitization processes, or the code is not properly escaped from processing by the browser. The code is then executed on the user's browser with their own access and permissions, allowing an attacker to redirect their web traffic, steal data from their session, or potentially access information on their own computer that their browser has the ability to access. This can cause a user to have their web traffic redirected through a system controlled by the attacker, thus allowing them to steal session and authentication information while the user thinks they are going to the legitimate website.

- **A4: Insecure Direct Object References**   This occurs when a developer has in their code a reference to something on the application side such as a database key, directory structure of the application, configuration information about the hosting system, or any other information that pertains to the workings of the application that should not be exposed to users or the network. If such a reference is discovered, an attacker could use it to access portions of the application directly without going through authorization. It is imperative that applications contain access controls and other validation methods to prevent references like this from being used if exposed. Also, the proper validation and sanitization of application code is needed to ensure any such references are not accidently included and exposed to users.

- **A5: Security Misconfiguration**   This occurs when applications and systems are not properly configured or maintained in a secure manner. This can be due to a shortcoming in security baselines or configurations, unauthorized changes to system configurations, or a failure to patch and upgrade systems as security patches are released by the vendor. This also includes ensuring that any default configurations or credentials that come with an application are changed prior to use and deployment. For example, most applications include default credentials for administrative access to platforms and environments as part of their distribution. Failure to change these, because they are public and very well known, immediately opens a system or application to access by an attacker using these known credentials. Having systems and processes in place to ensure baseline compliance and the prevention of unauthorized changes—through a strong change and configuration management process as well as through the use of monitoring tools on configuration items—will minimize the chances of misconfigurations from being deployed to the environment.

- **A6: Sensitive Data Exposure**   Many web applications regularly utilize sensitive user information, such as credit cards, authentication credentials, personally identifiable information (PII), and financial information. If this information is not properly protected through encryption and secure transport mechanisms, it can quickly become an easy target for attackers. Web applications must enforce strong encryption and security controls on the application side, but also require secure methods of communication with browsers and other clients that are used to accessing the information. With sensitive information, applications should ideally perform checks against browsers to ensure they meet security standards based on the versions and protocols supported.

- **A7: Missing Function-Level Access Control**   Many web applications perform verification of access and authorization when a user authenticates to the application, and makes the appropriate portions of the site visible to them within the user interface. However, it is imperative that applications also perform checks when each function or portion of the application is accessed as well, to ensure that the user is properly authorized to access it. Without continual checks, each time a function is accessed, an attacker could forge requests to access portions of the application where authorization has not been granted.

- **A8: Cross-Site Request Forgery (CSRF)**   A CSRF attack forces an authenticated client that a user has open to send forged requests under their own credentials to execute commands and requests that the application thinks are coming from a trusted client and user. Although an attacker cannot use this type of attack to steal data directly, because they have no way to see the results of the commands, it does open up other ways to compromise an application. If the authenticated user has permissions as a regular user of a system, CSRF could be used to execute any portion of the application where they have access. For example, if a user is authenticated to their online banking application, a CSRF attack could be used to transfer funds, change their contact information, and so on, which an attacker could then use to compromise their account directly. If the authenticated user has administrative or privileged access within the application, a CSRF attack could be used to compromise the entire application or make widespread changes to it.

- **A9: Using Components with Known Vulnerabilities**   No matter what the application or service is, it is built upon at least one component, but more likely multiple components, such as libraries, application frameworks, modules, and plug-ins. These components will run with varying levels of permissions and credentials on the host systems. However, even if they are properly run with least privileged access, at the very least they will have full access to the data used by the application, including any sensitive data or user data. As with any software or component, these pieces will all have regular updates and patches to fix bugs and known security vulnerabilities. If any components are not updated when security vulnerabilities are found, the entire system or application could be left vulnerable to attack and exploit. Unfortunately, a high number of successful attacks occur against systems running outdated and unpatched software and could have been prevented.

- **A10: Unvalidated Redirects and Forwards**   Many web applications offer redirect or forward pages where users can land on different, external sites. This is often done to allow users to link to outside information and authoritative sources, without a site or application having to reproduce or embed the data itself. However, this type of functionality, if not properly secured and validated, can allow attackers to use the application to forward users to sites for phishing or malware attempts. These attempts can often be more successful than direct phishing attempts, because users will trust the site or application that sent them there, and assume it has been properly validated and approved by the trusted application's owners or operators. It is incumbent on the web application owner to ensure that all redirect attempts are validated as proper and intended, and not leave their functions open to random injections from external users to leverage as a redirect or forwarding agent.

Cloud Software Assurance and Validation

As with any software implementation or development, those operating within a cloud environment must undergo auditing, testing, and validation to ensure that security requirements are being properly employed and verified.

Cloud-Based Functional Testing

Functional testing is a specific and focused test against a particular function or component of a system or application, as compared to full or regression testing, which is holistic in nature and consists of the entire application and all functionality. Application and software development within a cloud environment has all the standard considerations that are part of any project, plus additional considerations that are commensurate with the realities of cloud technologies. As part of testing and security, it is essential to consider any legal and regulatory requirements for the system when moving to a cloud. The particular jurisdiction where the cloud is hosted and the authorities to which it is subjected must meet the same requirements at a minimum for the application. The Cloud Security Professional must analyze the data being used and the application security requirements around it, making sure that the cloud provider selected or being considered can meet those requirements.

CAUTION Many data sets contain custody and access rules as to who can have such visibility from a legal and liability standpoint. For example, data may have requirements that only the data owners and their personnel have access to and visibility into those systems. Within a cloud environment, there is multitenancy to consider as well as the actual personnel of the cloud provider and what they are able to see and access based on how the system is implemented and secured.

Cloud Secure Development Lifecycle

The SDLC process is a set of phases that drive a software development project from conception and requirement gathering through development, testing, and maintenance. While the SDLC process is standardized and well known for all software development projects, adapting it for security within a cloud environment is a crucial responsibility of the Cloud Security Professional. The main focus in this instance is adapting an organization's perspective and approach to the realities of a cloud environment, where many of the standard security controls and system architectures are not applicable or feasible. Both security and cloud components must be included in the SDLC process from the onset, and retrofitting them later in the process after coding has begun (or has been completed) should not be attempted. Compared to a traditional SDLC process, the CSDLC process, much like most aspects of cloud computing in general, operates in a much more accelerated manner. This can often place considerable stress on established SDLC processes within an organization as well as on attempts to adhere to established timelines and development steps.

Security Testing

A few main types of application and security testing are followed within a cloud environment, and for the most part they have significant overlap with testing in a traditional data center from a methodology standpoint.

Dynamic Application Security Testing

Dynamic application security testing (DAST) is considered "black-box" testing of an application. It is run against live systems, and those running it do not have the benefit of special knowledge of the system. Unlike static application security testing (SAST), it must discover any information from the outside and attempt to discover its own paths and interfaces to test. DAST is used in conjunction with SAST to combine inside and outside methodologies and approaches to deliver a comprehensive test and evaluation of an application or system.

Pen Testing

Pen testing is typically a "black-box" test that is run in the same manner and with the same toolsets as an attacker would attempt to use against an application. It is designed to actively attempt to attack and compromise live systems in real-world-type scenarios. The purpose is to discover vulnerabilities and weaknesses using the same approach a malicious actor would employ against a system.

Runtime Application Self-Protection

Runtime application self-protection (RASP) is typically run against systems that have the ability to tune and focus their security measures based on actual environment variables and particular attack methods being used against them. It is designed to react to ongoing and active events and threats, and to tune and adapt the application to respond to and mitigate them at the time and against live production and running systems.

Static Application Security Testing

Static application security testing (SAST) is a method used to test and analyze the code and components of an application. It is considered "white-box" testing in that the ones running the tests have knowledge of and access to the source code and systems involved. The code is tested in an offline manner, and not against actual production systems. SAST is particularly good for catching programming errors and vulnerabilities such as SQL injection and cross-site scripting, and due to the knowledgeable and open nature of SAST, it tends to produce superior results to other types of testing that do not have the benefit of system knowledge.

Vulnerability Scanning

Vulnerability scans are those run by an organization against their own systems, using known attacks and methodologies to verify that their systems are properly hardened against them and that risk is minimized. These scans typically involve known tests and signatures, and they produce reports for management about discovered weaknesses and often include a risk rating or vulnerability rating based on their results. These ratings are typically based on the individual scans performed, and provide a risk rating for the application as a whole, incorporating all of the scan results across all signatures applied.

 EXAM TIP Make sure you know and understand the differences between dynamic and static application security testing.

Verified Secure Software

A key aspect of the selection of programming languages, software development platforms, application environments, and development methodologies is understanding the key components in a cloud environment that will promote and enforce security. With application code built on these frameworks and protocols, the decision to use toolsets and software packages that do not meet the security requirements in a cloud environment will ultimately have a detrimental impact on any software that is developed or implemented by an organization once it reaches a production state.

Approved API

With cloud-based applications heavily depending on APIs, the security of APIs is crucial to the overall security of the application. The introduction of APIs that are not adequately secured, especially with the integration of APIs that are outside the control or security boundary of the application, puts the entire data set within the application at risk of exposure or loss.

When considering the use of any external APIs, the Cloud Security Professional must ensure they undergo the same rigor of evaluation and security testing as any internal application and code would. Without a rigorous testing and validation process for external APIs, an application could end up consuming insecure API calls and data, thus possibly exposing itself to data compromises. Depending on the use of REST or SOAP, the appropriate security mechanisms for SSL/TLS or encryption, respectively, must be tested and validated to meet security requirements from both organizational policy and regulatory perspectives.

NOTE A Cloud Security Professional not only must verify that REST or SOAP APIs are using SSL/TLS or encryption, respectively, but also must ensure that those technologies are used properly to meet the guidelines and requirements set forth by any regulatory, legal, or oversight bodies.

Supply-Chain Management

Many cloud-based systems and modern web applications are composed of many different pieces of software, API calls, components, and external data sources. Modern programming techniques often require putting together different components that were authored by different sources, and leveraging their combined resources and capabilities to produce new applications. The integration of external API calls and web services allows an application to leverage enormous numbers of external data sources and functions, allowing for the integration of dynamic data and removing the need to store and maintain local data sources. Although this allows for much more efficient application programming and design, it also means the reliance on code that was not authored by the organization, or receiving data and functions from external sources. These external sources are outside of the control of the developers or organization, and in most instances, the design methodology, security models, data sources, and code testing and validation are unknown or even unknowable.

Community Knowledge

Open source software is very heavily used throughout the IT industry as a whole, and perhaps even more so with many cloud environments. Many developers in cloud environments heavily leverage open source software applications, development toolsets, and application frameworks. The most popular and widely used open source software packages have undergone extensive code review, testing, collaborative development, and a level of scrutiny that is not possible with proprietary software packages, which are closed source and protected. Given this level of scrutiny and the ability for any organization to evaluate and analyze the code from these packages, many consider them to be among the most secure and stable packages available in the industry. With the source being open and available, coupled with the number of people who analyze the code, security gets considerably improved over time and is woven into the code and build processes from the onset. When bugs or security vulnerabilities are discovered, collaborative coding can quickly and transparently address them and patches can be put out that can also be easily and quickly vetted for their success.

 NOTE The use of open source software for secure systems is often a hotly debated topic within the industry and across organizations. Many corporations and government agencies tend to shy away from open source software by default, whereas universities and nonprofits heavily rely on it. However, with any new software development or implementation, a thorough review of all software and sources is imperative regardless of past preferences, and neither open source nor proprietary software should be approached with any automatic assumption of having a higher degree of security or stability.

Understanding the Software Development Lifecycle (SDLC) Process

The SDLC process includes several steps in succession that form the framework for proper gathering, analyzing, designing, coding, testing, and maintaining of software development projects. It also includes practices and applications for maintaining and deploying systems in a standardized and enforceable manner.

Phases and Methodologies

Regardless of whether software development is being done for hosting in a traditional data center or a cloud environment, the overall steps and phases for the SDLC are the same.

Requirement Gathering and Feasibility

In the initial step, the high-level aspects of the project are gathered and specified. This includes the overall goals, the inputs available and the desired outcomes, the timing and duration of the project, the overall costs, and a cost–benefit analysis against the capabilities of current systems and the value derived from upgrade those systems or putting in new ones. This phase should include all stakeholders of the project as well as a sample of users and management to define what the application should do. As part of this initial high-level analysis, the risks and testing requirements are also defined, as well as an overview of the technologies available and the feasibility of the overall project's success. This step also takes into account all mandatory requirements as well as desired features and weighs the overall cost/benefit of incorporating them into the actual design. Security requirements should also be incorporated into the initial planning from the onset.

 NOTE It is essential that security be included in discussions and the SDLC process from the very initial stages. Many organizations try to incorporate security in later steps rather than from the onset, which can cause project delays or increased costs if previous decisions and directions need to be corrected or readdressed.

Requirement Analysis

After the initial high-level requirements are specified and the project has been approved, the next phase is to analyze those requirements and translate them into a real project plan with specific requirements and deadlines. This plan not only spells out the specific requirements for the features and functionality of the software, but also specifies the hardware and software platform requirements that the development team will build within. At the conclusion of this stage, the formal requirements and specifications for the project will be ready for the development team to turn into the actual software.

Design

The design phase takes the formal requirements and specifications and turns them into a plan and structure for the actual software coding, translating the requirements into an actual plan that can be applied to the programming language designated for the project. At this point of the project, the formal security threats and the requirements for risk mitigation and minimization are integrated with the programming designs.

Development/Coding

At the development stage, the project plan is broken down into pieces for coding and then the actual coding is done. As the requirements are turned into actual executable programing language, testing is completed on each part to ensure that it compiles correctly and operates as intended. Functional testing is completed by the development team as each portion of code is completed and tied into the larger project as a whole. This phase is typically the longest phase of the cycle.

 CAUTION Ideally, security scanning and testing should be done on sections of code as they are being developed and during incremental functional testing. Many organizations will wait until the whole package is together and then perform security scanning and testing. Doing so can lead to far greater complexity in fixes and project delays.

Testing

As part of the project design and specifications, a testing plan is also developed to ensure that all pieces are functioning properly and the desired outcome is achieved by the software. The test plan should have approval from management and include the appropriate allocation of system resources and personnel to complete the testing under the timeline established by the overall project plan. Testing is completed against the original design requirements and specifications to ensure that all objectives are met, from the perspectives of the major stakeholders and users. The testing includes security scans against the code and the completed application as it runs, as well as validations against the actual code for syntax errors and problems. As a deliverable, the testing phase will output a comprehensive results document that states any deficiencies or successes for each aspect of testing.

Maintenance

Once software has been successfully tested and put into production use, there will be continual updates for additional features, bug fixes, and security patches for the lifetime of the software. This is an ongoing and iterative process, and involves going through the overall SDLC process each time, progressing through requirements, analysis, design, coding, and testing.

EXAM TIP The exam always tends to include specific questions about the sequencing and phases of the SDLC process. Make sure that you fully understand them and review as part of your preparation process.

Business Requirements

With any system or software design, or even with changes to an existing one, gathering, analyzing, and understanding the business requirements is absolutely paramount to meeting organizational objectives and user expectations.

When a project is conceptualized, a thorough understanding of why it is needed, its goals, and the target audience will form the initial basis of business requirements. Getting input from as many stakeholders as possible will also increase the chances that all requirements are properly gathered and understood. If possible, potential users of the software should also be included, whether they are internal to an organization or part of the public. This will bring different perspectives and understandings for what management and internal populations are likely to expect, especially considering that the success of any software is ultimately dependent on its usability and end-user satisfaction.

Part of the gathering of business requirements is establishing and articulating the critical success factors for the project. These factors include specific feature sets and functionality, but also performance metrics and security standards. The critical success factors will play directly into the testing plan and provide the basis for measurable criteria to the stakeholders as to the success of the software development project.

Software Configuration Management and Versioning

With any environment, versioning and configuration management are extremely important. With the use of images and the rapid provisioning and auto-elasticity of a cloud environment, these factors become even more important to ensure system unity and cohesiveness. With traditional data center deployments, upgrades and patches are typically applied directly to servers and hosts. With a cloud environment, the process is typically to use new images and deployments to maintain systems and versions, rather than pushing out new changes, scanning to ensure their correct application, and then testing them. To maintain the versioning and proper system configuration throughout, the use of automated tools is almost a necessity with any cloud deployment.

For code development throughout the SDLC process, developers can utilize and leverage many tools for code collaboration, branching, and versioning. One of the more popular tools that is widely used is GitHub, which can be found at https://github.com/. It is an open source platform that allows for all of the features mentioned and is widely used by individuals, small businesses, government agencies, nonprofits, and corporations.

Two very popular tools for maintaining system configurations and versioning of software are Puppet (https://puppet.com/) and Chef (https://www.chef.io/chef/). Both solutions maintain server and system configurations, ensuring they are in the correct state based on policies that are centrally maintained and deployed. They can be used to push out new configurations, to change configurations, and, more importantly, to ensure that changes are not made on individual servers that will take them out of compliance with the other servers in the same pool of systems. If changes are detected on member systems that are contrary to the centralized policy, those changes will be reversed to main system unity and consistency with the set policies. Many organizations use these or similar products to handle code deployments and system configuration changes across the enterprise.

 NOTE A few examples of configuration and code management packages were given here, but far more are available, both open source and commercial products. The decision as to which to implement should be based on the particular needs and technologies used within a development project or system, because many benefits are based on the application platforms and operating systems used, which will determine their overall effectiveness and ease of use.

Applying the Secure Software Development Lifecycle

With a knowledge of that which comprises the Secure SDLC process, applying it requires an understanding of cloud-specific risks and the application of threat modeling to assess those risks and the particular vulnerabilities facing an application.

Cloud-Specific Risks

Whereas the OWASP Top 10 covers general application vulnerabilities for web applications, whether they are in a cloud or a traditional data center, the Treacherous 12, put out by the Cloud Security Alliance (CSA), covers risks that are specific to cloud-based applications and systems (https://cloudsecurityalliance.org/group/top-threats/). The following is a review of those 12 items (originally introduced in Chapter 2) and their specific relationship to cloud application security (see also Figure 5-2):

- **Data Breaches**   Any vulnerability in an application can lead to a data breach for that application, but also expose other applications hosted within the same cloud environment to threats due to multitenancy, especially if the cloud provider does not have appropriate segmentation and isolation between tenants. The threat is magnified in the event of a hypervisor or management plan compromise.

- **Insufficient Identity, Credential, and Access Management**   Without proper and strong access management and identity systems in place, a cloud environment and applications are exposed to many other threats on this list—in particular, data breaches and malicious insiders. The identity and access management implementation that a cloud environment or application uses is crucial to operations and features such as federation, which is covered later in this chapter.

- **Insecure Interfaces and APIs**   Cloud environments and many cloud-based applications rely heavily on APIs for automation and operations, so insecure APIs can lead to exposure and threat at both the cloud infrastructure and application levels.

- **System Vulnerabilities**   Any bugs found in the application-hosting framework are a potential vulnerability for the system. This includes any programming libraries and runtime environments that an application uses and relies on.

- **Account Hijacking**   Especially in instances where account sharing is permitted (it never should be!), accounts can be exposed and used by those wishing to compromise a system. Accounts should always be issued to an individual for their use only, with multifactor authentication systems in place to prevent another user from using an account, even if they do obtain the credentials for it.

Figure 5-2
The CSA
Treacherous 12

- Data Breaches
- Insufficient Identity, Credential, and Access Management
- Insecure Interfaces and APIs
- System Vulnerabilities
- Account Hijacking
- Malicious Insiders
- Advanced Persistent Threats
- Data Loss
- Insufficient Due Diligence
- Abuse and Nefarious Use of Cloud Services
- Denial of Service
- Shared Technology Issues

- **Malicious Insiders**   Any user who has legitimate access to a system or resources can use that access for unauthorized purposes. Active monitoring and auditing systems are needed at all times with sensitive systems and data to counter and catch unauthorized access and use.

- **Advanced Persistent Threats**   Advanced persistent threats occur any time a long-term program or malware is introduced into an environment to operate or steal data. In most cases, user education and training are effective countermeasures because most threats of this type require some degree of user action or intervention to allow the exploit to enter the system initially or to continue to operate.

- **Data Loss**   Within a cloud environment, data loss can come from the purposeful or accidental deletion of backups, a natural disaster or a physical event that causes actual loss of hardware systems that house the data, or when the key sets of an encrypted system are lost or destroyed. The deletion of data can occur by accident via authorized users and processes, or as the result of a malicious insider or external compromise.

- **Insufficient Due Diligence**   With any system or application, due diligence on the part of management, security personnel, and even users is required for optimal security and protection. Through active training and strong policies with enforcement mechanisms, many of the typical threats can be avoided and countered.

- **Abuse and Nefarious Use of Cloud Services**   Without proper application security controls in place, a malicious actor could infiltrate cloud applications or resources and use them to then attack other services or applications.

- **Denial of Service**   Flooding enormous amounts of traffic into a cloud environment has the potential to make an application slow or inaccessible. The impact might even be felt and experienced by all tenants hosted by the same cloud provider.

- **Shared Technology Issues**   With multitenancy and resource pooling, all cloud customers within a cloud provider use the same set of resources and technologies. By having technologies in place, including software applications, to serve a large number of customers, it is possible that not all components will be as secure as desired for all applications. This puts more of the onus on each cloud provider to layer on additional security and monitoring systems for their own applications.

Quality of Service

The quality of service (QoS) layer of SOA (service-oriented architecture) is focused on monitoring and managing both the business level and the IT systems levels. On the business side, QoS is focused on the measuring and monitoring of events, business processes, and key performance indicators (KPIs). On the IT systems side, QoS is focused on the security and health of systems, applications, services, storage, networking, and all other components that comprise the IT infrastructure. QoS is also concerned with the monitoring and enforcement of business policies in all areas, including security, access, and data.

Threat Modeling

Threat modeling is done on a system or application once it is live, and is used to determine and address any potential threats that face it. It is a very fluid and constant process because IT security and threats to IT systems are constantly changing. This is due to the rapidly changing technical landscape, where new tools and approaches for attacks are always evolving and system and application maintenance and upgrades are ongoing. Each time new code is introduced or configuration changes are made, the potential to impact threat assessments is a reality. Two prominent models recommended by OWASP are the STRIDE and DREAD threat models, though both were conceptualized by Microsoft.

STRIDE

STRIDE is a threat classification scheme in which the acronym STRIDE is a mnemonic for known threats in the following six categories (more information on STRIDE can be found at https://www.owasp.org/index.php/Threat_Risk_Modeling#STRIDE):

- **Spoofing Identity** This is a common risk for any application that uses an application-specific access control for the application and database, meaning that while users authenticate to the application with their own credentials and receive their own particular authorization based on their attributes, the application itself uses a single context to communicate with services and databases, such as a "service account" or other similar and uniform credential. With this configuration, it is important for the application to have proper controls in place that prevent any user from assuming the identity of another user, either to gain access to that user's information or to leverage their authorization levels to gain access to data.

- **Tampering with Data** Any application that sends data to the user faces the potential that the user could manipulate or alter it, whether it resides in cookies, GET or POST commands, or headers. The user could also manipulate client-side validations. If the user receives data from the application, it is crucial that the application validate and verify any data received back from the user. For example, if a user is applying for a loan and a proposed interest rate, package, or terms is sent to the user, it is possible that it could be manipulated (to a lower rate or more attractive terms) and then transmitted back to the application with an "acceptance" by the user. If the data is not verified by the application upon being sent back, it could be written into the database in altered form and have downstream effects on processing. Data received back from any user should never be accepted outright; it should always be validated to ensure it was the same data sent to the user, or that it matches acceptable possibilities within the application.

- **Repudiation** Applications must keep accurate and comprehensive logs of all user transactions. Without such logging, any transaction on the system is open to dispute or challenge by a user, who can claim they never performed the type of transaction the system says they did, or challenge the data contained on the system. For example, with a financial system, users can claim they paid certain bills already, made loan payments, never opened a credit line or credit card, or make any other type of dispute. If the financial organization cannot properly and accurately validate that certain transactions did or did not occur, they may be left with the responsibility for these transactions, leading to a charge-off or having to reimburse the user for transactions they claim they never made. Evidence can be in the form of logs, multifactor authentication mechanisms, or the integration of specific software packages designed to validate user credentials and keep comprehensive audit logs of transactions and verifications.

- **Information Disclosure**   Perhaps the biggest concern for any user is having their personal and sensitive information disclosed by an application. There are many aspects to consider within an application concerning security and protecting this information, and it is very difficult for any application to fully ensure security from start to finish. The obvious focus is on security within the application itself, and protecting the data and the storage of it. This is where strong controls can be put in place and audited. Where security can get more complex is with the client that the user of the application connects with. Although there are best practices from the application side, such as requiring secure communication channels, which can be enforced, there are others, such as sending directives not to cache pages or credentials, that are up to the client to enforce. Although many common browsers and clients will respect such directives, there is no way to enforce or require their compliance, and many times users can override such settings on their side.

- **Denial of Service**   Any application is a possible target of a denial-of-service attack. From the application side, the developers should minimize how many operations are performed for non-authenticated users. This will keep the application running as quickly as possible and using the least amount of system resources to help minimize the impact of any such attacks. The use of front-end caching technologies can also minimize the impact of attacks because they will remove many queries from the actual application servers.

- **Elevation of Privileges**   Many applications will have the same authentication and login processes for users, regardless of their status as a regular user or administrative user, with their role determining the functions and processes available to them once they have access the application. With this type of configuration, it is vital to re-verify administrative privileges when any functions are accessed. Without verifications, an application is susceptible to attacks where users are able to assume the role of administrator and elevate their own level of access, exposing the data as well as the entire application to unauthorized parties.

 EXAM TIP   The exam will almost certainly ask about the STRIDE model and what the specific letters stand for. Make sure that you memorize and review prior to the exam!

DREAD

The DREAD model is a bit different from STRIDE, in that it focuses on coming up with a quantitative value for assessing risks and threats. With a quantitative value, it can be compared with other systems and even itself over time. More information on DREAD can be found at https://www.owasp.org/index.php/Threat_Risk_Modeling#DREAD.

DREAD is based on the following algorithm, which computes the actual value based off of the quantification of risks in a few categories, using a value between 0 and 10, with the higher number meaning higher risk.

$$\text{Risk\_DREAD} = (\textbf{D}\text{amage} + \textbf{R}\text{eproducibility} + \textbf{E}\text{xploitability} + \textbf{A}\text{ffected users} + \textbf{D}\text{iscoverability}) / 5$$

- **Damage Potential**   This is the measure of damage to the system or data, should a successful exploit occur. On the low end, a value of 0 would signify no damage, with a high end of 10 signifying a total loss of data or systems. The determination of where on the scale a particular system would fall will be a subjective decision based on the classification and sensitivity of the data within it, as well as potential requirements and consequences from the regulatory or legal side.

- **Reproducibility**   The measure of how easy it is to reproduce an exploit. On the low end, a value of 0 signifies a near impossibility of exploit, even with administrative access. This would likely occur where other defensive measures prevent access or exploit. On the high end, a value of 10 signifies an easy exploit, such as simply accessing the application with a client, without needing authentication or other methods. Any value in the middle will be subjective and determined based on the particulars of the application, as well as any other mitigating factors from other defensive mechanisms.

- **Exploitability**   A measure of the skill level or resources needed to successfully exploit a threat. On the low end with a value of 0 are those exploits that require extensive knowledge or advanced tools. On the high end with a value of 10 would be those that require simple client access, with no specific knowledge or skill required for exploit, such as simply using a URL. The values in the middle are subjective and based on the specific circumstances of each application, the programming languages and libraries it is built on, as well as the security controls in place.

- **Affected Users**   This value indicates how much of the user base, based on a percentage of the total users of the application, would be affected by an exploit. This value ranges from 0 (no users affected) to 10 (all users affected), with values in the middle being subjective, based on the application.

- **Discoverability**   This is a measure of how easy or difficult it is to discover a threat. A low value of 0 would represent those threats that are very difficult or impossible to discover, and would typically require either administrative access of the actual application source code. On the high end, a value of 10 represents threats that are immediately noticeable from a client such as a web browser. Values in the middle can vary widely depending on the technologies used, how prevalent and visible they are, and how attractive the target is.

Cloud Application Architecture

Many tools and additional technologies are available that promote and ensure higher levels of security within a cloud environment. These are based on a defense-in-depth philosophy and offer layered security to expand upon traditional host or application security controls to allow for differing and additional types of security measures that go beyond what can be supported by just the application itself.

Supplemental Security Devices

While the security of the application itself is paramount on the actual system where the application resides, a layered security approach is vital to provide defense in depth. This supplements and complements the security from the system level to provide many layers of protection and monitoring of traffic and access before the application itself is reached. This not only provides far superior security and makes compromising a system far more difficult, but also removes the load for a lot of security hardening from the application, allowing for resources specifically dedicated to that purpose to handle the processing and network load. These technologies and devices can be focused on different layers and aspects of the communications, ranging from the inspection of the actual traffic and contents, to merely operating at the network level based on the source and destination of the traffic.

Firewalls

In a traditional data center, firewalls are physical network devices that are used at various strategic locations throughout the network to provide layered security. They are typically used at the border level as traffic first comes in to a data center, then at other multiple places as traffic traverses the internal network. A very common approach is to have independent firewalls between each zone of the application (presentation, application, data) as well as to have different firewalls between different types of applications or data within the network, providing a means of segregation and isolation.

Within a cloud environment, it is not possible for a cloud customer to implement physical devices on the network, so virtual (software-based) firewalls are required. Most major vendors of firewall appliances now offer virtual images of the same technologies that can be used within virtualized or cloud environments. These firewalls can be used with IaaS, PaaS, or SaaS implementations, and can be maintained either by the cloud customer, the cloud provider, or a third-party contracted specifically to do so.

Web Application Firewalls

A web application firewall (WAF) is an appliance or plug-in that parses and filters HTTP traffic from a browser or client and applies a set of rules before the traffic is allowed to proceed to the actual application server. The most common uses for a WAF are to find and block SQL injection and cross-site scripting attacks before they reach an application. Many WAF implementations are also very powerful tools that can look for patterns coming from similar hosts and report on them to administrators who can make reasoned decisions to augment or adjust rules, or even block the traffic outright. As an application is upgraded, and features or configurations change, a review of WAF rules should always be done to ensure they are still applicable and functional. With the nature of a WAF being applied to the web traffic itself, the tuning and maintenance of the WAF is an ongoing and iterative process. Because WAF rules are highly subjective and based on the application and how it operates, along with a heavy consideration given to the specific technologies of the application framework and programming languages employed, they should be created or modified with close coordination and input from the developers and those familiar with the application's functionality.

 CAUTION Although a WAF may provide very powerful tools for blocking a variety of attacks and thus significantly lower an application's vulnerability exposure, a WAF should never be used in place of proper security controls and testing of the application itself. This is especially critical if the WAF is part of the hosting provider's offerings. If security controls are relied on from a WAF and the hosting provider is changed, the application could be immediately vulnerable to a variety of threats.

XML Appliances

XML appliances come in a few forms that perform different operations and add different security and performance benefits to an application environment. Whatever the type or purpose of the specific XML appliance is, they all share some common features and functions. An XML appliance is used specifically to consume, manipulate, accelerate, or secure XML transactions and transaction data.

XML firewalls are commonly used to validate incoming XML code before it reaches the actual application. They are typically deployed in-line between the firewall and application server, and as such, traffic will pass through them before hitting the application. The XML firewall can validate data that is incoming, as well as provide granular controls to what systems and users can access the XML interfaces. While XML firewalls are typically a hardware appliance deployed in a data center, they are also available as a virtual machine appliance, and many have specific versions available for the most commonly used public cloud offerings.

XML accelerators are appliances designed to offload the processing of XML from the actual applications and systems and instead leverage optimized and dedicated appliances designed just for that purpose. In most instances, especially for a heavily used application, the use of an XML accelerator can drastically improve system performance and the possible security benefits as well having the XML processing done on a dedicated resource, separate from the actual application. This allows for the parsing and verification of inputs and values before hitting the actual application code, much in the same way that an XML firewall would.

Within a cloud environment, XML appliances are often used to broker communications between cloud services and enterprise applications. This is particularly useful in situations where enterprise applications may not be designed or equipped to handle the typical XML assertions and web services traffic that cloud applications often use, and it can provide for integration without the need for complete application changes or coding.

Cryptography

With a cloud environment being multitenant and much more open by nature, encryption is vitally important for the security of cloud-based applications, both in their implementation as well as operations. Different methods and technologies are available for data at rest versus data in transit or data in use.

With data at rest, the main methods for encryption are focused on either encrypting the whole instance, the volume storage that an application uses, or the individual file or directory. With whole instance encryption, the entire virtual machine and all its storage is encrypted. This method provides protection where the virtual machine is enabled and active or is sitting as an image. For volume encryption, either the entire drive or just parts of the drive can be protected, depending on the needs and capabilities of the application. This allows flexibility for either protecting the whole system or just select areas were sensitive code or data reside. Lastly, encryption can be done at the file or directory level, allowing very granular protection for just those files that are deemed the most sensitive or required by regulatory or government systems.

To accomplish encryption for data in transit, the most common and widely used technologies are SSL (Secure Sockets Layer), TLS (Transport Layer Security), and VPN (Virtual Private Network). SSL has been used extensively for many years, both for internal communications between application components as well as between the user's browser and the application itself. However, at this point much of SSL is being phased out or not permitted under regulatory requirements due to the compromise of the ciphers it uses or just because they are not as secure as required to meet modern threats. TLS has widely replaced SSL for encryption of network traffic and is required under many regulatory models. TLS ensures that communication is secured and remains confidential; it also ensures the integrity of the data being transmitted. With VPN technologies, a secure network tunnel is created from the user's system, over the public Internet, and connected to a secure private environment. This allows all communications into the private network to be secured while they traverse insecure systems, and is widely used to establish a presence on a private network from the outside, allowing the user to operate as if they were physically present at a corporate location and on the internal network.

Sandboxing

Sandboxing is the segregation and isolation of information or processes from others within the same system or application, typically for security concerns. Sandboxing typically is used for data isolation, such as keeping different communities and populations of users isolated from other similar data. The need for sandboxing can be due to internal reasons, such as policies, or come from external sources, such as regulatory or legal requirements. A good example of this would be a university keeping student data or affiliate data isolated and separate from faculty/staff or affiliate data. In this example, the drivers for segregation could serve system purposes, as each population has different needs for most uses, and the segregation makes access control easier to operate and control. However, segregation also helps fulfill privacy and regulatory requirements for the protection of student and academic data that go above and beyond those requirements for the protection of faculty/staff data.

Another use of sandboxing involves the testing of new code and application deployments, where a system maintainer or data owner would not want those systems accessible to production systems and would want to minimize the risk of any crossover. Within a cloud environment, where physical network separation is not possible, sandboxing is an even more important concept.

Application Virtualization

Application virtualization is a software implementation that allows applications and programs to run in an isolated environment, rather than directly interacting with the operating system. This works much in the same way as how a Type 2 hypervisor runs on top of an operating system; in the case of application virtualization, however, it is just the application itself running in a protected and segregated space. The application will appear to be running directly on top of the operating system, but depending on the software used for the application virtualization, it can be isolated to various degrees.

A crucial benefit of application virtualization is the ability to test an application on a system or environment while maintaining segregation from other applications. This is particularly important within a cloud environment to allow for the testing of new applications, code, or features in a manner that does not put at risk other applications within the same environment. The developers or system maintainers can then fully test and validate applications or upgrades on the same infrastructure or platform as their full systems run, but not put at risk their other systems or data. Application virtualization can also, in some cases, allow applications to run on an operating system that they were not designed for or implemented on, such as running Windows programs within a Linux operating system, or vice versa. This give developers additional flexibility to test their applications or code in a manner that is more agnostic of the underlying platform. Another big advantage of application virtualization is the far fewer resources and less time it takes to set up versus bringing online and configuring additional virtual machines for testing when needed.

However, not all applications are suitable for application virtualization. Anything that requires direct access to underlying system drivers or hardware will not work within a virtualized environment—the same issues with any applications that must use shared memory space to operate, such as older 16-bit applications. The testing of any security-related applications that require tight integration with operating systems, such as antivirus or other scanning software, will often not work in an application virtualized environment. A final complication can arise from properly maintaining all the various licenses required with an application virtualized environment, where both the host system and any virtualized applications must have proper licensing in place at all times.

 NOTE You may face considerable challenges trying to implement many traditional data center methodologies and technologies in a cloud environment. For example, an IPS (intrusion protection system) in a traditional data center will easily work inline with network flows, and even virtualized IPS appliances will do the same. However, this may make elasticity a big challenge to implement, and host-based solutions, rather than network-based solutions, may become necessary. This is just one example, but it showcases how changes in approach and methodology may be necessary to take full advantage of all cloud services and benefits.

Identity and Access Management (IAM) Solutions

Identity and access management is an aspect of security that ensures and enables the right individuals to access the right systems and data, at the right times, and under the right circumstances. Several factors and components make up an overall IAM solution.

Federated Identity

While most are familiar with how access and identity systems work within an application or organization, many are not familiar with federated identity systems. A big difference between a typical identity system and a federated one is that federated identity systems allow trust access and verification across multiple organizations.

In a federated system, each organization maintains its own identity and verification systems that are unique and separate from the other organizations, and only contain their population of users and information. In order for a federated identity process to work, all member organizations must each adhere to a common set of principles and policies. These typically are policies that involve how users have their identity verified to become part of the organization's system on the onset, but also security and hardening requirements and standards for their systems. With all member organizations adhering to common policies and standards, each member can have confidence in their systems and who they grant access to.

 NOTE A major federated identity system used in the academic and research world, and one that I worked on extensively in my previous job, is known as Shibboleth, which can be found at https://shibboleth.net/. It is an open source system that would serve as a good example for further learning about these types of systems. It also has a large library of pluggable authentication modules that can work with many common LDAP and authentication schemes.

With any federated identity system there has to be an accepted standard and means for the systems to communicate with each other. This would entail the applications that are granting federated access to be able to communicate with the identity providers of each member organization in a seamless and universal manner. To accomplish this, there are a few common and widespread standards that most systems use, with the Security Assertion Markup Language (SAML) being the most prevalent, but some previously mentioned technologies such as OAuth, OpenID, and WS-Federation are also used.

SAML

SAML 2.0 is the latest standard put out by the nonprofit OASIS consortium and their Security Services Technical Committee, and can be found at https://www.oasis-open.org/standards#samlv2.0. SAML is XML based, and it is used to exchange information used in the authentication and authorization processes between different parties. Specifically, it is used for information exchange between identity providers and service providers, and it contains within the XML block the required information that each system needs or provides.

The 2.0 standard was adopted in 2005 and provides a standard framework for the XML assertions and standardized naming conventions for its various elements. In a federated system, when an entity authenticates through an identity provider, it sends a SAML assertion to the service provider containing all the information that the service provider requires to determine the identity, level of access warranted, or any other information or attributes about the entity.

OAuth

OAuth was established originally in 2006 and is published in RFC 6749, found at http:// tools.ietf.org/html/rfc6749. The following is from the official RFC abstract:

> The OAuth 2.0 authorization framework enables a third-party application to obtain limited access to an HTTP service, either on behalf of a resource owner by orchestrating an approval interaction between the resource owner and the HTTP service, or by allowing the third-party application to obtain access on its own behalf.

OpenID

OpenID is an authentication protocol based on OAuth 2.0 specifications. It is designed to provide developers with an easy and flexible mechanism to support authentication across organizations and utilize external identity providers, alleviating the need to maintain their own password stores and systems. Developers can leverage OpenID as an open and free authentication mechanism and tie it into their code and applications, without being dependent on a proprietary or inflexible system. With a browser tie-in for authentication, OpenID provides web-based applications an authentication mechanism that is not dependent on the particular clients or devices that are used to access it. Information about OpenID and official specifications can be found at the OpenID website, http:// openid.net/.

WS-Federation

WS-Federation is an extension to the WS-Security standards, also published by OASIS. The following is from the official abstract of the WS-Federation 1.2 Specification, found at http://docs.oasis-open.org/wsfed/federation/v1.2/os/ws-federation-1.2-spec-os.html:

> This specification defines mechanisms to allow different security realms to federate, such that authorized access to resources managed in one realm can be provided to security principals whose identities and attributes are managed in other realms. This includes mechanisms for brokering of identity, attribute, authentication and authorization assertions between realms, and privacy of federated claims.

> By using the XML, SOAP and WSDL extensibility models, the WS-* specifications are designed to be composed with each other to provide a rich Web services environment. WS-Federation by itself does not provide a complete security solution for Web services. WS-Federation is a building block that is used in conjunction with other Web service, transport, and application-specific protocols to accommodate a wide variety of security models.

Identity Providers

In a federated system, two main components serve as its core. The first is the identity provider (IdP). The role of the identity provider is to hold authentication mechanisms for its users to prove their identity to the system to acceptable level of certainty. Once the user has successfully authenticated, the IdP can then assert to other systems, service providers, or relying parties the identity of the entity, thus proving authentication. The IdP can either return just a simple authentication success or an assertion containing a set of information about the entity, which can then in turn be used to process authorization and access within the system.

On the other side is the service provider or relying party. The relying party (RP) takes the assertion provided by the IdP and uses it to make a determination whether to grant the entity to a secure application, and, if so, what level and type of access is granted. The IdP and RP work together in an integral manner to facilitate authentication and authorization for a secure web-based application.

Single Sign-On

Single sign-on allows an entity to authenticate one time, at a centralized location that contains their information and authentication credentials, and then use tokens from that system to access other independent systems. This allows systems and applications to not have local credentials and maintain their own authentication systems, but rather to leverage centralized systems that are dedicated and secured for that sole purpose, allowing for more attention and hardened security controls to be applied. Once the entity has been properly authenticated, each system then uses opaque tokens to allow authorization, rather than passing over the network sensitive information or passwords. Within a federated system, this also is the mechanism by which identity providers pass tokens to relying parties to allow access to their systems with the minimal amount of information required while protecting the rest of the entity's identity or sensitive information and privacy.

Multifactor Authentication

Multifactor authentication, as its main principle, extends traditional authentication models beyond the system username and password combination, to require additional factors and steps to provide for more protection and assurance as to the entity's identity and their specific sensitive information.

With a traditional authentication system, and entity provides a username and password combination to prove their identity and uniqueness. While this system provides a basic level of security and assurance, it also greatly opens the possibilities of compromise, as both pieces of information can be easily obtained or possibly guessed based on information about the user, and once possessed can be easily used by a malicious actor until either changed or detected. In particular, many people will use the same username, or use their e-mail address as their username with systems where this is allowed, thus giving a malicious actor immediate knowledge of half of the information needed to authenticate. Also, out of habit, people use the same password for many different systems, opening up a grave possibility where a compromise of one system with lower security could ultimately lead to the compromise of a more secure system for which the individual happens to use the same password.

With multifactor authentication systems, the traditional username and password scheme is expanded to include a second factor that is not simply a piece of knowledge that a malicious actor could possibly obtain or compromise. A multifactor system combines at least two different requirements, the first of which is typically a password, but doesn't need to be. Here are the three main components, of which at least two different components are required:

- **Something the user knows**   This component is almost exclusively a password or a protected piece of information that in effect serves the same purpose as a password.
- **Something the user possesses**   This component is something that is physical possessed by the individual. This could be a USB thumb drive, an RFID chip card, an access card with a magnetic stripe, an RSA token with a changing access code, a text message code sent to the user's mobile device, or anything else along the same lines.
- **Something the user is**   This component uses biometrics, such as retina scans, palm prints, fingerprints, and so on.

Exercise

You have been hired as a new cloud security manager for a financial services firm that is looking to move its operations from a traditional data center to a cloud environment. The firm is in the very initial stages and has not selected a cloud provider or a cloud hosting model yet, and is just starting to analyze its systems for the move.

1. What are your main concerns with moving to a cloud environment?
2. What cloud hosting models would be most appropriate for a financial system?
3. What considerations need to be analyzed before such a move can be undertaken?
4. How will you educate management as to the likeliness of application changes needed before such a move can be done?

Chapter Review

Much attention has previously been devoted to the security of a system, and the data associated with it, within a cloud environment. Cloud application security, on the other hand, is focused on the knowledge, expertise, and training required to prepare developers and staff for deploying applications and services to a cloud environment. Not all systems are appropriate for a cloud, and even those that are may need substantial changes and updates before such a move is possible. All cloud environments come with their own set of APIs unique to their system, and the API sets offered may dictate which cloud providers and hosting models are appropriate for a specific application, keeping in mind that reliance on them may limit portability in the future. The Cloud Security Professional needs to fully understand the process of evaluating cloud providers and technologies and determining which are appropriate for a specific organization or application. A strong understanding of both the communication methods and authentication systems used within a cloud environment is also vital, as they are quite different from those typically used within an isolated traditional data center.

Questions

1. What are the two components to a federated identity system?

   A. Service provider and relying party

   B. LDAP and web server

   C. Identity provider and relying party

   D. Identity provider and password store

2. Which of the following security devices would enable a system to filter out attacks such as SQL injection before they reach the application servers?

   A. Firewall

   B. XML accelerator

   C. Sandbox

   D. WAF

3. Which type of testing would *NOT* be performed against an application that does not contain self-protection capabilities?

   A. RASP

   B. Pen

   C. SAST

   D. DAST

4. Which of the following could *NOT* be used in a multifactor authentication system along with a password?

   A. RSA token

   B. Retina scan

   C. Challenge-response with personal questions

   D. Fingerprint

5. Which of the following would be the *MOST* important reason to have the development and production systems in the same cloud environment?

   A. APIs

   B. Operating systems

   C. Programming libraries

   D. Programming languages

6. Which is the most commonly used assertion method with federated identity systems?

   A. OAuth

   B. SAML

   C. OpenID

   D. WS

7. Which of the following is *NOT* part of the OWASP Top 10 list?

   A. Cross-site request forgery

   B. Weak password requirements

   C. Injection

   D. Cross-site scripting

8. With a single sign-on system, what is passed between systems to verify the user's authentication?

   A. Tokens

   B. Masks

   C. Certificates

   D. Credentials

9. Which of the following is the only data format supported by SOAP?

   A. YAML

   B. SAML

   C. JSON

   D. XML

10. If you are running application security tests against a system where you have knowledge and access to the code, which type of test are you running?

   A. Dynamic

   B. Static

   C. Hybrid

   D. Open

11. What does the *S* in the STRIDE model refer to?

   A. Spoofing

   B. Security

   C. Sensitive

   D. SAML

12. Who would *NOT* be included for the initial requirements gathering for a software development project?

   A. Management

   B. Users

   C. Developers

   D. Security

Questions and Answers

1. What are the two components to a federated identity system?

   A. Service provider and relying party

   B. LDAP and web server

   C. Identity provider and relying party

   D. Identity provider and password store

   C. The identity provider and relying party are the two components of a federated identity system, with the identity provider handling authentication and providing information about the user, and the relying party accepting the authentication token and then granting access to some or all parts of an application. The other answers offer various components that are likely included with the implementation of the identity provider or relying party.

2. Which of the following security devices would enable a system to filter out attacks such as SQL injection before they reach the application servers?

   A. Firewall

   B. XML accelerator

   C. Sandbox

   D. WAF

   D. A WAF (web application firewall) sits in front of an application and has the capability to analyze and apply policies to incoming traffic and transactions based on their content. A very common use for a WAF is to detect and block common security threats such as injection attacks or cross-site scripting attacks. A firewall is used to deny or allow network traffic based solely on the source, destination, and port of the packets, and does not perform analysis of the packets or have the ability to inspect the packets for content. An XML accelerator performs XML processing before the data reaches an application server to offload the processing from the actual application. A sandbox is merely a segregated and isolated system configuration, and does not relate to network traffic or an analysis of it at all.

3. Which type of testing would *NOT* be performed against an application that does not contain self-protection capabilities?

   A. RASP

   B. Pen

   C. SAST

   D. DAST

> **A.** Runtime application self-protection (RASP) would only be performed against systems that contain self-protection capabilities. These systems have the ability to tune and refocus their security protections and controls based upon the actual attacks and methods being used against them in real time. Pen (penetration) testing, static application security testing (SAST), and dynamic application security testing (DAST) are all tests against any applications and do not pertain to self-protection capabilities at all.

4. Which of the following could *NOT* be used in a multifactor authentication system along with a password?

   A. RSA token

   B. Retina scan

   C. Challenge-response with personal questions

   D. Fingerprint

> **C.** A personal response challenge falls under the same category as a password, which is something the user knows, so it could not be used as part of a multifactor authentication system if the password was the other factor. The RSA token could be used along with a password as it constitutes something that is in possession of the user rather than something known. A retina scan or fingerprint also could be used as they both constitute biometric data.

5. Which of the following would be the *MOST* important reason to have the development and production systems in the same cloud environment?

   A. APIs

   B. Operating systems

   C. Programming libraries

   D. Programming languages

> **A.** APIs can differ greatly between cloud providers and, depending on how the applications are built or implemented, may make it difficult to seamlessly move from one environment to another. Also, unless there is a specific reason not to use the same cloud environment for development and production, separating them out only adds complexity and potential problems. The other choices, operating

systems, programming libraries, and programming languages, are all universal toolsets that would easily be available from different cloud providers as well.

6. Which is the most commonly used assertion method with federated identity systems?

   A. OAuth

   B. SAML

   C. OpenID

   D. WS

   B. SAML is the most commonly and widely used method for assertions within federated identity systems. WS is another protocol that was developed by a group of companies for use within their own projects, but it is not as widely or openly used as SAML. OpenID and OAuth are two single sign-on methods that are used with federated identity systems, but are not as widely used protocols within federated systems as SAML is.

7. Which of the following is *NOT* part of the OWASP Top 10 list?

   A. Cross-site request forgery

   B. Weak password requirements

   C. Injection

   D. Cross-site scripting

   B. Weak password requirements are not part of the OWASP Top 10. There is not a specific item in regard to password policies or requirements, but it would fall under some of the other topics as a mitigating factor for general security policies. The other choices, cross-site request forgery, injection, and cross-site scripting, are specific threats listed.

8. With a single sign-on system, what is passed between systems to verify the user's authentication?

   A. Tokens

   B. Masks

   C. Certificates

   D. Credentials

   A. Tokens are passed between systems, which enables the relying parties or service providers to verify back to the identity provider that a user has authenticated, as well as to obtain encoded information about the user to determine specific authorizations and roles within the application. Credentials are never passed with a federated system, as they are passed solely between the user and the identity provider, with only the tokens being used after that. Certificates are used for the encrypted connections in general, but are not passed as part of the primary functions of the system, and masks do not come into play at all with a federated identity system.

9. Which of the following is the only data format supported by SOAP?

   A. YAML

   B. SAML

   C. JSON

   D. XML

   D. SOAP only supports XML for data transfer and encoding. SAML is used within federated identity systems, while JSON is used for data exchange between applications, but not as part of SOAP. YAML is a data encoding protocol for use with scripting languages such as Perl and Python.

10. If you are running application security tests against a system where you have knowledge and access to the code, which type of test are you running?

    A. Dynamic

    B. Static

    C. Hybrid

    D. Open

    B. Static tests are done with knowledge of the system and security configurations, typically with the source code as well. This enables testers to perform on an offline system comprehensive analyses (such as scans of source code and evaluation of the coding and security mechanisms in place) that would not be possible from external tests without such knowledge. Tests can be directed to the specific protocols and technologies used, rather than applying general tests or having to discover what is being used. On the other end of the spectrum, dynamic testing is done without knowledge of the systems or code, and the testers must use tools and methods to discover anything about the environment to use with security evaluations. Open and hybrid are not terms that apply here at all.

11. What does the *S* in the STRIDE model refer to?

  A. Spoofing

  B. Security

  C. Sensitive

  D. SAML

> **A.** The *S* in STRIDE stands for "spoofing identity." This involves a user being able to assume the identity of, or make a system believe they are, another user and thus be able to use their level of authorization to access functions or data, typically at a higher level than they are authorized for themselves. The other answers are incorrect.

12. Who would *NOT* be included for the initial requirements gathering for a software development project?

  A. Management

  B. Users

  C. Developers

  D. Security

> **C.** Developers would not be part of requirements gathering, as their role does not begin until the project and scope are defined and ready for them to translate the design requirements and technology decisions into executable code. Management, users, and security staffers are crucial to design decisions and project requirements at all stages.

Operations

This chapter covers the following topics in Domain 5:
- The planning and design processes for a cloud data center
- How to implement, run, and manage both the physical and logical aspects of a data center
- How to secure and harden servers, networks, and storage systems
- How to develop and implement baselines
- How to conduct risk assessments of cloud systems
- ITIL service components to manage and comply with regulations
- How to secure and collect digital evidence from a cloud environment

The operations domain is focused on how to plan, design, run, manage, and operate both the logical and physical components of a cloud data center. We focus on the key components of each layer, including servers, network devices, and storage systems, as well as what makes them unique to a cloud data center versus a traditional data center. We also investigate the risk assessment process for a system and how it relates to cloud systems, as well as the collection of forensic evidence, along with the unique challenges and considerations that a cloud environment entails.

Support the Planning Process for the Data Center Design

While a traditional data center and a cloud data center share many similarities, there are many aspects and realities of cloud computing and the way cloud services are used and deployed that will drive considerations for data center design as well. Whereas a traditional data center design often focuses on the infrastructure to support cages and whatever hardware configurations customers will ultimately opt to deploy, a cloud data center must take into account the types of cloud models that will be offered, the potential targeted customers for the cloud environment, regulatory controls, and jurisdictions. A cloud provider will need to decide from the early planning stages which types of regulatory requirements or types of data classification they will focus on or be willing to host, as those decisions will have an impact on many of the physical and logical designs of their data centers.

Logical Design

The logical design area is what contains the most profound differences between a traditional data center and a cloud data center. Many of the key aspects of cloud computing will drive key data center design decisions, both with the design of the actual center as well as the location of it.

Virtualization

With virtualization being the key driver and technology base of a cloud environment, its use and specific security requirements are a primary concern when designing and building a cloud data center. The management plane is the most important component for security concerns with virtualization because a compromise of it can lead to a compromise of all hypervisors and hosted systems. Therefore, considerations of the use of secure communications, network separation, and isolation in a physical sense for the management plane are very important.

Another top consideration for virtualization at the design stage is how the system is going to handle storage concerns, specifically in regard to virtual machine images, meaning the actual storage of large volumes of data associated with these images as well as the security within the storage. Because virtual images are susceptible to attack regardless of whether they are running, the security of the system housing them and the manner in which it can be accessed are vitally important.

Also, business continuity and disaster recovery, including backup systems, have to be looked at differently than in a traditional data center and hardware model. Virtualized systems back up and replicate data and system configurations in different manners than standard server environments, and consideration of appropriate and specific concerns related to them is vital from the onset of any data center planning process.

Multitenancy

A key aspect of cloud computing is the capability to host many different tenants within a cloud environment, but that also raises security concerns because there will not be the physical separation of networks and infrastructure components that a traditional data center would afford. With physical separation not possible within a cloud environment, the cloud customer and cloud provider must rely on and leverage logical network separation for system and application isolation and segregation. While the physical network will be homogenous within a cloud environment, the use of virtual networks and logical networks allows the cloud provider to separate and isolate individual systems and applications, with the end result being only seeing one's own assets on the network and not being aware of or able to see other systems or network traffic. This logical network separation allows user and customer data to remain isolated and protected within a cloud environment, and minimize any chance of accidental exposure or modification.

Access Control

From a logical perspective, there are a few areas of access control that are very important to consider in regard to data center design. With a cloud environment, you have the actual virtual machines to consider, but also the management plane and hypervisor tiers.

This sets a cloud data center apart from a traditional data center because you are not planning for just access to physical machines, but also have to consider layers that have supervisory and administrative control over other systems. Planning for early states to keep separation from the various layers, allowing for the hypervisor and management plane layers to be completely shielded from systems and customer access, will promote stronger security controls. Additionally, planning for strong authentication and authorization controls, including multifactor authentication and strong verification requirements, to be implemented at the very least for administrative access will ensure stronger security. Along with strong access control designs, planning for strong logging, monitoring, and auditing of access control systems and mechanisms from the earliest stages of design is imperative from a security standpoint.

APIs

Within a cloud environment, the essential functions of applications and the management of the entire cloud infrastructure are based on APIs. The APIs must be implemented in a secure manner, but also be scalable and highly accessible for effective leveraging and dependency. This includes the use of appropriate network restrictions for accessing APIs, where possible or appropriate, as well as the use of SSL or TLS for API communications. Apart from the actual security of API access and communications, it is essential for the Cloud Security Professional to ensure that API calls are being appropriately logged with sufficient detail to audit security and appropriate use. These logs for API calls may also carry with them regulatory requirements for both the level of log detail and the required retention periods.

Physical Design

Much like systems and servers, data centers are made up of a common set of components and equipment, but all are different based on their needs, purposes, and goals, as set forth by the organizations building and maintaining the data centers. Many data centers will look and function very similar to others, but each is unique with its own issues and concerns.

Location

Location is the first primary physical consideration for a data center, and it applies to multiple different concerns. A major concern with location in regard to a cloud data center is the jurisdiction where it is located, including the applicable laws and regulations under that jurisdiction. The jurisdictional requirements could ultimately drive a lot of design considerations as well, especially in regard to physical security requirements for data protection and privacy, as well as retention and backup requirements. This will directly impact the needed resources for compliance, the space required, as well as environmental needs.

The physical location of a data center also drives many design requirements based on the realities of threats posed from the physical environment. Is the data center in a location that is susceptible to flooding, earthquakes, tornadoes, or hurricanes? Many locations have the threat of some of these possible disasters, which all directly impact many of the physical designs and protection requirements of the data center in different ways. While these natural disaster possibilities are never ideal for a data center location, it is very difficult to ever find a possible location that has very minimal risk, so the focus is on building and designing data centers to handle location realities, especially as other location consideration and organizational goals may dictate the necessity or desirability of such a location. The probability of each natural disaster will influence the data center design as well as the urgency and importance of business continuity and disaster recovery planning and testing. Many technologies can be employed to minimize or mitigate threats from natural disasters, such as dikes, reinforced walls, and vibration control.

Data centers need enormous environmental and utility resources as well. These needs include access to electrical grids that can handle the demands of a data center, access to water supplies, physical access for personnel, and access to telecommunications networks and the bandwidth that a data center requires. Just as important as having access to these crucial physical resources is having redundant resources. Data centers will ideally want duplicate connections and availability for each of these components, but especially for electrical and networking because they are core to the operations of the data center. With cooling as a major concern in any data center, access to a secure and accessible source of water is also imperative.

In regard to physical access, if a data center is located in a manner such that an incident can block the single point of access, it will run into major problems should that situation arise and critical staff members are not able to gain access to the data center. There is a trade-off with a single entry point, though. Although the single entry point can cause problems if it is blocked in any way, it also makes security easier because only one point of access needs to be secured and monitored. As with any physical attributes of a location, there are positives and negatives.

With any data center, physical security is also a paramount concern. Data centers should follow best practices for physical security and access. This means that perimeter security such as fences, gates, walls, and so on, are all deployed in a layered approach with monitoring capabilities as well. The location of a data center can significantly impact the types and layering of physical security available. If the data center is located in an open area, it is much easier to implement multiple layers of physical security in a perimeter, as well as the monitoring between them necessary. On the opposite side, if a data center is located in an urban area, it may be impossible to prevent vehicles and people from getting close to the building, making it susceptible to possible attacks, such as from explosives. A much higher probability of threat in an urban area is a fire in an adjacent building becoming a threat to the data center building.

Buy or Build?

When it comes to an organization requiring a new data center, the two main options available are to build a new structure or to buy an already existing one. For the purposes of our discussion, we will consider buying and leasing to fall under the same category, whether it pertains to a set amount of space or an entire data center. Each option has its own distinct advantages and disadvantages to an organization. Regardless of which option is ultimately chosen by the stakeholders and management, the requirements for security, privacy, regulatory adherence, and technological capabilities are the same.

Building a data center will give an organization the most input and control over all aspects of its setup, security mechanisms, location, and all other physical aspects, within the limitations of regulatory requirements or the organization's available budget. The organization can fully control the location, size, and features, all driven by their exact intended use and purpose for the data center. They can also ensure from the earliest stages of design that the data center will be fully compliant with all applicable regulatory requirements to which they are subject. The organization can fully involve all stakeholders, management, operations staff, and security staff in the data center design from the earliest stages of conception and planning. Although there are a lot of very strong positives involved with building a new data center and having full control over all aspects and planning, there are some very strong negatives as well. The most prominent of these is the extraordinary costs associated with building a new data center, but also the time everything takes, from conception through planning and construction, can be significant, especially in the rapidly changing and evolving IT world.

Buying or leasing space in a data center is the much quicker and easier option for an organization because it allows them to avoid the enormous initial investment in both time and money to plan and build a data center. The main drawback to buying or leasing space in a data center is the lack of control over the design and features that it will have. From a security perspective, buying or leasing space in a data center brings challenges with compliance for regulatory requirements. The focus on security requirements with buying or leasing space will shift to contractual and SLA enforcement for compliance. While this does pose an additional challenge, the difficulty with compliance will largely rest with the specific regulatory requirements pertinent to the hosted applications and data, and how prevalent they are throughout the industry. Many commercial data centers that lease or sell space have built their data centers to confirm compliance with the major regulatory requirements such as Payment Card Industry Data Security Standard (PCI DSS). If a data center has been built to specifications required by regulations, this will effectively serve as a certification of the underlying data center infrastructure and configurations, and leave the focus for compliance on the organization for their specific hardware and software implementations within the data center.

NOTE   In some cases, an organization can opt to buy or lease space in a data center where they are involved from the early planning stages as a key partner or stakeholder. In this instance, the organization would be acting in a community-type participation, likely with other similar organizations. This allows more input and involvement in the design, but also likely requires more commitment in time and money from the organization as well.

Design Standards

Apart from regulatory requirements that may end up dictating many design aspects of a data center, there are also industry design standards that cover the physical design, layout, and operational setups. Many standards are common throughout the world and cover specific aspects of physical design and data centers specifically. Although this is by no means an exhaustive or comprehensive list of data center design standards, here are a few of the most common:

- **BICSI (Building Industry Consulting Service International)**   BICSI issues certifications in the area of complex cabling for data systems as well as develops standards for them. Created in 1977, BICSI has members in over 100 countries. The most prominent of the BICSI standards is ANSI/BICSI 002-2014: Data Center Design and Implementation Best Practices. This standard is focused on cabling design and setups, and also includes specifications on power, energy efficiency, and hot/cold aisle setups. BICSI information can be found at https://www.bicsi.org/.

- **IDCA (International Datacenter Authority)**   IDCA has established the Infinity Paradigm, which is intended to be a comprehensive data center design and operations framework. It covers all aspects of data enter design, including location, cabling, utilities, security, connectivity, and even aspects such as lighting and signage. Apart from the actual physical design and components, the framework also covers many aspects of data center operations, such as storage, backup, recovering, mirroring, resiliency, monitoring, and network and security operations centers. A major focus of the Infinity Paradigm is also a shift away from many models that rely on tiered architecture for data centers, where each successive tier increases redundancy, and instead focusing on a paradigm where data centers are approached at a macro level, without a specific and isolated focus on certain aspects to achieve tier status. The IDCA Infinity Paradigm can be found at https://www.idc-a.org/infinity-paradigm.

- **NFPA (National Fire Protection Association)**   The NFPA publishes a large collection of standards regarding fire protection for almost any type of facility—from data centers to industrial companies, offices, vehicles, and more. Even for those without specific standards focused on them, the NFPA puts out general fire safety and design standards that can be applied. There are a few specific standards of note in regard to IT facilities and data center design. NFPA 75 and 76 are of particular importance for data center design. These two standards are titled "Standard for the Fire Protection of Information Technology Equipment" and "Standard for the Fire Protection of Telecommunications Facilities," respectively. Another standard of importance to data center design is NFPA 70, titled "National Electrical Code," which covers the overall electrical systems in a data center and crucial items such as emergency methods for immediately cutting electrical power, especially in a facility that has enormous electrical needs and load at all times. The NFPA information and standards can be found at www.nfpa.org/.

- **Uptime Institute**   The Uptime Institute publishes the most commonly used and widely known standard on data center tiers and topologies. It is based on a series of four tiers, with each progressive increase in number representing more stringent, reliable, and redundant systems for security, connectivity, fault tolerance, redundancy, and cooling. The standard also incorporates compliance tests to ensure adherence to the requirements of each tier and a means for data center owners or operators to measure and evaluate their configurations and designs. The Uptime Institute's tiered topology standard can be found at https://uptimeinstitute.com/research-publications/asset/tier-standard-topology.

NOTE   Due to the popularity and prevalence of the Uptime Institute's tiered methodology, it would be wise for the Cloud Security Professional to be familiar with it and its most important aspects. Overall, the principles of this methodology are largely "assumed" knowledge within the IT industry in regard to data center design and operations management.

Environmental Design

All data centers must account for key environmental considerations, including power, cooling, heating, ventilation, and the redundancy of these systems as well as network connectivity.

For optimal temperature and humidity levels in a data center, the following guidelines are commonly used, as established by ASHRAE (American Society of Heating, Refrigeration, and Air Conditioning Engineers):

- **Temperature**   64.4–80.6 degrees F (18–27 degrees C)
- **Humidity**   40–60 percent relative humidity

EXAM TIP   Make sure to memorize the values for temperature and humidity. These are often included as memorization-type questions on certification exams and are easy correct answers.

All data centers generate enormous amounts of heat from all the running electronic equipment, so adequate and redundant cooling is absolutely essential for any data center. This also represents one of the largest costs to a data center. The amount of energy and cooling required relates directly to the number of physical systems deployed in the data center, as well as whether optimal designs are used for air flow. A very common practice is to alternate rows of physical racks in order to have hot and cold rows for optimal airflow, and to have one row of racks pushing hot air directly into another row. Cooling systems are also highly dependent on the physical location of the data center and the environment around it; being in a warmer climate is going to require more extensive cooling inside the data center. To protect the physical assets of the data center, it is also imperative to have redundancy in both the cooling system and the power supplying it. With the heat that computing resources give off, especially in a dense setting like a data center, failed cooling will very quickly cause a shutdown.

Implement and Build the Physical Infrastructure for the Cloud Environment

The physical infrastructure for a cloud revolves around the key components of networks, servers, and storage. All these components need to undergo careful planning to work together with the key aspects of a cloud compared to a traditional data center, and done so with an eye toward security models and cloud considerations.

Secure Configuration of Hardware-Specific Requirements

While a cloud data center will have specific requirements that are unique to the cloud environment, the actual securing of hardware and systems is very similar to that of a traditional data center. Hardware and systems, much like software and applications, can carry an enormous number of configuration possibilities and requirements, due to the large numbers of possible combinations of operating systems and hardware, as well as the specific operating systems that run on appliances and hypervisor systems.

BIOS Settings

As with any physical hardware, virtualization hosts and trusted platform modules (TPMs) have BIOS settings that govern specific hardware configurations and security technologies to prevent access to them for the purpose of manipulation. Within a cloud environment, it is imperative that the cloud provider highly restrict and limit any access to BIOS-level systems, as well as put in place strong security measures to prevent them from both being accessed and altered, unless done by very limited privileged personnel and governed as part of the change management process. Each vendor will have specific methods and approaches for securing the BIOS of the physical assets, and the Cloud Security Professional should consult with the vendor documentation for best practices both on the physical device itself and any additional security layers that can be applied to it from the physical environment as a whole.

Network Devices

Within a cloud environment, both physical and virtual network devices play vital roles. The use of virtual network devices adds a layer of complexity above and beyond a traditional data center model. Although physical and virtual network devices may perform similar operations, they have very different considerations when it comes to security, potential problems, and their impact on a data center.

Physical Networks   Physical networks allow for total isolation of a system from other systems, as the actual physical cabling and switch ports are separate and isolated. Each server has a physical cable that is unique to itself and that goes to a unique port on the network switch; servers do not share cables or switch ports. While this allows for total isolation of network traffic and bandwidth, it also allows for the isolation of any potential hardware problems. If any cable or switch port goes bad from a hardware perspective, the impact is isolated to the host using those resources. Physical networking components also tend to offer very robust logging and forensic capabilities that allow complete introspection for all traffic and packets that traverse through them.

Virtual Networks   Virtual networking equipment attempts to replicate the capabilities and isolation of physical networking gear, but doing so as a virtual appliance and working within a virtualized system such as a cloud. The major difference between physical and virtual networking gear is the physical isolation that is afforded by cabling and switch ports. With a physical network, if a cable or a switch port goes bad, a single host or piece of gear is impacted by the outage. Even if the fix requires the replacement of an entire switch, that can be planned and scheduled to minimize downtime, and the affected host can be moved to a different switch or cabling in the interim period until a replacement or fix can be implemented. With a virtual network appliance, many hosts are tied to the same virtual switch, and because the hardware is all shared between them, a problem with a virtual network switch will impact all the hosts served by it. Also, because a virtual switch is running under a hypervisor, it creates additional load and consumes resources that are split among other hosts on the same system, whereas a physical network switch would not impact any hosts connected to it in regard to system resources and load. Also, the more virtual machines that are served by a virtual host, the more resources it will consume.

Servers

Securing servers overall involves the same process and principles, whether it's a physical server in a traditional data center or a virtual machine running within a cloud environment.

Servers must be constructed on a secure build methodology and secured using initial configurations that meet best practices and vendor recommendations. The build process should be incorporate the recommendations of operating system vendors as well as the requirements from regulatory bodies and organizational policies. Although the vendor of the operating system will typically issue recommendations for best practices and build requirements, many regulatory policies will extend these recommendations and require much more stringent configurations. This can also be largely dependent on the classification of data contained within the system. The more sensitive the data, the more stringent the initial configurations from regulatory requirements and organizational policy will be.

Beyond the actual build image used and the initial security configurations of a host, additional steps must be taken to harden and lock down the host. Hardening involves the removal of all nonessential services, software packages, protocols, configurations, and utilities from a host. Each of these components adds both complexity and potential attack vectors. By removing all nonessential components, you decrease the number of potential avenues for a successful attack, and allow both system monitoring and the systems support personnel to focus on just the core components and functions of the host.

TIP Many times system staff will want to simply disable components of a system that are nonessential rather than actually removing them completely from a system. Although this will serve to protect a system to a greater degree than if these components were left operational, it also leaves a system more at risk than totally removing them would. If these components are left in place, the possibility exists that they will be inadvertently started or made operational at a later date by systems staff or those with administrative access to a system. In this scenario, because the systems are assumed to not be using these components, additional security measures, such as monitoring, may not be enabled, thus leaving a system both increasingly vulnerable and without oversight of any potential compromises.

Once all nonessential components have been removed from the host, the components left must be locked down and restricted as much as possible to further reduce the number of possible avenues of exploit and vulnerabilities. Role-based access should be employed to ensure that only those users with appropriate need have access to a system, and once they do have access, that they are only allowed the minimal level needed to do their jobs. Servers should be configured to only allow secure access methods to ensure network sniffing cannot expose credentials or sensitive information, and network access should be restricted to only allow those appropriate networks, hosts, or protocols to reach a server. By restricting access at the network level, you can minimize the possible exposure to risks and threats to a specific set of networks or hosts where additional monitoring can be employed, rather than opening broad network access where potential threats could come from numerous possible origins. At no time should administrative or privileged access be directly allowed on a server from an external source, nor should the use of shared credentials or access be allowed where it is not possible to trace back the actual account activities to an individual.

Even when a server is appropriately built, configured, and hardened to minimize risks, those efforts are only valid at the specific time in which they are implemented or have successfully passed scanning requirements. Operating systems and software implementations are constantly responding to evolving threats and exploits, and the process of enhancements and updates is continual. Therefore, a strong patching and oversight program is essential to the ongoing security of a server. Systems staff should be actively and continually monitoring patches and exploit announcements from vendors to evaluate the risk and impact of each to their servers and the unique configuration circumstances of their implementations. Those patches that are particularly pertinent to their servers or the configuration of their servers should be utilized as soon as testing and validation are possible within their environments. This will minimize potential risks, especially as exploits are announced and become more familiar to those wishing to use them to compromise systems. In some instances, if the immediate patching is not possible based on the use and demands of the server, other mitigating efforts may be possible, such as restricting access or temporarily disabling some services or components, until patching can be undertaken and applied. This will serve to lower risk and exposure, depending on the classification of data within a system and the risk appetite of management. Patching in this sense applies to any and all software employed on a server, whether it is the operating system itself or software packages run within it.

 EXAM TIP   Make sure to remember the concept of applying mitigating factors where patching cannot be deployed immediately, such as temporarily disabling services or further restricting access points to services and APIs.

Along with patching, regular or continual scanning should be used with updated signatures to proactively discover any unpatched systems, validate whether patching has been successfully supplied, and potentially discover additional vulnerabilities through penetration testing.

Storage Communication

With a cloud environment being completely virtualized, all communications are done via networked devices and connectivity, and this also applies to storage devices and communication with them. With a traditional data center, physical servers and hosts have storage directly integrated with them on dedicated hardware, or are connected to storage networks via controllers or fiber channel networks. Much like with networks on physical appliances, storage communications with physical servers is done via dedicated hardware and cables that are not shared by other hosts; physical servers use their own cables and dedicated switch ports on storage networks.

With virtualized systems, storage traffic should, wherever possible, be segregated and isolated on its own LAN. Storage systems, because of their heavy network utilization and importance, should be considered LAN traffic and not WAN traffic, as latency issues are a major concern for storage systems versus typical network traffic, which is more resilient and flexible. While web service calls and general application traffic typically have encrypted communications capabilities built in, or can be added easily, this is often not the case with storage systems. In the instances where vendors supply this capability, it should always be used, but in the cases where it is not possible or supportable, having the storage traffic separated to a different LAN from application and user traffic will allow for great security and confidentiality of data transmissions.

The most prevalent communications protocol for network-based storage is iSCSI, which allows for the transmission and use of SCSI commands and features over a TCP-based network. Whereas a traditional data center will have SAN (storage area network) setups with dedicated fiber channels, cables, and switches, in a cloud data center this is not possible with the use of virtualized hosts. In this case, iSCSI allows systems to use block-level storage that looks and behaves like a SAN would with physical servers, but it leverages the TCP network within a virtualized environment and cloud.

iSCSI offers a lot of features that are ideal for a cloud environment and security. iSCSI traffic is recommended to be run over its own segregated networks for security reasons and protection of data privacy. However, iSCSI does support encrypted communications through such protocols as IPsec, and encryption should be used wherever possible to protect communications between virtual machines and storage networks. iSCSI also supports a variety of authentication protocols, such as Kerberos and CHAP, for securing communications and confidentiality within networks.

 NOTE It is important to remember that iSCSI must be protected with technologies such as those mentioned in this section, as iSCSI itself is not encrypted and must be protected through other means.

Installation and Configuration of Virtualization Management Tools

With a cloud environment entirely dependent on virtualization, the proper installation and configuration of the management tools that control the virtualized environment form one of the key core components of cloud data center security. Without proper controls and monitoring in place with hypervisors and the management plane, the entire environment may be insecure and vulnerable to a wide array of attacks. With a compromise or attack directed at virtualization management tools, the underlying data center infrastructure, and thus any hosts that reside within it, is vulnerable to threats and compromises.

With a variety of different virtualization platforms and software, each vendor will put out their own utilities and guidelines for how best to secure their implementations. Overall, the vendor responsible for the virtualization software will know the best practices for securing their own configurations. For a cloud provider, working as a partner with the virtualization vendor will promote the best understanding of security requirements. If possible, working with a vendor from the early planning stages will also allow the cloud provider to design their data center infrastructure in a way to best meet the security requirements of the virtualization platform, and specific requirements for security may ultimately have a significant influence on which virtualization platform is chosen by the cloud provider.

The process of securing the virtualized infrastructure will typically involve many different aspects of the data center and operations. The most obvious starting point involves the configuration and security options available within the virtualization platform itself. This involves role-based access, secure communication methods and APIs, and logging and monitoring of events and actions taken by privileged users within the software. However, outside of the actual configuration of the virtualization platform, using physical or logical methods of keeping the hypervisor and management plane isolated and separate from user traffic, and certainly from external network traffic, is also imperative for maintaining a secure environment.

TIP With the importance of vendor-supplied software and tools to secure the virtualized environment's management tools, it is imperative for the Cloud Security Professional to ensure that these are updated and patched regularly. This will include regular patching cycles that most vendors use, as well as ensuring that a cloud service provider has a documented and tested procedure for rolling out patches with urgency when required by the type of exploit discovered. It is important to design systems with sufficient redundancy to enable patching processes to occur without overall downtime to the application. Without this redundancy in design, there will likely be considerable tension between the application teams and the systems or security teams in regard to patching urgency and patching schedules.

The main principles applied to the security of any system also apply to the security of the virtualization management tools. The combination of security protocols between the actual virtual management devices with the use of network segregation and isolation is called defense in layers. By using strong role-based authentication and severely limiting the number of personnel who have access to the hypervisors and management plane, a strong access control presence is promoted within the system. As with any system, even with strong segregation and access control, active and thorough logging and monitoring are essential to ensuring that only the appropriate type of access and the appropriate system resources are being used by administrative personnel.

Run the Physical Infrastructure for the Cloud Environment

Running the physical infrastructure of a cloud environment involves the access control systems, the networking configurations, the availability of systems and resources, and the hardening of operating systems via baselines and compliance.

Configuration of Access Control for Local Access

Although a cloud data center may be based at the user level on virtual machines, which is where access control is typically focused, the same issues apply to access control for the underlying infrastructure and the components that form it. As with a traditional data center, physical access to servers and hardware should be severely limited in a cloud data center as well. This includes personnel access to data centers where the hardware is housed, but also to local access through terminals to hardware components. The two main considerations from a security perspective for local access are physical access through KVM (keyboard, video, mouse) and console access through the hypervisor. Regardless of which type of local access is used, multifactor authentication should be employed wherever possible, and comprehensive logging and auditing programs should be in place as well, all conforming to best practices for systems and security protection.

With the use of KVM for access, several best practices should be followed to ensure security protections. Much like with storage devices, KVM connectivity should be isolated on its own specific physical channels to prevent the leaking or exposure of communications packets. The KVM should have extensive physical protections to prevent updating or compromise of firmware, as well as a physical housing that is tamperproof. The housing should have both alarms and notifications in place if the physical panel is opened or compromised, or if any cabling has been exchanging or tampered with, to prevent the possibility of anyone installing components to steal credentials or gain access. The KVM should be configured to allow access to one host at a time and not allow any transfer of data between hosts through the KVM. Also, the KVM should be configured to not allow any USB devices to be connected to it and used, with the exception of any input devices such as a mouse or keyboard; no USB devices that allow storage or data transfers should be permitted access.

Console access to virtual machines is something that all hypervisor implementations offer, and it is crucial for administrators to be able to properly maintain their machines, especially in the event of a crash and for use in troubleshooting startup and shutdown problems. Console access, much like access through the management plane or administrative access through the hypervisor, must be protected and highly restricted because it gives a potential attacker enormous insight into and control over a virtual machine. Because console access is an integral part of the implementation from the hypervisor vendor, it also typically allows for strong access control mechanisms as well as logging and auditing capabilities. All of these should be implemented and regularly audited to ensure appropriate use and regulatory compliance of the environment and administrative/privileged user access.

Securing Network Configuration

The network layer is vital for overall system and data center security, and four main technologies are used for its security, as detailed next.

VLANs

Within a cloud data center, the concept of network isolation and segregation is very important to ensure optimal security. Because physical network isolation is not possible within a cloud data center in regard to virtual machines, the use of VLANs is essential. At the very least, all management and administrative networks should be completely isolated and segregated from other traffic. The same rule applies to storage networks and iSCSI traffic.

With regard to the actual virtual machines, the same type of segregation done in a traditional data center, where physical networks should be replicated with the use of VLANs. This includes the isolation of production and nonproduction systems, as well as the separation and isolation of application tiers—specifically the presentation, application, and data tiers or zones. With the proper configuration of machines grouped in a VLAN, they will only see the other servers in the same VLAN, so communication outside the VLAN can be more easily and greatly restricted, while allowing internal server-to-server communications in an easier and more efficient manner.

Although the use of VLANs will add additional granularity and security segregation, the same rules apply as far as monitoring and auditing are concerned with any other systems. Continual monitoring and auditing of network traffic and routing are essential to validate that the isolation and segregation afforded by the VLAN approach is in fact configured and operating properly, and that there is no unauthorized or unintended data access permitted between VLANs.

EXAM TIP   Make sure you have a thorough understanding of VLANs and the many different reasons to use them, such as segregating different cloud customers or different zones within an application.

TLS

TLS has replaced SSL as the default acceptable method for encryption of traffic across a network. It uses X.509 certificates to provide authentication and encrypt communications sent over the connection between two parties. With the transmission of the traffic being encrypted, TLS is a method for ensuring the confidentiality of information. TLS is used throughout all industry sectors, ensuring security of everything from web traffic, e-mail, messaging clients, and even Voice over IP (VoIP). TLS has two layers, as detailed next.

TLS Handshake Protocol   The TLS handshake protocol is what negotiates and establishes the TLS connection between the two parties and enables the secure communications channel to then handle data transmission. The protocol exchanges all information needed between the two parties to establish the connection by several messaging exchanges containing information and status codes for key exchange and establishing a session ID for the overall transaction. The certificates are used at this stage to authenticate and establish the connection to the satisfaction of both parties, and encryption algorithms are negotiated. The handshake protocol is done entirely before data is transmitted.

TLS Record Protocol   The TLS record protocol is the actual secure communications method for transmitting of data. The record protocol is responsible for the encryption and authentication of packets throughout their transmission between the parties, and in some cases also performs compression of the packets. Because the record protocol is used after the handshake and negotiation of the connection is successfully completed, it is limited to just the operations of sending and receiving. The handshake protocol can hold open the secure communications channel, at which point the record protocol will, as needed, utilize send and receive functions for data transmission. The record protocol relies entirely upon the handshake protocol for all parameters used during its transaction and function calls.

IPsec

IPsec is a protocol for encrypting and authenticating packets during transmission between two parties, which can be a pair of servers, a pair of network devices, or network devices and servers. The protocol will perform both authentication and negotiation of security policies between the two parties at the start of the connection and then maintain them throughout its use. A major difference between IPsec and other protocols such as TLS is that IPsec operates at the Internet network layer rather than the application layer, allowing for complete end-to-end encryption of all communications and traffic. This also allows the encryption and security to automatically be implemented by the systems or networks and not be dependent on the application framework or code to handle encryption and security, thus releasing the application developers from these requirements and allowing the requirements to be handled by dedicated staff that specialize in them.

There are some drawbacks of note to consider with IPsec as well. The first consideration is the load that IPsec adds to systems and a network. With small applications or a limited implementation, this load is likely not going to pose a major concern or risk, but in larger networks or systems with heavy traffic, especially when used across a data center for many systems and networks, the load at a cumulative level can become substantial and it will be incumbent on both the Cloud Security Professional as well as operations staff to ensure that the systems and networks can handle the load without unacceptable degradation to user or system performance. IPsec can add 100 bytes or more to each transmitted packet in overhead, so on a large network with substantial traffic the impact can be enormous on resources.

The second consideration is the implementation and support of IPsec throughout a system or data center. Because IPsec is not implemented at the application layer, it is incumbent on the systems or network staff to implement and maintain it. IPsec is also not a protocol that is typical enabled or installed by default on any systems, so it will incur additional effort and design considerations for the systems or networks where its use is desired. Within a cloud environment, this will be a contractual and SLA issue if desired by the cloud customer, and depending on whether the implementation is IaaS, PaaS, or SaaS, the support issues may be extremely expensive, complex, or even not something that the cloud provider is willing to support at all.

DNSSEC

DNSSEC is a security extension to the regular DNS protocol and services that allows for the validation of integrity of DNS lookups. It does not address confidentiality or availability, though, at all. It allows for a DNS client to perform DNS lookups and validate both their origin and authority via the cryptographic signature that accompanies the DNS response. DNSSEC relies on digital signatures and allows a client lookup to validate a DNS record back to its authoritative source, a process known as *zone signing*. When a client makes a request for a DNS lookup, the digital signature can validate the integrity of the DNS record, while otherwise performing the typical way DNS records are processed and cached, so modifications to applications and code are not required for the use of DNSSEC. It is important to understand that the integration of DNSSEC and the validation that it performs do not require any additional queries to be performed.

DNSSEC can be used to mitigate a number of attacks and threats. The main focus of DNS attacks is either on the integrity or availability of DNS resources. Although DNSSEC will not prevent or mitigate DoS attacks on DNS servers, it can be used to greatly mitigate or eliminate common integrity attacks. The most common attack using DNS protocols is to redirect traffic away from the appropriate host reflected in the DNS records and to a spoofed location instead. Because this traffic will be using a hostname for resolution via DNS, without other mechanisms in place to validate the integrity of the DNS record it receives in response, there is no way for an application or user to know they are being directed to a malicious site. With the use of DNSSEC, the DNS record can be validated to come from the officially signed and registered DNS zone, and not from a rogue DNS server or other process attempting to inject malicious traffic into the data stream.

OS Hardening via the Application of Baselines

The most common and efficient manner of securing operating systems is through the use of baselines, which are a standardized and understood set of base configurations and settings. When a new system is built or a new virtual machine is established, baselines will be applied to a new image to ensure the base configuration meets organizational policy and regulatory requirements. In many organizations, the baselines will have been applied to the virtual images before they are used, so that immediately upon the enabling and startup of a new host, the configurations are already set to a standard that has been scanned and verified previously. This allows for rapid deployment and auto-scaling in a cloud environment, and extends capabilities beyond what can easily be done with physical servers. Baselines can be applied to systems in a variety of ways, depending on organizational needs and capabilities, and of course dependent on the specific technologies and operating systems employed. In many cases they are integrated with build policies or post-build scripts. Also, an organization will employ a system such as Active Directory (Windows) or Puppet (multiplatform) to maintain baselines for all the servers and hosts under their control. The use of a system like this will apply baselines policies as well as serve as a mechanism to detect and report on any changes or deviations from them.

Availability of Standalone Hosts

Within a data center, hosts may be configured in a standalone or clustered configuration. With a traditional standalone model, a physical host is isolated in what it does from other systems; even if it's part of a pool of resources, it operates independently of the others. With the move to the virtualized environment of a cloud, this same configuration is certainly possible, and many organizations opt to continue to use it. This allows for easy porting of systems from a traditional data center to a cloud environment, without making system configuration changes or redesigning deployments. However, with such a move, these systems can leverage the underlying redundancy and high availability of a cloud. Although this will not mitigate failures of a single host if the application or software fails, which typically will be the preponderance of failures, it will mitigate hardware failures that can accompany physical servers.

Availability of Clustered Hosts

A *cluster* is a group of hosts combined physically or logically by a centralized management system to allow for redundancy, configuration synchronization, failover, and the minimization of downtime. With a cluster, resources are pooled and shared between the members and managed as a single unit. Clustering principles and technologies can be applied to a variety of computing resources, including applications, servers, networking appliances, and storage systems.

Distributed Resource Scheduling (DRS)

DRS is used within all clustering systems as the method for clusters to provide high availability, scaling, management, workload distribution, and the balancing of jobs and processes. From a physical infrastructure perspective, DRS is used to balance compute loads between physical hosts in a cloud to maintain the desired thresholds and limits on the physical hosts. As loads change, virtual hosts can be moved between physical hosts to maintain the proper balance, and done so in a way that is transparent to the users.

Dynamic Optimization (DO)

By nature, a cloud environment is a very dynamic one. Resources are constantly changing as the number of virtual machines is constantly in flux, as well as the load on the systems. With auto-scaling and elasticity, cloud environments are ensured to always be different from one moment to the next, and through automated means without any human intervention or action. Dynamic optimization is the process through which the cloud environment is constantly maintained to ensure resources are available when and where needed, and that physical nodes do not become overloaded or near capacity, while others are underutilized.

Storage Clusters

Much like the benefits derived from clustering servers, the clustering of storage systems allows for increased performance, availability, and cumulative capacity. Storage systems in a clustered configuration will allow a cloud provider to ensure SLA compliance for availability, especially in a cloud environment where the use of virtualization means that even machines are files residing on a storage system, so high availability and performance become absolutely vital. This also means that any problems can immediately impact large numbers of machines, and also very likely multiple cloud customers due to multitenancy.

Maintenance Mode

In regard to a cloud environment, maintenance mode refers to the physical hosts and times when upgrades, patching, or other operational activities are necessary. While in maintenance mode, no virtual machines can run under a physical host. This necessitates orchestration and movement of virtual resources to other physical hosts before one is placed into maintenance mode. In order to maintain compliance with SLA requirements for availability, all virtual resources should be either programmatically or manually moved before the use of maintenance mode, and in many instances this may be a fully automated process.

High Availability

A key component to a cloud environment—and one that has become almost synonymous with it—is the concept of high availability. With cloud environments, resource pooling and clustering are typically used to ensure high levels of redundancy for the systems and platforms that are hosted within them. In order to achieve high availability, all components that are necessary for making systems available and operational will need to be redundant and scaled. This includes servers, storage systems, access control systems, and networking components. Without all these aspects having high availably systems in place, the entire environment could lose high availably. With a cloud environment, the SLA between the cloud customer and cloud provider will articulate the expectations for availability, and it is incumbent on the cloud provider to ensure they are met. A cloud provider may also opt for having in place other cloud systems or environments to ensure high available requirements are met, which will allow SLA requirements in the event of failures to be maintained, if systems and processes can be failed over and migrated within the allotted times allowances.

Manage the Physical Infrastructure for the Cloud Environment

Managing the physical infrastructure for a cloud environment will cover several key areas, ranging from remote access, baselines and patch management, performance and hardware monitoring, backup and recovery, network security, logging and analysis, and overall management of the environment.

Configuring Access Controls for Remote Access

Regardless of the type of cloud implementation used or the type of hosting model, customers and users will need remote access to applications and hosts in order to do their jobs or access data. This can be for business purposes, public clouds offering personal services, or any other systems and data that people use IT services for. With the nature of a cloud implementation and the reliance on virtualization and broad network access, as far as customers and users are concerned, all access to systems falls under remote access. Unlike a traditional data center, customers will not have direct physical access to their systems at any time; even their administrative and systems personnel will rely on remote access to get their work done.

The Cloud Security Professional will need to ensure that appropriate users are able to authenticate and attain authorization to those systems and applications hosted in the cloud in an efficient and secure manner, as defined by organizational policies, while doing so in a manner that protects the principle of least privilege as well as the integrity and confidentiality of that data.

With a cloud environment being entirely remote and containing multiple tenants and broad network access, remote access controls are even more important because physical access controls or location controls cannot be used in a cloud. The use of encrypted communications methods is absolutely vital at all times in a cloud environment to ensure that other tenants and cloud provider personnel are not able to read or intercept data or credentials as they traverse the network. All of the physical security methods available should be used where appropriate or necessary, including network isolation and encrypted communications channels, both between the user and the cloud environment, but also within the cloud environment to reach the actual machines deployed in it.

Wherever possible, multifactor authentication should be used at all times, along with strong password requirements for both users and support staff. All user access should be logged and reviewed on a regular basis for any anomalies. Ideally, alerts should be in place to catch in real time large numbers of unsuccessful logins or login attempts coming from multiple originating IP addresses within short periods of times, in order to catch attack attempts before they are successful or data is exposed.

OS Baseline Compliance Monitoring and Remediation

Once baselines have been applied to a host, it is imperative to ensure that they were successfully and fully installed and enabled as intended. In most cases this will be done through automated scanning software that is loaded with baseline configurations. Then any hosts can be flagged that are out of compliance with any checks during scanning. Systems staff can then remediate where necessary to bring those hosts into compliance with the baselines, and, where necessary, determine how they came to be out of compliance in the first place. This step is important because it can uncover unauthorized changes being made by administrators or developers. It can also detect a gap in automated tools that are setting baselines and possible reasons as to why the deviation is occurring.

Another important part of the scanning process is allowing for approved deviations. These should have undergone approval through the organization's change management process, and all configuration and baseline deviations must be documented per organizational policy. Scanning should take place at regular intervals to maintain compliance, but also after system configuration changes, patching, upgrades, and new software installations, as all such activities introduce new potential weaknesses or may introduce deviations from accepted baselines. Over time, as new software and versions are introduced and configuration changes are made, baselines will continue to evolve at the same time, as some changes will become the new baseline under organizational policy.

 TIP Optimally, baseline deviations approved through change management can be applied to automated scanning tools. This will enable reports to not flag these deviations as a finding, but may still flag them as informational, with a notation that this is an approved change. If this is not possible, an approved list of deviations will need to be maintained so that any findings from future scans can be matched against approved deviations and removed as official findings in any reports generated.

Patch Management

All firmware and software, regardless of the type of system or application involved, will have regular patching needs. Patching is used to fix bugs found in software, address stability problems, introduce new features, and, most importantly, to fix security vulnerabilities. From a management perspective, patching involves a series of processes to properly validate, implement, and test patching in a way that protects operations and minimizes downtime or interruptions in service levels.

The first step in patch management is being aware of the patches available. Most vendors offer notification mechanisms or programs to send out notices to system maintainers or security personnel that a new patch has been released, along with information as to what is contained within it. This information will help an organization in setting priorities for implementation. If the organization has a well-established patching cycle that is done on a set regular basis, many patches will be added to this process, without requiring additional efforts. However, in the case of security patches that have already known or verified exploits, patching might require emergency or ad hoc cycles to get them in place more immediately. Even with emergency patching, an organization should have a well-documented and established procedure for testing and notification.

Once an organization is aware of patches being available for their systems or software, the next step is to actually acquire the patches. Depending on the vendor and software implementation, patches can come in a variety of forms. Many times they are downloadable files in various formats that personnel will use to perform the patching. This can be a ZIP file, a proprietary format, a script, or a binary executable. In some instances, patching utilities will go directly out to the vendors' systems and download the patches directly for implementation. However, this is not possible with many security setups, and overall should be avoided if possible, as it will require a system to have open outbound network connectivity across the Internet to systems that are outside the control of the organization or cloud provider. Many software vendors provide hash values for their software packages, and if provided they should always be used to ensure the patch file that has been downloaded matches and validates what the vendor has officially provided.

After the patch has been evaluated for implementation and the software or script obtained, the next step is the actual implementation of the patch. This should always be done on a nonproduction environment and thoroughly tested before being introduced with production systems. Depending on the type of appliance, this may not always be possible, but to the extent that it is, due diligence should always be thoroughly performed by any organization. In most cases automated software utilities will be used to deploy patches across multiple systems. Where these types of utilities are used, it is imperative to monitor the successful completion and implementation of patching to ensure that no hosts or appliances fail to properly install them. With cloud environments, many times patches are done by building new images for virtual machines or devices, then doing reimaging to the new baseline for each system with the new patches installed and tested. Either method is fine and dependent on the particular configurations and needs of the system, so long as policies and practices are established and documented.

After patches have been installed, the last (and very vital) step is to validate and verify the patches. Depending on the nature of the patches, this can be done a variety of ways. Care and attention should always be paid to the documentation put out by the software vendor that accompanies the patches. Many times scripts or instructions will be provided for verifying the patches. At the very least, the process for installing the patches should provide success or error responses back to the person or utility implementing them. Once patches have been successfully installed and verified, it is imperative that the hosted software and applications are also tested to ensure they are still performing as expected.

TIP Many times, organizations will not fully test applications after patches are deployed if they do not feel there could be an impact to the applications. For example, if the system is running a Java application and the patch is an operating system patch that does not touch the software at all, sometimes testing will be minimized due to lower risk. However, any changes to an operating system could have potential impact on an application, and testing of the application's functionality should be performed to the expected standards and to satisfy the risk appetite of the organization's management.

There are also many challenges to patching, especially within a cloud environment and for larger systems and implementations. Patch management solutions and processes that work in a traditional data center may not work correctly when moved into a cloud environment. This is also true for solutions moving from one cloud environment to another, or even across different hosting locations within the same cloud environment. Special care must be taken to ensure that a particular patch solution will work both within the environment and for the specific requirements of an organization and its systems. Even within a cloud environment, a patch solution used by one tenant will not necessarily work for another tenant, even within the same environment.

For large implementations within a cloud environment, the scalability of the patch management system will be a vital question. A further complication in this particular area concerns cloud implementations where auto-scaling is enabled, and each patch cycle will have different characteristics as far as the number and types of hosts at that particular point in time. There is also the question within a virtualized environment of hosts that are not currently enabled and active, but still exist as virtual machines within the storage solution. Because these hosts could be enabled at any time, even through automated processes, it is essential that they are managed under the same patching system and properly validated and tested as well.

Other complications for cloud systems include their large distributed nature and the timing of various systems based on the time zone and needs of the particular services. While a cloud provider may host from one or a small number of physical data centers, the virtual machines may be configured with a variety of time zones based on the actual users of the systems and their needs. This facet, as well as which hosts fall into which categories, is very important to consider when implementing a patching strategy because the particular time zone and peak times of each host will need to be taken into account as to when patching can be applied. With a large number of servers and user communities around the world, patching could quite possibly be a rolling process that covers virtually every hour of the day.

Performance Monitoring

For a cloud provider, it is essential to monitor the environment for performance metrics, as these are key components of contracts and SLAs between the cloud provider and cloud customer. The key physical components of a cloud environment also comprise the metrics for performance monitoring. The four key areas are CPU, disk, memory, and network. The cloud provider will need to ensure that adequate resources are available to meet current and possible future needs as well as that the resources are responding with sufficient speed and reliability to meet SLA requirements.

 EXAM TIP   Make sure to remember the four key areas of a physical cloud environment: CPU, memory, disk, and network. This question tends to show up on exams with different terminologies used.

With each of these four components, the vendor of the systems and software used will establish their own set of performance metrics, monitoring capabilities and techniques, and best practices for planning and implementation. The parameters and best practices, as established by the vendor, will play the major role in determining resource thresholds and planning for expected needs and growth. A cloud environment not only must ensure that it can fully support the requirements of each tenant currently but also support potential auto-scaling and growth. With auto-scaling done programmatically in response to changes in load demands, a sudden burst of traffic, either legitimate or responding to something like a DoS attack, can lead to a rapid increase in physical capacity demands throughout the environment.

Hardware Monitoring

While the focus in any cloud environment always seems to be directed toward the virtual infrastructure and the resources used by it, the reality remains that underneath it all is still physical hardware that has the same exact issues and concerns that physical hosts in a traditional data center would have. The same four components listed under performance monitoring also apply to these physical hosts.

As with applying monitoring to any system, following the recommendations and best practices of the hardware vendors should always be the starting point. Hardware, while similar among different vendors, is still unique enough that each vendor will have their own recommendations and utilities used to monitor their systems. Wherever possible, the tools and utilities provided by the hardware vendor should be used as the primary source of monitoring, with additional capabilities added on top, if possible. In most cases, this data or these utilities can be integrated into the same types of tools and reporting agents that are used to monitor virtual systems and other appliances throughout the environment. This integration allows the same personnel monitoring systems to look at everything at a holistic level as well as allows homogeny with monitoring reports and alerting.

Cloud systems by nature are built around the principle of redundancy, which also brings the added benefit of distributing load and having higher capacity than needed to run current operations. This also adds additional complexity to monitoring systems, as each physical host cannot be looked at in isolation, but must be analyzed in conjunction with the rest of the physical hosts serving the same clusters or redundant pools. It also means that alerting must be flexible and responsive to conditions where components of redundancy are removed or unavailable at any given time, due to either unexpected circumstances or planned outages for upgrades or maintenance. During these times, the overall pools of resources will be diminished, and monitoring and alerting will need to be able to recognize these periods and maintain overall system health even as the available pool of resources is in flux.

Backup and Restore of Host Configuration

As with any kind of data on any system, configuration data is extremely valuable and should be an integral part of any backup and recovery operations in a data center. This is another area where it is imperative to closely follow the recommendations and advice of the hardware vendors. For backups to work optimally with physical devices, vendors need to expose APIs or services to allow for backup systems to capture configurations. Any time information like this is exposed to any services or utilities, there is an inherent security risk of unauthorized access, so a thorough understanding of what can be exposed, as well as how it will be secured, is essential from the hardware vendor.

Depending on the cloud service model, the exposure of configuration data may also need to be negotiated between the cloud customer and cloud provider. This will largely depend on contractual and SLA requirements and should always be clearly defined as far as roles and expectations for exposure of any data, as well as ensuring that systems exposing configuration data are appropriately secured and isolated from other tenants or systems.

Implementation of Network Security Controls

Much like with a traditional data center model, network security for a cloud data center is also based on layered security and defense-in-depth principles. This is done through the use of a variety of technologies covering servers, appliances, and software implementations.

Firewalls

Firewalls control the flow of traffic in and out of networks based on rules configured on them. Firewalls control the traffic flow typically between trusted and untrusted networks by only allowing certain ports to connect between defined networks segments, which can be a single IP address, a VLAN, or a range of IP addresses. They can be either hardware or software implementations, depending on the needs, resources, and capabilities of the environment. Whereas a traditional data center will rely heavily on hardware-based firewall devices, within a cloud environment the use of virtual firewalls or host-based firewall software is necessary. For the most part, a virtual firewall device operates much the same as a hardware-based device. Regardless of whether a server is physical or virtualized, the software-based firewalls that come as part of the operating system package from the vendor or as an additional package or third-party package operate in the same manner. However, while host-based firewalls will accomplish a high degree of protection, they are not ideal compared to hardware-based or external firewalls. Having a firewall running as software on a host will add additional load to that host and consume resources that otherwise would be reserved for the application. From a security perspective, you also run the risk of a compromised host allowing the attacker to disable or alter the firewall running on the host. By having the firewall independent from the host, a compromised host cannot be exposed further with the segregation.

IDS (Intrusion Detection System)

An IDS is designed to analyze network packets, compare their contents or characteristics against a set of configurations or signatures, and alert personnel if anything is detected that could constitute a threat or is otherwise designated for alerting. With deep analysis of network packets, an IDS can detect and alert against a much broader range of threats than a firewall can, as a firewall is simply looking at the origin, destination, protocol, and port of the traffic. One of the biggest complaints and challenges with the use of an IDS is that it can often generate a high number of false positives. This can be reduced to a certain extent with a continual process of evaluation and tuning, but this also then adds enormous staff resources and requirements. As a positive, because of the packet analysis depth that an IDS is capable of, it can in some circumstances be used to assist in the troubleshooting of network or application problems. IDS systems are either host based or network based.

HIDSs (Host Intrusion Detection Systems)   An HIDS runs on a single host and only analyzes traffic for that host—both inbound and outbound traffic. Apart from network traffic, an HIDS system will typically monitor critical system files and configuration files for modification. This is especially important and valuable on production systems where changes will be minimal and should only occur when going through a rigorous change management process. Essentially speaking, any file modifications detected by an HIDS should be reactive in nature and should be predictable and knowable to administrators before the alerts are received from the HIDS. The main drawback with an HIDS is much like other devices similar to host-based firewalls: if the machine itself is compromised in a way that an attack has achieved administrative control over a system, there is nothing to prevent the attacker from disabling the HIDS or altering its configurations. A common approach to combating this possibility is to have the signatures and configurations for the HIDS on either read-only storage or accessed from an external system or external memory. The logs from an HIDS should also be configured to immediately be sent off to the individual host and to a log system collector or a SIEM system to detect any anomalies or prevent the logs from being altered by an attacker in an attempt to remove traces of their attack from the system.

NIDSs (Network Intrusion Detection Systems)   Whereas an HIDS is dedicated to a single host and does analysis of packets for that host, NIDSs are placed at various points in a network and can analyze all network traffic looking for the same types of threats. At this level, an NIDS can watch many systems and alert personnel based on potential threats and attack attempts, and can detect trends and attacks that might appear be a very small number if analysis is focused on each host, but looking from a holistic network level can see the scale and breadth of any such attempts. The biggest challenge with NIDSs is the size of the network and the high volume of traffic that flows through them. Typically, they will be placed around strategic assets or specific subnets with high-value data on them, rather than trying to monitor an entire network as a whole. However, with small implementations or where necessary by regulation or policy, larger-scale and more comprehensive monitoring can be employed.

EXAM TIP Make sure to remember both NIDS and HIDS approaches and what the acronyms stand for. Also, study the key challenges and benefits of both compared to the other.

IPS (Intrusion Prevention System)

An IPS works in much the same way as an IDS, with the major stark difference being the reactive nature of an IPS; it can immediately and automatically stop and prevent attacks as they occur, rather than sitting passively and just alerting personnel of possible issues. Because an IPS is able to do a deep analysis of network packets, it has a variety of methods available to block or terminate something that it determines to be an attack. It can block specific IP addresses, user sessions, traffic based on characteristics of the packets, or any other facet of the network traffic. With the ability to block based on specific characteristics of the packets, it enables an IPS to be effective at responding to distributed attacks, where blocking a large number of IP addresses would be neither practical nor desirable. It also has the ability to block portions of traffic or attacks while allowing the rest through. A prime example of this could be removing certain types of e-mail attachments that contain executable code or match signature aspects, while allowing the rest of the e-mail to proceed through. In some cases, if configured and allowed by organizational policies, the IPS may be enabled to automatically make configuration changes to firewalls or network routing to prevent or mitigate an ongoing attack, or even make configuration changes to individual hosts.

CAUTION An IPS and IDS face considerable challenges when dealing with encrypted traffic. With the packet contents encrypted, signature-based analysis is effectively eliminated because the system cannot perform inspection. A careful examination of the specific application or system will need to be performed by the Cloud Security Professional to determine if it is prudent or possible to decrypt all or some traffic at specific points in order to perform IDS/IPS inspection.

Honeypots

A honeypot is a system, isolated away from the production system, that is designed to appear to an attacker to be part of the production system and contain valuable data. However, the data on a honeypot is bogus data, and it is set up on an isolated network so that any compromise of it cannot impact any other systems within the environment. The intent is to lure would-be attackers into going after the honeypot instead the production system. This allows administrators to set up extensive monitoring and logging on the honeypot to watch the types of attacks and the methods employed in an attempt to compromise it. That knowledge can then be used to set up security policies and filters on the actual production system. By establishing a system identical to the production system but with dummy data, administrators can see the characteristics and origins of attacks being focused on their systems, and they also have the ability to evaluate the success (or possible success) of such attacks and to use that information to further refine their actual systems.

Vulnerability Assessments

Vulnerability assessments target systems with known vulnerabilities, and do so in a non-destructive way, to determine any problems that need immediate remediation or focus of efforts on those systems. While vulnerability assessments use known and common attempts on systems, they do not attempt to actually change data or carry the attacks to their conclusion, so as to not impact actual systems or data.

Vulnerability assessments can be done for a variety of reasons and for a variety of roles. They typically are based on the type of data contained on the systems and the relevant regulatory requirements that goes with it. This allows an organization to scope their vulnerability assessments to specific requirements and the types of tests based on those guidelines, and many times also serve as official audit reports and evidence of such tests being conducted as well.

From the physical infrastructure perspective, cloud customers will often have specific contractual and SLA requirements for the cloud provider to perform regular vulnerability scans of their systems. With any vulnerability assessment, the security of data and reports is essential because disclosure would put all tenants under the cloud provider at potential risk. All reports would be governed by contracts and certifications as to what can be disclosed and when, as well as by whom.

Typically, the contract and SLAs between the cloud provider and cloud customer will spell out the tools that are used for the assessments as well. Many assessment tools for vulnerability scanning are available now, and more and more are coming out that are focused on and designed specifically for cloud environments and their underlying infrastructure. Knowledge of which tools are used for the assessments is very important to a Cloud Security Professional so that they can evaluate the reputation and value of the specific tools.

 TIP　Always do a thorough investigation of the tools used for vulnerability assessments, including knowing which specific modules are used for each tool. It is not enough for a cloud provider to simply state they run assessments without knowing how they are conducted and certified. Without knowledge of the toolsets used, it is impossible to ensure comfort and confidence that the assessments are thorough and will hold up to scrutiny by regulatory oversight, or offer adequate liability protection for the cloud customer should their systems be breached, and they want to show due diligence was taken in protecting their systems and data.

In many cases, the cloud provider will obtain an external and independent auditor or security group to conduct their vulnerability assessments to add additional credibility and segregation to them. This is often a major selling point for the cloud customer as well, where the cloud provider can provide evidence of assessments performed and certified by reputable and independent auditors. Many cloud providers will also obtain certain industry or government certifications for their data centers and underlying infrastructure to facilitate cloud customers that require such certifications, and as a business point to use in sales to prospective customers.

While the cloud provider will undertake their own vulnerability assessments of their infrastructure, many customers may wish to undertake their own, independent assessments, or their regulatory requirements may dictate that they do so. If this is desired or required by the cloud customer, it must be clearly spelled out in the contractual requirements, along with the process and procedures for the assessments to be completed, as the cloud provider will have to be an integral part of any such independent assessments. This is something that not many cloud providers will be willing to do, as most will have a large number of tenants, and it is just not practical for them to have each doing their own assessments. It also means with each assessment, the cloud provider will have to disclose and open their systems to testing, and each time that is done, the potential for leakage of proprietary or sensitive information increases. The way most cloud providers will seek to mitigate this problem is having their cloud infrastructure certified on their own by well-known and industry standard bodies, and then allowing the cloud customers to inherit those certifications up to their own deployments within the cloud. This enables the cloud customer to conduct audits within their own scope and accept the certifications of the cloud environment as whole. This saves money for all tenants as well as the resources, privacy, and time of the cloud provider.

Log Capture and Analysis

Logging events, protecting the logs, and making them available for analysis are all vital for any security program and will be the main considerations and focus of the Cloud Security Professional.

Security Information and Event Management (SIEM)

SIEM systems serve to collect, index, and store logs throughout the multiple systems of an application, or even an entire data center, in a centralized location. This allows for the searching, reporting, and alerting of events that can be seen across systems and correlated together in a way that looking at a single system would not allow. For example, an attempted attack on a data center may only yield a small number of hits on each server, which, if you were alerting based on hosts, might not cross the alerting threshold. However, when you are looking at the data center level or a broader level, you would see these small number of attacks hitting many different hosts, which aggregated together would cause alerts to be generated. This also serves as a very powerful platform for troubleshooting because administrators with single searches can find events occurring on servers, firewalls, storage devices, and so on, allowing for problems to be discovered without administrators from all systems being engaged to look at these problems independently to try and discern where they may be occurring.

Centralizing logs on a SIEM solution also allows the abstraction of logs from systems that could potentially be compromised and have their logs altered or erased by an attacker in an attempt to cover traces of their activities. A SIEM solution that has real-time mirroring of systems logs would make this type of attempt moot and preserve evidence from an attack, or activities of a malicious insider using their access in an inappropriate way. The one drawback to centralizing log collections is the elevated security risk of the SIEM solution. Although it is log data and therefore should never contain sensitive information, if an attacker were to gain access to a SIEM solution, they could learn an enormous wealth of information about a system or infrastructure that could then be used to expose additional vulnerabilities.

Log Management

Throughout an environment, logs are generated in many places and in many different ways. Servers generate system logs and application logs; same with network devices, storage devices, and many various security devices such as IDS and IPS. A very important aspect to consider as a data center is configured and brought online is the logging capabilities of the physical assets. The Cloud Security Professional will need a thorough understanding of what logging is enabled by default from the vendor, as well as what logging capabilities exist beyond the default. In many instances, logging by default will be at a more information level or warning level, rather than capturing all events that are important or relevant to the particular organization or system.

A great deal of log exposure and availability in a cloud environment will depend on what cloud service model is used. This also extends to who has responsibility for collecting and managing log data. With an IaaS service model, most log collection and maintenance will be the responsibility of the cloud customer as far as virtual machines and application logs are considered. The SLA between the cloud customer and the cloud provider will need to clearly spell out what logs beyond those are available within an IaaS environment, who has access to them and the responsibility to collect them, who will be responsible for maintaining and archiving them, as well as what the retention policy is. With a PaaS implementation, the cloud provider will need to collect the operating system logs and possibly logs from the application as well, depending how PaaS is implemented and what application frameworks are used. Therefore, the SLA will need to clearly define how those logs will be collected and given to the cloud customer and to what degree support is available with such efforts. With a SaaS implementation, all logs will have to be exposed by the cloud provider via SLA requirements. With many SaaS implementations, logging to some degree is exposed via the application itself to administrators or account managers of the application, but those logs might be limited to a set of user functions or just high-level events. Anything deeper or more detailed will also need to be part of the SLA, though with a SaaS implementation, the cloud provider may be willing to expose very little cloud data unless they have APIs already designed to do so.

Another key aspect of log management is the retention of log files. The exact duration and type of retention will be dictated by regulatory requirements, which will set the minimum standards, and may or may not be expanded upon by organizational policy. Log retention will typically be for a set period of time, depending on the type of data the system stores and the sensitivity level of it. On top of the overall time required, retention policies usually also dictate the type of storage and accessibility of it. For example, the log retention policy may be for one year, where 30 days' worth of logs must be immediately accessible at all times, and the remainder kept on cheaper and slower storage, or possibly even written to tape and stored in long-term archival systems.

Management Plan

In a traditional data center, many operations will typically impact a single client or system, as most reside on physical hardware and are segregated from other systems. There are exceptions to this rule, of course, for enterprise-level services such as DNS, file servers, and so on. However, in a cloud environment, careful coordination and management are vital because many systems and different customers are directly impacted by operational decisions. With large cloud environments, careful planning and management are crucial in order to operate a system.

Scheduling

In a traditional data center with one customer impact, scheduling potential outages is much simpler because they can be performed at times when use is at its lowest—whether that is the time of the day, the day of the week, or during cyclical periods of heavy use on a system. With a cloud environment, due to the large number of possible tenants, this is not really possible, as it is unlikely that there will be a window that is agreeable to all tenants. In some instances, it might be possible to perform operations during times where the operations will minimally affect the main part of the business day, based on the time zone settings and locality of the cloud customer. At the same time, most major systems are now 24/7 in nature, and this type of downtime is not really available, regardless of the time of day or the date on the calendar. The cloud provider will have to determine the best course of action for their operations based on knowledge of their customers and the available resources of the cloud during any downtimes or when equipment is being rotated out for repairs. Regardless of the timing chosen, comprehensive communication with the cloud customers is imperative and should be outlined as far as expectations are concerned in the SLA.

Orchestration

Orchestration, as it relates to a cloud environment, pertains to the enormous use of automation for tasks such as provisioning, scaling, allocating resources, and even customer billing and reporting. Orchestration is a vital concept to consider when planning or executing any operational activities within a cloud environment because customers at any time can make configuration changes and expand their environments, without needing to involve personnel of the cloud provider at all. When maintenance activities are performed, or any operations undertaken that could impact the customer's ability to perform actions within the cloud, orchestration activities need to be carefully considered so as to not lead to a violation of SLA requirements.

Maintenance

As with any system and infrastructure, cloud systems need to undergo regular maintenance that could impact the operations of customers. With a large number of tenants on a system, and the virtualized nature of a cloud, maintenance becomes both easier in one sense and more challenging in another. For any virtualization host to be upgraded or patched, maintenance mode is typically required. With maintenance mode, no virtual systems can be active and served from that host, meaning they must either be stopped or moved to another host. In most instances, a cloud provider will opt to move to another host, to avoid any potential downtime or impact on customers. Although this is typically completely transparent to the customer, notification must be sent out about what is to be done, the steps the cloud provider is taking to avoid downtime, and what impacts could be expected, and the duration of the maintenance window. This notification should only be done after the cloud provider has undergone their own rigorous change management process and has received approval for all changes and actions as well as verification that the changes have been appropriately tested within the cloud environment already.

A major consideration for a cloud provider involves the use of maintenance mode and moving virtual machines to other hosts during the maintenance window. Although this aspect of a cloud is very attractive in that it should minimize or eliminate the impact to customers during this time, it also means that the cloud environment as a whole will be without a set of resources for the duration. Given the auto-scaling and self-provisioning of a cloud, the cloud provider will need to determine if they have enough resources to meet possible demands during the maintenance window as well as how much of their overall environment they can perform the maintenance on at any one time without causing potential problems.

Build the Logical Infrastructure for the Cloud Environment

Whereas the physical infrastructure of a cloud environment is focused on very specific and precise hardware and other physical assets, the logical infrastructure is much more abstract and is instead focused on the actual business needs of the customer. It removes the specifics of platforms and software, and instead focuses on the aspects that are important to customers, such as processes, roles, locations, and regulations.

Secure Configuration of Virtual Hardware–Specific Requirements

When configuring virtual hardware, it is important to be aware of the requirements of the underlying host systems. In many instances, specific settings and configurations will need to be employed on the virtual machines to match the capabilities and requirements of the physical hosts. These requirements will be clearly articulated by the virtual host vendors, and then will need to be matched by those building and configuring the images for the virtual devices. These settings allow for the proper allocation and management of CPU and memory resources from the host systems to the virtual machines running within then.

From the storage side, several steps should be taken for proper secure configuration. Immediately after the install, any default credentials supplied by the vendor should be changed immediately. These default credential sets are well known to any potential attackers and are typically one of the first targets used to compromise a system. All unnecessary interfaces and APIs should be immediately disabled to prevent any potential compromises, as well as to save on system resource overhead. Testing should be performed to ensure that storage controllers and systems can handle the expected load as well as meet the requirements for redundancy and high availability. As with any type of system or configuration, vendor recommendations for best practices should always be consulted and adapted to the particular environment.

 TIP   Always ensure that default credentials are changed immediately upon initialization of any system or platform that has them. They are very well known, and most hacking scripts and automated tools will try them immediately. Many administrators will minimize the importance of changing them, instead arguing that perimeter security methods are in place, and if the only access available to these interfaces is restricted to authorized personnel, then the need for immediate change is somehow lessened. The Cloud Security Professional should ensure that this practice does not persist within any environment, and if available, scanning for default credentials with automated tools should be done to all new hosts before put into use. This should be done regularly with continuing vulnerability assessments as well.

Within a cloud environment there are two main network models, with the appropriate model dependent on the particular needs and configurations of the cloud environment. The traditional networking model has physical switches combined with virtual networks at the hypervisor level. The converged networking model combines the storage and date/IP networks into one virtualized design and is intended for use with cloud environments. The traditional networking model can use regular security networking tools, whereas the converged networking model will use completely virtualized tools. However, due to the nature of a traditional networking model and the combination of physical and virtualized systems, there can sometimes be a disconnect between the two as it relates to full visibility with the virtualized networks. The converged networking model, being designed and optimized for cloud usage, typically maintains better visibility and performance under cloud operating loads.

Installation of Guest Operating System Virtualization Toolsets

Because the virtualized environment can run a variety of different operating systems within it, it is important to ensure that the appropriate toolsets are installed and available for it. Each operating system vendor will have their own virtualization tools and cloud utility sets that should always be used to ensure optimal compatibility and correct performance of the operating system within the environment. These can often be augmented with third-party and other toolsets, but following the recommended best practices and configuration guidelines put forth by the vendor will ensure optimal performance, security, and visibility into the guest operating systems.

Run the Logical Infrastructure for the Cloud Environment

In order to optimally run a solid, secure, and supportable logical environment within a cloud infrastructure, considerations for security at the network and operating system layers need to be properly planned for and designed. These designs are largely driven by a combination of characteristics of the cloud environment itself, such as the tenancy model and number of tenants, as well as the particular data classifications and regulatory requirements to which the likely cloud customers are bound. In most cases, there will be vendor-specific recommendations and guidelines to follow.

Secure Network Configuration

The following aspects of network configuration for a logical infrastructure are much the same as introduced in the physical networking section. However, some additional considerations for logical networks are added here, so refer back to the previous sections for more in-depth and comprehensive discussions.

VLANs

VLANs can be used in a cloud environment to provide the logical separation of different networks that would normally be accomplished by different physical networks and hardware in a traditional data center. This allows for the logical separation of management, storage, and security networks away from the actual production or customer networks. This also allows for greater security because traffic for these components will be isolated from the actual customer data flows. VLANs can also be used to separate and isolate the tiers of applications that would typically be done via separate hardware in a traditional data center. This isolates the presentation, application, and data tiers from each other, and from other tenants within the cloud environment.

TLS

TLS is used for encrypted data transfer between hosts. In a cloud environment where physical cabling and switching are not available, the use of a technology such as TLS is essential to protect data while it traverses the network between hosts. With the multitenancy of a cloud environment, TLS will be used to protect the confidentiality of data from other customers, even if the VLAN separation is not available from the cloud provider. This also prevents data from being sniffed or captured between multiple hosts if another host on the same VLAN is somehow compromised. TLS can also be used to allow external access into a cloud environment and to the virtual machines through VPN configurations and implementations.

DHCP

DHCP is essential for automation and orchestration within a cloud environment. Most people in the security world are well aware of the old adage that you never use DHCP with a data center and servers, and instead have IP addresses configured and set in a static manner.

This mentality has mostly passed, though, in favor of using DHCP with reservation. With DHCP, IP addresses are not always assigned dynamically from a pool. Within a cloud environment, the DHCP technology is used to centralize the issuance of IP addresses and maintain them in a static manner, where the IP, MAC address, hostname, and node names are set and not changed, and they are always assigned to the same virtual machine. This allows for far greater speed and flexibility with automation and removes the need for configurations such as network settings at the host level, which are instead centrally maintained and administered.

DNS

The security of DNS within a cloud is imperative because a compromise of DNS could allow an attacker to hijack and redirect traffic as it traverses the network. Locking down DNS servers and disabling zone transfers are best practices, and the use of DNSSEC will largely prevent the hijacking and redirecting of traffic because even if the DNS servers are compromised, there will be no way without the DNSSEC trust anchors established to get hosts to accept the new data.

IPsec

IPsec, much like TLS, can be used to encrypt and protect information between hosts within a cloud environment and as data traverses the network. It also can be used with VPN solutions to provide access to virtual machines and to allow for additional security such as IP-based restrictions and the use of multifactor authentication.

OS Hardening via Application of Baselines

The application of a baseline to operating systems is the same approach that's taken with physical assets, and is a widely used method to ensure security configurations. Any baseline, regardless of system, should be configured to only allow the minimal services and access required for the system to function, and it should meet all regulatory and policy requirements for security configurations. Each operating system, and possibly even version, will need to have its own baseline configurations and policies. Many organizations will also opt to establish baselines for different types of images within the same operating system. For example, if an organization has different images for a web server, database server, and so on, establishing different baselines can assist with quicker provisioning and better security protections from the initial build stage.

Regardless of the specific operating system, there is a sequence of steps for establishing a baseline to be used. The initial step is to use a fresh and clean install from the vendor of the operating system, using the latest build and version available, unless a specific version is required. After the initial install, all unnecessary software, utilities, and plug-ins should be removed, and all services that are nonessential should be stopped, disabled, or removed. Once all software and services have been removed, patching is applied to bring everything up to the most current versions and settings. Because all nonessential software and services are removed first, patching will be a more streamlined process. Once patching has been applied, all configuration items required by organizational policy or regulation are applied. At this point, the baseline image is complete from the configuration standpoint, but a full scan of the image, configured to ensure baseline compliance, should be run against the system to catch any configurations that were missed or set incorrectly. As a last step, full documentation should be established as to the creation, testing, and maintenance of the baseline. Also, documented configuration items should be captured for the change management process and inventory databases.

Depending on the platform and operating system, there may be additional considerations establishing a baseline. Operating system vendors also supply specific tools for managing their systems and performing maintenance activities, especially in the area of patch management.

Windows

Microsoft provides the Windows Server Update Service (WSUS) as a toolset to perform patch management on Windows systems. The tool downloads patches and hotfixes from Microsoft's servers, and then administrators can use it to update the Window machines under their control in a centralized and automated way. WSUS is a free service and a component of Windows.

Microsoft also offers the Microsoft Deployment Toolkit (MDT). MDT is a collection of tools and processes to facilitate the automation of server and desktop deployments through the use of system images, and it also can be used in a configuration management and security management role. These tools are often used to complement each other because they have different focuses, but ultimately can be used for a comprehensive strategy for managing and maintaining Windows environments.

Linux

Linux has many different flavors and builds, with different sets of tools and utilities that are part of the base build. These can range from very stripped-down and minimal distributions up to full-featured versions that have a full range of utilities and toolsets installed. The particular distribution and its attributes will largely drive the process and approach for establishing a baseline, because the particular build will drive the default services and configurations as well as the default security implementations to build the baseline on top of. To accomplish baselines with Linux, the Cloud Security Professional should utilize established baselining processes for Linux in general, and then apply changes where necessary based on the particular specific implementation. Not all Linux distros contain the same toolsets, utilities, applications, or configuration paradigms, so while the overall methodology for Linux will be consistent, the specific application of it will often be dependent on the distro to some extent.

VMware

VMware has built-in tools for doing baselines that are part of the vendor package. These can be leveraged to established baselines to meet organization or regulatory requirements, and an organization can also build a variety of different baselines for different types of systems and deployments within their data center. VMware comes with the vSphere Update Manager (VUM) utility. VUM can be used to automate patches of both vSphere hosts and virtual machines running under them. By comparing the status of hosts to established baselines, you can then perform updates to any systems to bring them into compliance.

VUM also provides a dashboard to allow for quick monitoring of the patching status across the entire infrastructure.

Availability of the Guest Operating System

One of the main benefits of a cloud environment is the redundancy and fault tolerance of systems to ensure availability. This is possible to a higher degree than using physical servers because the level of redundancy is so high, without the need for reliance on clustering to ensure availability. The needs and expectations for availability should be spelled out clearly in the contract and SLA.

There is a big difference between fault tolerance and high availability within an environment. High availability uses shared and pooled resources to minimize any downtime and quickly restore services when an outage does occur. Fault tolerance is different in that it involves specialized hardware that can detect faults and automatically switch to redundant systems or components, depending on the type of failure. Although fault tolerance promotes a very high degree of availability, due to the nature of having standby hardware available that is not otherwise in use, it comes at a much higher cost because the hardware is idle and unused much of the time. A big drawback to fault tolerance is that it is focused on hardware failures and does nothing to address software failures, which make up the vast majority of system availability issues.

Manage the Logical Infrastructure for the Cloud Environment

Managing the logical infrastructure of a cloud environment involves the same concepts and components as the physical environment, just focused with unique attributes and concerns on the logical infrastructure layer.

Access Control for Remote Access

Remote access to the physical infrastructure will be very highly restricted and reserved for administrative personnel of the cloud provider, whereas with the logical infrastructure, the need to allow remote access to virtual machines exists in regard to developers, customers, and other potential audiences as well. Because a wide audience will need remote access to the environment, a variety of security precautions and best practices can be employed to ensure a high level of security.

To promote the most secure access methods, TLS or a similar encryption technology should be used for all communications. The use of technologies such as Citrix will also greatly improve security of remote access. By requiring users to go through a secured server, rather than allowing direct access, an organization can eliminate many attack vectors for malware or other exploits, which is especially crucial for users who have personal and insecure devices. This narrows the security controls to the servers used for direct access rather than having to watch a large number of devices and different access methods and technologies. File transfers can also utilize the same mechanisms of passing through a secured Citrix server, where strong controls and scanning processes can be enforced from a centralized location.

With a centralized access method, strong monitoring and logging can also be integrated. All session data and activities will be under control of a centralized authority, which can also enforce stringent requirements for credentials and verifications. This also allows the easy termination of remote sessions when malware attempts are detected, or if users are found to be utilizing access in a manner in which they should not. This could include attempting to access data where that entitlement does not exist or when it appears that a user's credentials have been compromised. The use of a centralized access method will also enable the cloud provider or administrators to enforce a variety of limitations, if necessary or desired, such as time restrictions, session length restrictions, and termination of idle sessions.

Regardless of the specific centralized access method employed for a specific system or application, the use of multifactor authentication should be used at all times, unless there is a specific instance where it is not possible due to policy or technological limitations. In the instances where multifactor authentication is not possible to use, there should be formalized documentation and acceptance of that risk by management, and there should be a thorough investigation of any other technologies that can be used in lieu of it.

OS Baseline Compliance Monitoring and Remediation

Much like with monitoring and remediating variances from baselines, with a physical infrastructure the same requirements exist for the virtualized infrastructure and all hosts running within it. There are a variety of tools—some provided directly by vendors of the operating systems, and many more third-party applications and utilities. These tools should be in regular or continuous use throughout the environment to catch any deviations from baselines in a very responsive and time-effective manner, to ensure that at all times the environment is running with properly configured hosts.

When deviations are detected, processes need to be in place to determine the cause of the deviations and the steps needed to remediate them and return to the approved baseline. In some cases, and depending on the specific deviation, this can be a fully automated process where the remediation is done and notification is sent to administrative staff with full details. For other types of deviations and corrective actions needed, the change management process may be necessary to gain approval and a methodical approach taken for remediation.

Patch Management

Patch management for a logical infrastructure will closely follow the procedures necessary for the physical infrastructure. This includes the identification, planning, testing, rollout, and verification of patches throughout the environment. The roles and responsibilities for patch management within the virtualized environment will be largely dependent on the cloud service model used, but also on specific contractual and SLA requirements. For an IaaS model, patching will largely or solely be the responsibility of the cloud customer. For PaaS, patch management will largely be the responsibility of the cloud provider, to be done in coordination with the cloud customer. For a SaaS model, the entire responsibility resides with the cloud provider, and with proper redundancy and clustering can be accomplished with little or no impact on the cloud customer.

Performance Monitoring

Performance monitoring is a prime consideration for the cloud customer and their virtualized resources, and will also involve the cloud provider because those resource issues are tied back into the performance capabilities of the underlying physical infrastructure. Performance requirements and the metrics used to determine if they are met should be clearly articulated in the SLA between the cloud customer and the cloud provider. While it is easy to determine if resources for CPU and memory have been properly allocated during the provisioning process, determining if they are actually present and available is a main focus for SLA compliance and contractual obligations. This is especially important because measured service models will charge the cloud customer based on the resources they request and consume, so appropriate performance monitoring is crucial for ensuring contractual obligations are successful met and satisfied.

Backup and Restore of Guest OS Configuration

Regardless of which specific tools or utilities are used for backups of virtualized hosts, the Cloud Security Professional needs to ensure that backups are being performed successfully, as well as perform tests to ensure that restore processes are valid and successful. Vendors will put out recommendations and best practices for backing up their systems and software, and in many cases will also provide a recommended and supported tool for doing so. If another third-party utility is chosen instead, it will be incumbent on the Cloud Security Professional to independently validate and support that tool, as the operating system vendor will not have responsibility for ensuring its success.

Implementation of Network Security Controls

Networking requirements and technologies have been covered extensively throughout the book, and from the logical infrastructure perspective these are very similar to the physical infrastructure layer, with the difference being the reliance on virtualized network devices and appliances. The biggest point here to reiterate is the use of VLANs and methods to segregate and isolate network traffic and access for the virtualized hosts. This is one of the best defense-in-depth strategies available within a cloud environment, and it is a main responsibility of the Cloud Security Professional to test and validate the VLAN implementations that the cloud provider is utilizing to ensure isolation and protection of data.

Log Capture and Analysis

Similar to log requirements for the physical infrastructure, the logical infrastructure will have application and system logs that need to be collected and preserved to meet regulatory requirements. The same methodologies with centralized log collection and the use of SIEM technologies will also fulfill the requirements for log collection and retention in the logical environment. Depending on the cloud service model, a SIEM solution may serve as a SaaS application, where all the tenants are given access to their particular logs and systems. Alternatively, the SIEM may be set up by each tenant on their own virtual resources within the environment, or even sent offsite to either a traditional data center used by the cloud customer or another cloud provider completely. As the Cloud Security Professional, your job duties are to ensure that regulatory requirements are being met by the log collection and analysis processes, that all active alerts required are in place, and that retention requirements are being fully and successfully met.

Management Plan

Overall, the cloud customer is responsible for implementing their own management plan for the use and oversight of their cloud resources and implementations. The management plan will of course focus on the successful implementation of cloud resources and establishing production systems to an operational state, but once systems are in place, the Cloud Security Professional must keep abreast of changes in the cloud environment and perform a full analysis of the possible impact on the customer's systems, security operations, and data privacy and protection. This also includes staying current on security trends and emerging threats, and ensuring the customer's activities and those of the cloud provider are being adequately addressed in a timely manner.

Ensure Compliance with Regulations and Controls

One of the most crucial components of operations is compliance with regulations and controls. This is accomplished through a series of management components that together ensure proper documentation, auditing, and accountability procedures are being followed. These components ensure compliance with regulations and internal policies as well as form a structured operations management program that drives processes and implements governance of management oversight. Many of these components are encapsulated within ITIL (https://www.axelos.com/best-practice-solutions/itil). The following ITIL components are discussed in detail in this section:

- Change Management
- Continuity Management
- Information Security Management
- Continual Service Improvement Management
- Incident Management
- Problem Management
- Release Management
- Deployment Management
- Configuration Management
- Service Level Management
- Availability Management
- Capacity Management

Change Management

Change management is perhaps the most well-known component of IT operations and management oversight. Overall, it includes the processes and procedures that allow an organization to make changes to their IT systems and services in a structured and controlled manner, as well as fulfilling regulatory and policy requirements for documentation and auditing of all change processes and actors. The change management process strives to implement upgrades and changes to production systems, while minimizing any potential impact to users and customers.

Within the ITIL framework are subcomponents of change management that divide up the overall process into a granular series of events and objectives. The first component is the overall management process, which sets the stage and gathers the necessary information and policies that allow changes to proceed. This component provides the exact change management process to the organization, and typically offers a set of documents and processes that standardize the overall change management program.

Once changes are decided upon by management for implementation, the next component involves a high-level analysis of change proposals and requirements. The goal here is to evaluate the potential impact throughout the organization and enterprise and to determine if there are any potential problems that need to be considered from the early stages of design and implementation. The discovery and analysis of any potential dependencies are crucial at this stage before entering into the more formal change process and actionable items.

Once the high-level overview and dependency checks have been completed, if there are no major obstacles discovered, the next component is the creation of the formal request for change (RFC) and the official approval process. An official RFC ticket is created following whichever process and system the organization has in place. Many organizations will use software that handles their formal RFC process. These tickets contain all the information that is pertinent to the change request, such as originator, implementation timeline, official change details and reversal contingency plans, testing plans, and the stakeholders that must formally approve the request. Once entered into the official approval process, those stakeholders identified will evaluate the request to make sure all required information is present and valid, and that the timeline proposed and contingencies match up with policies from management. If all information is valid and appropriate, then each stakeholder within their own area will give approval, with the RFC considered officially approved once all necessary approvals have been obtained and recorded for audit purposes.

Official approvals involve stakeholders throughout the organization, which typically includes development teams, systems and operations teams, security, project managers, and management. Usually two formal approvals are dedicated specifically to the change process itself: the change advisory board (CAB) and the change manager. Both roles are designed to be dedicated to the enactment and oversight of the change process and policies, with both being removed from the groups doing the actual work and those with a vested stake in it. They are meant to be independent oversight and arbiter roles. The main distinction between the CAB and the change manager is the role they play in approving changes or modifications to changes. The CAB, made up of representatives from throughout the organization with different roles, has the authority to approve large and significant changes. The change manager plays a significant role with the CAB, but in most instances can approve only minor or corrective changes, without having to go through the full process with the CAB.

 NOTE One thing that many organizations opt to do is to have a full formal review of processes and procedures for minor changes, where the CAB will approve the actual process rather than the specific change. This usually applies to small and repeatable functions, such as patching, DNS changes, account creations, and so on. Once the CAB has approved the process, the change manager, or even the operations team, is authorized to approve changes and follow the necessary ticket and documentation requirements, without having to go through full CAB approval with each one. This allows for a streamlining of processes while still maintaining policy controls and documentation for audit purposes.

Once approvals have been obtained, the change moves into a process of scheduling and the actual building of the release. At this phase, the actual build package will be assembled, with all the various components required and their documentation for successful implementation. Upon completion of scheduling and the assembling of the build package, formal authorization is obtained for actually deploying the release and making the appropriate configuration changes. This also involves the functional testing and validation of the build package and deployment steps, using the testing plan developed earlier to ensure that all components are working as intended.

The final step in the change management process is to do a final review of the release after implementation has been completed and tested. This involves a review and analysis of the deployment and testing. This step serves a two-fold purpose. The first is to complete a lessons-learned debrief to improve the processes for the future to ensure better success and efficiencies. The second is to ensure that all documentation of the release have been successful completed for future audits or regulatory compliance.

Continuity Management

Continuity management, or business continuity management, is focused on planning for the successful restoration of systems or services after an unexpected outage, incident, or disaster. This can include security incidents that necessitate the shutting down of systems or services, physical problems with hardware systems or even an entire data center, loss of utilities or network connectivity, and widespread natural disasters that affect a large geographic region.

To develop a continuity plan, an organization must first identify and prioritize their systems and services. This will result in a full inventory of all services and the underlying systems and technologies that support them. This also serves to identify which systems are the most important to have restored quickly and which can endure longer outages or even remain down completely until the primary hosting facilities are restored. This is typically done through the development of a business impact analysis (BIA), which contains the identification of services and systems as well as the prioritization as set forth by management and stakeholders.

The business continuity plan outlines those events and incidents that will cause a triggering of the plan to be put into effect, as well as defines different severity levels. The plan should clearly define the roles and responsibilities of everyone involved in carrying it out should the need arise, as well as define the procedures and notification processes. For completeness, the plan should also define the procedures for restoring the production systems to their original state upon the successful closing of the incident, and the Cloud Security Professional should ensure that it is updated and tested at regular intervals, as most systems and services undergo continual change.

Information Security Management

Information security management is focused on the organization's data, IT services, and IT systems, and the assurance of their confidentiality, integrity, and availability. Under ITIL, security management encompasses the design of security controls, testing of security controls, managing security incidents, and continual review and maintenance of security controls and processes. Having security management as an integral part of the organization and the overall IT service components and processes ensures that security will be a part of all discussions and projects, from conception through planning and implementation, and not something that is added or considered at later stages when it is much more difficult or expensive to implement. Security management will be involved to varying degrees with all the other management components addressed in this section.

Continual Service Improvement Management

Continual service improvement is based on the ISO 20000 standards for continual improvement. The process applies quality management principles and the collection of a wide range of metrics and data. This is all combined into a formal analysis process, with a goal of finding areas within systems and operations to continually improve performance, user satisfaction, and cost effectiveness.

Incident Management

Incidents are defined as any event that can lead to a disruption of an organization's services or operations that impacts either internal or public users. Incident management is focused on limiting the impact of these events on an organization and their services, and returning their state to full operational status as quickly as possible. The main intent of the incident management program is to quickly respond to events and prevent them from evolving into large disruptions and more serious problems. A crucial part of any incident management program is to do a full analysis and lessons-learned debrief following an incident. This allows the organization to learn from the series of problems that caused the event, determine how to minimize the likeliness of occurrence in the future, and evaluate how the problem was responded to and corrected. A full understanding of these aspects will lead to a future occurrence of the incident being less likely, as well as a quicker and more efficient response should it happen again. Also, the steps that need to be taken to make the corrections and restore services will be well documented. These processes are typically handled in an organization by the incident response team (IRT) or the incident management team (IMT).

A major priority with any incident or event is the proper categorization and prioritization of it. This is based on the scale of the impact and the urgency to recover services. Typically, this is done by assigning a low, medium, or high designation to both the impact and urgency. This allows management to properly allocate resources and attention to the incident, and will often match up with previously designed response plans, which are then put into action.

An incident response process typically follows the same progression of sequences, regardless of the organization or categorization of the particular incident, as shown in Figure 6-1.

Problem Management

The focus of problem management is to analyze and identify potential issues, and put processes and mitigations in place to prevent predictable problems from ever occurring in the first place. This is done by collecting and analyzing data and reports from systems and applications, as well as reports from previous incidents, and then using that data to identify and predict potential problems. While the goal of problem management is to prevent predictable problems from occurring, through the identification of problem areas, processes and measures can be put into place to minimize the effect of those that cannot be prevented, or at minimum to have procedures in place to quickly recover from them when they do occur.

Figure 6-1
Incident
response cycle
and process

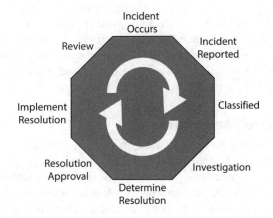

Release and Deployment Management

Release and deployment management involves the planning, coordinating, execution, and validation of changes and rollouts to the production environment. The main focus is on properly mapping out all steps required for a release and then properly configuring and loading it. This typically involves coordination between the business owner, developers, implementation team, and those who will validate and test the release after implementation. The release team will usually be involved at the early stages of planning a release, documenting the steps required and the stakeholders involved, and then working with the developers to build the release package and instructions. After the release has been deployed, the release management team will coordinate functional testing and the fixing of any minor defects. If there are any substantial defects found after the release, the team will coordinate discussions with management as to whether the release should be backed out, following plans established as part of the release instructions, should that step need to be taken. Upon successful completion of a release and functional testing and validation signoff, the release management team is responsible for closing out open tickets related to the release and ensuring that new baselines are established, reflecting the changes made during the release as the new production state.

Configuration Management

Configuration management tracks and maintains detailed information about any IT components within the organization. It encompasses all physical and virtual systems, and includes hosts, servers, appliances, and devices. It also includes all the details about each of these components, such as settings, installed software, and version and patch levels. This information applies to a traditional data center or systems hosted within a cloud environment.

The configuration management process is an ongoing and iterative one. When new systems are brought online and configured, they are immediately added to the configuration database. As changes occur over time, updates are constantly made to configuration information, and the configuration management process becomes an integral part of many other processes, such as change management and release management. Also, the information contained within the configuration databases becomes crucial to processes such as incident management, security management, continuity management, and capacity management. The information contained within the configuration management database will also be used to monitor and ensure that no unauthorized changes have been made to systems.

Service Level Management

Service level management is focused on the negotiation, implementation, and oversight of SLAs. This component, while focused on SLAs, is also responsible for overseeing operational level agreements (OLAs) and underpinning contracts (UCs). You know from previously in this book that an SLA is a formal agreement between the cloud customer and cloud provider that maps out minimal performance standards for elements detailed in the contract. An OLA is similar to an SLA, but it has as its two parties two internal units of the same organization, rather than the customer and an external provider. A UC is a contract agreed upon between an organization and an external service provider or vendor. The major focus of service level management is the enforcement and metrics of SLAs to ensure contract compliance and the meeting of customer expectations.

Availability Management

Availability management is focused on making sure system resources, processes, personnel, and toolsets are properly allocated and secured to meet SLA requirements for performance. Availability management defines the objectives for the availability of IT services, as well as how those objectives will be measured, collected, reported, and evaluated. IT also strives to ensure that the way IT systems are configured and provisioned is consistent with the organization's availability goals or requirements.

Capacity Management

Capacity management is focused on the required system resources needed to deliver performance at an acceptable level to meet SLA requirements, and doing so in a cost-effective and efficient manner. Capacity management is a very important aspect to running any IT system overall. If a system is under-provisioned, then services and performance will lag, which could lead to the loss of business or reputation. If a system is over-provisioned, then the organization is spending more money than needed to maintain their services, thus leading to lower revenues and profits.

Conduct Risk Assessment for the Logical and Physical Infrastructure

Risk measures the threats an organization, their IT systems, and their data face. Risk assessment evaluates the organization's overall vulnerability level, the threats they face, the likeliness a threat will succeed, and any mitigation efforts that can be undertaken to further minimize the risk level. Ultimately, the organization can try to decrease and minimize the level of risk facing a system, or the organization will have to accept the level of risk.

The risk evaluation, assessment, and acceptance methodology comprises four main components and phases. Figure 6-2 shows the risk assessment processes and components.

Framing Risk

Framing risk sets the stage for the rest of the risk management processes and serves as its basis. At this stage, the organization will determine what risk and levels they want to evaluate, based on the unique characteristics of their systems, the requirements of their data, and any specific details about implementations or specific threats they wish to determine. Decisions made at this point will guide how the risk assessment is approached and its overall scope.

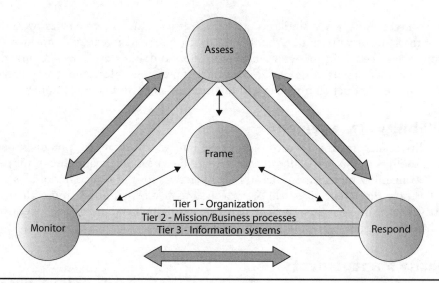

Figure 6-2 Risk assessment processes and components (source: NIST SP 800-39: Managing Information Security Risk)

Assessing Risk

The formal risk assessment process involves several steps of measurement and evaluation, combined with assigning numerical values to categories, ranging from low risk to high risk, typically on a scale of 1 to 5, with 5 being the highest risk.

The first step is to determine the specific threats the organization and their systems face. This entails analyzing the type of data and its sensitivity, to determine the value to an attacker and the types of efforts they will employ in an attempt to compromise it. The threat analysis will also be focused on what kinds of groups and attackers are determined to compromise the systems, which in turn determines the sophistication of likely attacks and the types of methods employed during it.

The second part is to assess the vulnerabilities of a particular system. Vulnerabilities can be internal or external in nature, and both should be included with the assessment. Internal vulnerabilities focus on configuration issues, known weaknesses in security measures, particular software used, or any other type of item an organization is aware of. External vulnerabilities can include natural and environmental issues facing a data center and operations, as well as social engineering attacks.

The third key component to a risk assessment is evaluating the potential harm that an attack can cause to an organization's systems, data, operations, or reputation. This is based on the vulnerabilities and threats already established and the potential damage that could be caused by them.

The last main component is the likelihood of a successful attack and the harm it could cause. While there will be a variety of possible vulnerabilities identified, not all carry the same likelihood of being successful exploited by an attack, and even within individual attacks, there can be varying degrees of exploitation and damage.

TIP An often overlooked aspect of potential harm is the loss of reputation to an organization. The focus tends to be on the loss of uptime or business, but impaired services or news stories about data leaks or systems problems can do far more damage over the long term than short-duration outages.

After the four main components have been identified and documented, the actual assessment of risk and testing can be performed. The actual tests performed fall into one of two categories: qualitative or quantitative.

Qualitative Assessments

A qualitative risk assessment is done against nonnumerical data and is descriptive in nature, rather than data driven. Qualitative assessments are typically used when an organization does not have the money, time, data, or sophistication to perform a full quantitative assessment. They typically involve the review of documentation for operational procedures and system designs, as well as interviews with system maintainers, developers, and security personnel. Once all data is gathered from interviews and documentation and technical specifications have been reviewed, the findings of threats, vulnerabilities, impact, and likeliness can be matched to the system implementations and operational procedures. From this synthesis, reports can be generated for management as to a risk evaluation and categorization, from low to high, for areas such as risk, likeliness, and damage possibilities.

Quantitative Assessments

Qualitative assessments are typically used when an organization has the money, time, data, and sophistication to perform them. Quantitative assessments are data driven, where hard values can be determined and used for comparison and calculative measure. Whereas quantitative assessment is considered its own type, qualitative assessment is always part of a quantitative one because not all data can be numerical, and key aspects of operations and systems will be missed if only numerical methods are utilized.

The following measures and calculations form the basis of quantitative assessments:

- **SLE** The SLE is the single loss expectancy value. The SLE is defined as the difference between the original value of an asset and the remaining value of the asset after a single successful exploit. It is calculated by multiplying the asset value in dollars by what is called the exposure factor, which is the loss due to a successful exploit as a percentage.

- **ARO** The annualized rate of occurrence value. The ARO is an estimated number of the times a threat will successfully exploit a given vulnerability over the course of a single year.

- **ALE** The annualized loss expectancy value. The ALE is the value of the SLE multiplied by the ARO, so the ALE = SLE × ARO.

By calculating the ALE and assigning a numeral dollar value to the expected loss from a single vulnerability, the organization can now use that value to determine the cost–benefit implications of available countermeasures. If the ALE is higher than the cost to mitigate the vulnerability, it makes sense for the organization to spend the money on mitigation. However, if the ALE is less the cost of mitigation, the organization may soundly decide to accept the risk and the cost from dealing with successful exploits, as doing so will cost less money than the cost of mitigation. Management can use the ALE to make sound judgments on investments in security countermeasures for their systems.

For example, an organization may calculate the SLE for the failure of a particular feature of their application at $50,000 in loss of business based on its usage and the time it will take to recover. Based on analysis and trends, they anticipate that such an outage will occur potentially three times a year. This means on an annual basis, the organization can expect to lose $150,000 in revenue from these outages. If there is a piece of additional software that could mitigate this outage, and the cost to license the software is $100,000 per year, then this would be a sound investment as the cost to mitigate is lower than the cost of the outages. However, if the software to mitigate were to cost $200,000 per year, then management may soundly decide to accept the risk as the costs to prevent it would be greater than the loss of revenue. Of course these considerations must take into account potential loss of reputation and trust, above and beyond just the loss of revenue during the outages.

 CAUTION   The ALE, while useful for evaluating the spending of funds to mitigate risk, also has to be considered within the context of any data that is covered under regulatory rules. While the cost to mitigate a vulnerability may outweigh the direct risk to the organization to deal with it if it occurs, regulatory rules can impose stiff fines or even the denial of operating on contracts or services that use protected data. The potential cost for exploits under regulatory requirements must also be heavily factored into any decisions on cost–benefit analyses.

Responding to Risk

After the identification and evaluation of risk, combined with the potential mitigation efforts and their costs, an organization must decide on the appropriate course of action for each risk. There are four main categories for risk responses, as detailed next.

Accept the Risk

An organization may opt to simply accept the risk of a particular exploit and the threats posed against it. This occurs after a thorough risk assessment and the evaluation of the costs of mitigation. In an instance where the cost to mitigate outweighs the cost of accepting the risk and dealing with any possible consequences, an organization may opt to simply deal with an exploit when and if it occurs. In most instances, the decision to accept a risk will only be permitted for low-level risks, and never for moderate or high risks. The decision to accept a risk must be taken very seriously, as any successful exploit may transcend simple dollar values in remediation—it could have lasting impact on an organization's reputation and user base. Any decisions to accept risk must be clearly documented and official approvals granted by management.

Avoid the Risk

An organization may opt to take measures to ensure that a risk is never realized, rather than accepting or mitigating it. This typically involves a decision to not utilize certain services or systems. For example, if a company decides that integrating direct purchasing through their website, rather than requiring faxed or phone orders, will pose a significant risk to their systems and data protections, they can opt to not enable ordering from their website at all. While this obviously could lead to significant loss of revenue and customers, it allows an organization to avoid the risk altogether. This is typically not a solution that an organization will undertake, with the exception of very minor feature sets of systems or applications, where the disabling or removal will not post a significant impediment to the users or operations.

Transfer the Risk

Risk transfer is the process of having another entity assume the risk from the organization. One thing to note, though, is that risk cannot always be transferred to another entity. A prime example of transfer is through insurance policies to cover the financial costs of successful risk exploits. However, it should be noted that this will not cover all issues related to risk transference. The direct financial costs may be able to be transferred via insurance policies, but this will not cover the loss of the organization's reputation. Also, under some regulations risk cannot be transferred, because the business owner bears final responsibility for any exploits resulting in the loss of privacy or confidentiality of data, especially personal data.

Mitigate the Risk

Risk mitigation is the strategy most commonly expected and understood. Through risk mitigation, an organization takes steps—sometimes involving the spending of money on new systems or technologies—to fix and prevent any exploits from happening. This can involve taking steps to totally eliminate a particular risk or taking steps to lower the likeliness of an exploit or the impact of a successful exploit. The decision to undertake risk mitigation will heavily depend on the calculated cost–benefit analysis from the assessments.

NOTE As a Cloud Security Professional, you will need to be aware of the concept of residual risk. In short, no matter what efforts an organization takes, and no matter how much money they can decide to spend, they will never reach a point were all risks are mitigated or removed. This remaining risk falls into the category of residual risk.

Monitoring Risk

Once risks have been identified, possible directions to deal with them have been analyzed and decisions made, they will need to be tracked and monitored continually. The first main focus of risk monitoring is an ongoing process of evaluation to determine if the same threats and vulnerabilities still exist in the same form as when the assessment was undertaken. With the rapidly changing world of IT systems and services, both the threats and vulnerabilities will also be in a constant state of flux. Understanding the changing dynamic of risks, threats, and vulnerabilities will enable the risk monitoring process to evaluate whether risk mitigation strategies are still effective. It also serves as a formal process to monitor changing regulatory requirements and whether the current risk evaluations and mitigations still fulfill and meet their expectations.

Understand the Collection, Acquisition, and Preservation of Digital Evidence

The term *digital forensics* has become more prevalent in recent years as techniques for collecting data and preserving data have improved, in addition to the increase in legal and regulatory requirements for performing deep analysis of events. Forensics in a broad sense just means the application of science and scientific methods to an analysis.

Due to the complexities of a cloud environment and its fundamental differences from a traditional data center, it is imperative for an organization to have a comprehensive understanding of how the cloud provider handles data, and how they will format and preserve data in the event of a court order. This should be articulated in the contract, as well as the specific roles and responsibilities on behalf of both the cloud provider and the cloud customer should such an order be received. No data or systems should be moved to a cloud environment without an understanding of and agreement on how such an order will be handled and processed if received. Failure to do this prior to moving any data will put an organization at substantial regulatory and legal risk should an order be received.

Proper Methodologies for the Forensic Collection of Data

The same requirements that are followed for normal evidence collection and preservation also apply to digital evidence. This relates to a very formal and tightly controlled chain of custody, as well as methods for preserving the original integrity of the data. Whereas data collection has well established methods and practices in a traditional data center, a cloud environment brings a whole new set of challenges.

The first major challenge in a cloud environment is the location of the data. In a traditional data center, the data is located either on physical drives within servers, or on network-based storage that has physical connections and is located in the same data center. With a cloud environment, all data storage is virtualized and can be located anywhere throughout the cloud data center (or data centers). It can be a big challenge ensuring that all locations of data are known, or all locations of virtual machines and services. Before any data collection and preservation can be undertaken, knowing the full locations and collection points is absolutely vital.

Ownership of data is also a huge concern in a cloud environment for forensic data collection. With a traditional data center, the organization will fully own the systems and storage devices, and know exactly where they are located and how they are configured. Depending on the cloud service model, the cloud customer will have varying degrees of ownership over data and access to it. With IaaS, the customer has a high degree of access and control over virtual machines and everything built on them. With PaaS and especially with SaaS, the cloud customer's access and control are extremely limited, if not completely removed. Regardless of which model is used, though, the cloud provider will be the sole owner and controller of many infrastructure-level systems and data, such as networking gear and storage systems. The contract and SLA between the cloud customer and the cloud provider must clearly articulate access, support, and response timelines for the collection of forensic data, should the need or desire for it arise. It is impossible in any model for the cloud customer to fully undertake data collection of this type, so the support of the cloud provider and their administrative staff is crucial.

In a cloud environment, data and systems are very rapidly changing and dynamic. In a traditional data center, there is no question about the physical location and possession of systems and data. In a cloud environment, virtual machines can be in a large number of locations at any time, and can also change at any time, making the collection of data and the preservation of the chain of custody very tricky. It also can add complexity to chain-of-custody issues with regard to the time zones of where the data was located at the time of the incident and where the data was collected from, which all needs to kept in sync and documented.

Cloud systems are completely based on virtualization and the use of virtual machines. This makes it more imperative for data to be collected in the right way. With all session and other information running in virtual memory space versus on physical hardware, turning off any virtual machines will cause a loss of crucial data that will be integral to any collection of evidence.

Multitenancy can also cause problems with data collection and preservation. Because different customers can have their data located within the same physical hosts and the same devices as other customers, data captures can potentially contain records from different customers. In order for the validity of data to be maintained and admissible in court, separation will have to be maintained and documented between captured data of the systems in question and any potential data from other customers that may be mingled in with it.

The big issue of data ownership and access will create the biggest problem for the Cloud Security Professional in the collection and preservation of data and evidence. The cloud customer is totally dependent on the cloud provider for the collection of data, which is where contract and SLA requirements become so crucial. The cloud provider is responsible for ensuring that the customer's data is collected and comprehensive, and that it is separated from other tenants' data. This also includes maintaining the initial chain of custody and securing of data from evidence collection. This is a crucial aspect later for ensuring the integrity of data and the admissibility of evidence.

Evidence Management

Maintaining of the integrity of data and the chain of custody is vital to the management and preservation of evidence collected. Without the proper controls and processes in place, the data could possibly be later scrutinized and deemed invalid or inadmissible as evidence. The Cloud Security Professional should always ensure that any collection of data and evidence is limited to the scope of what is requested or required, and not to go beyond that with extra data. Limiting the scope to the specific request will allow the minimal disclosure and reduce the potential for sensitive data from being exposed. It will also serve to provided documented evidence for any regulatory oversight that the only data exposed tightly conforms to the exact request received. In some cases, if the requestor is a government source or part of a sensitive criminal investigation, the processes and the request itself may be deemed confidential, and as such, the staff involved with its collection should be strictly limited. The same issue also arises with disclosure of collection activities or processes in a multitenant environment. The cloud customer should never disclose any collection requirements, requests, or activities to any other tenants. If the cloud provider has any such contractual or SLA requirements to do so, that will be handled by the cloud provider through their communications channels and policies, and should never be disclosed by the cloud customer to other cloud customers or potential customers.

Manage Communication with Relevant Parties

Communication is always vital and important between parties with any business or type of operation, but especially so with IT services. Cloud services add another layer of complexity and considerations on top of regular communications. For communications to be effective and foster optimal relationships, they need to be both concise and accurate. The constructs of details that most learn as a young child are the same for communications at this level as well: who, what, when, where, why, and how.

Vendors

Communication with vendors will be driven almost exclusively through contract and SLA requirements. Both articulate communication requirements, from the perspectives of types of communications and the frequency of them. This will typically be done through the requirement of reports, the content to be contained within them, as well as the frequency that they must be supplied. Vendor communication is crucially important for the entire duration of the relationship, and will cover everything from initial onboarding and configuration, production run and maintenance phases, to even communication throughout any decommission or contract-termination process.

Customers

Because there are a variety of audiences and interests, understanding customers' particular needs and being able to scope what is communicated is essential. From the perspective of IT operations or the Cloud Security Professional, customers can be either internal or external, depending on how the services are offered and delivered. A crucial element of customer communication is understanding where roles and responsibilities fall. If there is a gap between what a provider expects the customer to maintain, or vice versa, the likely result is a strained customer relationship, service interruptions, or working in opposition to each other and causing conflicts. In many cases, communications about availability, changing policies, and system upgrades and changes will be the most crucial to the relationship between the provider and customer.

Partners

Partners are a bit different with regard to communication than vendors, because there isn't a contractual relationship in the same sense between organizations as there is between a cloud customer and a cloud provider. The most prevalent example of partnerships within a cloud environment is through the use of federated services and federated access to resources and systems. A formal agreement is typical between federated organizations and will articulate requirements and expectations for the partnership. In order for this partnership to operate and be successful, communication about expectations, system changes, security incidents, and availability is very important. With federated systems, it is crucial to ensure that both proper onboarding and offboarding policies and procedures are clearly communicated and understood.

Regulators

Whether IT operations are hosted within a traditional data center or a cloud provider, communication with regulators is essential. When an organization is considering deploying IT services and operations to a cloud environment, this is even more critical. Many regulatory requirements are based on geography and jurisdiction, which are both straightforward in their approach when hosting in a traditional data center. However, with a cloud environment, where services can be moved easily or even spread across multiple data centers, these concepts become significantly more complex and muddled. Undertaking early communication with regulatory bodies and auditors when considering such a move will allow an organization to find any potential problems or considerations very early on, before time and resources have been expended on planning or moving IT services. Many regulatory bodies are also now adopting and publishing cloud-specific requirements and recommendations that could help drive the direction an organization decides to pursue with cloud hosting.

Other Stakeholders

Depending on the project or application, there may be other stakeholders that need to be involved in communication processes that are either specific to that project or specific to regulatory requirements. The Cloud Security Professional needs to evaluate each set of circumstances to determine whether there are other appropriate stakeholders, as well as determine what type of communication is required and its frequency.

Exercise

Your boss has just asked you, a Cloud Security Professional, to evaluate whether your company should continue to buy services from a cloud provider or consider turning the current traditional data center into a cloud-based data center for the company's own private cloud.

1. How do you approach this analysis?

2. What key considerations do you need to analyze from your traditional data center to evolve it into a cloud-based data center?

3. What internal teams and groups would need to revamp their processes to make this work?

4. Which stakeholders do you need to communicate with and for what reasons?

Chapter Review

In this chapter, you learned about the operational components that allow a cloud data center to function. The cloud data center is focused on logical and physical systems, but there are great similarities between their features and considerations. You learned about the ITIL components that allow for overall system and service management, as well as how to conduct risk assessments, communicate with relevant parties, and perform the collection of digital information and evidence for regulatory compliance or investigations.

Questions

1. What is the first step in the process of creating a baseline image?

   A. Patch the operating system to the latest level.

   B. Update all software and utilities on the image.

   C. Perform a clean install with a base operating system.

   D. Disable nonessential services.

2. Which networking concept allows for segregation and isolation of systems in a cloud environment?

   A. VLAN

   B. WAN

   C. LAN

   D. PLAN

3. What is the *MOST* important security reason for centralizing log collection?

   A. Minimize storage needs on hosts

   B. Prevent log manipulation or deletion on a host

    C. Encrypt logs that contain sensitive information

    D. Immediate response for eDiscovery requests

4. What type of application allows centralized log searching and reporting?

    A. LSRT

    B. SIEM

    C. SAMS

    D. CLSR

5. Which of the following concepts is focused on preventing potential issues from occurring within a system or process?

    A. Incident management

    B. Continuity management

    C. Availability management

    D. Problem management

6. What is the order for the four components of a risk management process?

    A. Framing, monitoring, assessing, responding

    B. Responding, assessing, framing, monitoring

    C. Framing, monitoring, assessing, responding

    D. Responding, assessing, framing, monitoring

7. What is the name of the Microsoft tool for performing patches on systems?

    A. WUSU

    B. MPMT

    C. MSPT

    D. WSUS

8. What does the acronym SLE stand for?

    A. Server loss exception

    B. System loss expectancy

    C. Single loss expectancy

    D. System load emergency

9. To automatically detect and block attacks against systems, which type of device would you employ?

    A. IDS

    B. NIDS

    C. HIPS

    D. IPS

10. What are the four possible responses to risk?

    A. Accept, avoid, transfer, mitigate

    B. Deflect, avoid, transfer, ignore

    C. Avoid, insure, remediate, nullify

    D. Accept, deflect, ignore, cancel

11. Who has responsibility for forensic collection of data in an IaaS implementation?

    A. Cloud provider

    B. Cloud customer

    C. Cloud broker

    D. Cloud administrator

12. Risk transfer is often equated to what type of service?

    A. Banking

    B. Policing

    C. Insurance

    D. Inspection

13. Which of the following is *NOT* part of the management plan for operations of a cloud environment?

    A. Orchestration

    B. Maintenance

    C. Planning

    D. Scheduling

14. Which of the following is concerned with ensuring enough resources are available to meet SLA requirements?

    A. Capacity management

    B. Allocation management

    C. Availability management

    D. System management

15. Which type of assessment is based on observations and documentation rather than data and numbers?

    A. Quantitative

    B. Cursory

    C. Documentary

    D. Qualitative

Questions and Answers

1. What is the first step in the process of creating a baseline image?

    A. Patch the operating system to the latest level.

    B. Update all software and utilities on the image.

    C. Perform a clean install with a base operating system.

    D. Disable nonessential services.

    C. When creating a new baseline image, you always want to start with a clean operating system install. This allows configuration settings to be applied from the bottom up, and without the possibility of other changes from previous images impacting the new image, or having to clean up an old image and remember to reset everything to the original. Once a new operating system install is used, it can have all nonessential services disabled and brought to the latest patching level, have updated software and utilities installed, and have all security and configuration requirements set.

2. Which networking concept allows for segregation and isolation of systems in a cloud environment?

    A. VLAN

    B. WAN

    C. LAN

    D. PLAN

    A. A VLAN allows for network isolation in a cloud environment by establishing virtual network segments, with their own IP space and firewall settings, that are segregated from other network segments. Wide area network (WAN) and local area network (LAN) are both network concepts that speak to networks as a whole, and not to segments within a network and separation, while PLAN is an extraneous choice.

3. What is the *MOST* important security reason for centralizing log collection?

    A. Minimize storage needs on hosts

    B. Prevent log manipulation or deletion on a host

    C. Encrypt logs that contain sensitive information

    D. Immediate response for eDiscovery requests

    B. Preventing log manipulation or deletion on a host is a main reason for log aggregation. By sending or copying the logs from hosts into a central system, it prevents those with system or administrative access on host servers from altering the logs to cover traces of unauthorized access, or the wholesale deletion of logs.

This enables separation of duties as well, where the security team and auditors can have access to the aggregated logs, and the system administrators have access to the actual systems, but not to each other. Although minimizing storage on systems and allowing more aggressive log rotation and cleanup are benefits of a SIEM solution, they are not a main reason for it or a security-focused benefit. Encryption of log files can be done at any level if needed or desired, though, in general, sensitive information should not be written to log files, and a SIEM solution may assist with eDiscovery orders, but it would depend on the scope of the order and it is not a primary reason for a SIEM solution.

4. What type of application allows centralized log searching and reporting?

   A. LSRT

   B. SIEM

   C. SAMS

   D. CLSR

   B. A security information and event management (SIEM) solution allows centralized searching and reporting of log files or any other event data that has been collected and aggregated into it. The other examples are extraneous acronyms to the question.

5. Which of the following concepts is focused on preventing potential issues from occurring within a system or process?

   A. Incident management

   B. Continuity management

   C. Availability management

   D. Problem management

   D. Problem management is focused on preventing issues from occurring within a system or process in a proactive manner. Incident management is focused on the response and mitigation of problems or incidents after they have occurred in a reactionary manner. Continuity management is focused on the resiliency or restoration or services after an unexpected outage or event, and availability management is focused on meeting SLA requirements for performance and availability of systems.

6. What is the order for the four components of a risk management process?

   A. Framing, monitoring, assessing, responding

   B. Responding, assessing, framing, monitoring

C. Framing, monitoring, assessing, responding

D. Responding, assessing, framing, monitoring

C. Framing, monitoring, assessing, and responding are the four components of a risk management process, and in that order. The other choices contain components that are not part of the risk management process.

7. What is the name of the Microsoft tool for performing patches on systems?

A. WUSU

B. MPMT

C. MSPT

D. WSUS

D. Windows Server Update Services (WSUS) is the name of the Microsoft tool for performing patches on a Windows system. The other acronyms are extraneous.

8. What does the acronym SLE stand for?

A. Server loss exception

B. System loss expectancy

C. Single loss expectancy

D. System load emergency

C. SLE stands for single loss expectancy, which is the difference in the value of an asset from before a successful exploit to after one has occurred. It is calculated by multiplying the value of an asset in dollars by the exposure value, which is a percentage of loss based on a successful exploit.

9. To automatically detect and block attacks against systems, which type of device would you employ?

A. IDS

B. NIDS

C. HIPS

D. IPS

D. An intrusion prevention system (IPS) is used to detect and automatically block attacks against a system, as opposed to an intrusion detection system (IDS) which is designed to detect and alert on potential attacks. The other options are specific types of either device; an HIPS is a host-based IPS and NIDS is a network-based IDS device.

10. What are the four possible responses to risk?

    A. Accept, avoid, transfer, mitigate

    B. Deflect, avoid, transfer, ignore

    C. Avoid, insure, remediate, nullify

    D. Accept, deflect, ignore, cancel

    A. Accept, avoid, transfer, and mitigate are the four possible responses to risk. Accept occurs when an organization decides that cost of mitigation exceeds the costs of the risk and decides to leave the risk in place. Avoid is when an organization takes other mitigating steps to avoid an exploit happening at all, such as placing other technologies like network devices to block traffic that can exploit an application rather than applying fixes to the application itself. Transfer is when an organization can get a different party to accept liability for a successful exploit, most commonly in the form of insurance. Mitigate is when an organization can fix the actual exploit so that it cannot occur. The other options are not the correct four possible risk responses.

11. Who has responsibility for forensic collection of data in an IaaS implementation?

    A. Cloud provider

    B. Cloud customer

    C. Cloud broker

    D. Cloud administrator

    A. Since a cloud provider controls the physical and underlying systems within a cloud and is the only party that has full administrative and system access to everything, they are responsible for forensic data collection within the environment. Expectations and requirements should be established within the contract between the cloud customer and cloud provider to govern the collection and timeline to do so.

12. Risk transfer is often equated to what type of service?

    A. Banking

    B. Policing

    C. Insurance

    D. Inspection

    C. The transfer of risk is when an organization gets another entity to assume liability for all or some of the impact and loss as a result of a successful exploit. The most common example of this kind of transfer is through the use of insurance to cover any losses.

13. Which of the following is *NOT* part of the management plan for operations of a cloud environment?

   A. Orchestration

   B. Maintenance

   C. Planning

   D. Scheduling

   C. The three main building blocks for a cloud environment and the management plan for it are orchestration, maintenance, and scheduling. Planning would occur before systems or applications are deployed to a cloud environment and thus is not part of the actual management plan for cloud operations.

14. Which of the following is concerned with ensuring enough resources are available to meet SLA requirements?

   A. Capacity management

   B. Allocation management

   C. Availability management

   D. System management

   A. Capacity management is concerned with ensuring that sufficient resources are available to meet the needs of cloud customers throughout the environment, as established through their SLAs. Availability management is ensuring that systems and services are available and accessible when needed by users. System management is concerned with the overall management of IT systems and assets within an environment. Allocation management is not one of the principles of ITIL.

15. Which type of assessment is based on observations and documentation rather than data and numbers?

   A. Quantitative

   B. Cursory

   C. Documentary

   D. Qualitative

   D. A qualitative assessment is based on a review of documentation in regard to system design, policies, and procedures. It is not based on hard numbers or data in the way that a quantitative assessment is. Both cursory and documentary choices are not types of assessments.

Legal and Compliance Domain

This chapter covers the following topics in Domain 6:

- Legal risks and controls relating to cloud computing
- eDiscovery and forensic requirements
- Laws pertaining to PII
- Audit types
- Audit processes in a cloud environment
- Risk management as it pertains to the cloud
- Outsourcing to a cloud and overseeing the contract

Cloud computing presents many unique challenges on the legal and policy front because it often crosses jurisdictional lines that have different rules and regulations as to data privacy and protection. Although auditing all IT systems is a very critical and sensitive process, a cloud environment presents unique challenges and requirements for auditing, as a cloud customer will not have full access to systems or processes in the same manner they would in a traditional data enter. Risk management also poses unique challenges in a cloud, as it expands the realm of operations and systems for an organization. Also, the realities of a cloud environment introduce additional risks and complexities, especially with multitenancy. We will also touch on the requirements for managing outsourcing and contracts with cloud providers.

Legal Requirements and Unique Risks Within the Cloud Environment

Cloud environments often cross jurisdictional lines and create a wealth of complex issues regarding applicable laws and regulations from the policy side, as well as technological issues for data collection and discovery requirements.

International Legislation Conflicts

With the global nature of computing services and applications, it is almost certain that international boundaries and jurisdictions will be crossed from both policy and techno- logical perspectives. When operating within a global framework, a security professional runs into a multitude of jurisdictions and requirements that many times might not be clearly applicable or might be in contention with each other. These requirements can include the location of the users and the type of data they enter into the systems, the laws governing the organization that owns the applications and any regulatory requirements they may have, as well as the appropriate laws and regulations for the jurisdiction hous- ing the IT resources and where the data is actually stored, which might be in multiple jurisdictions as well.

With systems that span jurisdictions, it is inevitable that conflicts will arise when incidents occur, especially concerning the laws requiring reporting and information collection, preservation, and disclosure. Many times the resolution is not clear, because there is no international authority to mediate the problems that has full jurisdictional control at this time, so such incidents can become very complex and difficult legal matters to resolve. In many instances, legal proceedings in multiple jurisdictions are required, which may or may not have complementary outcomes and rulings, making orders and investigations increasingly difficult, especially with the move toward cloud computing.

Appraisal of Legal Risks Specific to Cloud Computing

Cloud computing adds an extra layer of complexity from a legal perspective. With a traditional data center, the organization will own and control the environment, systems, and resources, as well as the data that is housed within all of them. Even in environments where support and hosting services are contracted out to a third party, the contracting organization will still hold control over their own systems and data, and typically will be physically segregated within a data center from a network standpoint as well as in cages on the data center floor. This makes the legal requirements and the parties to them very clear for any types of issues that should arise.

With a cloud environment, the cloud customer is reliant on the cloud provider that actually owns and operates the overall system and services. The main difference that distinguishes a cloud environment from a legal perspective is the concept of multitenancy—that is, having cloud customers sharing the same physical hardware and systems as each other. This makes the cloud provider not only contractually bound to your organization, but also to all the other organizations using the same hosting environment. This precludes the cloud provider from simply capturing systems and turning over any and all data to investigators or regulatory agencies because they will need to ensure that no data or logs are captured from other customers and potentially exposed to additional parties.

Regardless of where a system and its services are hosted, an organization is legally responsible for all data they use and store. When a cloud provider is used for these services, the contract will need to ensure that the cloud provider accepts and complies with the same regulatory and legal requirements that pertain to the cloud customer. This includes jurisdictional requirements based on the locations of customers or data, but also regulatory requirements such as HIPAA and Sarbanes–Oxley (SOX) that apply to applications and their data, based on the type of application and what the data is used for, regardless of the specific physical location of the data and the services that contain and process it.

Legal Controls

With the complexities of cloud environments and the geographically disparate realities, any systems and applications hosted within a cloud will be subjected to a variety of different laws and legal controls.

In the United States, there are a myriad of federal and state laws and regulations that a system must conform to. On the federal level, there are regulations like HIPAA and SOX, as well as federal regulations based on the particular type of commerce and the data involved is concerned. With any systems that interact with federal agencies in any way, there are extensive requirements under FISMA for compliance with security controls required by the federal government, depending on the classification of the system and the data it uses. On the state level, there can be additional requirements placed on systems, also dependent on the type of commerce involved and the type of data being used and stored. Specific requirements can also arise from contractual language and the specific rights and responsibilities required within the jurisdictions.

Other countries have their own regulatory and legal requirements that may or may not be similar in nature to those of the United States. The most prominent of those requirements are put forth by the EU, which has a very strong focus on personal privacy and data protection. In fact, many countries and jurisdictions around the world have adopted the EU or U.S. guidelines and regulatory requirements, even if they reside outside of their jurisdiction, as a model to use. However, the EU guidelines are far more commonplace in this regard.

While not directly legal in nature, many standards organizations have adopted rules that mirror or closely align with actual legal requirements. This applies to regulatory and standardization models such as PCI-DSS and the various ISO/IEC standards. These typically dictate specific requirements for security controls as well as operational procedures and policies for handling specific types of data and applications. They usually are included as contractual requirements from the organization level as well as between the cloud customer and the cloud provider.

eDiscovery

eDiscovery is the process of searching, identifying, collecting, and securing electronic data and records, to ultimately be used in either criminal or civil legal proceedings. With a traditional data center, the collection and identification is typically easier and less complex because physical systems are known and can be easily isolated or brought offline and preserved. With a cloud environment, all systems and data are virtualized, and because of this, additional challenges and complexity exist within cloud environments.

Within a traditional data center, when a request or requirement for eDiscovery is received, it is substantially easier to determine the scope and systems involved because they will be all under tight control and typically on-premises, with well-known configurations and systems involved. The security team, working with a company's legal and privacy teams, can present the eDiscovery request to the application and operations teams, determine which server and systems are involved, and begin the data collection and preservation processes without much need for external involvement in most cases. Within a cloud environment, this information is scattered over virtual machines and storage devices, which may be dispersed across different physical data centers and jurisdictions as well. A further complication is that these systems have multiple tenants hosted on them, making isolation and collection more complex, and the privacy and confidentiality of other tenants' data are required as well. Within a cloud environment, systems cannot simply be physically isolated and preserved.

Legal Issues

A few aspects of eDiscovery from a legal perspective make bringing a cloud environment into compliance more complex. These legal realities are found in the United States in the Federal Rules of Civil Procedure (FRCP) and the Federal Rules of Evidence (FRE). These rules must be followed for evidence to be identified, collected, and preserved in a manner that will make it admissible in court proceedings.

One major aspect is that eDiscovery is focused on information that is in the "possession, custody, or control" of an organization, per the Federal Rule of Civil Procedure 34(a) of the United States. For a traditional data center, this is a very easy issue to address because all information is on dedicated servers and storage for the particular company or organization. Even in instances where data center space is leased, each client will have their systems and assets on isolated physical servers and contained in locked cages that are particular to their own systems and protected from other clients' systems. When information is contained in a virtualized environment, especially a cloud environment, questions about control and possession can become legally pertinent between the cloud customer and cloud provider. The big question as to who actually possess and controls the information is something that should be articulated in the contract and terms of service with the cloud provider. While this is a complex question for private clouds, it is even more so in public clouds, which are much larger, open to anyone, and contain in many instances large numbers of tenants.

A second major issue from FRCP is that data custodians are assumed and expected to have full knowledge of the internal design and architecture of their system and networks. With a traditional data center, where full ownership and design is already established, this is trivial for an organization to comply with. With a cloud environment, and even with an IaaS implementation, the cloud customer will only have rudimentary knowledge of the underlying systems and networks. With a PaaS implementation and certainly with a SaaS implementation, the cloud customer's knowledge will be extremely limited. This is another crucial area where the contract and SLA between the cloud customer and cloud provider will have to establish the roles and responsibilities, as well as the required timelines, for support of eDiscovery requirements and any other legal or regulatory requirements to which the organization is subjected.

Conducting eDiscovery in the Cloud

With the need to rely on the cloud provider to assist or conduct any eDiscovery investigations and respond to orders, it is vital for the cloud customer and their security personnel to have a good relationship with the support teams of the cloud provider. This relationship should be cultivated from the early days of the contract and hosting arrangement so that familiarity with processes and procedures can be established and understood while not under the pressure of an actual incident or order. Part of this relationship should also entail gaining a rudimentary understanding of the underlying cloud fabric and infrastructure. Although this will not be comprehensive or detailed for investigations, it will lay the groundwork and serve as a basis of understanding to enable more rapid and efficient work when an actual order is being processed.

Part of the contract should articulate where the potential hosting areas for data and applications are within the cloud environment. When data discovery and collection operations are being conducted, it is very possible in a cloud that data will reside in multiple different jurisdictions, and quite likely in different countries that may have drastically different laws and requirements from each other. Having an understanding of possible scenarios and contingency planning in place allows for a more structured approach to eDiscovery orders and serves a basis of starting them with various facts and templates already prepared. Understanding different laws, jurisdictions, and expectations is vital for the Cloud Security Professional to effectively conduct and ensure eDiscovery. Depending on the nature, scope, and jurisdictions impacted by the eDiscovery order, it is also possible that some requirements clash with each other and need to be rectified in a manner that respects local laws as well as enables the organization to comply with the order.

The exact approach and method to eDiscovery in the cloud will be determined by the contractual requirements between the cloud customer and cloud provider as well as largely driven by the cloud model employed. Regardless of the cloud model used, the cloud provider will have to play a central role in any eDiscovery process. While the cloud customer has the greatest level of control, access, and visibility within an IaaS implementation, even under that model the cloud customer will be limited in their collection and isolation abilities. In most instances, the access to the toolsets and utilities needed for eDiscovery collection will be limited to the cloud provider because more extensive access to the underlying systems and management tools will be necessary. With a PaaS implementation, the burden for eDiscovery compliance will largely fall on the cloud provider because access from the cloud customer will be very limited in nature, and access to any sort of management toolsets or utilities will likely be nonexistent. With a SaaS implementation, the cloud customer will need to completely rely upon the cloud provider for eDiscovery compliance. Although the cloud customer might have a degree of data access, and perhaps even the ability to export data from the application, it will almost certainly not be in a format that would be acceptable as evidence under an eDiscovery order.

eDiscovery Against the Cloud Provider

While the discussion and focus thus far has been on eDiscovery of cloud customers, their applications, and their data, there is also the perspective of eDiscovery orders against the cloud providers themselves. In this instance, the eDiscovery requirements would be in regard to the cloud environment itself, and this has the potential to impact many different cloud customers and data sets. Depending on the scope and requirements of the eDiscovery order against the cloud provider, there may be the need to turn over data or physical assets from the environment, which could include systems and data that is part of, or impacts directly, cloud customers. Due to this reality, the Cloud Security Professional will need to ensure that language is in the contract with the cloud provider pertaining to how such issues will be approached, addressed, and handled by the cloud provider, should the need emerge.

ISO/IEC 27050

ISO/IEC 27050 strives to establish an internationally accepted standard for eDiscovery processes and best practices. It encompasses all steps of the eDiscovery process, including the identification, preservation, collection, processing, review, analysis, and the final production of the requested data archive. It attempts to address the enormous volume of data that organizations produce and hold, the complex and disparate methods by which this data is stored and processed, as well as the challenges with how quickly and easily electronic data and records can be produced, stored, shared, and destroyed. With cloud computing very often crossing jurisdictional boundaries—either with the customer base or the distributed nature of cloud computing and the cloud provider using geographically diverse hosting locations—an internationally published and accepted standard will give both cloud providers and cloud customers a contractual component and basis for standardization. This allows cloud providers to structure their support and operations around the framework and best practices put forward, and to advertise that compliance to cloud customers and potential customers.

CSA Guidance

The Cloud Security Alliance has published, as part of their "CSA Security Guidance" series, a publication that addresses eDiscovery titled "Domain 3: Legal Issues, Contracts, and Electronic Discovery." This document outlines specific cloud-based concerns for eDiscovery, issues specific to the cloud provider and cloud customer, and approaches to take to ensure compliance with eDiscovery orders and the pitfalls and challenges that occur because of them.

A big challenge with eDiscovery compliance is that orders for data collection and preservation are focused on data that an organization owns and controls. With a traditional data center, this is a lot clearer because the organization controls and owns the systems—from the hardware and network level, all the way through the application level. With a cloud environment, even with IaaS, the cloud customer only owns and controls a subset of data, with the cloud provider maintaining ownership and control over the rest, usually without any access provided automatically to the cloud customer. With this setup, in many jurisdictions, one eDiscovery order may be required for the cloud customer and another for the cloud provider, in order to get the entire set of data. The contract between the cloud customer and cloud provider should clearly delineate the responsibilities of both parties as far as data ownership and collection, and what mechanisms and requests are necessary should an eDiscovery order be received. In some jurisdictions, or depending on the contracts and expectations of other tenants within the same cloud, separated court orders or eDiscovery orders may be necessary to gain access to the infrastructure-level data and logs.

Another big factor is the additional time that may be required in a cloud environment for data preservation and collection. This is due to the complexities of a cloud environment, but also due to the particular tools and access levels available to the cloud customer. In a traditional data center, the system administrators and privileged staff will have full access to the entire system and all components of it, including the network layer. With full access, a wide assortment of eDiscovery tools and utilities are available, both open source and proprietary. With a cloud environment, many of these tools will not be available to the cloud customer due to access restrictions, and may need to be loaded and executed by a cloud administrative user instead. Accounting for the time it will take to make separate requests to the cloud provider for information and assistance, the cloud customer will need to be prepared to properly respond to a requesting authority as to how long data collection will take, as well as when to request extensions for requests that are too aggressive on time requirements.

Cost is also a big factor in regard to the resources required for the preservation of data—namely, storage costs within a cloud. Depending on the size and scope of an eDiscovery order, the possibility exists that substantial storage space could be required to collect and consolidate all of the data, especially if it involves forensically valid full system images or binary data, which does not carry the benefit of compression. The SLA and contract between the cloud provider and cloud customer should spell out how costs and operations are handled during eDiscovery orders, as well as the time length limitations, if any, of that temporary data use and preservation. Apart from storage costs, some cloud environments are also built on pricing models that incorporate the amount of data transferred into and out of the resources consumed by the cloud customer. If large amounts of data need to be transferred out to fulfill the eDiscovery order, the SLA and contract should spell out how those costs are handled under the circumstances and if it differs at all from the typical pricing and metering that applies to the cloud customer.

A major factor from a legal standpoint, as well as one that will be of critical importance to the cloud customer, is notification of receiving any subpoena or eDiscovery order. The contract should include requirements for notification by the cloud provider to the cloud customer upon the receipt of such an order. This serves a few important purposes. First, it keeps communication and trust open between the cloud provider and cloud customers. More importantly, though, it allows the cloud customer to potentially challenge the order if they feel they have the grounds or desire to do so. Without immediate notification by the cloud provider upon the receipt of such an order, it may eliminate or make more difficult a challenge by the cloud customer against the requesting body. Of course there may be instances where a legal order specifically precludes that cloud provider from notifying the cloud customer, and upon receipt of such an order, that is an area that will override the terms of the contract and require compliance by the cloud provider.

Forensics Requirements

Forensics is the application of scientific and methodical processes to identify, collect, preserve, analyze, and summarize/report digital information and evidence. It is one of the most powerful tools and concepts available to a security professional for determining the exact nature, method, and scope of a security incident within any application or system.

With a traditional data center, where the organization has full access and control over systems (especially the physical aspect of those systems), forensic collection and analysis are far more simple and straightforward than in a cloud environment. Determining the location of the data and systems involved within a traditional data center will be far easier, as will isolating and preserving systems or data during collection and analysis.

Within a cloud environment, not only is determining the exact location of systems and data far more complex, the degree of isolation and preservation is also a lot different from a traditional server model. With forensic data collection processes being at the management or administrative level of a system, the involvement and cooperation of the cloud provider is absolutely essential and crucial, regardless of the specific cloud hosting model employed by the cloud customer.

With forensics in the cloud, the complexities and challenges spelled out previously with eDiscovery are also applicable. The particular challenge with forensics is that cloud providers may be unable or unwilling to provide information of this nature to a cloud customer because it might violate the agreements, privacy, or confidentiality of other cloud customers that are tenants within the same systems. However, with eDiscovery, and the nature of court orders and subpoenas, cloud providers are required to provide information to comply with the order. With forensics, if it is only at the request of the cloud customer for their own investigations or purposes, it is quite possible the cloud provider will decline to provide such information if there are concerns about the impact on other tenants. This is a main reason why it is vital for the Cloud Security Professional to ensure that contractual requirements will empower the cloud customer to obtain the information they might need; otherwise, they must accept the risk and realities of not being able to provide the same level of forensic investigation as they would in a traditional data center environment.

Privacy Issues and Jurisdictional Variation

Privacy issues can vary greatly among different jurisdictions. This variation can pertain to the types of records and information protected as well as the required controls and notifications that apply.

Difference Between Contractual and Regulated Personally Identifiable Information (PII)

Whether a system and its data are hosted in a traditional data center model or in a cloud hosting model, the owner of the application is responsible for the security of any PII data that is processed by or stored within their application and related services. While the concept of PII is widely understood, regardless of jurisdictional or legal requirements, there are two main types of PII, and they have differing approaches and requirements.

Contractual PII

Contractual PII has specific requirements for the handling of sensitive and personal information, as defined at the contractual level. These specific requirements will typically document required handling procedures and policies to deal with PII. These requirements may be in specific security controls and configurations, policies or procedures that are required, or limitations on who may gain authorized access to data and systems. With these requirements being part of the contract, auditing and enforcement mechanisms will be in place to ensure compliance. Failure to follow contractual PII requirements can lead to penalties with contract performance or a loss of business for an organization.

Regulated PII

Regulated PII has requirements put forth by specific laws or regulations. Unlike contractual PII, where a violation can lead to contractual penalties, a violation of regulated PII can lead to fines or even criminal charges in some jurisdictions. PII regulations can depend either on the jurisdiction that applies to the hosting location or application or on specific legislation based on the particular industry or type of data that is used. Regulated PII will typically have requirements for reporting any compromise of data, either to an official government entity or possibly to the impacted users directly.

Country-Specific Legislation Related to PII and Data Privacy

While many countries have laws that protect and regulate PII and data privacy, there can be significant variance among various jurisdictions as to what is required or allowed. The following is not an exhaustive or complete list of all countries and regulations; instead, it is a sampling of the major and most prominent jurisdictions and their respective regulations.

United States

The United States lacks a single law at the federal level addressing data security and privacy, but there are multiple federal laws that deal with different industries and types of data that the Cloud Security Professional needs to be aware of. It is also important to note that, unlike many other countries, the United States has very few laws on housing of data within geographic areas, so data can often be housed on systems outside the United States, even though the individuals the data pertains to, as well as the applications, are accessed from within the borders of the United States.

The Gramm–Leach–Bliley Act (GLBA)   The Gramm–Leach–Bliley Act (GLBA), as it is commonly called, based on the names of the lead sponsors and authors of the act, is officially known as "The Financial Modernization Act of 1999." It is specifically focused on PII as it relates to financial institutions. There are three specific components of GLBA, covering various areas and use, on top of a general requirement that all financial institutions must provide all users and customers with a written copy of their privacy policies and practices, including with whom and for what reasons their information may be shared with other entities. The first component is the Financial Privacy Rule, which regulates overall the collection and disclosure of financial information of customers and users. The second component is the Pretexting Provision, which prevents an organization for accessing, or attempting to access, PII based on false representation or pretexts to customers or potential customers. The last component is the Safeguards Rule, which puts a requirement and burden on financial institutions to enact adequate security controls to protect the privacy and personal information of their customers.

The Health Insurance Portability and Accountability Act of 1996 (HIPAA) HIPAA requires the Federal Department of Health and Human Services to publish and enforce regulations pertaining to electronic health records and identifiers between patients, providers, and insurance companies. It is focused on the security controls and confidentiality of medical records, rather than specific technologies that are used, so long as they meet the requirements of the regulations.

Safe Harbor The Safe Harbor regulations were developed by the Department of Commerce and are meant to serve as a way to bridge the gap between privacy regulations of the European Union and the United States. Due to the lack of an adequate privacy law or protection from the federal level, European privacy regulations general prohibit the exporting or sharing of PII from Europe with the United States. Participation in the Safe Harbor program is voluntary on behalf of an organization, but it does require them to conform to specific requirements and policies that mirror those from the EU, and as such, can possibly fulfill requirements for data sharing and export, and allow American businesses to serve customers in the EU as well. Those organizations that do voluntarily submit themselves to Safe Harbor policies and requirements also must agree to allow audits and official dispute-resolution processes as a condition of participation, to bring them in line with similar protections in the EU.

The Sarbanes–Oxley Act (SOX) SOX is not an act that pertains to privacy or IT security directly, but rather it regulates accounting and financial practices used by organizations. It was passed to protect stakeholders and shareholders from improper practices and errors, and sets forth rules for compliance, as regulated and enforced by the Securities and Exchange Commission (SEC). The main influence on IT systems and operations are the requirements it sets for data retention, specifically in regard to what types of records must be preserved, and for how long. This will impact IT systems as far as the requirements for data preservation and the ability to read it, and in particular with cloud computing, the need to ensure that all required data can be accessed and preserved by the cloud customer, or the acceptance of that burden by the cloud provider. SOX also places substantial requirements—in some cases well beyond those already required from other regulatory or certification requirements—on virtually all aspects of a financial system's operations and controls. These apply to networks, physical access, access controls, disaster recovery, and any other aspect of operations or security controls.

European Union (EU)

The EU has some of the most stringent and specific requirements as far as data privacy and protection of the confidentiality of PII are concerned, as well as strict requirements that the data not be shared or exported beyond its borders to any jurisdiction that does not have adequate and similar protections and regulations of its own. This can have an enormous impact on cloud hosting, as it places the burden on an organization to know exactly where their processes or data will be housed at all times, and to ensure that it does not violate the requirements for geographic and jurisdictional hosting that does not conform to EU requirements. This can be very difficult in large cloud implementations, which often span many geographic areas.

Directive 95/46 EC   Adopted in 1995, this directive establishes strong data protection and policy requirements, and it declares data privacy to be a human right. It establishes that an individual has the right to be notified when their personal data is being access or processed, that it only will ever be accessed for legitimate purposes, and that their personal data will only be accessed to the exact extent that it needs to be for the particular process or request.

General Data Protection Regulation   This regulation, which will be enforced starting in 2018, aims to strengthen and expand on personal privacy protections, as well as add official restrictions on the exporting of data outside of the EU. The main goal is to ensure that individuals have full ownership and control over their data, and that all of the EU is operating under identical data privacy laws and regulations in a uniform manner.

Russia

Effective as of September 1, 2015, Russian Law 526-FZ establishes that any collecting, storing, or processing of personal information or data on Russian citizens must be done from systems and databases that are physically located within the Russian Federation.

Differences Among Confidentiality, Integrity, Availability, and Privacy

The big three core aspects of security are confidentiality, integrity, and availability. As more data and services have moved online, especially with the explosion of mobile computing and apps that utilize sensitive information, privacy has become a fourth key aspect. All four work closely together, and based on the particular specifics of the application and data that it utilizes, the importance of some versus the others will change and adapt in their degree of importance.

Confidentiality

In short, confidentiality involves the steps and effort taken to limit access to sensitive or private information. The main goal of confidentiality is to ensure that sensitive information is not made available or leaked to parties that should not have access to it, while at the same time ensure that those with appropriate need and authorization to access the same information can do so in a manner commensurate with their needs and confidentiality requirements.

When it comes to granting access to appropriate users, there can be different levels of access; in other words, confidentiality is not an all-or-nothing granting of data access to users. Based on the particular data sets and needs, users can have different access or requirements for more stringent security, even within an application based on different data types and classifications. With some applications, even for users with approval to access particular data fields or sets, there may be further technological limitations or restrictions on access. For example, a privileged user may have access to an application and sensitive data within it, but certain data fields may have requirements that the user access through a particular VPN or a particular internal network. Other data within the application may be available even from outside those requirements, but the enhancements are applied to particular portions of the application or particular data sets or fields.

While a main focus of confidentiality revolves around technological requirements or particular security methods, an important and often overlooked aspect of safeguarding data confidentiality is appropriate and comprehensive training for those with access to it. Training should be focused on the safe handling of sensitive information overall, including best practices for network activities as well as the physical security of the device or workstation used to access the application. Training should also focus on specific organizational practices and policies for data access, especially if any aspect of data storage or persistence is a factor with the specific application or types of data it utilizes. Although it should be evident, best practices such as strong passwords, at a minimum, should be stressed with general security training specifically geared toward confidentiality. Training should also include awareness of social-engineering-type attacks to fill in the gaps beyond technological security measures.

Integrity

Whereas confidentiality focuses on the protection of sensitive data from disclosure, integrity is focused on the trustworthiness of data and the prevention of unauthorized modification or tampering. The same focus on the importance of access controls applies to integrity as well, but with more of an emphasis on the ability to write and modify data, rather than simply the ability to read the data. A prime consideration for maintaining integrity is an emphasis on the change management and configuration management aspects of operations, so that any and all modifications are predictable, tracked, logged, and verified, whether they are performed by actual human users or systems processes and scripts. All systems should be implemented in a manner so that all data modification operations and commands are logged, including information as to who made the modification.

With many systems, especially where downloading of data, executable code, or packages is permitted or desired, the ability to maintain the integrity of those downloads is very important to the end users. To facilitate this verification, technologies such as checksums are in widespread use. With a checksum, a hashed value is made of the specific package, with that known hash published by the entity offering the data. The user downloading the data can then perform the same hashing operation on the file they have downloaded and compare that to the published value from the vendor. Any discrepancy in values will be an immediate indication that the file, as downloaded by the user, is not the same file being offered from the vendor. This is especially important with scripts or executable code to ensure that no malware has been injected into the package and that no modifications have been made by a malicious actor at some point in the process.

NOTE A common misconception is that integrity and confidentiality are always used together or correlated together with a data set. However, this is not always the case. For example, the medicare.gov website offers downloads of quality rating databases for researchers or anyone else who might desire the data. These are complete sets of data, the same as that used by the tools on the website. As such, these data sets have no level of confidentiality attached to them at all. However, the integrity of them is extremely important. While the data is freely and completely available to anyone, the altering of the data could have enormous impact on healthcare facilities or providers. Consider a hospital that is graded on a one-to-five-star rating from a quality perspective. A hospital that has a high rating, such as a 4 or 5, could find themselves facing considerable negative publicity should the website now display a rating of 1 or 2 stars, due to either inadvertent or purposeful modification of the intended data.

Availability

Availability is often not understood as part of security in that it is often viewed as part of operations. However, in order for a system to be considered secure and operate in a secure manner, it must provide robust accessibility to those who are authorized to have it, and do so in a trustworthy manner. There are a few different components that make up the concept of availability.

The first and most obvious consideration is the availability of the live production system. This is accomplished through redundancy of hardware, networks, data storage systems, as well as supporting systems such as authentication and authorization mechanisms. Apart from redundancy, in order to ensure availability, production systems must also have adequate resources to meet their demands within acceptable performance metrics. If the system is overloaded or unable to handle attacks such as a denial of service, then redundancy will not matter in the larger scheme of things, because the system will be unavailable to users and services that rely on it or its data. The ability to mitigate such attacks is also a prime reason why availability falls under security concepts. Redundancy also is vital for proper maintenance and patching of systems. Without appropriate redundancy to perform those functions without incurring downtime, organizations will delay doing vital security and system patching until later when downtime is more palatable to management. Doing so can expose systems and data to higher risk because known security vulnerabilities are left in place.

Disaster recovery and business continuity are also vital concerns with availability. Within security, they ensure the protection of data and continuity of business operations. If data is destroyed or compromised, having regular backup systems in place as well as the ability to do disaster recovery in the event of a major or widespread problem will allow operations to continue with an acceptable amount of time and data loss for management, while also ensuring that sensitive data is protected and persisted in the event of a loss or corruption of data systems or physical storage systems. Cloud services offer unique opportunities to have distributed data models and a lack of dependency on physical locations and assets over traditional data centers, making the reliability of systems and disaster recovery options more streamlined and robust.

Privacy

Privacy used to be considered part of confidentiality, but with the prevalence of online services and especially mobile computing, the need for a separate category for privacy has become imperative. The growth of strong personal privacy laws in many jurisdictions has also created the necessity for a unique focus. The concept of privacy overall relates to an individual's control over their own information and activities, versus the information that an organization would have in their own data stores, which is governed under confidentiality.

A central concept of privacy is the right to look at things online anonymously, but also the right to be forgotten by a system once you are done using it. This includes any information about yourself, your means of access, location, and so on. The most stringent protections and privacy requirements currently employed are those from the European Union, with other jurisdictions and regulatory requirements being less stringent or enforced. With many applications needing information about a user's location, device, or client used for access, there is a constant battle between utilizing and storing the information needed to conduct services and data access, while at the same time enabling users to have control over their own privacy and personal information in a way that complies with regulatory requirements.

Audit Processes, Methodologies, and Required Adaptions for a Cloud Environment

Many audit practices and requirements are the same, whether the system is deployed in a traditional data server model or within a cloud environment. Regulations and laws are written in a way that are agnostic to the underlying hosting model, and they focus on the ways applications must be secured and data protected. However, with a cloud environment having unique qualities, features, and challenges, there are different approaches and strategies to successfully conducting audits within it.

The Cloud Controls Matrix, published by the Cloud Security Alliance, provides a detailed approach and framework for cloud customers, with a focus on controls that are pertinent and applicable to a cloud environment. Many of the certifications that are well known throughout the IT industry are also very applicable and adaptable to cloud environments.

Internal and External Audit Controls

With any data center and application, there will be a variety of both internal and external controls that are vital and required for security. These controls must be audited and evaluated regularly to ensure continued applicability, but also for compliance. Internal audits can be used to ensure corporate polices and mandates are being properly executed and adhered to for the satisfaction of management. They are also useful for gauging the efficiencies and effectiveness of internal policies and procedures, and for allowing management to find new ways to expand on the implementation of controls and policies, or to rectify problems that are causing additional costs or overhead. Internal audits are also very useful for planning future expansions of services or upgrades within the environment.

Independent external audits of controls will be necessary for customer assurance and compliance with regulatory or certification programs. An external audit will evaluate the IT system and policy controls, but will not address the same types of issues that an internal audit will, such as operating efficiency, costs, and design or expansion plans.

Impact of Requirements Programs by the Use of Cloud

The use of a cloud environment will likely have a profound effect on how auditors have traditionally operated and conducted audits. A typical component of many legacy audits is having the audit team on location at the data center or physically on the same network, where they can directly scan and probe systems, without going over the public network. However, in a cloud environment, this is not possible because the organization will not have the level of control or access over the physical environment; coupled with the reality of geographic distribution of cloud environments, this makes being on site virtually impossible. Another big difference with the cloud environment is the use of virtual servers and images, which can and will change often over time. This makes repeated audits or later verification significantly more difficult, as the state of a system in its current form may look substantially different than when the original audit was conducted. What's more, the virtual machine that was originally tested may no longer exist at all.

Assurance Challenges of Virtualization and Cloud

Virtual machines and cloud environments pose enormous challenges to auditing and scanning as compared to traditional data centers. Many application audits within a virtualized environment will span many virtual machines and often different geographic locations. Even those within the same physical location will span multiple different physical servers, with different hypervisors controlling some subset of the overall environment. The challenge presented is how to audit and ensure compliance without testing the entire environment, which can also be very fluid and change rapidly. This is further complicated with a lack of access to the physical environment within a cloud, where the cloud customer and auditors working on behalf of the cloud customer will have very limited access, or even no access at all, to the underlying physical environment.

In order to map out an audit plan, an auditor also needs to have full and complete documentation as to the structure and architecture of a system or application. While this is very easy to do within a traditional data center, it poses a significant challenge within a cloud environment. The cloud customer will not be aware of the underlying architecture, and almost no cloud provider will be willing to disclose this information either, because doing so exposes information and security controls that pertain to all the other tenants within the same cloud environment. The main strategy to deal with this is to rely on audits and certifications for the underlying environment that are done in conjunction with the cloud provider, and thus can be used by all tenants as the basis for their own audits.

Audits of the underlying cloud environment will test and validate the security hardening and configurations of the physical assets and their associated systems, such as hypervisors. The cloud provider can then publish to their customers, or to the public, the audit reports and some information about their baseline configurations. The vast majority of information and audit reports will likely be restricted to only current customers or potential customers, and only after the signing of nondisclosure agreements to protect the underlying environment and other tenants. The use of accepted industry standard certifications will also give customers an immediate insight into the type of testing and controls in place without the need to see specific audit reports and results, as the standards and evaluation criteria are public and well known.

Apart from providing audit reports and certifications, a cloud provider can build customer assurance by conducting patching and upgrades in a timely manner. With security risks and vulnerabilities changing and emerging on a continual basis, this is an important area that needs constant attention. Although this is largely governed through the use of contracts and SLAs, the verification of adherence is the important part. Therefore, the cloud provider will need to establish a program that is satisfactory to their customers to provide this assurance.

Types of Audit Reports

Several different audit reports have been standardized throughout the industry. Although they differ some in approach and audience, they have a similar design and serve a similar purpose.

SAS

The Statement on Auditing Standards (SAS) Number 70, which is commonly known as SAS 70, is a standard published by the American Institute of Certified Public Accounts (AICPA) and is intended to provide guidance for auditors when analyzing service organizations specifically. Within this context, the definition of a "service organization" is intended to include those that provide outsourced services to an organization, where the services provided impact data and processes within their controlled and secured environment (in this case, the specific application is in regard to hosted data centers). It is also known commonly as a "service auditor's examination."

There are two types of reports under SAS-70. Type 1 reports are focused on an evaluation by the auditor as to the service organization's declarations and to the security controls they have put in place, as well as an opinion on the side of the auditor as to the effectiveness of the design of the controls to meet the objectives stated by the service organization. With a Type 2 audit, the same information and evaluation is included, but additional evaluations and opinions on behalf of the auditor are added as to the effectiveness in actually meeting the control objectives on behalf of the service organization. So whereas a Type 1 audit focuses on how effective the design of the controls are in meeting objectives, the Type 2 audit adds an additional qualitative assessment as to the actual effectiveness of the controls as implemented.

There are multiple reasons for why an organization would undergo an SAS 70 audit. A primary reason is to present audit reports to current or potential customers as to the state of controls designed and implemented. The report would serve as an independent and outside evaluation of the environment as a way of gaining the approval of customers and providing assurance. This is the intended application of the audit reports and their design. However, many service organizations have expanded their use beyond this for other purposes as well. Many regulatory and legal systems have requirements for audits and reports from organizations as to their controls and effectiveness. In some instances, these requirements are based on the organization providing evidence that they are implementing adequate oversight for data protection and privacy, and these types of reports can be used to fulfill and meet those requirements. Some examples of regulatory schemes are Sarbanes–Oxley (SOX), ITIL, and COBIT, but there are many others where these types of audit reports can fulfill requirements for providing assurances with independent oversight.

 NOTE SAS 70 reports have been standard for many years, but were replaced in 2011 by the SSAE 16 reports, which are covered in the next section. However, because they are so well known and were standardized in the industry, the information is provided here for historical context, as well as to show the evolution of auditing and oversight with regulatory requirements. The Cloud Security Professional should have a sound understanding of the past use and intent of SAS 70 reports, even though they have been deprecated.

SSAE

The Statements on Standards for Attestation Engagements (SSAE) 16 replaced the SAS 70 as of 2011, and is the standard that most in the United States now use. Rather than focusing on specific control sets, the SSAE 16 is focused on auditing methods. Much like the SAS 70 reports, the SSAE 16 reports are largely used to help satisfy regulatory requirements for auditing and oversight of financial systems, such as Sarbanes–Oxley (SOX).

Whereas the SAS 70 was known as the "service auditor's examination," the SSAE 16 is known as the Service Organization Control (SOC) report, and there are three different types: SOC 1, SOC 2, and SOC 3.

SOC 1 SOC 1 reports effectively are the direct replacement for the SAS 70 reports and are focused specifically on financial reporting controls. SOC 1 reports are considered restricted-use reports, in that they are intended for a small and limited scope of controls auditing, and are not intended to be expanded into greater use. They are focused specifically on internal controls as they relate to financial reporting, and for uses beyond financial reporting, the SOC 2 and SOC 3 reports should be used instead.

The audience for these restricted-use reports is defined as follows:

- The management and stakeholders of the company or organization having the SOC 1 reports done, known in this instance as the "service organization."
- The clients of the service organization having the reports done.

- The auditors of the financial organization having the SOC 1 reports done. This is where the use of SOC 1 reports to assist in compliance with regulations, such as SOX, comes into play.

SOC 1 reports, like SAS 70 reports, also have two subtypes:

- **Type 1 reports**   These are focused on the policies and procedures at a specific and set point in time. They evaluate the design and effectiveness of controls from an organization, and then verify that they were in place at a specific time.
- **Type 2 reports**   These are focused on the same policies and procedures, as well as their effectiveness, as Type 1 reports, but are evaluated over a period of at least six consecutive months, rather than a finite point in time.

To instill confidence in the viability of the audit reports, most users and external organizations will only accept Type 2 reports, as they are more comprehensive than the single-point-in-time Type 1 report.

SOC 2   SOC 2 reports expand greatly on SOC 1 reports and apply to a broad range of service organizations and types, whereas Type 1 reports are only for financial organizations. The basis of SOC 2 reporting is a model that incorporates "principles." With the last update to SOC 2 in 2014, five principles were established. Under the guidelines, the security principle must be included with any of the following four to form a complete report:

- **Availability**   The system has requirements and expectations for uptime and accessibility, and it is able to meet those requirements within parameters set by contract or expectation.
- **Confidentiality**   The system contains confidential or sensitive information, and information is properly safeguarded to the extent required by regulation, law, or contract.
- **Processing integrity**   The system processes information, and it does so in a manner that is accurate, verified, and done only by authorized parties.
- **Privacy**   The system uses, collects, or stores personal and private information, and does so in a manner that conforms to the organization's stated policy privacy, as well as any pertinent regulations, laws, or standards requirements.

The security principle itself is then made up of seven categories:

- **Change management**   How an organization determines what changes are needed as well as how they are approved, implemented, tested, and verified. The goal is to ensure that all changes are done in a methodical and controlled manner with appropriate approvals, with safeguards to prevent unauthorized changes.

- **Communications** How an organization communicates all aspects of its operations to stakeholders and users, including policies, procedures, outages, system statuses, or any other contractually obligated or expected communications.

- **Logical and physical access controls** How an organization implements controls related to physical and logical access to systems and applications, including policies and procedures related to the granting, authorizing, and revoking of access.

- **Monitoring of controls** How an organization oversees and verifies the controls they have implemented, ensuring their correct configuration and application, as well as looking for methods to improve upon them.

- **Organization and management** How the organization is structured and managed, as well as oversight over individual personnel. This includes how personnel are selected, verified, and supervised within their environment and perform their jobs duties.

- **Risk management and design and implementation of controls** How an organization handles risks that may impact their systems and data, from identifying, evaluating, designing, and responding to them to, in some cases, accepting them.

- **System operations** How an organization implements and monitors all of their IT systems and applications, as well as ensures they are running properly and performing to expectations or requirements.

Similar to SOC 1 reports, the SOC 2 reports are considered "restricted use" for the internal review of the organization. They also contain two subtypes:

- **Type 1 reports** These reports are focused on the systems of a service organization, coupled with the design of the security controls for it and an evaluation as to their suitability from a design and intent standpoint.

- **Type 2 reports** These reports are based on the design and application of security controls on the service organization's systems and an evaluation as to their effectiveness from an operational standpoint.

SOC 3 SOC 3 reports are similar to the SOC 2 reports in scope, design, and structure. The main difference between SOC 2 and SOC 3 is the audience they are intended for. Whereas SOC 2 reports are meant to be internal or restricted to an organization or regulatory oversight body, SOC 3 reports are designed to be for general use. This basically means that SOC 3 reports will not contain sensitive or proprietary information that a service organization would not want open or available to release and review.

ISAE

The International Auditing and Assurance Standards Board (ISAE) 3402 reports are very similar in nature and structure to the SOC Type 2 reports, and are also designed to be a replacement for the SAS 70 reports. Given that they serve the same function and have mostly the same structure, the largest difference in use between the SOC and ISAE reports is that SOC is mostly used in the United States, and ISAE is used more internationally.

Similar to SOC reports, the ISAE reports have two subtypes:

- **Type 1 reports**   These are aligned with SOC Type 2 reports, in that they are based on a snapshot of a single point in time.

- **Type 2 reports**   These are also aligned with SOC Type 2 reports in scope and intent, and are done typically for six months to show the management and use of controls over that period of time.

Restrictions of Audit Scope Statements

Before any audit can be undertaken, it is vital for the organization and their auditors to define the scope of the audits, as well as any restrictions on what is covered by and subjected to the audit process and testing. This is done during the initial stages of the audit process, where an audit scope statement will be developed.

The audit scope statement is done by the organization, and serves to define to the auditors what exactly will be covered and required as part of the audit. This will incorporate organizational goals and expectations, as well as any audit requirements specified by regulation or law. The audit scope typically includes the following items:

- **Statement of purpose**   An overall summation and definition for the purpose of the audit. This serves as the basis for all aspects of the audit, as well as the audience and focus of the final reports.

- **Scope of audit**   Defines what systems, applications, services, or types of data are to be covered within the scope of the audit. This is an affirmative statement of inclusion, informing the auditors of the structure and configuration of the items to be audited, but it can also list any exclusions or scope limitations. Limitations can apply broadly to the entire audit or exclude certain types of data or queries.

- **Reason and goals for audit**   There can be more than one reason for an audit, such as for management oversight internal to an organization, to assure stakeholders or users, and as a requirement for compliance with regulations or laws.

- **Requirements for the audit**   This defines how the audit is to be conducted, what tools or technologies are to be used, and to what extent they are to be used. Different tools and technologies will test systems and applications to different levels of impact or comprehensiveness, and it is vital to have an agreed-upon approach, as well as to prepare and monitor any systems and applications during testing.

- **Audit criteria for assessment** This defines how the audit will measure and quantify results. It is vital for the organization and auditors to clearly understand what type and scale of rating system will be used.

- **Deliverables** This defines what will be produced as a result of the audit. The main deliverable will of course be the actual report, but what format or structure the report is presented in needs to be defined. The organization may have specific format or file type requirements, or regulatory requirements may specify exact formats or data types for submission and processing. This area also includes what parties are to receive the audit report.

- **Classification of audit** This defines the sensitivity level and any confidentiality requirements of the audit report and any information or documents used during the preparation or execution of the audit. This can be either organizationally confidential or officially classified by the government as Confidential, Secret, or Top Secret.

Apart from the audit scope statement, the limitations and restrictions on the audit scope are also very important. These will define what exactly is subjected to the audit by placing limits on where the auditors can test and expand into based on what they discover during the course of testing. They are also very important for the impact on current systems and operations, and to ensure that the audit does not negatively impact the systems or data. Most audits are more focused on operational design, policies, and procedures rather than actual technical testing and evaluations.

If actual technical testing is to be performed, to limit and restrict impact on systems and operations it is important to declare times when audit testing can be done, as well as what types of methods are to be used. If an audit is expected to cause increased and noticeable load on a system, leading to performance degradation or user impact, then it is vital to schedule the audit for off-peak times and when system utilization is at its lowest. If possible, testing should always be done against nonproduction systems with nonproduction data. This will remove the possibility of data corruption or impact on users as far as the system's availability and performance are concerned. In most instances, organizations will strictly prohibit any such testing done against live or production systems, and regulations may prevent testing against any systems that contain real or sensitive data, especially if the testing could lead to any type of potential data leakage or exposure.

Gap Analysis

A gap analysis is a crucial step that is performed after all information has been gathered, tested, and verified through the auditing process. This information comes from reviews of documentation, tools for discovery of IT systems and configurations, interviews with key personnel and stakeholders, and the actual audit testing to verify the information provided through these processes. The desired configuration or requirements can come from a variety of sources, including organization policy, contractual requirements, regulatory or certification requirements, and applicable legal requirements.

The gap analysis is then performed to determine if the results found from information discovery and testing match with the configuration standards and policies. Any resulting deviation from them will be considered a finding, or a "gap" between the desired state of a system or its operations and the actual verified current state.

 EXAM TIP Remember that a gap analysis and the presentation of audit findings should always be from an impartial and independent actor. While many organizations conduct internal audits, these should be considered for their own purposes or fact-finding efforts, and should never be used for certifications or compliance. Only findings done by someone external and independent, who has no financial or other interests in the results of the audit, should be considered valid and trustworthy. Under virtually all regulatory and certification programs, only audits performed by an independent actor, sometimes with certification requirements of their own, will be accepted as a valid for the purposes of compliance.

Audit Plan

The overall audit plan falls into a series of four steps, each with important and sequenced components that drive the overall process to meet the objectives and requirements.

Here are the four steps in the audit plan:

- Define objectives
- Define scope
- Conduct the audit
- Lessons learned and analysis

Define Objectives

Defining the objectives of the audit includes several steps to lay the groundwork for the entire audit process, and will drive the process of defining the scope for actually conducting the audit. This step clearly defines and articulates the official objectives of the audit and produces a document attesting to them. The objectives take into account the management priorities and risk acceptance to ensure they are aligned with what is desired from the audit. They also define the format or formats of the audit report and any other deliverables that will be produced as a result of it. Based on the requirements and the scale of the audit, this process also defines the number of staff needed to conduct the audit, not only on behalf of the auditing group, but also the systems and application teams that need to be available to produce data, answer interview questions, and run whatever scripts or grant access needed from the audit team's perspective.

EXAM TIP Make sure you understand that audits can be conducted for different purposes and audiences. In some instances, depending on the regulatory requirements, there may be several different audits that seemingly overlap. This is especially true with government contracts, where many different regulations and agencies share responsibility for oversight of security and enforcement of policies. It is possible that some findings will require remediation that causes other audits to be in conflict for similar requirements; therefore, some coordination and negotiation may be necessary.

Define Scope

The definition of the audit scope is one of the most important (and most tedious) aspects of the audit process. This is where a very detailed set of rules and information gathering occurs that ultimately and completely drives the entire audit process. If done correctly, a well-defined and detailed scope makes the actual performance of the audit straightforward and efficient, as well as ensures that it successfully meets the goals and objectives set forth by the organization concerning the purpose for conducting the audit.

The following are many key concepts and information points for an audit scope. While it is impossible to fully encapsulate all aspects of all audits, because systems, applications, and objectives can differ wildly, this list will form the basis for the overwhelming majority of audits and points of consideration:

- **Audit steps and procedures**   The process and procedures for the actual audit will be clearly documented and agreed upon. This is the primary grouping for all aspects of the audit plan, and the other components support and carry out the purpose and initiatives from it. The overall steps and sequence of the audit will be defined and broken into stages for a methodical approach, ranging from information gathering, to the actual audit, reviewing results, making recommendations, and enacting responsive changes or actions based on findings.

- **Change management**   During the audit, the change management process and controls will be evaluated for effectiveness and documentation. Any changes since the last audit should be evaluated for their effectiveness in meeting their goals, and a sampling of change requests should be verified to ensure that the process has been followed. This should include systems and technological changes as well as operational and policy changes and how they are handled throughout the entire process.

- **Communications**   There are a few different aspects to communications in regard to audits, and they are absolutely crucial at all levels to ensure the audit is successfully completed and done so in a smooth and efficient manner. A major component of the communications plan that will be done early on is the gathering and documenting of the key points of contacts, as well as backups, of all parties involved. This should include the audit team, the cloud customer, cloud provider, and all support staff that will be assisting with the audit under each group. The communications plan also documents the methods of communications to be used and their frequency. Note that these may differ by audience and party involved. In order to ensure timely responses and progression of the audit, escalation contacts and plans should be included as part of the communications plan.

- **Criteria and metrics**   The metrics used to evaluate the effectiveness of controls, as well as the methodology for their evaluation, need to be fully understood, agreed upon by all parties, and clearly documented in the audit plan. As part of this component, it is also important to verify that any metrics and criteria are consistent with contractual and SLA requirements, especially in a cloud environment where the cloud customer does not have full control over or access to all available metrics and data points.

- **Physical access and location**   Where the audit will be conducted from and what level of access will be used or required are key components of audit planning. Many applications or systems have controls in place to limit where connections can be made from, especially if means of access other than those used by typical users are to be utilized by the auditors. Some systems also have geographic restrictions based on the type of data, such as United States federal government contractors having requirements that they must physically be located and present within the borders of the United States to work on or interact with the systems. It is also important to define how the audit team will be located to conduct their tests. Will they be located together as a team or work remotely? Will the staff from the organization be present, or just be available as a resource when needed?

- **Previous audits**   When a new audit is being conducted, it is imperative to review previous audits for any high or critical findings. The new audit should comprehensively test those previous findings to verify they have been mitigated and officially closed. Under any regulatory or auditing requirements, repeat findings are typically considered very serious, so special attention to previous findings should always be used to verify final disposition of them.

- **Remediation**   After the audit has been completed and all findings documented and reported, the organization must develop a plan to address and remediate all findings. The plan to remediate can be to fix the actual finding, to put in other compensating controls to reduce the level of the finding, or for management to accept the risk and leave the finding in place. Not all findings will be up to management to determine remediation decisions, as regulation or law may dictate the approach that that must be taken, depending on the type of data and its classification level. The audit plan should also articulate the process that will be used to document and track findings for remediation.

- **Reporting**   The audit plan must clearly define and document the requirements for the final report, including format, how it will be delivered, and how it will be housed long-term. The organization will either demand reports be delivered in their format, and later processed and packaged for the official report copy, once resolved findings have been verified and all language from the course of the audit is cleaned up, or require a final polished report from the auditors themselves once all clarifications and closures have been completed. The audit plan will also document who should receive reports, what information will be in them, as well as the required dates for their dissemination to all parties.

- **Scale and inclusion**   The systems, applications, components, and operations to be included within the scope of the audit are vital to planning the actual execution of it. At this point, everything will be clearly documented as to what is included, as well as any boundaries and limitations on it. Within a cloud environment, this is highly dependent on the cloud service model used, as that will dictate how deep and far the audit can be conducted with the access that an auditor or cloud customer has. This also includes exactly which computing resources are subjected as part of the audit, such as storage, processing, and memory.

- **Timing**   With any system and operation, there are likely to be time restrictions and limitations as to when testing can be done. Special care should be taken to not schedule audits or testing for busy times of the year for the organization or during peak usage times. In regard to calendar limitations, audits should not be scheduled during peak times of the year where systems and staff have heavy demands based on their organization and services, which could include holiday periods, cyclical peak times of usage, special initiatives, and during system upgrades or new rollouts. For regular times, tests against systems, if they are against live systems, should be done to avoid peak processing times and user load during the day or week, deferring instead to off hours and lower utilization times to avoid impacting current operations or users.

Conduct the Audit

Once the audit plan has been completed and signed off by all parties, the actual audit will be conducted based on the agreed parameters and timelines. While the audit is being conducted, it is important to monitor the timelines, staff requirements, and any potential impact on systems. Although all effort to minimize user impact would have been taken during the audit planning process, there can still be unintended or unforeseen consequences while the actual audit is being conducted. If such circumstances arise, management will have to work closely with the audit team to determine if the audit will proceed as planned, or if some changes need to be made to the audit plan to mitigate further or continued negative impact on users or systems.

Lessons Learned and Analysis

Once the audit has been completed, management and systems staff will analyze the process and findings to determine what lessons have been learned and how continued improvement processes can be applied to further harden systems or improve upon processes and operations. There are multiple areas for focus and analysis after an audit:

- **Audit duplication or overlap**   Once the audit has been completed, since many organizations undergo multiple audits from different auditors, an analysis should be done to compare the scope of each and any overlap or duplication.

With some audits that are mandated by regulation, there may be nothing the organization can do about duplication. However, with other types of audits, it might be possible to alter the scope or get the auditors to accept specific evaluation of controls from other audits, rather than repeating the same tests. This will lead to a costs savings, both in the costs of the audit, but also in the staff time that must be dedicated during an audit and potential systems impact and downtime.

- **Data collection processes** The first time most audits are performed, there is a considerable amount of manual data collection and processing. As audits are completed, methods for automation and proactive collection should be explored wherever possible, which can provide an organization with a better handle on its data and processes, but also make future and additional audits much more expedient and efficient. It is also very important to look at the specific data elements that were collected for analysis, with the intent on determining if more data was collected than was needed and can be eliminated in future efforts.

- **Report evaluation** After the report has been completed and submitted, it should be reviewed for structure and content as well. It should be evaluated for how findings and information are presented and the format they are presented in, to ensure that management and stakeholders can effectively use them to make improvements in systems or processes, but also to ensure that users or regulatory groups will find them useful and appropriate for their needs.

- **Scope and limitations analysis** Once the audit has been completed and reports submitted, there should be a look back at the original scope and limitations documents to determine if they were correct and appropriate. During many audits it will become clear that some items included in the scope were really not necessary, or that some things not included, or even explicitly excluded, should have been included. This process will enable an organization to have a solid scope and limitations document already prepare for future audits, and will enable a more efficient updating process rather than starting from scratch for future audits. If possible, the document should be incorporated into the change management process so that any appropriate changes can be made in an iterative and incremental manner, rather than a wholesale concentrated effort when needed.

- **Staff and expertise** With any audit, there are considerable investments in staff and the particular skills sets of that staff in order to complete the audit, including the collection and presentation of data. The number of staff involved and dedicated to the audit, as well as the particular skill sets of that staff, should be evaluated for need in regard to future audits. In many instances, adjustments can be made in either skill sets or numbers to lower the costs for and impact on the operations of an organization during audits.

Standards Requirements

Standards are established by industry groups or regulatory bodies to set common configurations, expectations, operational requirements, and definitions. They form a strong body of understanding and collaboration across jurisdictional boundaries, and allow for users and cloud customers to evaluate services and cloud providers based on external and independent criteria, with an understanding that the awarding of a certification ensures that standards have been met and verified by an external party.

ISO/IEC 27018

ISO/IEC 27018 is an international standard for privacy involving cloud computing. It was first published in 2014 and is part of the ISO/IEC 27001 standards, and is a certification that cloud providers can adhere to. The standard is focused on five key principles:

- **Communication** Any events that could impact security and privacy of data within the cloud environment are clearly documented with detail, as well as conveyed per requirements to the cloud customers.

- **Consent** Despite all information being on systems that are owned and controlled by the cloud provider, no data or information about the cloud customer can be used in any ways, including for advertising, without the express consent of the cloud customer. This also extends to any users and cloud customers being able to use the cloud resources without having to consent to such use of information as a precondition of the cloud provider.

- **Control** Despite being in a cloud environment, where the cloud provider owns and controls the actual infrastructure and storage systems, the cloud customer retains complete and full control over their data within the environment at all times.

- **Transparency** With the lack of full control within a cloud environment by the cloud customer, the cloud provider bears the responsibility for informing them about where their data and processes reside, as well as any potential exposure to support staff, and especially to any subcontractors.

- **Independent and yearly audit** To assure cloud customers and users as to their certification and protection of data privacy, the cloud provider must undergo a yearly assessment and audit by a third party.

Generally Accepted Privacy Principles (GAPP)

GAPP is a privacy standard, focused on managing and preventing risks to privacy, that was developed by a joint privacy task force of American Institute of Certified Public Accountants (AICPA) and the Canadian Institute of Chartered Accountants (CICA). The standard contains ten main privacy principles, as well as over 70 privacy objectives and associated methods for measuring and evaluating criteria. The ten generally accepted privacy principles form a basis for security and privacy best practices for an organization.

Here are the ten GAPP principles:

- **Management** As an organization, privacy policies and procedures are clearly documented, reviewed, and communicated to the necessary parties, and official measures and criteria for accountability are established.

- **Notice** Whether by regulation, law, or best practices, the organization publishes and makes available to interested or required parties their privacy policies, including what information they collect, store, share, and securely protect or destroy after use.

- **Choice and consent**   With any systems or applications that collect or use personal information, the choice is clearly presented to the user to decide if they want to disclose their information. This ideally will require active consent on behalf of the user to share information, but it should also make clear to users what limitations they will have if they chose not to disclose information as far as use and processing of information through the application or system.

- **Collection**   The organization has policies and procedures in place to ensure that any personal information that is collected is used only for the express purposes stated and known to the user, and any additional use is prohibited without additional informed consent.

- **Use, retention, and disposal**   Any personal information that is collected, and collected only after affirmative consent, is only used for the purposes stated, and as soon as it is no longer needed, the information is securely removed following security best practices or any requirements from regulation or law.

- **Access**   As required by regulation or policy, the organization makes available to an individual the personal information that they have collected on them for review, and then allows for any modifications, updates, or removal requests.

- **Disclosure to third parties**   With many modern applications, external services or components are often used and integrated throughout an application. Where personal information needs to be shared with third parties in this manner, that notice is made to the user and their consent is required for such a disclosure.

- **Security for privacy**   Any information that is used or stored by a system or application is protected with stringent security measures to ensure its confidentiality.

- **Quality**   Whereas security protects the confidentiality of sensitive and personal information within a system or application, the quality principle is focused on integrity and ensuring that the organization has accurate and correct information on individuals that use it, and that it is correctly processed and used.

- **Monitoring and enforcement**   As with any policy or best practice, proactive and accurate monitoring is required to ensure it is applied correctly and enforced. This also includes having processes in place to resolve compliance problems or complaints and disputes from users about the use of their information.

Internal Information Security Management System (ISMS)

An internal information security management system (ISMS) includes the policies that establish a formal program in an organization, focused on reducing threats and risks against their IT resources and data in regard to confidentiality, integrity, and availability. The main purposes for an ISMS are minimizing risks, protecting the organizations reputation, ensuring business continuity and operations, and reducing potential liability from the exposure of security incidents. The protection of reputation and the higher degree of confidence it can bring applies to users, customers, and stakeholders of any system or application.

In order for an ISMS to have measurable validity and accepted structure, it should be formed and implemented along the lines of an accepted and established standardization, such as ISO/IEC 27001. The ISO/IEC 27001:2005 standard specifically outlines steps to create an ISMS for any organization. To start with an ISMS, an organization must first define their security policies, which should be in place already from normal operations and audit requirements. This will lead into the formulation of an ISMS scope, which must have management support and be matched specifically to the organization's goals and objectives.

The most important part of the ISMS is then to undertake a risk assessment and determine how to address those risks to meet the requirements and expectations of management or regulations. The risk assessment and risk management will be highly subjective and specifically tuned to each system or application based on the type of data and management oversight and expectations, as well as any applicable regulatory requirements or laws. Without taking into consideration the full range of risk requirements and expectations, an organization is likely to end up with an ISMS that is either ineffective or does not meet requirements to bring value to the organization.

Once a comprehensive risk assessment has been completed and management decisions have been made concerning how to approach the organization's risk, the selection and implementation of controls can be made to address the risk. Because there are so many possible permutations of risk and it is so subjective to a specific system, application, or organization, no two risk assessment or risk management plans will look the same. The selection and implementation of additional or different controls will be geared specifically towards the specific instance and risk appetite of management.

In order for an ISMS to be successful, several factors need to be consistent across organizations, regardless of their specific considerations or unique needs and requirements. The full and continued support of management and stakeholders will be absolutely crucial with any security implementation or policy. The ISMS must be applied consistently and uniformly across the entire organization, in order to fully implement and adhere to the overall strategy and risk appetite. All business processes and management processes must include the ISMS as a key and central component to maintain consistency and standardization. Whenever business demands or policies change, the ISMS must be included and adjusted and adapted as needed to remain consistent. The personnel of the organization, as well as any outsiders or subcontractors that work on the organization's systems must be fully trained and aware of the ISMS and how it is implemented and designed. Finally, as with any type of management policy, the ISMS must be a continuous process, and one that is implemented in a way that complements and supports the staff and operations, rather than preventing or obstructing them.

Internal Information Security Controls System

The ISO/IEC 27001:2013 standard puts forth a series of domains that are established as a framework for assisting with a formal risk assessment program. These domains cover virtually all areas of IT operations and procedures, making ISO/IEC 27001:2013 one of the most widely used standards in the world.

Here are the domains that comprise ISO/IEC 27001:2013:

- **A.5** Management
- **A.6** Organization
- **A.7** Personnel
- **A.8** Assets
- **A.9** Access Control
- **A.10** Cryptography
- **A.11** Physical Security
- **A.12** Operations Security
- **A.13** Network Security
- **A.14** Systems Security
- **A.15** Supplier/Vendor Relationships
- **A.16** Incident Management
- **A.17** Business Continuity
- **A.18** Compliance

 EXAM TIP While ISO/IEC 27001:2013 is the most widely used international standard, make sure you are aware of other standards that have their own domain sets that organizations either choose to or are required to use. These can include PCI for financial, HIPAA for healthcare, and FedRAMP for U.S. federal government assets. There are many others, depending on the jurisdiction and type of application or system as well as the data that it uses.

Policies

Policies document and articulate in a formal manner the desired or required systems and operations standards for any IT system or organization. They are crucial to correctly and securely implementing any system or application, and they are the basis for how an organization operates and governs their activities, hiring practices, authorization for access, and compliance. For an organization, especially a large organization, there can be a large number of policies put in place following a granular model, but together form a cohesive overall program and framework to govern their systems and activities, and will complement and depend on each other.

Organizational policies govern how an organization is structured and how it operates. They are done with a goal of efficiency and profit, as well as protecting the organization's reputation, legal liabilities, and data they collect and process. These policies form the basis for the implementation of IT and functional policies to govern the actual detailed operations and activities of an organization. Of great importance to any organization is the minimization of legal liabilities and exposure. This is where the focus on security and privacy comes into play, but it also shows the important of hiring and authorization policies and practices. Without strong control over hiring staff who are trusted and verified, and only granting access to those individuals who are trusted based on management's or regulatory standards, the entire organization and their data can be placed at immediate risk from malicious actors, or even those who are just sloppy with their security duties and practices.

IT policies govern all aspects of IT systems and assets within an organization. These include access control, data classification, backup and recovery, business continuity and disaster recovery, vendor access, segregation of duties, network and system policies, and virtually any aspect of an IT organization that you can think of. Some of the most prominent policies that even nontechnical staff are well aware of are password policies and Internet use policies, and while many will complain about restrictions and requirements in both of these areas, they represent the first and most visible layer of security within many organizations, and are crucial to the success of the security program overall.

With the introduction of cloud computing, the need for making modifications to current policies or crafting new policies has become very important. Many policies that organizations already have for operating within a traditional data center will require substantial modification or addition to work within a cloud environment, as the underlying structure and realities of a cloud are far different from operating in a controlled and private physical environment. With the lack of control over assets and access, policies will need to be augmented to allow for cloud provider access and any compensating changes needed for the realities of multitenancy.

Identification and Involvement of Relevant Stakeholders

With any IT system or operation, the proper and correct identification of stakeholders is absolutely vital. With the correct list of stakeholders, proper communications can be ensured to reach all relevant and important parties—and in a timely manner. To properly identify stakeholders, multiple audiences need to be addressed. The most obvious are those support members of the actual organization, including management. With a cloud environment, this will also need to include the cloud provider, as they will be responsible for many facets of the IT services hosting and implementation, and will have access, insight, and responsibilities that expand far past the limited scope of the cloud customer. Apart from the actual organization and other support services they use, stakeholders include users and consumers of the system or application. These groups are highly and crucially dependent on the availability and security of the services they are leveraging, and will need to be informed of any changes or risk exposure, as this will directly impact their own systems or initiatives as well. Lastly, depending on the type of data and any pertinent regulations, there may be additional bodies or auditors who need to be kept in continual communication as well.

Once the proper stakeholders have been identified, the level of involvement by them must be documented and developed. A key challenge is determining where and when each stakeholder needs to be involved or sent communications. Any IT environment, especially a cloud environment, will likely be highly complex and have many different possible sections or processes that need their own communications process and have different stakeholders. The challenge is also then to determine, in a highly complex and integrated environment, which issues affect which stakeholders when the impact is felt across multiple levels or components. Regulations, contracts, and SLAs will highly impact how communications and stakeholder involvement play out as well, especially in regard to the timeliness of involvement.

Specialized Compliance Requirements for Highly Regulated Industries

With any environment or system there will be jurisdictional requirements for security and privacy, as well as audit requirements and oftentimes reporting and communications environments. However, for specific types of data or systems, there are additional requirements that pertain to the specific data and processes that involve them, regardless of physical location or hosting model used. With highly sensitive data models, such as healthcare, financial, and government systems, there are additional compliance requirements in the form of HIPAA, PCI, and NIST/FedRAMP, respectively. When hosting in a cloud environment, all of these regulations still apply the same as a traditional data center, and with cloud being a much newer technology, not all regulatory requirements have been fully updated or adapted to cloud environments either. In this case, there may be some specific changes to the configurations needed to comply, or waivers for some requirements may need to be documented and requested. However, most major regulatory systems have been either partially or fully updated for cloud at this point, and it will be a matter of compliance and auditing rather than adapting and engineering.

Impact of Distributed IT Model

Modern applications, especially mobile and web-based applications, are a stark departure from the traditional server model, where there are presentation, application, and data zones, and the lines between each and the communications channels are obvious and well understood. Modern applications rely on very complex systems that are built on a variety of different components and technologies, many times located across several geographic areas, and they rely on web service calls and APIs rather than direct network connections, function calls, and tight integration. The introduction of cloud computing has made this complexity even more pronounced, as the reliance on consumable services, rather than owned and maintained systems, has increased at a rapid pace. While this has made building systems and scaling systems far cheaper and easier than ever before, it has also introduced significant changes for security, auditing, and compliance.

With distributed models, security is always a top challenge and concern. With the reliance on so many different components, many of which are external web services and features, it is impossible for an organization to have a full grasp on security at every layer of an application like they would in a traditional data center, where they have full control and ownership over the entire system. With this type of configuration and distribution, the importance of audit reports and certifications of systems are even more vital, as they serve as one of the few ways the provider and owner of a web service can promote confidence and verify security to external parties. The stated and published privacy policies of a web service and provider are also very important, which is where audit reports can also serve to promote confidence in their controls and adherence to policies. When choosing to use an external web service or provider, the Cloud Security Professional must ensure that SLAs and other agreements are in place to handle security incidents should they arise, and have a clear understanding of what levels of support and services will be offered by that provider should a security incident occur.

Another complication that arises with a reliance on external services is coordination of versions, upgrades, patching, and compatibility of features and APIs. With large external services that potentially have thousands of systems and users dependent on them, it is impossible for a service provider to meet all requests and demands, especially in regard to the timeliness of patches and upgrades. The lack of control over the patching and upgrade cycle for components, some of which may be core and central components to an application, can lead to versioning problems and configuration matching, thus exposing to the organization to increased risk.

With a distributed model, communication can also be a big challenge for many of the same reasons. The identification of stakeholders and key communications needs are always a challenge to obtain and keep updated with any organization or system, but with the reliance on outside resources and components, the difficulty of having proper and timely communications becomes even more pronounced. With the application owners now becoming consumers of other services, they will no longer have the type of internal control and management authority that they would in a traditional data center, and instead must rely on SLAs and other mechanisms for communication and assurance.

Perhaps the biggest and most impacting difference with a distributed model is the crossing of jurisdictional and geographical locations. With a traditional data center model, the location of data and services is well known and static, with any potential moves being under the control and initiative of the organization. This allows for extensive research and planning for any potential move, including the vetting of jurisdictional changes and requirements, allowing management to make an informed decision before authorizing and approving any such change. An organization can also purposely choose locations of data centers and data storage to take advantage of beneficial jurisdictional requirements. With a distributed cloud model, or reliance on external services, an organization loses some (or even all) control over where the systems are located overall or at any specific point in time. Cloud services can and will move all the time between geographical locations, or span multiple jurisdictions at any given point in time. With external services, it may be completely unknown where the services are located and operated from, and with these services not being under the control of the organization and management, they can move at any point in time, or span multiple jurisdictions in an ever-changing dynamic.

Implications of Cloud to Enterprise Risk Management

As with any other component of IT services and management, cloud computing will have a definite impact on an organization's risk management program and practices, adding an additional layer of complexity that must be taken into account.

Assess Providers Risk Management

With a move to any hosted environment, it is crucial to understand and evaluate the risk management program and processes with the provider. Since the cloud customer will be housing their services and data within that environment, the risk management processes and risk acceptance of the hosting provider will directly impact the security and risk management programs of the customer as well. This is another area where certification is so valuable for the cloud provider because it will largely tell the cloud customer the type of risk management programs and policies in place with the cloud provider, and what level of risks are allowed to be accepted or are required to be mitigated.

Difference Between
Data Owner/Controller vs. Data Custodian/Processor

To understand risk as it pertains to data, it is important to first understand the different roles and responsibilities as they pertain to data. In many organizations, these roles have formal titles and dedicated responsibilities. At the same time, many regulatory and certification bodies require specific individuals to be named as data owner and data custodian, and they bear responsibility for their jobs and roles when it comes to liability, auditing, and oversight. For these purposes, the roles can be defined as follows, with some variance allowed depending on the particular organization and audience for the definition:

- **Data owner**   The data owner is considered the individual who bears responsibility for controlling the data and determining the appropriate controls for it, as well as the appropriate use of it. In some cases, there may be an additional role of a data steward to oversee access requests and the utilization of the data, ensuring that organizational policies are being adhered to and access requests have the correct approvals.

- **Data custodian**   The data custodian is anyone who processes and consumes data that is owned or controlled by the data owner, and must adhere to policies and oversight while conducting business with the use of the data.

The data owners and custodians work with the management of the organization to establish the overall risk profile for their systems and applications. The risk profile will document and identify the level of risk that management is willing to take, as well as how risk is evaluated and approved for appropriate use requests. With a cloud environment, the risk profile can become a lot more complicated with the amount of systems and services that are outside the control of the organization—not to mention the reliance on mitigating technologies and systems needed to have the same level of security controls in a cloud that a dedicated traditional data center would enjoy.

The willingness of management to take and accept strategic risks forms the organization's risk appetite, which is the overall culture of security and how much allowance there is for using specific systems and services when coupled with the classification of data that is being used. An understanding of an organization's risk appetite will allow systems staff and application managers to make quick decisions for development and operations, without having to consult management for every decision. This allows for efficient operations while adhering to the organization's overall security and privacy strategy.

Risk Mitigation

The results of audits, whether internal or external, form the basis for evaluating risk within an organization and their computing environments. When audits are done, each finding or issue is categorized as low, medium, or high, which directly relates to the level of risk it entails. The level of risk is based on the potential damage from a successful exploit or vulnerability, combined with the likeliness that a threat will be successfully exploited. Risk mitigation is the process of augmenting security controls or making configuration changes to lower the risk level. The lowering of the risk level can be accomplished by increasing the security controls in place to make exploits more difficult or by putting controls in place to make the likelihood of them happening lower, or some combination of both approaches.

EXAM TIP Keep in mind that no matter what approach is taken to lower or mitigate risk, the elimination of all risk is not possible. No matter what, some level of risk will still exist for any system or application. With a cloud environment, it is even trickier to mitigate or reduce risk because you will not have full control over the environment, and you are relying on the cloud provider to keep systems secure and tenants isolated from each other. During your exam, keep in mind the unique challenges with risk mitigation in the cloud.

Different Risk Frameworks

Three prominent risk frameworks pertain to cloud and are in widespread use throughout the IT world.

European Network and Information Security Agency (ENISA)

In 2012, ENISA published a general framework for risk management in regard to cloud computing titled "Cloud Computing: Benefits, Risks, and Recommendations for Information Security." This publication outlines a series of 35 risks that organizations face, as well as a "Top 8" list of risks based on their probability of occurrence and potential impact on an organization.

ISO/IEC 31000:2009

The ISO/IEC 31000:2009 standard focuses on risk management from the perspectives of designing and implementing a risk management program. Unlike other ISO/IEC standards, it is not intended to serve as a certification path or program, but merely a guide and a framework. It advocates for risk management to be a central and integral component of an organization's overall IT strategy and implementations, similar to how security or change management is integrated throughout all processes and policies.

The ISO/IEC 31000:2009 standard puts forth 11 principles of risk management:

- Risk management as a practice should create and protect value for an organization.
- To be successful and comprehensive, risk management should be part of all aspects and processes of an organization and an integral component.
- Risk management should be a component to all decisions that an organization makes to ensure that all potential problems are considered and evaluated.
- With all organizations there is uncertainty at all times. Risk management can be utilized to mitigate and minimize the impact of uncertainty.
- To be effective, risk management must be fully integrated and efficient in providing information and analysis; it cannot slow down the processes or business of an organization.
- As with any type of decision making, risk management needs to ensure that it is using accurate and complete data; otherwise, any evaluations will be inaccurate and possibly counterproductive.
- While there are multiple general frameworks for risk management, they must be tailored to the particular needs and realities of each organization to be effective.
- While risk management is always heavily focused on IT systems and technologies, it is essential to consider the impact and risk of human elements as well.
- To instill confidence from staff, users, and customers, an organization's risk management processes and policies should be transparent and visible.
- With IT systems and operations being highly dynamic, the risk management program needs to be responsive, flexible, and adaptive.
- As with all aspects of an organization, risk management should be focused on making continual improvements in operations and efficiency.

National Institutes of Standards and Technology (NIST)

NIST published Special Publication 800-146, titled "Cloud Computing Synopsis and Recommendations," in 2012, which has components focused on risk in a cloud environment and recommendations for their analysis, among many other aspects of cloud computing and security. This document is the U.S. version of the ENISA document and pertains to U.S. federal government computing resources. While it only officially applies to the United States and computing resources of the federal government, it can serve as a general reference for other computing systems, and many organizations and regulatory bodies around the world use it as a guide and framework.

Metrics for Risk Management

Risks are almost always rated and presented as a score that balances the impact of a successful exploit, weighed against the likeliness of occurrence. Through the application of additional controls or configuration changes, the risk level can often be lowered to where it can be accepted by management. In addition, many organization policies or certification requirements will only allow the acceptance of risks at certain levels.

Here are the most commonly used categories of risk:

- Minimal
- Low
- Moderate
- High
- Critical

Assessment of the Risk Environment

To adequately evaluate risk in a cloud environment, multiple different levels need to be assessed. The particular application, system, or service is the first component, and involves a similar analysis to hosting in a traditional data center, with the addition of cloud-specific aspects added into the mix. The cloud provider must also be evaluated for risk, based on their track record, stability, focus, financial health, and future direction.

Outsourcing and Cloud Contract Design

Many organizations have shifted IT resources to outsourced and hosting models for many years now. This typically has involved an organization not owning and controlling their own data center, but leasing space, and possibly also contracting for support services with a hosting and IT services organization. The economies of scale always made it cheaper for many organizations to have space within data centers that were owned by other organizations, where the physical facilities and requirements could be done on a larger scale, with the cost shared by all of the customers, rather than each organization needing to build and control their own physical data center. With leased space, an organization still has full control over their systems and operations, as their systems and equipment are physically isolated from other customers. However, with outsourcing to cloud environments, there is significant additional complexity to contracts that needs to be addressed, and many organizations likely lack expertise and experience in managing cloud contracts.

 NOTE With traditional data centers, an organization has to build out systems to have sufficient capacity to handle their highest expected load, because it is cumbersome and expensive to add additional capacity and is not realistically feasible to do so for short periods of time. Cloud environments alleviate that problem, but also introduce new complexities to contracts and funding models. This is especially true with government contracts, where strict funding is set in advance, and many contract models do not support the elastic nature of cloud, especially with auto-scaling, where additional costs are fluid and potentially unpredictable.

Business Requirements

Before an organization can consider moving systems or applications into a cloud environment, they must first ensure that they have a comprehensive understanding of how their systems are currently built and configured, and how they relate to and interact with other systems. This understanding will form the basis for an evaluation as to whether a system or application is even appropriate for a cloud environment. It is very possible that current systems or applications may need extensive code changes or configuration retooling before they will effectively work in a cloud environment, as well as the possibility of enormous impacts on compliance programs and requirements.

This analysis forms the basis of articulating and documenting specific business requirements for a cloud environment. It enables an organization to begin to explore cloud offerings with an eye toward meeting those requirements. As with any outsourcing endeavor, it is likely that not all business requirements can be met by a vendor completely, and a thorough gap analysis will need to be performed by both the operations staff and the security staff of an organization to determine the level of risk associated with a move towards cloud. The risk must then be evaluated by management to determine if it fits within acceptable levels. During this analysis, the business continuity and disaster recovery plans of the organization should also be considered, and what impact, either positive or negative, a move toward cloud would have on them, and what degree of updating and modification would need to be undertaken on them. These are all substantial costs in both time and money to an organization, and they must be considered beyond just the actual costs of hosting and computing resources.

As with any contract, SLAs are of vital importance between the organization and their service providers, but with a cloud environment, there is an even greater level of importance for SLAs. With a traditional data center, an organization will have broad access to their systems and equipment, and many aspects that would fall under a cloud SLA can be handled by their own personnel, with their own management fully in control over allocation of staff resources. However, in a cloud environment, not only is the cloud provider fully responsible for their own infrastructure, the customer will not have this same level of access, nor will the cloud provider solely answer to them as a customer because the cloud provider will potentially have a large number of other customers as well. With this in mind, the SLA is vitally important to ensure the cloud provider allocates sufficient resources to respond to problems and gives these problems the needed prioritization to meet management's requirements.

Vendor Management

Once a decision has been reached to move toward a cloud solution, the process of selecting a cloud provider must be approached with care and exhaustive evaluation. Cloud computing is still a relatively new technology on the IT landscape, and as such, many companies are scrambling to offer cloud solutions and to become part of the explosive growth in the industry. While the level of competition is certainly beneficial to any customer, it also means that many new players are emerging that do not have long-established reputations or track records of performance to evaluate. It is crucial to ensure that any vendor being considered is stable and reputable to host critical business systems and sensitive data with. The last thing any organization wants is to give critical business systems to a cloud provider that is not mature enough to handle the growth and operational demands, or to a small startup that might not be around when the contract has run its course. Although major IT companies are offering cloud services and have extensive track records in the IT industry, the startups trying to gain a share of the explosion in cloud services may offer very attractive pricing or options in an attempt to establish a strong presence in the industry based on the number (or importance) of customers using their services.

Many factors need to be evaluated before selecting a cloud provider. The following is a list of core factors an organization must consider in the selection process:

- What is the reputation of the cloud provider? Are they are a long-established IT company or a newer startup? Is cloud computing their core business, or is it something they have added along the way, like a side project? What is the financial situation and future outlook for the company?

- How does the company manage their cloud services? Are the services all handled by staff employed by the company, or do they contract out support services and their management? Is their support model or strategy likely to change in the future during your contract with them?

- What types of certifications does the company have? Do they have current cloud, security, or operations certifications? Do they intend to get additional ones? Do the certifications they have match up with the regulatory requirements of your business? Are they willing to get additional certifications or conform to additional certifications if required by a cloud customer?

- Where are the facilities located for the cloud provider? What jurisdictional requirements would apply? Are there limitations based on the specifics of the application or its data that would preclude specific cloud providers based in certain physical locations?

- How does the company handle security incidents? What is their process and track record with incidents, and are they willing to provide statistics or examples of them? Have they had publicly disclosed or high-profile security incidents or loss of availability?

- Does the cloud provider build their platform on standards and flexibility, or do they focus a lot more on proprietary configurations? How easy is it to move between cloud providers or move to a different one if desired by management? Will you get locked in with a specific provider and limit your options?

Apart from the major operational and technological questions with selection, certifications will play a very prominent role, especially as regulatory compliance becomes increasingly important and public. The Common Criteria framework serves as a strong starting point for evaluating the security posture of any service provider, and it's based on standards from ISO/IEC. By using such standards and their associated certifications, a potential cloud customer can be assured that a provider is adhering to a well-understood and verified set of security controls, and can use these independent certifications as a way of comparing different providers to a common baseline. Certifications can also ensure that a cloud customer will be in full compliance with any regulatory requirements they may be subjected to. Depending on the type of application and data, the certifications may be a required component for them.

TIP A common issue that arises between cloud providers and cloud customers involves the certifications the cloud provider holds or is willing to obtain. In many instances, a cloud provider may already have in place all controls and procedures to meet the requirements of a particular certification, but has not actually done so, or is even unwilling to. A cloud customer should not assume that a cloud provider will be agreeable to obtaining additional certifications, as they require considerable expense and staff time. A Cloud Security Professional must remember that most cloud environments contain a large number of customers, and the cloud provider must balance the needs and requirements of each against the others. The cloud provider must take the best approach for their business model and their customers, even if that means they are not able to meet the needs of a number of specific customers.

Contract Management

As with any service arrangement or hosting situation, a sound and structured approach to contract management is a necessity, and being in a cloud environment does not make contract management any easier—and in many cases, it makes it more complex and involved. A thorough understanding of the organization's needs and expectations has to be done through a discovery and selection process before the contract is drawn up. Those requirements, combined with specific regulatory or legal requirements, will form the basis of the initial contract draft. The main components and considerations for the contract are as follows (note that this is not an exhaustive list, and depending on the system, application, data, or organization, there may be additional elements to the specific contract):

- **Access to systems**   How both users and the cloud customer will get access to systems and data is a key contract and SLA component. This includes multifactor authentication requirements, as well as supported identity providers and systems. From the cloud customer perspective, this defines what level of administrative or privileged access they are granted, depending on the cloud model used and the services offered by the cloud provider.

- **Backup and disaster recovery**   How systems and data will be backed up and how the cloud provider will implement disaster recovery. The disaster recovery requirements of the cloud customer must also be specified. This includes the acceptable times for recovery, as well as to what extent the systems must be available during a disaster situation. The contract should also document how backup and disaster recovery procedures will be tested and verified, as well as the frequency of the verifications and testing.

- **Data retention and disposal** How long data will be preserved and ultimately disposed of is a crucial piece to a contract. This is even more important in a cloud contract, as the cloud customer will be dependent on the cloud provider for backup and recovery systems to a degree they would not be with a traditional data center. The contract must clearly document how long data is to be preserved and in what format, as well as the acceptable methodologies and technologies used for data sanitizing after removal. Upon secure removal and sanitization, the contract should document what level of proof must be presented to the cloud customer by the cloud provider to meet either regulatory requirements or their own internal policies.

- **Definitions** The contract should include agreed-upon definitions of any terms and technologies. Although it may seem obvious to people in the industry what various terms mean, having them in the contract formalizes the definitions and ensures that everyone has the same understanding. Without doing this, issues could arise where expectations are different between both parties, with no clear recourse if the contract has not clarified the terms and set expectations.

- **Incident response** How the cloud provider will handle incident response for any security or operational incidents, as well as how communication will be provided to the cloud customer. This forms the basis of an SLA between the cloud provider and cloud customer, and it documents the cooperation between the incident response teams from both sides.

- **Litigation** From time to time, the cloud customer could be the subject of legal action, which would likely also impact the cloud provider and require their involvement. The contract will document the responsibilities on behalf of both parties in such a situation, as well as the required response times and potential liabilities.

- **Metrics** The contract should clearly define what criteria is to be measured as far as system performance and availability are concerned, and the agreement between the cloud customer and cloud provider as to how the criteria will be collected, measured, quantified, and processed.

- **Performance requirements** The contract, and more specifically the SLA, will document and set specific performance requirements of the system and its availability, and this will form the basis for determining the success of and compliance with the contract terms. The specific performance requirements may also impact the ultimate system design and allocated resources as well. The performance requirements will also set expectations for the response time for system requests and support requests.

- **Regulatory and legal requirements** This section details any specific certifications that are required, or any specific set of laws or regulations that the cloud customer is subjected to. This includes the specific steps taken by the cloud provider to comply with these requirements, as well as the response to legal orders such as eDiscovery, and the process that the cloud provider will use to audit and verify compliance. The cooperation of the cloud provider for application- and system-specific audits that will be done by the cloud customer is also included in this section of the contract.

- **Security requirements**   This includes technology systems and operational procedures that are in place from the cloud provider, but also includes requirements for personnel who work on systems from the cloud customer and have access to their systems and data. This includes background checks and employee policies, and may have an impact on cloud providers from a regulatory standpoint. For example, contractors for U.S. federal government contracts typically must have all personnel located within the United States, and for some cloud providers, this may be an eliminating factor.

- **Termination**   Should the need arise, the contract must clearly define the terms under which a party can terminate the contract, and what conditions are required as part of doing so. This will typically include specific processes for formal notice of nonperformance, remedy steps and timelines that can be taken, as well as potential penalties and termination costs, depending on the reasons for and timing of such action.

Executive Vendor Management

For managing outsourced and cloud services, the SLA is crucial in documenting the expectations and responsibilities of all parties involved. The SLA dictates specific requirements for uptime, support, response times, incident management, and virtually all operational facets of the contract. The SLA also articulates specific penalties for noncompliance and the impact they will have on the overall contract and satisfactory performance of it.

Supply-Chain Management

With the nature of modern applications built on a myriad of different components and services, the supply chain of any system or application is rapidly expanding to a scale far outside a single organization. This complexity makes security of systems increasingly difficult, as a breach of any component of the supply chain can impact all other components, or the overall system or application itself. No matter how many stringent security controls and policies are in place, attackers will find the weakest component and attempt to use that to gain further access. This means the Cloud Security Professional must not only worry about systems under their control, but also the security posture and exposure from all components and external services that are being leveraged.

The best approach to take from the perspective of the Cloud Security Professional is to fully document and understand each component being used and to perform an analysis as to the extent of exposure and vulnerability each represents to the overall application. This allows for a risk assessment for each component as well as for the possibility of designing additional controls or verifications for each connection point to ensure data and processes are operating securely and not performing actions outside of their intended purpose.

Exercise

The company you work for is based in the United States but is looking to expand services to European countries. However, management is very happy with the setup and systems currently in place and does not want to operate additional hosting from other locations during this expansion, which would increase the complexity of their systems.

1. What issues from a legal and regulatory standpoint will this type of situation incur?

2. What technical concerns and issues will likely come into play with this scenario?

3. How would you update and augment the risk management program of the organization to account for this additional expansion?

4. What new policies or procedures are likely to be needed with this effort from a regulatory standpoint?

Chapter Review

In this chapter, you learned about the various laws, regulations, and complexities of hosting in a cloud environment and how they pertain to data protection and privacy. You learned about how eDiscovery and forensics work in a cloud environment, as well as who has authority and responsibility for conducting them. We talked about how audits are defined and performed in a cloud environment, and their importance for ensuring confidence in security and operations within a cloud environment. We also talked about how risk management programs are crucial to any organization, and what unique factors cloud computing brings to a risk management program, as well as the unique challenges of managing outsourced contracts with cloud services.

Questions

1. Which of the following regulations specifies the length that financial records must be kept?

   A. HIPAA

   B. EU

   C. SOX

   D. Safe Harbor

2. Which type of audit report would be suited for the general public to review to ensure confidence in a system or application?

   A. SAS-70

   B. SOC 1

   C. SOC 2

   D. SOC 3

3. Which of the following would *NOT* be part of an audit scope statement?

    A. Deliverables

    B. Cost

    C. Certifications

    D. Exclusions

4. Which of the following would be appropriate to include in an audit restriction?

    A. Time when scans can be run

    B. Type of device the auditors use

    C. Length of audit report

    D. Training of auditors

5. What is the correct sequence for audit planning?

    A. Define objectives, define scope, conduct audit, lessons learned

    B. Define scope, conduct audit, prepare report, remediate findings

    C. Conduct audit, prepare report, remediate findings, verify remediation

    D. Define objectives, conduct audit, prepare report, management approval

6. Which of the following is *NOT* a domain of ISO/IEC 27001:2013?

    A. Personnel

    B. Systems

    C. Network

    D. E-mail

7. Which of the following is *NOT* a specialized regulatory requirement for data?

    A. HIPAA

    B. FIPS 140-2

    C. PCI

    D. FedRAMP

8. Which of the following is the best definition of "risk profile"?

    A. An organization's willingness to take risk

    B. A publication with statistics on risks taken by an organization

    C. A measure of risks and possibility of successful exploit

    D. An audit report on an organization's risk culture

9. Which of the following is responsible for data content and business rules within an organization?

    A. Data custodian

    B. Data steward

    C. Database administrator

    D. Data curator

10. When can risk be fully mitigated?

    A. After a SOC 2 audit

    B. When in compliance with SOX

    C. When using a private cloud

    D. Never

11. Which of the following shows the correct names and order of risk ratings?

    A. Minimal, Low, Moderate, High, Critical

    B. Low, Moderate, High, Critical, Catastrophic

    C. Mitigated, Low, Moderate, High, Critical

    D. Low, Medium, Moderate, High, Critical

12. Which of the following is *NOT* one of the major risk frameworks?

    A. NIST

    B. ENISA

    C. GAPP

    D. ISO/IEC 31000:2009

13. What does ENISA stand for?

    A. European National Information Systems Administration

    B. European Network and Information Security Agency

    C. European Network Intrusion Security Aggregation

    D. European Network and Information Secrecy Administration

14. Where does Russian data privacy laws allow for data on Russian citizens to reside?

    A. Anywhere that conforms to Russian security policies

    B. Russian or EU hosting facilities

    C. Any country that was part of the Soviet Union

    D. Russian data centers

15. In a cloud environment, who is responsible for collecting data in response to an eDiscovery order?

    A. The cloud customer

    B. The cloud provider

    C. The data owner

    D. The cloud customer and cloud provider

Questions and Answers

1. Which of the following regulations specifies the length that financial records must be kept?

   A. HIPAA

   B. EU

   C. SOX

   D. Safe Harbor

   C. SOX specifies how long financial records must be kept and preserved, as well as many other regulations for transparency and confidentiality protection. The EU and HIPAA guidelines are for European Union privacy protections and healthcare data protection, respectively. The Safe Harbor program is not a series of regulations, but rather a voluntary program to bridge the gap between privacy rules and laws between the United States and Europe.

2. Which type of audit report would be suited for the general public to review to ensure confidence in a system or application?

   A. SAS-70

   B. SOC 1

   C. SOC 2

   D. SOC 3

   D. SOC 3 audit reports are meant for general consumption and to be shared with a wider and open audience. The other types of audit reports listed—SAS-70, SOC 1, and SOC 2—are all restricted use audit reports that are only used internally, with current customers, or with regulators.

3. Which of the following would *NOT* be part of an audit scope statement?

   A. Deliverables

   B. Cost

   C. Certifications

   D. Exclusions

   B. Cost would not be part of an audit scope statement. The audit scope statement covers the breadth and depth of the audit, as well as the timing and tool sets used to conduct it. Cost is not part of the audit scope at this level, nor part of the planning and discussion between management and the auditors. The deliverables, exclusions, and certifications covered or required are all part of the audit scope statement.

4. Which of the following would be appropriate to include in an audit restriction?

   A. Time when scans can be run

   B. Type of device the auditors use

   C. Length of audit report

   D. Training of auditors

   A. Specifying the time when scans can be run would be appropriate for an audit restriction, so as to ensure they do not impact production operations or users. The type of devices that the auditors use, the length of the final report and deliverables, as well as the particular training of the audits would not be part of audit restrictions.

5. What is the correct sequence for audit planning?

   A. Define objectives, define scope, conduct audit, lessons learned

   B. Define scope, conduct audit, prepare report, remediate findings

   C. Conduct audit, prepare report, remediate findings, verify remediation

   D. Define objectives, conduct audit, prepare report, management approval

   A. Define objectives, define scope, conduct audit, lessons learned is the correct sequence for audit planning. The other options have either incorrect choices, choices that are really subsections of the real sections, or incorrect ordering.

6. Which of the following is *NOT* a domain of ISO/IEC 27001:2013?

   A. Personnel

   B. Systems

   C. Network

   D. E-mail

   D. E-mail is not a domain covered under ISO/IEC 27001:2013. The other options—personnel, systems, and network—are all separate and distinct domains under the standard.

7. Which of the following is *NOT* a specialized regulatory requirement for data?

   A. HIPAA

   B. FIPS 140-2

   C. PCI

   D. FedRAMP

   B. FIPS 140-2 is a certification and accreditation program for cryptographic modules, not a specialized regulatory requirement for data. HIPAA for healthcare records and systems, PCI for credit cards and financial systems, and FedRamp for United States Federal Government cloud systems are all specialized regulatory requirements.

8. Which of the following is the best definition of "risk profile"?

   A. An organization's willingness to take risk

   B. A publication with statistics on risks taken by an organization

   C. A measure of risks and possibility of successful exploit

   D. An audit report on an organization's risk culture

   A. The "risk profile" is an organization's willingness to take risks and how they evaluate and weigh those risks. The other choices are all incorrect with regard to what a risk profile is.

9. Which of the following is responsible for data content and business rules within an organization?

   A. Data custodian

   B. Data steward

   C. Database administrator

   D. Data curator

   B. The data steward is responsible for overseeing data content and ensuring that applicable policies are applied to access controls, as well as for ensuring that appropriate approvals have been obtained before access is granted. Data custodian is another term for the data owner. Although the data custodian (owner) has overall responsibility for data and its protection within a system or application, the data steward is the one who handles the actual operations processes of granting access and ensuring policies are followed. The database administrator role is a technical position that does the actual administration of a database, but is not responsible for setting policy or granting access to data. Data curator is an extraneous answer.

10. When can risk be fully mitigated?

    A. After a SOC 2 audit

    B. When in compliance with SOX

    C. When using a private cloud

    D. Never

    D. Risk can never be fully mitigated within any system or application. Risk can be lowered and largely mitigated, but can never be fully mitigated, as any system with users and access will always have some degree of possible successful exploit.

11. Which of the following shows the correct names and order of risk ratings?

    A. Minimal, Low, Moderate, High, Critical

    B. Low, Moderate, High, Critical, Catastrophic

    C. Mitigated, Low, Moderate, High, Critical

    D. Low, Medium, Moderate, High, Critical

    A. Minimal, Low, Moderate, High, Critical are the correct names and order of risk ratings for a system or application, based on the classification of the data and the specific threats and vulnerabilities that apply to it. The other answers are either out of order or contain invalid names for risk ratings.

12. Which of the following is *NOT* one of the major risk frameworks?

    A. NIST

    B. ENISA

    C. GAPP

    D. ISO/IEC 31000:2009

    C. The Generally Accepted Privacy Principles (GAPP) is not a major framework for risk to a system or application, but is instead focused on principles of privacy risks. NIST, ENISA, and ISO/IEC 31000:2009 are all specifically focused on systems, threats, and risks facing them directly.

13. What does ENISA stand for?

    A. European National Information Systems Administration

    B. European Network and Information Security Agency

    C. European Network Intrusion Security Aggregation

    D. European Network and Information Secrecy Administration

    B. ENISA stands for European Network and Information Security Agency.

14. Where does Russian data privacy laws allow for data on Russian citizens to reside?

    A. Anywhere that conforms to Russian security policies

    B. Russian or EU hosting facilities

    C. Any country that was part of the Soviet Union

    D. Russian data centers

    D. Russian laws require data on Russian citizens to be kept in Russian data centers only, based on Russian Law 526-FZ, which became effective September 1, 2015. It requires specifically that any collection, storing, or processing of personal information or data on Russian citizens must be done on systems that are physically located within the political borders of the Russian Federation.

15. In a cloud environment, who is responsible for collecting data in response to an eDiscovery order?

   A. The cloud customer

   B. The cloud provider

   C. The data owner

   D. The cloud customer and cloud provider

   D. In a cloud environment, both the cloud provider and cloud customer are responsible for collecting data in response to an eDiscovery order. Depending on the scope of the eDiscovery order, as well as the specific cloud service category used, the degree to which it falls on either party will differ a bit.

Exam Review Questions

The following are comprehensive exam review questions taken from the entirety of the six domains of material for the CCSP.

Questions

1. Your organization has just been served with an eDiscovery order. Because the organization has moved to a cloud environment, what is the biggest challenge when it comes to full compliance with an eDiscovery order?

   A. Virtualization

   B. Data discovery

   C. Multitenancy

   D. Resource pooling

2. Your organization is considering a move to a cloud environment and is looking for certifications or audit reports from cloud providers to ensure adequate security controls and processes. Which of the following is *NOT* a security certification or audit report that would be pertinent?

   A. FedRAMP

   B. PCI DSS

   C. FIPS 140-2

   D. SOC Type 2

3. You are developing a new process for data discovery for your organization and are charged with ensuring that all applicable data is included. Which of the following is *NOT* one of the three methods of data discovery?

   A. Metadata

   B. Content analysis

   C. Labels

   D. Classification

4. Management has requested that security testing be done against their live cloud-based applications, with the testers not having internal knowledge of the system. Not attempting to actually breach systems or inject data is also a top requirement. Which of the following would be the appropriate approach to take?

   A. Static application security testing

   B. Penetration testing

   C. Runtime application self-protection

   D. Dynamic application security testing

5. Which of the following cloud categories would allow for the *LEAST* amount of customization by the cloud customer?

   A. IaaS

   B. SaaS

   C. PaaS

   D. DaaS

6. Which phase of the risk management process involves an organization deciding how to mitigate risk that is discovered during the course of an audit?

   A. Assessing

   B. Framing

   C. Responding

   D. Monitoring

7. During the testing phase of the SDLC, which of the following is *NOT* included as a core activity of testing?

   A. User testing

   B. Stakeholder testing

   C. Vulnerability scanning

   D. Auditing

8. You have decided to use SOAP as the protocol for exchanging information between services for your application. Which of the following is the only data format that can be used with SOAP?

   A. SAML

   B. OAuth

   C. XML

   D. HTML

9. A cloud provider is looking to provide a higher level of assurance to current and potential cloud customers about the design and effectiveness of their security controls. Which of the following audit reports would the cloud provider choose as the most appropriate to accomplish this goal?

   A. SAS-70

   B. SOC 1

   C. SOC 2

   D. SOC 3

10. At which stage of the software development lifecycle is the most appropriate place to begin the involvement of security?

   A. Requirements gathering

   B. Design

   C. Testing

   D. Development

11. Which of the following is *NOT* one of the main considerations with data archiving?

   A. Format

   B. Regulatory requirements

   C. Testing

   D. Encryption

12. While an audit is being conducted, which of the following could cause management and the auditors to change the original plan in order to continue with the audit?

   A. Cost overruns

   B. Impact on systems

   C. Regulatory changes

   D. Software version changes

13. Which of the following threat models has elevation of privilege as one of its key components and concerns?

   A. DREAD

   B. STRIDE

   C. HIPAA

   D. SOX

14. What type of risk assessment is based on a documentation review and making informed judgment calls about risk from operational procedures and system designs?

   A. Computational

   B. Quantitative

   C. Qualitative

   D. Cursory

15. With a SOC 2 auditing report, which of the following principles must always be included?

   A. Security

   B. Processing integrity

   C. Privacy

   D. Availability

16. Which of the following would be used to isolate test systems from production systems within a cloud environment for testing or development purposes?

   A. Sandboxing

   B. Application virtualization

   C. Firewalling

   D. Puppet

17. Which of the following is *NOT* as aspect of static application security testing (SAST)?

   A. Access to source code

   B. Offline system

   C. Knowledge of system configurations

   D. Live system

18. Which of the following are the four cloud deployment models?

   A. Public, private, hybrid, and community

   B. Public, private, internal, and hybrid

   C. Internal, external, hybrid, and community

   D. Public, private, hybrid, and organizational

19. Which of the following is a commonly used tool for maintaining software versioning and code collaboration?

   A. GitHub

   B. Chef

   C. Puppet

   D. Nessus

20. Which of the following is *NOT* a core component of an SIEM solution?

   A. Correlation

   B. Aggregation

   C. Compliance

   D. Escalation

21. Which of the following threat types is the *MOST* difficult for an organization to defend against and detect?

   A. Data loss

   B. Malicious insiders

   C. Insecure APIs

   D. Account hijacking

22. Which of the following storage types are used with Infrastructure as a Service (IaaS)?

   A. Structured and unstructured

   B. File and database

   C. Object and volume

   D. Block and striped

23. Which of the following data-sanitation approaches are always available within a cloud environment?

   A. Physical destruction

   B. Shredding

   C. Overwriting

   D. Cryptographic erasure

24. Which of the following technologies will often make elasticity a bigger challenge in a cloud environment?

   A. IPS

   B. XML accelerator

   C. Vulnerability scanner

   D. Web application firewall

25. Which of the following concepts involves the ability of cloud customers to easily move services from one cloud provider to another?

   A. Interoperability

   B. Portability

   C. Multitenancy

   D. Measured service

26. What does the *S* stand for in the STRIDE threat model?

 A. Secure

 B. Structured

 C. Standard

 D. Spoofing

27. Which of the following is *NOT* a major concern with encryption systems?

 A. Integrity

 B. Confidentiality

 C. Efficiency

 D. Key management

28. Which of the following types of data is the United States' HIPAA regulations concerned with?

 A. Financial

 B. Historical

 C. Healthcare

 D. Hybrid cloud

29. Which of the following in a federated environment is responsible for consuming authentication tokens?

 A. Relying party

 B. Identity provider

 C. Cloud services broker

 D. Authentication provider

30. Which phase of the cloud data lifecycle involves processing by a user or application?

 A. Create

 B. Share

 C. Store

 D. Use

31. Which of the following is *NOT* a state of data that is important for security and encryption?

 A. Data in use

 B. Data in transit

 C. Data at rest

 D. Data in archive

32. Which of the following is a standard and certification for cryptographic modules?

    A. FIPS 199

    B. FIPS 140

    C. FIPS 201

    D. FIPS 153

33. The use of which of the following technologies will *NOT* require the security dependency of an operating system, other than its own?

    A. Management plane

    B. Type 1 hypervisor

    C. Type 2 hypervisor

    D. Virtual machine

34. Which of the following threats involves sending untrusted data to a user's browser in an attempt to have it executed using the user's permissions and access?

    A. Cross-site scripting

    B. Injection

    C. Unvalidated redirects

    D. Man in the middle

35. Which of the following involves assigning an opaque value to sensitive data fields to protect confidentiality?

    A. Obfuscation

    B. Masking

    C. Tokenization

    D. Anonymization

36. Which of the following is *NOT* one of the security domains presented within the Cloud Controls Matrix?

    A. Financial security

    B. Mobile security

    C. Data center security

    D. Interface security

37. Which ISO/IEC standards set documents the cloud definitions for staffing and official roles?

    A. ISO/IEC 27001

    B. ISO/IEC 17788

    C. ISO/IEC 17789

    D. ISO/IEC 27040

38. Which of the following pieces of information is *NOT* included as part of PII as a direct identifier?

  A. Address

  B. ZIP Code

  C. Biometric records

  D. Phone number

39. Which concept pertains to the risk an organization entails in regard to the ability to move between cloud providers at a later date?

  A. Interoperability

  B. Reversibility

  C. Portability

  D. Broad network access

40. Which of the following is *NOT* one of the core building blocks of cloud computing?

  A. CPU

  B. Memory

  C. Storage

  D. Hardware

41. You have been tasked with creating an audit scope statement and are making your project outline. Which of the following is *NOT* typically included in an audit scope statement?

  A. Statement of purpose

  B. Deliverables

  C. Classification

  D. Costs

42. With a multifactor authentication system, which of the following would *NOT* be appropriate as a secondary factor after a password is used?

  A. Fingerprint

  B. RSA token

  C. Text message

  D. PIN code

43. Which of the following ISO/IEC standards pertains to eDiscovery processes and best practices?

  A. ISO/IEC 27050

  B. ISO/IEC 17789

  C. ISO/IEC 27001

  D. ISO/IEC 17788

44. Which of the following is *NOT* one of the cloud computing activities, as outlined in ISO/IEC 17789?

   A. Cloud service provider

   B. Cloud service partner

   C. Cloud service administrator

   D. Cloud service customer

45. Which act relates to the use and protection of PII with financial institutions?

   A. SOX

   B. GLBA

   C. HIPAA

   D. PCI DSS

46. Which of the following is *NOT* one of the cloud service capabilities?

   A. Infrastructure

   B. Network

   C. Platform

   D. Software

47. Which of the following would *NOT* be used to determine the classification of data?

   A. Metadata

   B. PII

   C. Creator

   D. Future use

48. What is the prevailing factor for determining which regulations apply to data that is housed in a cloud environment?

   A. PII

   B. Classification

   C. Population

   D. Location

49. Which concept involves applying standardized configurations and settings to systems to ensure compliance with policy or regulatory requirements?

   A. Images

   B. Repudiation

   C. Baselines

   D. Interoperability

50. Your company has just been served with an eDiscovery order to collect event data and other pertinent information from your application during a specific period of time, to be used as potential evidence for a court proceeding. Which of the following, apart from ensuring that you collect all pertinent data, would be the *MOST* important consideration?

   A. Encryption

   B. Chain of custody

   C. Compression

   D. Confidentiality

51. Which of the following concepts will ensure that no single host or cloud customer can consume enough resources to impact other users on the same system?

   A. Limits

   B. Multitenancy

   C. Reservations

   D. Shares

52. Which of the following roles is responsible in many organizations for overseeing access requests for data utilization and ensuring that policies are followed and proper approvals are granted?

   A. Data owner

   B. Data steward

   C. Data processor

   D. Data controller

53. Which of the following is directly part of the "metered" costs associated with PaaS?

   A. Staffing

   B. Development

   C. Licensing

   D. Auditing

54. Many highly regulated data types and systems will have specialized regulatory requirements that extend further than the regulatory requirements that apply to all data. Which of the following is *NOT* a specialized regulatory framework that has its own compliance requirements?

   A. FedRAMP

   B. HIPAA

   C. FIPS 140-2

   D. PCI DSS

55. Which cloud deployment model offers the most control and ownership over systems and operations for an organization?

  A. Private

  B. Public

  C. Community

  D. Hybrid

56. Which of the following is encryption *MOST* intended to address?

  A. Integrity

  B. Availability

  C. Data loss

  D. Confidentiality

57. To test some new application features, you want to isolate applications within the cloud environment from other applications and systems. Which of the following approaches would be the *MOST* appropriate to accomplish this?

  A. Sandboxing

  B. Application virtualization

  C. Honeypot

  D. Federation

58. Which of the following would *NOT* be included as input into the requirements gathering for an application or system?

  A. Users

  B. Management

  C. Regulators

  D. Auditors

59. Which phase of the SDLC process includes the selection of the application framework and programming languages to be used for the application?

  A. Requirement gathering

  B. Development

  C. Design

  D. Requirement analysis

60. Which regulations were designed to try and bridge the gap in privacy laws between the United States and the European Union?

  A. Safe Harbor

  B. HIPAA

  C. SOX

  D. GLBA

61. Which concept involves the maintenance of resources within a cloud environment to ensure resources are available when and where needed?

    A. Dynamic optimization

    B. Auto-scaling

    C. Elasticity

    D. Resource pooling

62. Which type of storage with IaaS will be maintained by the cloud provider and referenced with a key value?

    A. Structured

    B. Object

    C. Volume

    D. Unstructured

63. When an audit plan is being prepared, four distinct steps are done in sequence. Which of the following is the second step, after the defining of objectives?

    A. Define scope

    B. Conduct audit

    C. Identify stakeholders

    D. Gather documentation

64. Which of the following technology concepts is listed specifically as its own domain as part of ISO/IEC 27001:2013?

    A. Firewalls

    B. IPS

    C. Honeypots

    D. Cryptography

65. What are the two main types of APIs used with cloud-based systems and applications?

    A. REST and SOAP

    B. XML and SOAP

    C. REST and XML

    D. HTTPS and REST

66. You have been tasked by management to offload processing and validation of incoming encoded data from your application servers and their associated APIs. Which of the following would be the most appropriate device or software to consider?

   A. XML accelerator

   B. XML firewall

   C. Web application firewall

   D. Firewall

67. What is used with a single sign-on system for authentication after the identity provider has successfully authenticated a user?

   A. Token

   B. Key

   C. XML

   D. SAML

68. Which document will enforce uptime and availability requirements between the cloud customer and cloud provider?

   A. Contract

   B. Operational level agreement

   C. Service level agreement

   D. Regulation

69. Which of the following concepts makes repeated audits and verification much more difficult in a cloud environment versus a traditional data center?

   A. Multitenancy

   B. Resource pooling

   C. Elasticity

   D. Virtualization

70. The security principle of the SOC 2 reports consists of seven categories. Which of the following is *NOT* one of the seven categories?

   A. Monitoring of controls

   B. Legal compliance controls

   C. Change management

   D. System operations

71. Which privacy standard was developed as a joint effort between AICPA and the CICA?

    A. GLBA

    B. HIPAA

    C. GAPP

    D. ISO/IEC 27001

72. Which cross-cutting aspect relates to the ability for a cloud customer to remove their data and systems from a cloud provider and be afforded assurances that it has been securely removed?

    A. Portability

    B. Reversibility

    C. Sanitation

    D. Wiping

73. Which protocol is the current default and industry standard for encrypting traffic across a network?

    A. TLS

    B. SSL

    C. IPsec

    D. DNSSEC

74. Which network concept is used within a cloud environment to segregate and isolate network segments from other systems or applications?

    A. Subnets

    B. VLANs

    C. Gateways

    D. IPsec

75. Which jurisdiction, through Directive 95/46, enacted in 1995, declared data privacy to be a human right?

    A. United States

    B. European Union

    C. Russia

    D. Japan

76. What type of encryption allows for the manipulation of encrypted data without having to first unencrypt it?

    A. Homomorphic

    B. Symmetric

    C. Asymmetric

    D. Public key

77. Which of the following threat models includes discoverability as a key component and concern?

    A. DREAD

    B. SOX

    C. STRIDE

    D. CSA Treacherous 12

78. From a legal perspective, data that is covered under eDiscovery falls into three different categories. Which of the following is *NOT* one of the three?

    A. Possession

    B. Shared

    C. Control

    D. Custody

79. Which of the following would be covered by an external audit and *NOT* by an internal audit?

    A. Security controls

    B. Costs

    C. Operating efficiency

    D. System design

80. What is the most prevalent communications protocol for network-based storage solutions within a data center?

    A. iSCSI

    B. TCP

    C. TLS

    D. NetBIOS

81. Which of the following security responsibilities is always solely under the cloud provider?

    A. Infrastructure

    B. Data

    C. Physical

    D. Application

82. Your organization has made it a top priority that any cloud environment being considered to host production systems have guarantees that resources will always be available for allocation when needed. Which of the following concepts will you need to ensure is part of the contract and SLA?

   A. Limits

   B. Shares

   C. Resource pooling

   D. Reservations

83. Which is the most commonly used standard for information exchange within a federated identity system?

   A. OAuth

   B. OpenID

   C. SAML

   D. WS-Federation

84. Which of the following common threats involves an organization not placing sufficient controls and oversight on their systems and data protection?

   A. Data loss

   B. System vulnerabilities

   C. Insufficient due diligence

   D. Advanced persistent threats

85. Which of the following groups would *NOT* be appropriate to share a SOC 1 report with?

   A. Regulators

   B. Potential customers

   C. Current customers

   D. Management

86. With data in transit, which of the following will be the *MOST* major concern in order for a DLP solution to properly work?

   A. Scalability

   B. Encryption

   C. Redundancy

   D. Integrity

87. Which of the following, if important to the cloud customer or required by regulation, is something that must be addressed by a contract, versus an SLA, to ensure compliance?

    A. Certifications

    B. Availability

    C. Incident management

    D. Elasticity

88. Which of the following aspects of the physical environment is considered an external redundancy issue?

    A. Generators

    B. Cooling chillers

    C. Power distribution units

    D. Storage systems

89. Which of the following methods is often used to obscure data from production systems for use in test or development environments?

    A. Tokenization

    B. Encryption

    C. Masking

    D. Classification

90. As part of an audit, systems and processes are tested to evaluate whether they are in compliance with regulatory or organizational policy requirements. What is the official term for determining any discrepancies between the real and desired states?

    A. Audit findings

    B. Gap analysis

    C. Audit deficiency

    D. Compliance analysis

91. In a cloud environment, apart from confidentiality, what is the *MOST* important factor to consider with a key management system?

    A. Integrity

    B. Nonrepudiation

    C. Availability

    D. Archiving

92. Which of the following top security threats involves attempting to send invalid commands to an application in an attempt to get the application to execute the code?

    A. Cross-site scripting

    B. Injection

    C. Insecure direct object references

    D. Cross-site request forgery

93. Which of the key aspects of security is concerned with ensuring information and data is in its intended format and has not been altered?

    A. Integrity

    B. Confidentiality

    C. Availability

    D. Privacy

94. Which of the following has user training as a primary means of combating and mitigating its success against a cloud application?

    A. Data breaches

    B. Account hijacking

    C. Advanced persistent threats

    D. Malicious insiders

95. You have been tasked with developing a list of requirements for cabling design in a new data center as well as ensuring that any designs developed by the networking team meet standards. Which standard should you consult?

    A. IDCA

    B. BICSI

    C. Uptime Institute

    D. NFPA

96. Which network protocol is essential for allowing automation and orchestration within a cloud environment?

    A. DNSSEC

    B. DHCP

    C. IPsec

    D. VLANs

97. Which of the following tools has the ability to analyze incoming traffic for patterns and content and take appropriate actions based on them before the traffic reaches the actual applications?

    A. XML accelerator

    B. XML firewall

    C. Web application firewall

    D. Firewall

98. The ISO/IEC 27018 standard focuses on privacy in cloud computing and consists of five main principles. Which of the following is *NOT* one of the principles established in the standard?

    A. Communication

    B. Consent

    C. Yearly audit

    D. Penalties for privacy violations

99. Which of the following concepts of cloud computing necessitates the logical separation of systems that would normally be done by physical separation in a traditional data center?

    A. Resource pooling

    B. Multitenancy

    C. Elasticity

    D. Measured service

100. Which common threat is mitigated by the use of DNSSEC?

    A. Spoofing

    B. Snooping

    C. XSS

    D. DDoS

Quick Answers

1. B	**26.** D	**51.** A	**76.** A
2. C	**27.** A	**52.** B	**77.** A
3. D	**28.** C	**53.** C	**78.** B
4. D	**29.** A	**54.** C	**79.** A
5. B	**30.** D	**55.** A	**80.** A
6. C	**31.** D	**56.** D	**81.** C
7. D	**32.** B	**57.** B	**82.** D
8. C	**33.** B	**58.** D	**83.** C
9. D	**34.** A	**59.** D	**84.** C
10. A	**35.** C	**60.** A	**85.** B
11. D	**36.** A	**61.** A	**86.** B
12. B	**37.** B	**62.** B	**87.** A
13. B	**38.** B	**63.** A	**88.** A
14. C	**39.** C	**64.** D	**89.** C
15. A	**40.** D	**65.** A	**90.** B
16. A	**41.** D	**66.** A	**91.** C
17. D	**42.** D	**67.** A	**92.** B
18. A	**43.** A	**68.** C	**93.** A
19. A	**44.** C	**69.** D	**94.** C
20. D	**45.** B	**70.** B	**95.** B
21. B	**46.** B	**71.** C	**96.** B
22. C	**47.** D	**72.** B	**97.** C
23. D	**48.** D	**73.** A	**98.** D
24. A	**49.** C	**74.** B	**99.** B
25. B	**50.** B	**75.** B	**100.** A

Questions and Comprehensive Answer Explanations

1. Your organization has just been served with an eDiscovery order. Because the organization has moved to a cloud environment, what is the biggest challenge when it comes to full compliance with an eDiscovery order?

   A. Virtualization

   B. Data discovery

   C. Multitenancy

   D. Resource pooling

   B. Data discovery in a cloud environment encounters significant challenges due to the distributed nature of cloud computing. A primary concern with eDiscovery is determining all of the applicable data and locating it for collection and preservation. Within a cloud environment, locating the data and ensuring that all locations have been found can be a difficult process and will require the cooperation of both the cloud provider and the cloud customer, with procedures outlined in the contract and SLAs.

   A is incorrect because while virtualization forms the backbone of a cloud environment, the actual use of virtual machines does not increase the difficultly of data discovery, even if it does mean that assistance may be needed from the cloud provider for the actual data collection. With physical hardware, it is very easy to fully isolate and gather information because support staff will have full control of and access to the systems at all levels.

   C is incorrect because multitenancy involves hosting different systems and applications, from different organizations, within the same cloud environment and sharing resources between them. Although this can pose an additional challenge, depending on the scope of the eDiscovery order and the data it pertains to, data discovery as a broad topic is the more appropriate answer.

   D is incorrect because resource pooling is the sharing of resources between many different customers and systems, allowing for the aggregation of resources and the sharing of load across them. This will not have any impact on data-discovery processes.

2. Your organization is considering a move to a cloud environment and is looking for certifications or audit reports from cloud providers to ensure adequate security controls and processes. Which of the following is *NOT* a security certification or audit report that would be pertinent?

   A. FedRAMP

   B. PCI DSS

C. FIPS 140-2

D. SOC Type 2

C. FIPS 140-2 is a security standard from the United States federal government that pertains to the accreditation of cryptographic modules. While this is important to security processes and controls, it is not a certification or audit report that is responsive to overall security controls, policies, or operations.

A is incorrect because the Federal Risk and Authorization Management Program (FedRAMP) is a program under the U.S. government for ensuring adequate security policies, practices, and configurations when using cloud-based resources and services. It offers certifications at different classification levels for federal agencies to use in their security monitoring and auditing and ensures they comply with specific, established security standards.

B is incorrect because the Payment Card Industry Data Security Standard (PCI DSS) is an industry security standard for organizations that process and handle credit card transactions from the major credit card vendors and platforms. PCI DSS certification can be obtained, or required, by complying with and verifying security standards and policies.

D is incorrect because the Service Organization Control (SOC) Type 2 reports focus on the nonfinancial aspects of an organization's systems, specifically related to security, privacy, availability, processing integrity, and confidentiality. They are produced after thorough audits and reviews, and can be used to assure clients of security controls and policies meeting specific standards and requirements.

3. You are developing a new process for data discovery for your organization and are charged with ensuring that all applicable data is included. Which of the following is *NOT* one of the three methods of data discovery?

   A. Metadata

   B. Content analysis

   C. Labels

   D. Classification

   D. Classification is the overall process of using certain attributes about data and then applying appropriate security controls to that data. Classification is applied after data discovery has been completed, and it pertains only to the application of security controls, not the actual process of discovering or determining data.

   A is incorrect because metadata is essentially data about data. It contains information about the data, such as the type, how it is stored, how it is organized, how it was created, or how it is used. Metadata can also include headers and organizational markings, such as column or field names in a database or a spreadsheet.

B is incorrect because content analysis is actually looking at the data itself to make decisions based on what it is. This can include a person actually looking at it manually, or the use of tools like checksums, heuristics, or statistical analysis to determine its content and data discovery.

C is incorrect because labels are groupings or categorizations that have been applied to data either by personnel or automated means. They are typically done based on characteristics or content of data, and then matched against criteria to be included under such a label. Unlike metadata, labels are only as good as how standardized and thoroughly they are used throughout an environment. If they are not used in a standardized way, or done comprehensively across all data sets, their usefulness to data discovery will be greatly diminished.

4. Management has requested that security testing be done against their live cloud-based applications, with the testers not having internal knowledge of the system. Not attempting to actually breach systems or inject data is also a top requirement. Which of the following would be the appropriate approach to take?

   A. Static application security testing

   B. Penetration testing

   C. Runtime application self-protection

   D. Dynamic application security testing

   D. Dynamic application security testing is done against a system or application in its actual runtime state, and where the testers do not have specific knowledge about the configurations or technologies employed on it. Unlike static application security testing, dynamic testing must discover all interfaces and paths to test, but unlike penetration testing, it does not attempt to actively exploit vulnerabilities that could cause system outages, impact to users, or damage to the system or data.

   A is incorrect because static application security testing is done against offline systems, where the testers have knowledge ahead of time about the application and its configuration. This can include documentation about system design and the specific technologies used, as well as access to the source code and programming libraries that the application was built upon. Because the testing is done against offline systems, it does not have the ability to impact production systems or users while the testing is being completed.

   B is incorrect because penetration testing is done against an application where the testers do not have any particular knowledge of the system or application. They would not know the specific technologies or toolsets used in the development of the application, or information about the runtime environment and the technologies it is built upon. Penetration testing is done using the same toolsets and tactics that hackers would use to attack the system in a real situation, and it is intended to determine security vulnerabilities in a proactive manner, allowing for patching or mitigation before hackers are able to discover the same exploits and successfully use them.

C is incorrect because runtime application self-protection is the ability of a system or application to detect and respond to security threats and attacks in an automated manner. It is intended for applications to be able to respond to real-world attacks and scenarios in real time and apply mitigation tactics to stop the attacks immediately, allowing personnel to review when available and provide further tuning or to investigate further.

5. Which of the following cloud categories would allow for the *LEAST* amount of customization by the cloud customer?

   A. IaaS

   B. SaaS

   C. PaaS

   D. DaaS

B. Software as a Service allows the least amount of customization by the cloud customer. With the entire system and application under control of the cloud provider, the cloud customer will only have minimal options for customization, which typically is limited to branding or the selection of default options or settings.

A is incorrect because Infrastructure as a Service allows the most customization by the cloud customer. While the cloud provider is solely responsible for the physical infrastructure and appliances of a cloud environment, the cloud customer has enormous control over storage, network settings, virtual machines, and identity and access control systems. With this level of control, the cloud customer can choose which technologies and configurations to use, typically without any involvement from the cloud provider.

C is incorrect because Platform as a Service, while not allowing full control to the operating system level like IaaS, allows tremendous control over application environments and configurations, as well as sole control over the code that is deployed and configured for the applications. PaaS allows the cloud customer to choose the underlying operating system, application frameworks, and programming libraries and interfaces that are used within the environment.

D is incorrect because Desktop as a Service works as a virtual desktop where configurations and installations are stored remotely and accessed over the network. It offers substantial security and recoverability features because the device is no longer the holder of data or software. Although it is centrally maintained, it offers more flexibility as far as configuration, software packages deployed, and customization than a SaaS solution offers to users.

6. Which phase of the risk management process involves an organization deciding how to mitigate risk that is discovered during the course of an audit?

   A. Assessing

   B. Framing

   C. Responding

   D. Monitoring

   C. Responding is the stage of the risk management process where an organization will determine, based on the exact nature of the risk finding, as well as the potential costs and efforts involved with mitigation, which is the appropriate direction to take. The organization may decide to accept the risk "as is," which is typically an option when the finding is of a low or possible moderate classification. They can opt to avoid the risk by employing countermeasures or changes in operations so that the risk is never realized, which is typically accomplished by disabling or blocking access to certain function or interfaces. They can also opt to transfer the risk to another entity, which, although not always possible, will typically be in the form of insurance. Lastly, they can decide to mitigate the risk through the use of applicable technologies, configuration changes, or code changes to remove or lessen the vulnerability or exposure.

   A is incorrect because the process of assessing risk involves evaluating potential vulnerabilities, coupled with the likeliness of occurrence and the possible damage from successful exploit, and then assigning a risk classification value (ranging from minimal to critical). In some instances, the assigning of a risk level will be automatically dictated by regulatory requirements, depending on the type of data and application involved. This value and rating will then be used in the responding phase to determine the appropriate course of action based on the risk exposure, the risk appetite of the organization, and the costs associated with mitigation.

   B is incorrect because the framing stage of the risk management process is where the overall risk assessment is defined and scoped. The organization will determine during framing what risk and levels they want to evaluate, based on specific threats, regulation, or the type of data that is used. This will guide the overall risk assessment process from start to finish.

   D is incorrect because the main purpose of the monitoring phase is to track risks and evaluations of them over time to determine if they are still applicable, and if the same level of risk classification still applies. This will also incorporate changes from the regulatory perspective and ongoing threats, and can serve as a continual risk management and assessment process for the organization.

7. During the testing phase of the SDLC, which of the following is *NOT* included as a core activity of testing?

   A. User testing

   B. Stakeholder testing

C. Vulnerability scanning

D. Auditing

D. Although many different types of testing are done at this phase, auditing is not one of them. Testing, as part of the SDLC process, is highly focused on functional and operational readiness, both from a stability perspective and a meeting functional requirements perspective. The testing phase does include security scanning as part of it, but not to the extent of formal audits and evaluations.

A is incorrect because user testing involves having actual users test the application to see if it performs as expected and desired. This is very important overall because it will be a similar experience for all users of the application, and any features that are difficult to use or any aspects that are confusing to users will come to light, and possible fixes can be explored before the application is released to all users. With most testing, application developers and stakeholders are so involved in the application and how it is supposed to work, it is difficult for them to do proper testing and see things from the perspective of actual users, especially those who are new to the application or are encountering the new features being deployed. This will also bring out any user actions and behaviors that cause error conditions or incorrect data inputs that were not considered when the application and error checking were defined and coded.

B is incorrect because stakeholder testing involves management, strategic partners, internal experts, and possibly customers if done as part of a contract for development. These groups are the core investors and administrators of the system or application as well as those who have a vested interest in it and an intimate knowledge of it and how it should operate. Testing by this group should be thorough, using scripted regression testing that evaluates all aspects of the application, including specific targeted testing for new and updated features as part of the code release.

C is incorrect because while much of the testing phase is focused on functional and usability testing by populations of users and stakeholders, vulnerability scanning is also crucial at this stage. Although not a comprehensive audit, scanning should be done using standard tools with full signature sets to detect any common vulnerabilities, especially any code or functions that are vulnerable to XSS or injection attacks.

8. You have decided to use SOAP as the protocol for exchanging information between services for your application. Which of the following is the only data format that can be used with SOAP?

A. SAML

B. OAuth

C. XML

D. HTML

C. The SOAP protocol only uses XML as a data format for exchanging information. XML is a free, open standard for encoding documents and data in a format that is both machine and human readable. XML is designed to be extremely flexible and to handle any type of data formatting, which makes it ideal for web services. XML is widely used across all platforms and many different application frameworks and programming languages.

A is incorrect because SAML is a free, open standard that is built on XML, and is intended to be used for authentication and authorization data exchange between identity and service providers. While it is similar to and built on top of XML, it is used for the specific purposes of authentication and authorization and is not appropriate to use for general web services, specifically within the SOAP protocol, which requires XML.

B is incorrect because OAuth is an authentication mechanism that allows users to authenticate to many different applications or web services using commonly used credentials, such as Google, Facebook, Twitter, and so on. It enables users to use credentials they already have, without having to create an account on each system or application, and without their credentials ever being exposed. It is an open standard that any system or application is free to use and leverage.

D is incorrect because HTML forms the backbone of web pages and web design, and is used as markup language to enable web browsers to render and display content. Although it is widely used and will be crucial to any web-based application, it is not used to encode information to be used by web services or protocols such as SOAP.

9. A cloud provider is looking to provide a higher level of assurance to current and potential cloud customers about the design and effectiveness of their security controls. Which of the following audit reports would the cloud provider choose as the most appropriate to accomplish this goal?

   A. SAS-70

   B. SOC 1

   C. SOC 2

   D. SOC 3

D. SOC reports are done to test controls in place within an organization for financial or other systems. SOC 3 reports specifically are intended for general use and exposure, so they would be appropriate to use for potential cloud customers or put out for public consumption and review.

A is incorrect because SAS-70 reports have largely been phased out and replaced by SOC 1 reports. When they were in routine use, SAS-70 reports were considered "restricted audience," and as such, would not be appropriate for potential customers or current customers. They were intended for internal audit or regulatory compliance review.

B is incorrect because SOC 1 reports are considered restricted-use reports, much the same as their predecessor, the SAS-70 reports. They would not be appropriate for use with potential customers, because they are restricted for internal use only, and are also focused only on financial controls.

C is incorrect because SOC 2 reports are very similar to SOC 3 reports, in that they cover security controls and go beyond the financial control limitation of SOC 1 reports. However, SOC 2 reports are not meant for general use and, in this particular example, potential customers.

10. At which stage of the software development lifecycle is the most appropriate place to begin the involvement of security?

   A. Requirements gathering

   B. Design

   C. Testing

   D. Development

A. Security should be involved at all times in the SDLC process, including from the very initial stages of requirements gathering. Security can provide guidance on requirements from the regulatory perspective and the necessary security controls that they dictate. By not involving security from the earliest stages, an organization can incur substantial risk for software development because security controls and requirements may be missed or inadequate, requiring later revisions or fixes. This can add additional costs and time to software development projects that are largely avoidable by including security from the onset. It also serves to foster better cooperation and to limit the perception prevalent in many organizations that security is a hindrance or roadblock in development and operations.

B is incorrect because at the design stage, specific decisions are made as to which technologies and programming languages will be used with development. At this point, requirements have already been gathered and scoped, and it is very possible that security requirements have been missed or misunderstood. Although this is still early in the process, and changes are much easier to make at this stage than at later stages, it still adds additional time and costs that could have largely been avoided.

C is incorrect because by the testing stage, development has been either mostly or completely finished, and it is far too late to start the involvement of security. Although security will play a role in the testing phase as far as vulnerability scanning and evaluation of security controls and their implementations go, many security concerns or requirements will likely have been missed throughout the overall development. Because this stage occurs as a final approval before release to production is approved, any changes in design or code based on discovered security concerns will likely incur substantial costs and delays, and depending on the release and any publicity that may have been done, or requirements to meet required deadlines, these delays can carry significant risk to an organization.

D is incorrect because during the development stage, actual coding and implementations are done, based on requirements and decisions made during the design phase. At this stage, the lack of security could lead to a return to the design phase to mitigate concerns or deficiencies, which will in turn delay the project, and will likely add additional costs to the overall project.

11. Which of the following is *NOT* one of the main considerations with data archiving?

    A. Format

    B. Regulatory requirements

    C. Testing

    D. Encryption

    D. Although encryption will be used in many archiving solutions and implementations, it is not always a requirement, and will be largely subjective, based on the type of data and the archiving method chosen. It is not considered, by itself, to be a major consideration with archiving.

    A is incorrect because the format of archives is very important to consider, both at the time of archiving and for the long-term considerations involved. The format chosen will have to be one that properly ensures archiving and readability. Failure to pick a format that is recoverable for the duration of the required archiving term will expose an organization to substantial risk for noncompliance with data-retention requirements.

    B is incorrect because in most instances, requirements for data retention, and possibly even archiving methods, will come from regulatory requirements. Depending on the type of data and its use, regulations will typically require minimum periods of archiving and data retention. In some instances, regulatory requirements will also dictate the time of recovery, in which case regulations will play a large role in the exact methods and technologies chosen for archiving. Also, an organization needs to ensure that they can recover data for the duration of the retention requirements. It serves no purpose and doesn't satisfy compliance requirements if the data being archived for a period of time cannot be recovered.

    C is incorrect because in order for an archiving system to be considered valid and sound, it must be tested to ensure restoration and access are functional. Without this level of assurance, there is no point in having the archives in the first place. Testing should be done at regular intervals and follow the same procedures as those used for actual recoveries and restorations.

12. While an audit is being conducted, which of the following could cause management and the auditors to change the original plan in order to continue with the audit?

    A. Cost overruns

    B. Impact on systems

C. Regulatory changes

D. Software version changes

B. During an audit, even after extensive planning and scoping, there may end up being negative impacts on the environment and the performance of systems. Although testing should ideally be done against offline systems, that is not always possible in all environments, and may cause potential service interruptions or slowdowns with the systems being tested. If this were to occur, it will be a decision by management as to whether to continue with the audit or to modify the scope or approach.

A is incorrect because cost issues and budgeting would be completed before the audit begins. Once the audit has begun and the original scope and process are followed, costs should not be a dynamic value and should have no impact on the audit proceeding as planned.

C is incorrect because regulatory changes during an actual audit would have no impact on the current audit. Since the audit scope and requirements are done before the audit begins, any changes after that would be captured by future audits. Also, regulatory changes happen over time, and even if new regulations were released during an audit, they would almost certainly have a future implementation and enforcement date.

D is incorrect because software changes or releases would be suspended during auditing periods within any organization. Organizations almost always use an audit period as a freeze for configuration and version changes so that the environment is consistent and static while undergoing testing. The exception to this would be limited changes to mitigate auditing findings during the actual audit so that they can be closed before becoming official, but those changes would be very specific and limited in scope.

13. Which of the following threat models has elevation of privilege as one of its key components and concerns?

   A. DREAD

   B. STRIDE

   C. HIPAA

   D. SOX

B. The *E* in the acronym for the STRIDE threat model stands for "elevation of privilege." Elevation of privilege occurs as a threat to applications and systems that use a common login method and then display specific functions or data to users based on their role, with administrative users having the same initial interface as regular users. If the application is not properly coded and performing authorization checks within each function, it is possible for users to authenticate and change their level of access once they are within the application, even gaining administrative access if access controls are not properly enforced.

A is incorrect because the DREAD model does not include elevation of privilege. While the DREAD model also contains an *E* with its acronym, in this instance it represents "exploitability," which is a quantitative measure of the skills and sources needed for someone to successfully exploit a weakness. The value will be within a range of 0 to 10, with 0 representing extensive knowledge and resources to exploit and 10 representing no specific knowledge or skill required to exploit.

C is incorrect because HIPAA refers to the U.S. Health Insurance Portability and Accountability Act of 1996. It covers the privacy and security of patient medical information.

D is incorrect because SOX refers to the U.S. Sarbanes–Oxley Act of 2002. SOX is intended to protect the public and shareholders from accounting and fraudulent practices by corporations. In addition, it requires that certain information be disclosed to the public.

14. What type of risk assessment is based on a documentation review and making informed judgment calls about risk from operational procedures and system designs?

   A. Computational

   B. Quantitative

   C. Qualitative

   D. Cursory

C. Qualitative risk assessments are based on documentation and other data about systems and applications that are not easily converted into numerical values for comparison. They are often done in situations where an organization does not have the time or money to complete a more exhaustive quantitative assessment. After a thorough review of documentation, systems design, policies, and operational practices, risk categories can be assigned for management review based on the likeliness of threats being exploited, as well as the potential damage that could occur if they were successfully exploited.

A is incorrect because computational is not a type of risk assessment.

B is incorrect because quantitative risk assessments are based on numerical data and metrics. With the availability of quantified data and risks, real calculations can be performed during a quantitative assessment. This will include the values for single loss expectancy (SLE), the annualized rate of occurrence (ARO), and the derived annualized loss expectancy (ALE). These values and calculations can give management hard data and cost numbers to make informed risk mitigation or acceptance decisions.

D is incorrect because cursory is not a type of risk assessment.

15. With a SOC 2 auditing report, which of the following principles must always be included?

A. Security

B. Processing integrity

C. Privacy

D. Availability

A. The SOC 2 auditing reports are built on a set of five principles: security, processing integrity, privacy, availability, and confidentiality. A SOC 2 audit can include any number of these principles, but under the official guidelines, the security principle must always be included. Within the security principle are seven categories: change management, communications, logical and physical access controls, monitoring of controls, organization and management, risk management and design and implementation of controls, and system operations.

B is incorrect because while processing integrity is one of the five principles of the SOC 2 audits, it is not required to be included with any of the other principles. The processing integrity principle is focused on ensuring that data is in its correct format, accurate, and verified, and that it has not been altered or modified by unauthorized parties or means.

C is incorrect because while privacy is one of the five principles of the SOC 2 audits, it is not required to be included with any others during audits. The privacy principle is focused on personal and private information, and ensuring that it is handled per the organization's policies, as well as per any applicable regulations or laws, during all times—whether it is either created, stored, processed, or disposed of by a system or application.

D is incorrect because like processing integrity and privacy, availability is one of the five principles of the SOC 2 auditing reports, but it is not a required principle to be included while auditing any others. The availability principle evaluates whether data or functions are available to authorized parties when needed, and in such a manner that meets requirements and policies. These requirements and policies can come from either business needs and expectations or in some instances legal or regulatory mandates.

16. Which of the following would be used to isolate test systems from production systems within a cloud environment for testing or development purposes?

A. Sandboxing

B. Application virtualization

C. Firewalling

D. Puppet

A. Sandboxing involves isolating systems and applications from others within the same environment. This is typically done to keep data segregated and inaccessible from other systems, such as keeping production and nonproduction data segregated from each other. This can also be done within environments to keep production data isolated, such as keeping employee data and customer data completely segregated from each other, or in an academic setting, keeping student data and faculty/staff data isolated from each other. The need for isolation can sometimes come from organizational security policies, but in many instances it will be required by regulation.

B is incorrect because while application virtualization will keep applications isolated away from operating systems and other applications, it is restricted to the application layer and cannot be used for overall systems. Also, application virtualization will typically be within the same host systems, so any potential compromise of the host system could expose data between the two virtualization containers.

C is incorrect because firewalling is used to limit or restrict specific network traffic from making successful inbound or outbound connections, usually with specific ports as well. Although a firewall is a security tool for protecting and isolating traffic, it is not used for segregating and isolating systems or applications as an overall concept like sandboxing is.

D is incorrect because Puppet is a tool for maintaining configurations and deployments across systems and applications, as well as for enforcing rules and requirements for the configurations. It is not a concept for segregating and isolating systems or applications with an environment.

17. Which of the following is *NOT* as aspect of static application security testing (SAST)?

    A. Access to source code

    B. Offline system

    C. Knowledge of system configurations

    D. Live system

D. SAST is always done against systems that are not live and operational to users or customers. SAST is done by testers with extensive knowledge of systems and how they were coded, and as such, will typically produce superior results as compared to other types of testing that must discover and scan to try and determine how systems are put together.

A is incorrect because the testers performing SAST will have access to the source code, and in many instances full knowledge of the SDLC process that the application went through. It is intended to expose programming errors and typical security deficiencies related to coding, such as XSS and injection.

B is incorrect because SAST testing is always done against nonproduction systems; these systems will not have production data or users interacting with them. This enables testers to do more invasive and deeper testing than what can be done against live systems because the risk of data corruption or negatively impacting users will not exist with SAST.

C is incorrect because one of the key aspects of SAST is the knowledge on the part of the testers of the systems' configurations and the technologies used. With other types of testing, where this inside knowledge is not present, the testers are limited to the information they are able to expose or glean from scanning and other discovery tools. Relying on scanning and discovery will always pose significant challenges because many other layers of security and complementary systems will likely limit or prohibit a high degree of success from these tools.

18. Which of the following are the four cloud deployment models?

   A. Public, private, hybrid, and community

   B. Public, private, internal, and hybrid

   C. Internal, external, hybrid, and community

   D. Public, private, hybrid, and organizational

A. The four cloud deployment models are public, private, hybrid, and community. Public cloud deployments are operated and maintained by companies that offer services to the public as a whole, without needing to be part of a special group or population. Many of these offerings are free or mostly free, and many are very commonly known to the public and in widespread use. Someone wanting to leverage a public cloud just needs network access and typically a credit card to purchase services or add-ons. Private clouds are run either by cloud service providers or by the organizations using them. They are not available to the general public, and will necessitate a contractual or partnership relationship with the cloud customer. Hybrid clouds are a mixture of two or more of the other cloud models, typically public and private cloud offerings used together. The community cloud model is where cloud services are maintained and offered by an organization or company, which may or may not be a member of the specific community, but services are restricted to a certain population or type of cloud customer, such as universities or members of professional organizations.

B is incorrect because while public, private, and hybrid are correct cloud deployment models, there is no "internal" model for cloud deployments. Instead, the correct cloud deployment model is community.

C is incorrect because while hybrid and community are correct cloud deployment models, there are not "internal" and "external" cloud models. The other two correct cloud deployment models are public and private.

D is incorrect because while public, private, and hybrid are correct cloud deployment models, there is not an "organizational" cloud deployment model. Instead, the correct cloud deployment model is community.

19. Which of the following is a commonly used tool for maintaining software versioning and code collaboration?

   A. GitHub

   B. Chef

   C. Puppet

   D. Nessus

> **A.** GitHub is an online code repository that works from both command-line and web-based interfaces. It provides robust access control and many different toolsets for code collaboration, including bug tracking, management tools, and wikis. For code collaboration and management, it offers extensive versioning and branching capabilities and is in widespread use throughout the IT industry.
>
> **B** is incorrect because Chef is a software tool for handling infrastructure configurations. It will often be used in conjunction with GitHub to form a comprehensive management solution for systems and applications, but by itself it does not handle code versioning and collaboration.
>
> **C** is incorrect because Puppet is also a software application for handling infrastructure configurations. It works much in the same way as Chef, and is used to manage configurations and standards in regards to systems configuration, not to handle code versioning and collaboration.
>
> **D** is incorrect because Nessus is a tool for conducting vulnerability scans, and it does not have anything to do with code collaboration and versioning. Nessus works by taking a large ensemble of known vulnerabilities and scanning against systems to determine if they are vulnerable to them. With the results, application developers and security teams can proactively discover and mitigate security vulnerabilities before a malicious actor is able to exploit them.

20. Which of the following is *NOT* a core component of an SIEM solution?

   A. Correlation

   B. Aggregation

   C. Compliance

   D. Escalation

> **D.** Escalation is the process of moving issues or alerts along a predefined path to others responsible for remediation and action if those prior to them in the chain do not respond. This is done to bring the issues to the attention of management. While SIEM solutions can trigger alerts based on predefined conditions, the full workflow of escalation is handled by an external tool or application, and the role of the SIEM solution would be the initial identification and alert.

A is incorrect because correlation is a key component and use of SIEM solutions. An SIEM solution has as a primary function: collecting logs from many systems throughout an infrastructure. With having data from many different systems, an SIEM solution can easily detect the same pattern or other details across those systems, whereas relying on log files from particular servers would require each server to be analyzed independently. The SIEM solution also allows for the identification of the same types of issues, traffic, or events across a heterogeneous environment. For example, if an IP address is suspected of attempting to attack a system or application, an SIEM solution can correlate the traffic and events across networking devices, servers, firewalls, IPSs, and so on, which otherwise would require different teams and substantial resources to search, and would typically take much longer than the rapid nature of a security incident.

B is incorrect because a core component of an SIEM solution is the aggregation of events and data from many disparate systems into a single searching and reporting platform. Without an SIEM solution, log data would be held through a data center environment on many different devices, and likely in many different formats. An SIEM solution will collect and aggregate all of that data into a single system that can be searched in a uniform and consolidated manner. This allows an organization to see the same particular traffic or details across their enterprise, without having to search many different systems, as well as being able to search logs (which are likely in many different formats) from a single interface using the same commands. Aggregation in this way allows an organization to analyze data in a much more rapid and efficient manner than would be possible without aggregation.

C is incorrect because an SIEM solution is a crucial tool in many organizations for compliance activities. Almost all regulatory systems require activities such as periodic review of log data for specific types of activities. This could include invalid login attempts, account creations, access control changes, and many other types of data points. With an SIEM solution, this reporting is easy to do using the robust search and reporting features, as well as leveraging correlation and aggregation to allow a single reporting tool to generate reports across the enterprise and many diverse and disparate systems.

21. Which of the following threat types is the *MOST* difficult for an organization to defend against and detect?

    A. Data loss

    B. Malicious insiders

    C. Insecure APIs

    D. Account hijacking

B. A malicious insider is any user of a system, though typically someone with elevated access, who uses their otherwise authorized access for unauthorized means. Because a malicious insider uses authorized access, it is very difficult for an organization or monitoring tool to detect such a vulnerability. Typically, such an attack will only become obvious after it has already been completed and the damage is done. Although possessing authorized access, a malicious insider in most instances will also have extensive knowledge of the system or application, as well as the data contained within it, and will know what has the most value and the best ways to compromise it.

A is incorrect because data loss can typically be prevented by having in place redundant systems, as well as appropriate business continuity and disaster recovery plans. While redundancy can help prevent data loss from happening at all, having robust and comprehensive backups, as well as the means to restore them quickly, will largely mitigate or minimize the effects of any data loss.

C is incorrect because proper validation, certification, and testing of APIs will largely mitigate vulnerabilities and prevent successful exploits from ever occurring. Because the APIs of a system are known and selected prior to use, secure requirements and standards can be used in their selection and implementation, ensuring everything is done in a secure manner. The use of appropriate monitoring tools will also go a long way toward preventing insecure APIs from being successfully exploited and mitigating the damage should such exploitation occur.

D is incorrect because many methods and tools are available to minimize or prevent account hijacking. Through the use of technologies such as multifactor authentication, the possibility of credentials being stolen and successfully used to access data is very minimal. Even if passwords and user IDs are successfully stolen and obtained by a malicious actor, they will not be in possession of the second factor needed to access the systems or data. Other approaches such as active alerting for users attempting to access systems from unknown or unique locations can also make such an attack much more difficult. For example, systems can monitor for the location or origination of login attempts, and any attempt made from outside a typical geographic region (especially from a foreign location) can cause logins for that user to be disabled until they can be validated, even in instances where multifactor authentication is not used.

22. Which of the following storage types are used with Infrastructure as a Service (IaaS)?

    A. Structured and unstructured

    B. File and database

    C. Object and volume

    D. Block and striped

C. IaaS uses object and volume storage types. With volume storage, a logical storage unit will be allocated to the virtual machine, and it will appear to the system, applications, or users as part of the file system. It can then be used as normal storage would in a physical server model, complete with file system organization, permissions, data structures, and any other aspects of a file system. With object storage, data is kept in a flat structure and accessed through the use of opaque tokens, rather than a filename or through a directory structure. This type of storage is often used for media objects such as images, videos, and audio files, as well as where cloud providers store system images and virtual machine files.

A is incorrect because structured and unstructured storage types belong to PaaS, not IaaS. Structured storage is done typically through systems such as databases, which have a set, defined data-organization scheme and are maintained by the cloud provider, with data inserted or created by the cloud customer. Unstructured data does not follow platform-defined structures and is open to the data structures defined by the cloud customer. This will typically be used for web-based systems within a PaaS environment, where the web objects, media files, and components are stored and accessed via the application framework.

B is incorrect because while file and database are two common storage methods or concepts, they are higher-level concepts that many other data structures fit within, and are not part of the formal data structures that IaaS uses.

D is incorrect because while block and striped are concepts in computing that relate to data storage and structure, they are not data types themselves, nor are they used and defined within IaaS or other cloud models.

23. Which of the following data-sanitation approaches are always available within a cloud environment?

   A. Physical destruction

   B. Shredding

   C. Overwriting

   D. Cryptographic erasure

   D. Cryptographic erasure is a means to ensure data is no longer accessible, and it can always be used within a cloud environment because it is purely a software approach and not dependent on the infrastructure. Rather than a traditional means of overwriting or destroying physical media, cryptographic erasure is performed by encrypting data and then destroying the keys that were used to encrypt it, thus rendering it inaccessible and unreadable. This method, especially where data is already encrypted, is extremely fast and efficient. Whereas deleting large volumes or numbers of files on a system can often take substantial time to complete, in addition to the significant time required for overwriting or ensuring it is deleted, keys can be deleted instantaneously and from where they are housed, sometimes without even accessing the systems holding the actual data. If the data was encrypted with strong encryption, the chances of it ever being accessed again are extremely low; for the most part, it's virtually impossible.

A is incorrect because physical destruction of media is virtually impossible within a cloud environment. With multitenancy and resource pooling, you can be assured that every physical device houses more than one cloud customer. Due to this, the idea of having the cloud provider destroy the physical media housing the data is an impossibility. Also, with how much data is always moving and being balanced within a cloud environment, it is almost impossible to fully determine all the physical locations of data at any one point so that such destruction could even be requested.

B is incorrect because shredding is a form of physical destruction of media and, as explained for answer A, would not be possible within a cloud environment.

C is incorrect because the realities of a cloud environment, with the use of virtualization and constant balancing and migrating of data, make it impossible to perform overwriting in a manner where it could be ensured that all data is overwritten. It also would be virtually impossible to isolate a particular customer's data, even if one could determine all the locations of that data, and perform overwriting in a manner that would not impact other tenants within the same environment.

24. Which of the following technologies will often make elasticity a bigger challenge in a cloud environment?

   A. IPS

   B. XML accelerator

   C. Vulnerability scanner

   D. Web application firewall

A. The use of IPS systems can be complicated with elasticity and auto-scaling; as systems are expanded programmatically, it is difficult to ensure that traffic is accurately routed through IPS systems and that the correct signatures, policies, and rules are applied. Within a traditional data center, network pathways are known and routing, as well as physical network connections, will ensure that the correct paths are always taken. In cloud environments, where the infrastructure is in a constant state of flux, this is far more difficult to achieve. The primary means to implement IPS to get around the shortcomings of virtual network-based IPS is through the use of host-based IPS systems in a cloud environment.

B is incorrect because XML accelerators will be placed around load balancers and will automatically be added as systems are expanded programmatically. This differs from IPS because it relates to where in the network flow XML accelerators are placed and how the network is routed. XML accelerators also are used in conjunction with established web services, which, regardless of the number of virtual machines accessing them, will remain the same.

C is incorrect because elasticity will have no impact on vulnerability scanners, other than changing the number of systems that must be scanned. However, through auto-scaling and elasticity, the server type and purpose will be known, and it is easy to ensure that these systems are added to the lists for vulnerability scanning.

D is incorrect because web application firewalls (WAFs) are used based on the purpose of the server, which will be known through auto-scaling. Also, they are often placed in front of servers at the load balancer level, so the number of servers behind the load balancer will not have any direct impact on the use of WAFs.

25. Which of the following concepts involves the ability of cloud customers to easily move services from one cloud provider to another?

   A. Interoperability

   B. Portability

   C. Multitenancy

   D. Measured service

B. Portability is the feature that allows a system to easily move between different cloud providers. This is accomplished by relying on standardized tool sets and platforms and avoiding the use of propriety APIs or other toolsets that will end up binding an organization to a particular cloud provider, making the cost of moving to another substantial, in both time and money.

A is incorrect because interoperability is the ability of a system or application to reuse components. This allows organizations to avoid particular ties to vendors or other systems for the components or functions of their own systems and applications. This can also be related to the use of standardized data structures and formats to avoid vendor lock-in.

C is incorrect because multitenancy relates to a cloud environment hosting applications and systems from different customers within the same physical systems. While this concept would make it easy for any cloud customer to establish systems in a new cloud provider, it is does not address at all the ability of a customer to move from one cloud environment to another.

D is incorrect because measured service relates to a cloud customer only paying for the resources that they consume, and only for the duration of the time in which they are consuming them. Although this makes it easier and cheaper to get set up in any environment and scale outward as needed, it does not address the ability of systems or applications to move from one environment to the other beyond just the initial setup costs required to do so (not from a technical perspective).

26. What does the *S* stand for in the STRIDE threat model?

    A. Secure

    B. Structured

    C. Standard

    D. Spoofing

D. The *S* in the STRIDE threat model stands for spoofing, or more specifically, spoofing identity. This involves applications that have unique access controls for individual users and administrators, but then within the application they use service accounts or common credentials to communicate with databases, APIs, or other services. In this instance, it is possible for a user to assume the identity of another within the application once authenticated, and then make it appear as if that user is accessing resources through the application. To mitigate this threat, systems should continually check the access of a user as they move between interfaces or functions to ensure they have the proper level of access, as well as check that the identity the system assumes they have actually matches the identity that they used to initially authenticate and access the system or application.

A is incorrect because the *S* stands for "spoofing identity" and not for "security." While security is obviously a large part of the STRIDE threat model at a high level, and is the overarching concept, it is not the actual term used here.

B is incorrect because the *S* stands for "spoofing identity" and not for "structured." The term *structured* typically applies to data types, especially for PaaS implementations, where structured and unstructured are the two official data types.

C is incorrect because the *S* stands for "spoofing identity" and not for "standard." While *standard* is a term used a lot within security and IT in general, especially as it relates to certifications and best practices, it is not applicable in this instance as part of the STRIDE threat model.

27. Which of the following is *NOT* a major concern with encryption systems?

    A. Integrity

    B. Confidentiality

    C. Efficiency

    D. Key management

A. Encryption is intended to protect the confidentiality and privacy of data first and foremost. While encryption can certainly prevent the unauthorized altering of data at rest, that is not its intended purpose.

B is incorrect because confidentiality is the main concern and focus of encryption. It is intended to prevent the unauthorized exposure or leakage of data to parties that are not authorized to have it. In order to read data that is encrypted, a party would need to have access to the keys used to encrypt it.

Encryption is focused solely on the ability to read data, so it is not used to prevent the encrypted volumes from being intercepted specifically—just the reading and access of the data contained with them.

C is incorrect because in order for an encryption system to be usable in a real environment and within applications, it must be easy and efficient to use. That is one of the main benefits and features of encryption. Although an encryption system is virtually unbreakable with current technology and capabilities, if you are in possession of the correct keys, it takes very little overhead to decrypt and read the data. In order to integrate into applications, especially those open to the public and that have larger user bases, this speed and efficiency is absolutely crucial.

D is incorrect because key management is one of the central challenges and components of any encryption system. The keys are central to encrypting and then decrypting data, and the corruption, loss, or exposure of the keys will either render the security useless or make the data unrecoverable. Each organization will have to carefully analyze their systems and applications where encryption is used, and based on the particulars of each system and application, where it is hosted, how it is accessed, and many other factors, make the most appropriate decision on how keys will be secured and managed.

28. Which of the following types of data is the United States' HIPAA regulations concerned with?

   A. Financial

   B. Historical

   C. Healthcare

   D. Hybrid cloud

C. The Health Insurance Portability and Accountability Act of 1996 (HIPAA) in the United States is concerned with the protection of patient privacy and the security involved with the protection of medical records. While a major part of the law protects workers and their families from losing health insurance when they change or lose their jobs, the other major parts of the law that are important in this context are the protection of patient data, the requirements to establish electronic healthcare transactions, and the attempt to standardize identifiers with healthcare institutions.

A is incorrect because HIPAA is concerned with healthcare data, not financial data. Other major regulatory and standards systems are concerned with financial data, such as SOX and PCI DSS.

B is incorrect because HIPAA has nothing to do with historical data beyond how it relates to healthcare data. As with most regulatory systems, there are requirements for data retention that establish minimum periods of time to maintain data, but the overall focus of the regulations is not "historical" in any sense.

D is incorrect because HIPAA was established long before cloud computing came into existence, and it is not focused on specific technologies but rather on the overall handling of records and security requirements. While HIPAA will certainly apply to any healthcare systems hosted in a hybrid cloud environment, that is not the purpose or focus of the law.

29. Which of the following in a federated environment is responsible for consuming authentication tokens?

    A. Relying party

    B. Identity provider

    C. Cloud services broker

    D. Authentication provider

A. The relying party in a federated environment is the actual service provider that gives access to secure systems or data. The relying party consumes authentication tokens that are generated by an acceptable identity provider and then grants authorization to access the systems or data based on the successful authentication, and possibly based on specific attributes about the user or entity that are provided by the identity provider, by enabling the relying party to make decisions about roles.

B is incorrect because the identity provider is the generator of authentication tokens in a federated system, not the component that will consume and process them. The role of the identity provider is to perform authentication on users who are known to it, and in many instances provide additional attributes and information about those users to the relying party so that it can make authorization decisions that are appropriate for the user and the data access they are attempting to use.

C is incorrect because a cloud services broker does not play any role in a federated system or environment. The role of a cloud services broker is to take the cloud services offered by public or private cloud providers and then extend or add value to them through integration, aggregation, or by providing customized interfaces or data fields.

D is incorrect because *authentication provider* could be another term for identity provider. Thus, the authentication provider would not be a consumer of authentication tokens, but rather a generator or provider of them.

30. Which phase of the cloud data lifecycle involves processing by a user or application?

   A. Create

   B. Share

   C. Store

   D. Use

D. The "use" phase of the cloud data lifecycle is where the data is actually processed or consumed by an application or user. During the "use" phase, data will transition between the data-at-rest and data-in-use states and will require additional security as it is exposed and accessed by systems. Therefore, it must be presented in an unencrypted state. This also extends the data security concerns from the server or storage aspect to the client aspect and the security of the specific device or client being used to access the data. Compared to some other phases, the "use" phase is considered read-only because any modification or creation would fall under a different phase.

A is incorrect because the "create" phase is when data is first entered into a system, or modified from a previous form, and thus new data has been created. At the "create" phase, the important initial decisions as to data classification are made so that security controls can be immediately placed on the data from the point of conception. These decisions will impact all later phases for the data and will govern much of its use and processing for its lifetime.

B is incorrect because the "share" phase is where data is made available for systems or applications outside of the original intended ones for the data. Because the data will be leaving the original system and its security enclave, security becomes an important aspect as it is incumbent on the receiving party to secure it from that point onward. This is typically accomplished from auditing reports and operating agreements that establish security standards and requirements for all parties that will consume and accept the data.

C is incorrect because the "store" phase is where the data is official recorded and entered upon its creation. This is usually a simultaneous process, or one that happens immediately after the creation of the data. Data can be entered in many different types of storage, including databases and file systems. Storage must be done with respect to the classification of the data, ensuring that appropriate security controls are in place immediately upon the data being entered. This is also the phase where concepts such as redundancy and backup methods are used on the data.

31. Which of the following is *NOT* a state of data that is important for security and encryption?

   A. Data in use

   B. Data in transit

C. Data at rest

D. Data in archive

D. Data in archive is not one of the official states of data as it applies to security and encryption. Although the other three states of data in use, data at rest, and data in transit will have implications and applicability to archiving, the concept of archiving is found within them and is not considered a state in and of itself.

A is incorrect because data in use is an official state of data. During this state, data is actually consumed and processed by a system or application. As such, additional security controls need to be applied compared to when the data is in static storage. This also exposes the security from the client side because it will be what is viewing the data and in some instances processing the data as well.

B is incorrect because data in transit is also an official state of data. During this phase, data will traverse networks and systems, typically between storage and processing entities. During this phase, particular security concerns arise because the data will usually cross systems and networks that are not under the control or security perimeter of the originating organization. This will often be mitigated by the use of encryption, where the entities on both sides are knowledgeable of the keys. This prevents any systems in the middle, or anyone who manages to capture the data, from being able to read or modify it.

C is incorrect because data at rest is an official state of data. With this state, the data is contained within storage systems and is not actively being processed or consumed. This is typically the easiest state in which to secure data because technologies such as encryption and isolation can be used to prevent the access or exposure of data.

32. Which of the following is a standard and certification for cryptographic modules?

    A. FIPS 199

    B. FIPS 140

    C. FIPS 201

    D. FIPS 153

B. FIPS 140, specifically the current revision of FIPS 140-2, is a processing standard published by the United States government pertaining to the certification of cryptographic modules that are used within systems. Following this standard, which is contained in four levels, will ensure varying degrees of confidence in the security of cryptographic modules used to encrypt and decrypt data on systems.

A is incorrect because FIPS 199 is a U.S. government standard that defines security categories of systems that are used by the government and are not specifically related to cryptographic modules. The FIPS 199 standard establishes low, moderate, and high categories for information systems, and requires all agencies of the government to evaluate and rate their systems into one of the categories for confidentiality, integrity, and availability security concerns. The highest rating from any of these three areas becomes the overall rating of the system. For example, if a system is rated moderate for confidentiality and availability, but a high for integrity, then the system as a whole will be considered a high system.

C is incorrect because FIPS 201 is a U.S. government standard that establishes guidelines for personal identity verification (PIV) for any employees or contractors of the federal government. The requirements apply to all federal government information systems and applications, with the exception of national security systems, which are covered under their own separate regulations and policies. The PIV standard advocates for the use of smartcard technology as a requirement for any identification systems, extending beyond the typical password requirements into the multifactor realm.

D is incorrect because FIPS 153 is a standard relating to 3D graphics and has no impact on or role in cryptographic modules.

33. The use of which of the following technologies will *NOT* require the security dependency of an operating system, other than its own?

    A. Management plane

    B. Type 1 hypervisor

    C. Type 2 hypervisor

    D. Virtual machine

B. Type 1 hypervisors run directly attached to the underlying hardware of the host and do not have any software between them or dependencies on external operating systems. With configuration, the Type 1 hypervisor is highly optimized for its intended functions, and all code is removed by the vendor, with the exception of the code explicitly required for it. This removes the complexity and flexibility of operating systems, which even with all unnecessary services and functions disabled or removed will still contain large amounts of code or components that are unneeded to operate the hypervisor. The direct tie between the hypervisor and hardware allows the vendors to lock down and patch specific to threats and exploits in their software only, without the need to rely on other libraries or components from operating systems, including being at the mercy of the operating system vendors to appropriately patch their own systems within a reasonable timeframe.

A is incorrect because the management plane is a web portal or utility for managing hypervisors that runs within its own systems and software. This creates dependencies on operating systems and application frameworks that will run the portal or utilities, potentially introducing many security vulnerabilities and requiring the reliance on those vendors for timely and comprehensive patching. Because the management plane is used to manage and control hypervisors throughout the environment, any security exploit of it will potentially expose an entire infrastructure or data center to threats and exposure.

C is incorrect because Type 2 hypervisors are software-based applications that reside on a host system and then launch virtual machines within them. With this type of configuration, the hypervisor is dependent on the operating system of the host, rather than running directly on top of the hardware with a Type 1 hypervisor. Due to this dependency, the hypervisor is potentially vulnerable to any security exploits that occur with the underlying operating system. Operating systems are also designed to support a wide range of applications and uses. Therefore, they will have large amounts of code and components that are not necessary for the use of the hypervisor, potentially exposing far more possible vulnerabilities to protect and monitor than if the hypervisor was dedicated and running on the hardware directly.

D is incorrect because as part of their nature, virtual machines run under host systems, and therefore are dependent on them and are largely at their mercy from a security perspective. Any compromise of the host system can potentially render any virtual machines hosted by it vulnerable as well.

34. Which of the following threats involves sending untrusted data to a user's browser in an attempt to have it executed using the user's permissions and access?

A. Cross-site scripting

B. Injection

C. Unvalidated redirects

D. Man in the middle

A. Cross-site scripting involves injecting scripts into web pages that are then executed on the client side by the browser. This allows an attack to run scripts using the permissions of the browser and any authenticated sessions to execute. This can expose web applications to potential attacks by allowing the bypassing of some security controls such as same-origin policies, as well as utilizing the credentials of a valid user to execute.

B is incorrect because injection attempts involve sending segments of code through input fields in order to have the code executed by the system or application. This is done to attempt to access information and bypass security controls when the input fields are not properly validated or sanitized when submitted by the user. For example, a field may call for the user's e-mail address, but an attacker may send SQL code in the input field. If the application does not properly validate the input fields, the application may either directly run the code or insert it into the database and then execute it later when a SQL command is run against that field. This can be used by an attacker to expose other database areas beyond those intended, or even dump entire database fields or file system information back to the malicious actor.

C is incorrect because unvalidated redirects occur when an application does not properly validate input and sets up a situation where users can be redirected through this untrusted input to external sites. Through this kind of attack, it is possible for the attacker to steal user credentials and attempt phishing attacks against users as well. Because the user went through a trusted application and was redirected by it, they may not be aware they are no longer sending input to the trusted application and are thus exposing their private data or privileged access.

D is incorrect because a man-in-the-middle attack involves the interception of communications between two parties. The attacker attempts to read, alter, or redirect the data flows in a manner that the parties are unaware it is happening and continue to use the transmissions as normal.

35. Which of the following involves assigning an opaque value to sensitive data fields to protect confidentiality?

   A. Obfuscation

   B. Masking

   C. Tokenization

   D. Anonymization

C. Tokenization is the process of replacing sensitive data with an opaque or random value, with the ability to map back the value to the original real value. This allows an application to operate in the same manner in which it was coded and to use the same values as keys, but without using the actual real value, which may contain PII or other sensitive data. This can allow an application to conform to confidentiality or privacy requirements without the need for other, more expensive and intensive implementations such as encryption. With the ability to map back tokenized values to the original sensitive values, the system that contains the original mappings or is responsible for generating them must be protected and secured to prevent exposure.

A is incorrect because obfuscation involves replacing sensitive or protected data fields with random information, typically for generating data sets for testing in nonproduction systems or other purposes similar in nature. The difference between tokenization and obfuscation is that, with obfuscation, the original mappings to the protected data are not maintained, nor are they important. Although this will be more secure than tokenization because the original mappings are not preserved anywhere, it also means that the data cannot be used in any meaningful way beyond functional testing or development purposes.

B is incorrect because masking is another term for obfuscation.

D is incorrect because anonymization involves replacing data so that it cannot be successfully mapped back to an individual. It is built on the concept of direct and indirect identifiers. Indirect identifiers are those attributes that by themselves cannot map to a single individual, but a combination of many indirect identifiers could lead to the identification of a specific individual. Anonymization is often used in conjunction with the obfuscation or tokenization of sensitive fields as a way of removing the indirect identifiers to ensure the data sets cannot be mapped back successfully through any means.

36. Which of the following is *NOT* one of the security domains presented within the Cloud Controls Matrix?

   A. Financial security

   B. Mobile security

   C. Data center security

   D. Interface security

A. Financial security is not one of the specific security domains presented as part of the Cloud Controls Matrix (CCM). While many other domains will play into the protection of financial information, there is not a domain that is specifically related to it. This also includes the inclusion of costs as a factor in security, because only security controls and policies are a part of the CCM.

B is incorrect because mobile security is one of the specific domains outlined in the Cloud Controls Matrix.

C is incorrect because data center security is one of the specific domains outlined in the Cloud Controls Matrix.

D is incorrect because interface security is one of the specific domains outlined in the Cloud Controls Matrix, specifically labeled as application and interface security.

37. Which ISO/IEC standards set documents the cloud definitions for staffing and official roles?

    A. ISO/IEC 27001

    B. ISO/IEC 17788

    C. ISO/IEC 17789

    D. ISO/IEC 27040

B. ISO/IEC 17788, specifically the latest revision ISO/IEC 17788:2014, provides an overview and vocabulary for cloud computing. It defines much of the commonly used cloud terminology, such as service categories and cloud deployment models.

A is incorrect because ISO/IEC 27001 is a general security standard that can apply to any type of system in any type of hosting environment.

C is incorrect because ISO/IEC 17789 is focused on cloud computing and the reference architecture, including the common features that define cloud computing such as measured service, broad network access, multitenancy, on-demand self-service, rapid elasticity and scalability, and resource pooling.

D is incorrect because ISO/IEC 27040 is focused on security techniques as they relate to storage security.

38. Which of the following pieces of information is *NOT* included as part of PII as a direct identifier?

    A. Address

    B. ZIP Code

    C. Biometric records

    D. Phone number

B. As they relate to PII, ZIP Codes would not be considered a protected piece of information. A ZIP Code, being a broad geographic area, would not meet the definition required for PII because it solely cannot be used to identify an individual. However, combined with other various pieces of information, a ZIP Code could be used to narrow down information and possibly identify or distinguish an individual from others with similar attributes.

A is incorrect because an address relates to a specific resident or location and, as such, can directly identify an individual.

C is incorrect because biometrics can immediately and directly identify an individual, and most biometric markers will be unique to a single individual.

D is correct because a personal phone number, and in many instances even a business phone number, can be directly tied to a specific individual and, as such, is definitely considered PII.

39. Which concept pertains to the risk an organization entails in regard to the ability to move between cloud providers at a later date?

    A. Interoperability

    B. Reversibility

    C. Portability

    D. Broad network access

C. Portability is the concept that allows a cloud customer to easily move between cloud providers at a later date. Portability takes into account the characteristics and features of a system or application that can lead to vendor lock-in and therefore are aspects that should be avoided. For example, if a cloud customer builds their systems or applications around specific APIs or features that are proprietary to a specific cloud provider, it will be almost impossible for the cloud customer to later move to a different cloud provider without incurring substantial costs in both time and money to change their applications, which would also expose them to significant risk for such an undertaking.

A is incorrect because interoperability refers to the ability of a system or application to reuse components from previous versions or other applications in new ways. With this ability, developers can save time and money building applications and components through the use of code that not only is already written, but also tested and verified by both users and security scanning.

B is incorrect because reversibility refers to the ability of a cloud customer to remove all systems, applications, and data from a cloud environment, as well as to ensure that all traces of them have been securely deleted. This is governed by contract terms for the level of assistance that the cloud provider must provide as well as the timeliness of having all tasks completed and verified.

D is incorrect because broad network access is one of the core components of cloud computing, but it does not relate at all to moving between cloud providers. Broad network access refers to the ability to access cloud resources and systems from anywhere and over the public internet, rather than through restricted network tunnels or specific physical networks.

40. Which of the following is *NOT* one of the core building blocks of cloud computing?

    A. CPU

    B. Memory

    C. Storage

    D. Hardware

D. Hardware is not considered one of the core building blocks of cloud computing. With cloud computing specifically, hardware should not be a concern at all for cloud customers, because they will never interact with it or even have a need to really know what it is. All cloud services are segregated from the hardware layer, and cloud customers are only buying computing resources that are consumable in nature and specific to their computing needs.

A is incorrect because CPU is a core building block of cloud computing. When new virtual machines or virtual appliances are provisioned in a cloud environment, one of the main selections made is in regard to their CPU resources. The measured service costs associated with each virtual machine and the aggregate total of CPU resources will tie directly into the costs of hosting with the cloud environment. With the cloud built entirely on virtual and logical infrastructure from the perspective of the cloud customer, CPU allocations per virtual machine can easily be changed with stopping and starting of a virtual machine after configuration changes have been made through the service portal. CPU is part of the resource pooling and is shared between the tenants of the cloud environment.

B is incorrect because memory is a core building block of cloud computing. Much like CPU resources, memory is configured per virtual machine, and the individual or aggregate totals will tie into the cost structure for the cloud customer. Memory can also be changed after the provisioning configurations have been updated by a simple stopping and starting of the virtual machine instance. Memory is part of the resource pooling and is shared among the tenants of the cloud environment.

D is incorrect because storage is also part of the pooled resources of a cloud infrastructure, and it shares similar qualities to memory and CPU as far as ease of changes and modifications after initial builds. Depending on the cloud service category, storage will come in different formats, and billing may differ as a unit cost based on the type of storage selected.

41. You have been tasked with creating an audit scope statement and are making your project outline. Which of the following is *NOT* typically included in an audit scope statement?

   A. Statement of purpose

   B. Deliverables

   C. Classification

   D. Costs

D. The audit scope statement focuses on the reasons and goals for conducting the audit, and the costs associated with the audit are handled under different processes. By the time an audit scope statement is being worked out between the organization and the auditor, costs will have already been determined and the scope will focus on the technical and procedural details of the audit.

A is incorrect because the statement of purpose is the first step in the audit scope statement. The statement of purpose covers the reason for the audit. Typically, audits can be conducted either for internal purposes of the organization and at the organization's own request, or they can be conducted to fulfill requirements from regulations. In the case of regulations, the statement of purpose, as well as many aspects of the audit scope as a whole, may be dictated by the regulatory requirements pertinent to the type of application or date under review.

B is incorrect because deliverables are a key component to an audit scope statement. While all audits will ultimately result in the production of certain reports, these reports can differ greatly based on the audience or purpose of the audit. The scope will cover the format of the deliverables, which can be textual reports, presentations, or even formatted specifically for import into software applications for tracking. This also includes who should receive the reports in the end. In most instances, even if they are done for regulatory reasons, unless the auditors are tied directly to the regulators, the reports will first go to management for review and will then be made known to the regulators.

C is incorrect because the classification of the data, as well as the reports produced, is a key consideration of an audit scope. Under most regulatory systems, the classification of the data will directly tie into the type and scope of audit, as well as to what degree specific security controls are tested and what is required of them. When the report is ultimately produced, it could fall under classification requirements as well, depending on the system and data. Audit reports should be well protected at all times because they essentially contain information about verified and perceived weaknesses of the security controls employed on a system, as well as information pertaining to specific threats and the likeliness of their successful exploit.

42. With a multifactor authentication system, which of the following would *NOT* be appropriate as a secondary factor after a password is used?

    A. Fingerprint

    B. RSA token

    C. Text message

    D. PIN code

D. A PIN could not be used as part of a multifactor authentication system if a password is also used because a PIN is essentially a type of numeric password, so both would be in the same category of authentication types—in this case, something "known" to the user.

A is incorrect because a fingerprint could be used along with a password for multifactor authentication. The password would be something "known" to the user, while the fingerprint would be something in the user's possession, as well as being a biometric factor.

B is incorrect because an RSA token could be used as secondary factor with multifactor authentication if a password is used as well. The RSA token represents a PIN code, and the user would need to be in possession of the token in order to know the regularly changing PIN code that the token has at the time the PIN code needs to be entered. This would satisfy the multifactor requirements because the password would constitute something "known" to the user and the RSA token would be something in possession of the user.

C is incorrect because the use of a text message as a secondary factor along with a password would satisfy the requirement for multifactor authentication. To receive the text message with a secondary code, the user would need to be in possession of a preregistered device, which would be something in their possession. Because the device would have to be preregistered with the system to receive the text code, this also is a robust security system because it would negate someone from getting a new device and then trying to use it to access the system.

43. Which of the following ISO/IEC standards pertains to eDiscovery processes and best practices?

   A. ISO/IEC 27050

   B. ISO/IEC 17789

   C. ISO/IEC 27001

   D. ISO/IEC 17788

A. ISO/IEC 27050 is a standard focused on eDiscovery processes and how best to approach an order. The goal of the standard is to establish common terminology, give an overview of the eDiscovery process, and then provide guidance and best practices for conducting the data collection, including discovery, preservation, and analysis.

B is incorrect because ISO/IEC 17789 provides a reference architecture for cloud computing and is focused on general cloud computing design and implementation. While some information contained would be useful in some instances of eDiscovery, the standard itself does not address eDiscovery at all or provide any guidance toward it.

C is incorrect because ISO/IEC 27001 is focused on general security principles and best practices, and does not have any specific guidance or focus on eDiscovery processes or anything that is involved with them.

D is incorrect because ISO/IEC 17788 provides terminology and definitions for cloud computing in general, but does not have any focus or sections pertaining to eDiscovery at all.

44. Which of the following is *NOT* one of the cloud computing activities, as outlined in ISO/IEC 17789?

   A. Cloud service provider

   B. Cloud service partner

C. Cloud service administrator

D. Cloud service customer

C. The activity of a cloud service administrator is not one of the defined cloud computing activities in ISO/IEC 17789.

A is incorrect because the cloud service provider is an official role established in ISO/IEC 17789. The cloud service provider is the entity that makes cloud services available to users or customers, regardless of the cloud deployment model or hosting model used.

B is incorrect because the cloud service partner is an official role established in ISO/IEC 17789. The cloud service partner is defined as an entity that assists either the cloud service customer or the cloud service provider in the delivery of cloud services, or both.

D is incorrect because the cloud service customer is an official role established in ISO/IEC 17789. The cloud service customer is defined as any entity that has a business relationship for the use of cloud services.

45. Which act relates to the use and protection of PII with financial institutions?

   A. SOX

   B. GLBA

   C. HIPAA

   D. PCI DSS

B. The Gramm–Leach–Bliley Act (GLBA), also known as the Financial Modernization Act of 1999, is specifically focused on the use of PII by financial institutions and the necessary requirements for the protection of it. The Act contains what is known as the Safeguards Rule, which puts the specific requirements and burdens on financial institutions to protect the privacy and personal information of their customers. The Act also requires regular notification of the privacy practices of financial institutions as well as with whom they share personal information and for what purposes.

A is incorrect because the Sarbanes–Oxley Act (SOX) is focused on the protection of stakeholders and shareholders from financial irregularities, improper practices, and errors by organizations. The act also outlines specific requirements for data retention and preservation of financial and system records.

C is incorrect because the Health Insurance Portability and Accountability Act (HIPAA) is focused on privacy and personal information as it relates to healthcare and health records, and has no bearing on financial institutions at all.

D is incorrect because PCI DSS is a financial industry regulation as it pertains to organizations that accept credit card payments from the major credit network providers. It is focused on security requirements and records retention for those types of transactions specifically, and does not apply to personal data or the financial sector in general.

46. Which of the following is *NOT* one of the cloud service capabilities?

    A. Infrastructure

    B. Network

    C. Platform

    D. Software

B. Network is not a defined cloud service capability. Network services are a major component of cloud computing in general, and all service capabilities heavily use and depend on network services, but network is not a standalone category.

A is incorrect because infrastructure is one of the three cloud service capabilities. This is why Infrastructure as a Service is one of the three main cloud service categories, where the cloud provider is responsible for the physical environment and making services available, but the cloud customer is responsible for the virtual machines, configurations, storage, and almost all aspects of maintenance.

C is incorrect because platform is one of the three cloud service capabilities. Platform as a Service, being one of the main cloud service categories, is where the cloud provider makes available to the cloud customer virtual machines with application frameworks installed and configured, where the cloud customer just needs to load their application code and data. The cloud service provider is responsible for the patching and maintenance of the virtual machines and the associated frameworks running on them.

D is incorrect because software is one of the three cloud service capabilities. Software as a Service is one of the main cloud service categories, and one where the cloud provider is responsible for the infrastructure up through the fully functional application. The cloud customer may have limited configuration or default settings to leverage but otherwise is responsible for importing or loading applicable data and then for user account management.

47. Which of the following would *NOT* be used to determine the classification of data?

    A. Metadata

    B. PII

    C. Creator

    D. Future use

D. The future use or intended use of data should have no bearing on the classification of it. The classification of data should be based on the sensitivity of the data, any regulatory requirements, and the potential risks and costs associated with compromise. Applications and services that intend to use data must adapt their security controls and policies to the classification of the data. The data should not be classified based on the demands or needs of specific applications or users.

A is incorrect because metadata is one of the keys for classifying data. Information about the creation of data, the time of creation, who created the data, where and how it is stored, and the specific fields involved all play heavily into data classification, and all fall under the concept of metadata.

B is incorrect because any data that contains PII will automatically have legal or regulatory requirements placed on it for data classification. In most regulatory systems, the inclusion of PII will have automatic ramifications on the classification level of the data and the necessary security controls that must be used on it.

C is incorrect because the creator of data can definitely have an impact on the classification level of it. For example, if the creator of data is a doctor's office, and the nature of the data is healthcare related, then the data will automatically assume certain data classification requirements.

48. What is the prevailing factor for determining which regulations apply to data that is housed in a cloud environment?

   A. PII

   B. Classification

   C. Population

   D. Location

D. The location of the data, and any jurisdictions that the location fall under, will always be the prevailing factor for determining which regulations apply to it, regardless of what type of data it is.

A is incorrect because while PII will have a definite impact on the regulations that apply to data, it is a subsection of the overall data classification requirements.

B is incorrect because the classification of the data will always have a major impact on the regulations that apply to it, but the jurisdiction, based on location, is ultimately what makes that determination.

C is incorrect because while the population of the data can certainly have an impact on the regulations that apply to it, it is a subset of the overall data classification requirements.

49. Which concept involves applying standardized configurations and settings to systems to ensure compliance with policy or regulatory requirements?

   A. Images

   B. Repudiation

   C. Baselines

   D. Interoperability

C. Baselines are set configuration standards and requirements that apply to a system or application. Baselines are often part of regulatory or legal requirements and oftentimes follow published industry standard guidelines.

A is incorrect because images form the basis for virtual machines, but are the end result of applied configurations and requirements, not the mechanism for applying or ensuring their compliance.

B is incorrect because repudiation deals with the verifiability of an individual and proof of their activities, and does not have any impact or bearing on system configurations or regulatory requirements, though repudiation and nonrepudiation may certainly be themes of regulatory requirements.

D is incorrect because interoperability has to do with the ability of systems or applications to reuse components or code to make development simpler, more granular and efficient, and less costly. It does not have anything to do with regulatory requirements or their enforcement.

50. Your company has just been served with an eDiscovery order to collect event data and other pertinent information from your application during a specific period of time, to be used as potential evidence for a court proceeding. Which of the following, apart from ensuring that you collect all pertinent data, would be the *MOST* important consideration?

   A. Encryption

   B. Chain of custody

   C. Compression

   D. Confidentiality

B. When a company is dealing with eDiscovery orders, the chain of custody is extremely important as it pertains to official legal proceedings. The chain of custody documents everyone who has had possession of the data, in what format, and for what reasons. For data to be admissible for legal proceedings, the chain of custody is vital in showing that nothing has been tampered with and that everyone in possession of the data can be questioned and investigated, if needed.

A is incorrect because although encryption may be used as part of eDiscovery to sign, preserve, and protect any evidence that is collected and turned over, especially if the data is sensitive, in general it is not a required element of eDiscovery.

C is incorrect because although compression may be used when preserving and submitting evidence pursuant to the order, it is not a requirement element and will have no bearing on the overall process of eDiscovery.

D is incorrect because confidentiality may or may not be a factor with eDiscovery, depending on the nature of the data requested and the types of systems involved.

51. Which of the following concepts will ensure that no single host or cloud customer can consume enough resources to impact other users on the same system?

    A. Limits

    B. Multitenancy

    C. Reservations

    D. Shares

A. Limits are put in place to enforce the maximum amount of compute resources that any one tenant or system can consume. The limits can be placed on various levels and units, ranging from a specific virtual machine to a cloud customer for the aggregate of their utilization across all systems. They are designed to ensure that no single host or customer can utilize enormous resources that will ultimately make the cloud provider unable to properly allocate resources and serve the needs of other cloud customers.

B is incorrect because multitenancy is the larger concept that deals with hosting multiple, different cloud customers within the same cloud environment. While it is certainly the driving reason why the need for balancing resource allocations is necessary, that concept itself does not play into the specific details of implementations like this.

C is incorrect because a reservation is the minimum amount of resources guaranteed to a cloud customer within the environment. A reservation will typically guarantee to a cloud customer that they will have the minimum required resources necessary to power on and operate their services within the environment. Reservations also offer insurance against denial-of-service (DoS) attacks or other customers using such large amounts of resources that the cloud customer cannot operate their services.

D is incorrect because shares are focused on cloud customers requesting more resources for allocation and provisioning than are currently available in the environment. Shares establish a prioritization and weighting system, defined by the cloud provider, that determines which systems, applications, and customers will receive priority for additional resource requests when utilization is high and resources are limited.

52. Which of the following roles is responsible in many organizations for overseeing access requests for data utilization and ensuring that policies are followed and proper approvals are granted?

    A. Data owner

    B. Data steward

    C. Data processor

    D. Data controller

B. The data steward is responsible for overseeing an organization's policy in regard to data access, as well as for evaluating access requests and matching them with organizational policy to ensure compliance and proper use. If the business purpose is acceptable, the data steward is responsible for ensuring that appropriate approvals have been obtained and documented as well.

A is incorrect because while the data owner has final authority and responsibility over data policies and access, the data steward is the position officially designated for directly carrying out those duties. The data owner is responsible for establishing the risk management approach to data security and access in conjunction with management and then matching this to the organizational policies or regulatory requirements.

C is incorrect because the data processor is the one who actually uses the data within an application or service. As the consumer of the data, the data processor does not play a role in granting data access or policy enforcement.

D is incorrect because the term *data controller* is synonymous with data owner; they have the same duties and responsibilities.

53. Which of the following is directly part of the "metered" costs associated with PaaS?
    A. Staffing
    B. Development
    C. Licensing
    D. Auditing

C. With PaaS, the cloud provider is giving the cloud customer a fully functioning environment, including the operating system and any middleware or application framework components. As part of the services, the licensing costs and tracking are the responsibility of the cloud provider and are factored into the metered costs of the cloud customer.

A is incorrect because staffing comes in many different forms, with many different parties involved. Within cloud computing, although the cloud provider has staffing to maintain the environment, due to self-service provisioning, staffing is not needed as additional virtual machines are brought online or new services provisioned; this is all handled through automated processes.

B is incorrect because development is not part of the services from a cloud provider, nor is it included in the costs from the cloud provider for cloud services. Development would be done under its own contract, or possibly even under contracts that incorporate the costs of the cloud hosting services as well. However, it would not be a direct part of the metered services from the cloud provider as additional resources are allocated or provisioned.

D is incorrect because auditing is part of all cloud server categories and is documented in the contract and SLA requirements. It is not a specific part of any one category over another, though it can differ in scope based on the specific category used. Regardless, it does not relate to the metered costs of any cloud category.

54. Many highly regulated data types and systems will have specialized regulatory requirements that extend further than the regulatory requirements that apply to all data. Which of the following is *NOT* a specialized regulatory framework that has its own compliance requirements?

    A. FedRAMP

    B. HIPAA

    C. FIPS 140-2

    D. PCI DSS

C. FIPS 140-2 is a certification for cryptographic modules based on the specific needs and requirements for the level of encryption and the protection of it. It is based on both software and hardware requirements and the level of control, features, and protections that each have. It is not a regulatory framework with compliance requirements.

A is incorrect because FedRAMP is a regulatory framework that the United States federal government uses to assess and certify cloud services for their use by federal agencies. As part of FedRAMP, there is a certification process for low and moderate systems, as well as high systems of 2016, to meet requirements and auditing. One aspect of FedRAMP is that it was designed for use by any federal agency once a provider had been certified, removing the need for each agency to conduct their own certifications and audits of the cloud services provider. FedRAMP is available for use by civilian agencies and can be used for data and systems other than those for national defense.

B is incorrect because HIPAA relates to regulated healthcare and personal data within the United States, and sets strict and extensive requirements for how it must be protected. It is specialized for healthcare data and supersedes any other regulatory requirements to which a system or data might be subjected. As part of HIPAA regulations, data controllers are subjected to increased scrutiny for the methods and processes they use to protect personal and patient data.

D is incorrect because PCI DSS is an industry-specific regulation and oversight framework, established by the major credit card companies and networks, and is a requirement for any business that conducts transactions over those networks.

55. Which cloud deployment model offers the most control and ownership over systems and operations for an organization?

   A. Private

   B. Public

   C. Community

   D. Hybrid

A. Private clouds offer the most control and ownership for an organization. With a private cloud, an organization will either have sole ownership or be a strategic paying partner with the entity running the cloud and thus have much more influence and input into decisions and policies than any other model affords.

B is incorrect because an organization would have very little say, or possibly even no say, in how a public cloud operates or functions. Public clouds typically offer free services to the public at large, or offer services to any customer that is willing to pay. With the large number of customers or free services offered, it is not possible for a public cloud to take into account individual demands from customers or for customers to expect any reasonable likeliness of their demands being met. Public clouds are intended to serve mass populations and to do so cheaply and efficiently. They are not intended for a large degree of customization or for adapting to the particular needs of individual customers.

C in incorrect because while a community cloud will typically offer customers a higher degree of input and influence than a public cloud, it will not match what a private cloud can offer. While a community cloud will usually have a smaller subset of users, who share many common traits, it is still bound to serve multiple different customers with their own needs, desires, and expectations. Any requested changes by one customer would almost certainly have an impact on other customers, so it is difficult to allow customers to have significant influence for particular needs or requests.

D is incorrect because a hybrid cloud itself is not an entity that an organization could have influence over; it is a concept that involves the use of multiple cloud deployment models. As such, the positives and negatives of each environment would be combined within a hybrid cloud and ultimately would minimize the level of influence a cloud customer could have.

56. Which of the following is encryption *MOST* intended to address?

   A. Integrity

   B. Availability

   C. Data loss

   D. Confidentiality

D. The purpose of encryption, first and foremost, is to prevent the unauthorized viewing of data. While encryption can be a useful tool when used in conjunction with other tools (for digital signing and nonrepudiation, for example), the protection against unauthorized access to data is its primary intended use and focus. With the use of modern and strong encryption techniques, along with the proper protection of keys, data can easily and efficiently be rendered inaccessible and virtually unbreakable.

A is incorrect because encryption is not focused on integrity, or useful to protect it, in any reasonable sense. Encryption is focused solely on the confidentiality aspect of security overall. While it will prevent a user from accessing the data to modify it, especially while the data is at rest, it is not a tool that can be used with an application or live environment to prevent the unauthorized modification of data once it is accessible.

B is incorrect because encryption will not promote or assist in availability at all. The use of encryption will not enhance the availability or accessibility of data at all; instead, it is merely designed to protect the confidentiality of data.

C is incorrect because encryption will not prevent the destruction or deletion of data at all.

57. To test some new application features, you want to isolate applications within the cloud environment from other applications and systems. Which of the following approaches would be the *MOST* appropriate to accomplish this?

   A. Sandboxing

   B. Application virtualization

   C. Honeypot

   D. Federation

B. Application virtualization allows you to run parallel application deployments in the same environment for the purposes of testing new features or patches. It differs from sandboxing because it does not require distinct systems or segregated networks to function, and can be focused purely at the application level. It takes far fewer resources to set up and use than sandboxing.

A is incorrect because sandboxing goes far beyond isolating applications for testing. With sandboxing, you are setting up totally separate and distinct virtual machines, and in most cases network isolation as well. Although sandboxing could be used to test new features for applications, it goes far beyond that mandate. Therefore, application virtualization is a more appropriate approach to take.

C is incorrect because a honeypot does not have anything to do with the testing of new application features or the isolation of them. A honeypot is a security concept of setting up servers and data that appear to be legitimate production systems in order to entice attackers to go after them instead of the real systems.

The security team can then use the attacks and traffic they see going against the honeypot to block sources or refine security controls and configurations of the actual production systems.

D is incorrect because a federation is a concept within identity and access management and does not have any relationship to or impact on application isolation or testing.

58. Which of the following would *NOT* be included as input into the requirements gathering for an application or system?

   A. Users

   B. Management

   C. Regulators

   D. Auditors

D. Auditors would not be included or considered during the collection of requirements for an application or system. While auditors will play a role later in any new design or modification by ensuring compliance with regulation and policy, they would not be involved at an early stage at all. The role of an auditor is to validate configurations, policies, and practices against the regulations they are designed to comply with, and to establish a gap analysis between the desired and actual state of the system or application, not to be involved with design or development decisions.

A is incorrect because users would be a primary concern and focus during the requirements-gathering stage of a system or application. Input from users, as the ultimate consumers of the system, is vital for a system to work efficiently and easily, with features that consumers find beneficial and productive. Without the input of users, stakeholders and developers are left to assume their decisions are what people will ultimately desire and need, and substantial gaps between their perceptions and the perceptions of users are very likely. This could lead to a system that does not meet expectations, or even ultimately fails to catch on with consumers.

B is incorrect because management has the major financial role and responsibility to both shareholders and users of a system or application. While the users and their satisfaction will ultimately decide the fate or success of an application, management sets the direction and desired features of the application, as well as ensures compliance with regulators. Management also has the responsibility for protecting both personal and financial data, and needs to be heavily involved at all stages to set priorities and budgets for development, as well as to make decisions as to which requirements to focus on and which might be deferred to a later version or update.

C is incorrect because regulators and the regulations they enforce will have a strong influence on all aspects of an application in regard to security and policies. Many of the features and configurations of a system or application will be driven directly by regulations, or at least choices in approach will be limited by regulations.

59. Which phase of the SDLC process includes the selection of the application framework and programming languages to be used for the application?

   A. Requirement gathering

   B. Development

   C. Design

   D. Requirement analysis

   D. The requirement analysis phase is where the specific hardware and software platforms with which the programmers will work are decided, along with the specific functionality and features that are expected. This will then be used during the design phase for the programmers to plan the actual coding and methodology to develop the application around to meet the design requirements.

   A is incorrect because the requirement-gathering phase is where the mandatory requirements and success criteria for the development and overall project are decided. This involves representation from all stakeholder groups, and an analysis of any regulatory requirements that must be adhered to as well. The overall budget and timeline for the project are also decided as this phase.

   B is incorrect because the development phase is where the actual coding of the application occurs and where the executable code is compiled. As each segment of code is completed and each milestone reached, functional testing is completed against the code to ensure that it functions as designed and required. The development phase is typically the longest phase of the SDLC process.

   C is incorrect because the design phase is where the requirements for and decisions on platforms and technologies are combined to form a project plan to create the actual code. This phase also includes the merging of security and risk management concerns into the overall plan, as well as the testing and validation to be completed during the development phase.

60. Which regulations were designed to try and bridge the gap in privacy laws between the United States and the European Union?

   A. Safe Harbor

   B. HIPAA

   C. SOX

   D. GLBA

A. The Safe Harbor regulations were developed and implemented by the Department of Commerce to serve as a way to bridge the gap between the privacy laws of the United States and the European Union. The European Union has very strong privacy laws enforced at a high level, while the United States does not have a specific privacy law at the federal level. The EU regulations prohibit the export of PII information from Europe to jurisdictions that do not have the equivalent privacy laws with the same strict requirements as they do, so the voluntary program was developed for organizations to adhere to as a means to show the same strict scrutiny and protection requirements as the EU. Part of the Safe Harbor program is that those organizations must also submit to audits and dispute-resolution processes to bring them in line with EU requirements and equivalent processes.

B is incorrect because the Health Insurance Portability and Accountability Act (HIPAA) is focused on healthcare data and the privacy and protection of patient data by covered healthcare professionals, and does not pertain the privacy regulations regarding the European Union.

C is incorrect because the Sarbanes–Oxley Act (SOX) pertains to financial and accounting records and their transparency to regulators and shareholders. It involves reporting requirements and data-retention requirements, and does not pertain to the privacy of individuals or interactions with the European Union at all.

D is incorrect because the Gramm–Leach–Bliley Act (GLBA) pertains to PII and financial institutions. It requires that financial institutions provide all users and customers with a copy of their privacy policy and practices, including when and with whom customer information may be shared with. It also puts the burden on financial institutions for adequate security controls and oversight of any personal data they collect or store from customers.

61. Which concept involves the maintenance of resources within a cloud environment to ensure resources are available when and where needed?

   A. Dynamic optimization

   B. Auto-scaling

   C. Elasticity

   D. Resource pooling

A. Dynamic optimization is the continual and automatic process within a cloud environment of shifting resources and virtual machines between physical hosts and resources to ensure a proper balance is maintained. This ensures that a single physical host or a subset of physical hosts does not become maxed out on resources and thus impact other customers or virtual machines on the same host. This ensures availability and auto-scaling and makes sure any provisioning requests are able to be met as they come in from customers.

B is incorrect because auto-scaling pertains to the automatic and programmatic mechanisms for scaling up or down a system or application based on load and demand. It pertains only to the system or application in question and does not pertain to the resources of the overall environment or to meeting the needs of each tenant.

C is incorrect because elasticity refers to the ability of the environment to provision and de-provision resources to meet current needs in a programmatic and automated way. If elasticity is implemented correctly, the systems and applications should ideally have the exact resources they need at any time and not have an excess or deficit of resources.

D is incorrect because resource pooling refers to the overall sharing of the aggregate resources available in a cloud environment between all the individual tenants of the environment. It refers to the overall allocation of resources and is not related to the ability to adapt to specific situations or demands on a system or application.

62. Which type of storage with IaaS will be maintained by the cloud provider and referenced with a key value?

   A. Structured

   B. Object

   C. Volume

   D. Unstructured

B. Object storage is a type of IaaS storage where files and objects are physically stored on a separate system and are referenced by a key or token value. It differs from traditional storage as it does not contain any organizational or hierarchical capabilities; instead, everything is stored in a flat system with a token or key as the only reference for access. It is heavy used for media objects such as pictures and videos, or for the storage of larger files where organization is not relevant, such as virtual machine image files.

A is incorrect because structured is a type of storage under Platform as a Service, and is typically related to storage types such as databases that have defined structures and rules pertaining to how the data is organized and stored.

C is incorrect because while volume storage is a type used under IaaS, it involves and resembles traditional storage, with a file system and tree structure where data can be organized and accessed in the same manner as a traditional server (by pathname and filename).

D is incorrect because unstructured is a type of storage under PaaS that is used for handling data objects that will not fit within a structured system. This includes websites and web pages, their associated components, media files, images, or anything else that will not fit within a typical database paradigm.

63. When an audit plan is being prepared, four distinct steps are done in sequence. Which of the following is the second step, after the defining of objectives?

A. Define scope

B. Conduct audit

C. Identify stakeholders

D. Gather documentation

A. After the objectives within an audit have been defined, the defining of the scope is the next step. This involves the specifics of what is to be tested as well as all the details about how and when it will be tested.

B is incorrect because conducting the audit occurs after both the scope and objectives have been defined, which will serve as the roadmap for the actual audit.

C is incorrect because the identification of stakeholders will be done as part of initially defining objectives, and will then be refined some during the defining of the scope.

D is incorrect because gathering documentation is not a step itself and is done as part of both the defining objectives and defining scope steps.

64. Which of the following technology concepts is listed specifically as its own domain as part of ISO/IEC 27001:2013?

A. Firewalls

B. IPS

C. Honeypots

D. Cryptography

D. Cryptography as an overall concept is a specific domain of ISO/IEC 27001:2013, which covers all of the various aspects and methods where cryptography is used within IT services and operations.

A is incorrect because firewalls are covered under network domains and are not a specific domain themselves.

B is incorrect because IPS is covered under network and application security and is not a domain itself.

C is incorrect because a honeypot is a security mechanism for capturing and analyzing attack attempts against systems that uses a similar-looking server with fake data that is designed to entice attackers. The application owners can then use the exploit attempts that are directed toward the honeypot to refine and augment security controls on the actual production systems.

65. What are the two main types of APIs used with cloud-based systems and applications?

　A. REST and SOAP

　B. XML and SOAP

　C. REST and XML

　D. HTTPS and REST

A. Representational State Transfer (REST) and Simple Object Access Protocol (SOAP) are the two main types of APIs used within cloud-based systems. SOAP is focused on providing a structured information exchange system for web services, and REST is a protocol for using HTTP requests to access and manipulate data.

B is incorrect because although SOAP is one of the two methods, XML is a protocol for encoding and representing data, and is not one of the two main API types for cloud-based systems.

C is incorrect because although REST is one of the two methods, XML is a protocol for encoding and representing data, and is not one of the two main API types for cloud-based systems.

D is incorrect because although REST is one of the two methods, HTTPS is a protocol for secure communication extensions to the HTTP web protocol, and is not one of the two types of APIs used by cloud-based systems.

66. You have been tasked by management to offload processing and validation of incoming encoded data from your application servers and their associated APIs. Which of the following would be the most appropriate device or software to consider?

　A. XML accelerator

　B. XML firewall

　C. Web application firewall

　D. Firewall

A. An XML accelerator is designed to sit in front of application servers or services and APIs for the purpose of offloading processing and validation of incoming XML. They are highly scaled and tuned appliances to handle their specific purpose and will allow the backend service providers to focus on business logic, rather than processing and validating the incoming data.

B is incorrect because an XML firewall is designed to protect systems and scan data as it is coming in and out of an application or data center for validity, but does not provide the processing capabilities and application interaction of an XML accelerator.

C is incorrect because a web application firewall is designed to inspect web traffic coming into an application to detect security exploit attempts or other signatures of the traffic and take specific action against it based on what policies are matched. This can include redirecting or blocking the traffic before it reaches the application.

D is incorrect because a firewall is designed to control network communications between sources and destinations, as well as the ports they are communicating over. It does not perform content inspection on packets.

67. What is used with a single sign-on system for authentication after the identity provider has successfully authenticated a user?

   A. Token

   B. Key

   C. XML

   D. SAML

A. With a single sign-on system, once the user has successfully authenticated, they are issued an opaque token that can then be used to access systems that are part of the federation. Each system can validate the token back to the identity provider to ensure it is current and to gain information about the user to then make informed decisions on authorization within the application.

B is incorrect because a key would typically refer to encryption and is not used to refer to maintaining the session and presence within a single sign-on system.

C is incorrect because XML is a standard for data encoding and presentation, and would not be used for proving identity after successful login.

D is incorrect because SAML is used within a federated system to pass information about the user for authorization or registration purposes, but would not be used to validate the authentication in the way that the token would be.

68. Which document will enforce uptime and availability requirements between the cloud customer and cloud provider?

   A. Contract

   B. Operational level agreement

   C. Service level agreement

   D. Regulation

C. The SLA will determine and document the requirements and expectations for factors such as uptime and availability within a cloud environment that are expected to be met by the cloud provider. This will be done on a percentage basis that represents how much unscheduled or unplanned downtime is allowable within a specified period of time, and will be specific to the applications and systems in question.

A is incorrect because the contract is the high-level formal agreement between the cloud provider and the cloud customer that documents the requirements for policies and resources that are covered for an agreed-upon price, but does not specify operational details such as availability and uptime requirements like the SLA would, or the metrics used to evaluate them.

B is incorrect because an operational level agreement is similar to an SLA, but is used internally between components of the same organization to document duties and responsibilities, and would not pertain to the relations or arrangements between the cloud customer and the cloud provider.

D is incorrect because regulations may serve as the inputs or requirements for specific performance metrics, but not how they would be enforced as part of the business relationship. They would be captured within the SLA, where their requirements and metrics are established.

69. Which of the following concepts makes repeated audits and verification much more difficult in a cloud environment versus a traditional data center?

    A. Multitenancy

    B. Resource pooling

    C. Elasticity

    D. Virtualization

D. Virtualization makes repeated audits and verifications difficult within a cloud environment because it is almost impossible to ensure that the system being tested now is the same as the previous one. In a virtual environment, images are changed often and systems reimaged for patches or other changes. This differs from a traditional data center where servers are physical assets that can easily be verified as being the same system as before, even if upgrades and features have changed over time.

A is incorrect because multitenancy refers to the hosting of multiple customers within the same cloud environment and within the same pool of resources, and would not play into the ability to audit or ensure consistency over time.

B is incorrect because resource pooling refers to the aggregation of resources from the entire cloud environment and how they are made available to all the customers within the cloud environment, and would not be a factor in auditing consistency over time.

C is incorrect because elasticity refers to the ability for systems to automatically scale up or down to meet current demands without having an excess or deficiency of resources at any given point.

70. The security principle of the SOC 2 reports consists of seven categories. Which of the following is *NOT* one of the seven categories?

    A. Monitoring of controls

    B. Legal compliance controls

    C. Change management

    D. System operations

B. The SOC 2 reports do not contain the legal compliance controls as a factor, because they can differ greatly from one jurisdiction to another, and each regulatory system will have its own compliance requirements and auditing demands.

A is incorrect because the monitoring of controls is one of the main seven categories under SOC 2 and pertains to organizations effectively testing and verifying their controls are adequately addressing their intended threats, as well as ensuring that mechanisms put in place are still in place and have not been changed through unintended or unauthorized means.

C is incorrect because change management is a core component of SOC 2 reports and how an organization oversees and verifies the process of changes within their environments. This includes documentation, approvals, and risk management evaluations for all proposed changes, as well as tracking their completion and the signoff from functional testing and validation.

D is incorrect because system operations and how an organization runs their systems through policies and procedures is a core component of evaluation under the SOC 2 reports.

71. Which privacy standard was developed as a joint effort between AICPA and the CICA?

    A. GLBA

    B. HIPAA

    C. GAPP

    D. ISO/IEC 27001

C. The Generally Accepted Privacy Principles (GAPP) was established by a joint effort between the American Institute of Certified Public Accountants (AICPA) and the Canadian Institute of Chartered Accountants (CICA). It serves to assist organizations and their management in developing strong privacy programs that address risk and regulatory requirements.

A is incorrect because the Gramm–Leach–Bliley Act (GLBA) was established by the United States federal government to deal with financial organizations and the way they handle personal and private information.

B is incorrect because the Health Insurance Portability and Accountability Act (HIPAA) was established by the United States federal government and pertains to the protection of private health information and records.

D is incorrect because the ISO/IEC 27001 standards on security were established by the joint technical committee between the International Organization for Standardization (ISO) and the International Electrotechnical Commission (IEC).

72. Which cross-cutting aspect relates to the ability for a cloud customer to remove their data and systems from a cloud provider and be afforded assurances that it has been securely removed?

    A. Portability

    B. Reversibility

    C. Sanitation

    D. Wiping

B. Reversibility refers to the ability for a cloud customer to withdraw their data and configurations from a cloud environment quickly and efficiently. The cloud provider must also provide assurances and a timeline for securely and completely removing the data from within their environment.

A is incorrect because portability refers to the ability for a system or application to move between different cloud providers, but does not relate to the ability to securely remove its data and configurations from one environment as it moves to another. Instead, portability is purely focused on the ability to move or migrate.

C is incorrect because sanitation commonly refers to the ability to ensure that data has been securely deleted and wiped from a system, but does not pertain to the ability to extract data or configurations from an environment.

D is incorrect because wiping would be the same concept as sanitation in this case, and it would have the same limitations and concepts apply to it.

73. Which protocol is the current default and industry standard for encrypting traffic across a network?

    A. TLS

    B. SSL

    C. IPsec

    D. DNSSEC

A. Transport Layer Security (TLS) is the standard protocol used for sending encrypted traffic over a network between two parties. It has replaced SSL, which is no longer considered secure enough for general usage. TLS supports much stronger and more robust encryption ciphers.

B is incorrect because SSL was the predecessor to TLS and has been replaced as the standard method for encrypting communications over the network. At this point, SSL is considered insecure because it uses weaker and older ciphers that no longer provide adequate protection or assurance of security.

C is incorrect because IPsec is a communications method that is used to encrypt traffic between two hosts. However, it is not in widespread use due to resource limitations and demands. It also requires known hosts to be configured to use it, and it is not a general-purpose encryption method that is widely available.

D is incorrect because DNSSEC is used to verity the integrity and authority of DNS resolution and lookups back to their intended issuer. It digitally signs DNS resolutions that can be verified back to their source, preventing the spoofing or redirecting of network traffic by sending out incorrect IP address resolutions to hosts.

74. Which network concept is used within a cloud environment to segregate and isolate network segments from other systems or applications?

   A. Subnets

   B. VLANs

   C. Gateways

   D. IPsec

B. Because cloud environments do not have the ability to physically separate networks the same way a traditional data center would, they rely on logical separations with VLANs to keep systems isolated from others. This enables security to be controlled within the VLAN and allows similar systems and applications to communicate with each other within a secure enclave where the separation of physical networks and cabling is not possible.

A is incorrect because subnets break up larger networks into logical sections for IP addressing and organization, but do not contain the protections and segregations that VLANs afford and allow.

C is incorrect because gateways are where systems send data when they do not know the specific route. The gateway can determine how to route the packets to the correct destination and can serve as a router on the network.

D is incorrect because IPsec is an encryption protocol that is applied to each and every packet sent between two systems over the network, and does not play a role in the segregation of networks without a logical framework.

75. Which jurisdiction, through Directive 95/46, enacted in 1995, declared data privacy to be a human right?

   A. United States

   B. European Union

C. Russia

D. Japan

> **B.** The European Union issued Directive 95/46, which established data privacy of personal information to be a human right. Following this directive, Europe has had some of the strictest privacy controls and requirements in the world.
>
> **A** is incorrect because the United States does not currently have a federal-level policy on data privacy and personal information protection in a general sense, but it does for more specific applications such as healthcare and financial data.
>
> **C** is incorrect because Russia did not issue Directive 95/46, but it does has its own laws focused on protecting the privacy of information for Russian citizens, including restrictions that require all data on Russian citizens to be housed on servers that reside within the political boundaries of the Russian Federation.
>
> **D** is incorrect because Japan was not party to Directive 95/46.

76. What type of encryption allows for the manipulation of encrypted data without having to first unencrypt it?

   A. Homomorphic

   B. Symmetric

   C. Asymmetric

   D. Public key

> **A.** Homomorphic is a new cutting-edge type of encryption that allows a system or application to read and manipulate encrypted data without first having to unencrypt it. This allows for enhanced security because the data does not need to reside on a system in unencrypted format at any point, so even a compromise of a system will not reveal data to the malicious actor, because they would still need the encryption keys to read it, even on a live system that is accessing the data.
>
> **B** is incorrect because symmetric encryption refers to the situation where both parties of a secure communication have the same key pairs and they are exchanged prior to communications being established. This allows for very fast communications over encrypted channels, but does require both parties to be known and familiar with each other before attempting communication so that the keys can be exchanged.
>
> **C** is incorrect because asymmetric encryption is done through the use of keys and certificates issued by known authorities that are trusted by both parties. This requires reliance on the third-party authority to establish trust, and enables communications over secure channels where the parties don't know each other and haven't already exchanged keys.
>
> **D** is incorrect because *public key* is another term for asymmetric encryption.

77. Which of the following threat models includes discoverability as a key component and concern?

    A. DREAD

    B. SOX

    C. STRIDE

    D. CSA Treacherous 12

    A. The DREAD threat model includes discoverability as the second *D* in the acronym. In this sense, discoverability refers to the likeliness or possibility that a malicious actor will discover that a specific vulnerability exists and have the ability to exploit it.

    B is incorrect because the Sarbanes–Oxley Act covers companies and the way they handle financial transactions, records, retention, and the transparency of their practices and compliance. The concept of discoverability does not directly play a role in SOX.

    C is incorrect because the STRIDE threat model does not include discoverability as one of its key components. With the STRIDE acronym, the *D* stands for denial of service.

    D is incorrect because the Cloud Security Alliance Treacherous 12 does not include discoverability as one of its 12 key components.

78. From a legal perspective, data that is covered under eDiscovery falls into three different categories. Which of the following is *NOT* one of the three?

    A. Possession

    B. Shared

    C. Control

    D. Custody

    B. From the perspective of eDiscovery, who data is shared with is not a primary concern or one of the main principles of it. Data collection is the responsibility of the authoritative source or systems that use it, but logging and preservation are focused on the data owner or the one who controls and makes the data available to consumers.

    A is incorrect because possession of the data is one of the three main components of eDiscovery, and the party that possesses the data will likely be the first recipient of the eDiscovery order.

    C is incorrect because control of the data is one of the main components and principles of eDiscovery. This is of particular concern within a cloud environment because the boundaries will blur between the cloud customer and cloud provider with most cloud implementations.

D is incorrect because custody is one of the main principles and components of eDiscovery. Within a cloud environment, custody is very important and can be complex because the duties for custody fall on both the cloud provider and the cloud customer, and depending on the type of cloud implementation, the duties may fall on one party more than the other.

79. Which of the following would be covered by an external audit and *NOT* by an internal audit?

   A. Security controls

   B. Costs

   C. Operating efficiency

   D. System design

A. Security controls and testing are crucial aspects of an external audit and typically the focus of one. While internal audits may perform some level of security controls validation, they are not considered to be valid audits, because there is no independent external auditor to evaluate them. Independent and external testing for audits is paramount to instill trust in a system, and is a required component for regulatory compliance and certification programs.

B is incorrect because costs would be considered part of an internal audit of operation policies and procedures. External audits are focused on regulatory compliance or certifications, as well as on ensuring customer requirements for security controls and validation, and are not concerned with costs. They are only concerned with the compliance (or lack thereof) with requirements and regulation.

C is incorrect because operating efficiency is a major component of internal auditing and a crucial input for management oversight and decision making. An external audit would not be concerned with operating efficiency, but rather only with compliance with regulatory or certification standards and the validation of security controls and policies.

D is incorrect because system design overall is internal to an organization. While an external audit will likely include a review of system design, it is for the purposes of establishing knowledge of how security controls are designed and implemented, not with the soundness of efficiency or customer satisfaction beyond the security controls requirements and validation.

80. What is the most prevalent communications protocol for network-based storage solutions within a data center?

   A. iSCSI

   B. TCP

C. TLS

D. NetBIOS

A. iSCSI is a protocol that sits on top of the TCP stack and enables the sending of SCSI commands over a network, rather than through the traditional method in a physical environment where storage devices are directly attached to the server. Within a cloud data center especially, iSCSI is crucial because virtual machines and other virtual appliances will not have any direct physical connections to storage systems.

B is incorrect because TCP is the general protocol for network communications and is not specifically related to storage systems or the direct carrier of storage communications or commands. TCP does play a central role given that iSCSI is dependent on it, but by itself TCP is not an appropriate answer here.

C is incorrect because TLS is a secure communications and encryption protocol for network traffic, but it's not specifically related to storage systems or the carrying of storage solution communications.

D is incorrect because NetBIOS is a program that allows applications to communicate over a local area network with each other, and is not specifically related to storage communications.

81. Which of the following security responsibilities is always solely under the cloud provider?

    A. Infrastructure

    B. Data

    C. Physical

    D. Application

C. Regardless of the cloud service category employed, the cloud provider will always be responsible for the management and operations of the underlying physical environment. Even with IaaS, the cloud customer is not responsible for, or involved with, the physical environment at all.

A is incorrect because infrastructure is the sole responsibility of the cloud provider with PaaS or SaaS, but is a shared responsibility with the cloud customer for IaaS.

B is incorrect because data is always the responsibility of the cloud customer, who is responsible for the maintaining and loading of data as well as ensuring the appropriate use of it and access to it. Even within a SaaS implementation, the cloud customer as the data owner is always responsible for the data.

D is incorrect because only in the SaaS service category is the cloud provider responsible for the applications. With both PaaS and IaaS, the cloud customer loads, configures, and maintains the applications at all times.

82. Your organization has made it a top priority that any cloud environment being considered to host production systems have guarantees that resources will always be available for allocation when needed. Which of the following concepts will you need to ensure is part of the contract and SLA?

    A. Limits

    B. Shares

    C. Resource pooling

    D. Reservations

    D. A reservation is a set-aside and guaranteed amount of resources that will always be available to a system or application. Typically, reservations represent the minimal amount of resources required to power on and operate a cloud customer's systems, but may not provide for increased provisioning as needed.

    A is incorrect because limits are upper boundaries on the amount of resources that a system, application, or customer can consume within a cloud environment, and are not a guarantee that a specific minimum of resources will be available at any given point.

    B is incorrect because shares are a means of prioritizing the allocation of requested resources for times when there may be limitations on what can be allocated. This allows the cloud provider to establish a weighting system based on contract, system, application, or any other factor that they need to for their systems to follow when resources are requested. Those with the highest priority will receive what is requested first and foremost, and those at the lower end will receive resources last, or possibly not at all.

    C is incorrect because resource pooling represents the overall aggregation and allocation of compute resources throughout the entire cloud environment, as well as the sharing of all of these resources by any cloud customers hosted within the environment. Resource pooling applies to the overall concept of aggregating and sharing resources, rather than the actual allocation and management of them.

83. Which is the most commonly used standard for information exchange within a federated identity system?

    A. OAuth

    B. OpenID

    C. SAML

    D. WS-Federation

    C. The Security Assertion Markup Language (SAML) is the standard protocol for information exchange within federate identity systems. It is used for exchanging both authentication data and information to be used for authorization purposes. SAML is based on XML standards and is widely used throughout the industry to ensure compatibility between identity providers and service providers or relying parties.

A is incorrect because OAuth is a standard for providing login services to online sites and applications through the use of a user's credentials on a third-party system such as Google or Facebook. Through OAuth, the user can authenticate and gain access to an application without exposing their login credentials or creating a new account on that system. However, it is not the common standard for information and authentication exchange within federated systems.

B is incorrect because OpenID is similar to OAuth, in that it allows a user to use their own authentication system to log in to a new system, but it is not the standard protocol used with federated systems. OpenID allows a user to use accounts such as Google and Facebook to authenticate to new applications, without the need to create a new account or expose their login credentials to it.

D is incorrect because while WS-Federation is also a federated identity system, it is one that was developed by a select group of companies for use within their systems and is not used in a widespread manner as a standard for the federated identity systems that are commonly used.

84. Which of the following common threats involves an organization not placing sufficient controls and oversight on their systems and data protection?

    A. Data loss

    B. System vulnerabilities

    C. Insufficient due diligence

    D. Advanced persistent threats

C. Insufficient due diligence is where an organization does not properly evaluate, plan, design, operate, or secure their systems and applications or the data that they house. Any of these areas can cause security exposure if sufficient due diligence is not applied to them, and can lead to any other sorts of vulnerabilities and attacks being possible as a result.

A is incorrect because data loss occurs when data is corrupted or deleted, either intentionally or through the actions of malicious actors, or even malicious insiders. While a security breach will often be the result of not placing sufficient oversight or security controls in place, that is not the focus of the data loss vulnerabilities, so it is not the best answer in this case.

B is incorrect because system vulnerabilities can occur in many forms, and are not necessarily the result of insufficient oversight or controls. They can occur in software or configurations, even those done following best practices, because exploits can be found nonetheless.

D is incorrect because advanced persistent threats involve a malicious actor establishing a presence in an environment and gathering information or data over a long term; these are often caused by insiders being susceptible to social engineering attacks such as phishing. In many circumstance, the cause of this threat is a lack of training and not a deficit of security controls or oversight.

85. Which of the following groups would *NOT* be appropriate to share a SOC 1 report with?

    A. Regulators

    B. Potential customers

    C. Current customers

    D. Management

    B. SOC 1 reports are considered restricted-use reports and are limited in the audience they can or should be exposed to. Potential customers, which do not currently have a contractual or business relationship with a cloud provider, would not be included within the restricted-use classes.

    A is incorrect because regulators are a key audience of SOC 1 reports and one of the primary groups that will receive and review them.

    C is incorrect because current customers are a key audience for SOC 1 reports. They do have a contractual agreement with a cloud provider and, as such, have the necessary nondisclosure agreements and understandings that come with it.

    D is incorrect because regardless of the type of audit requested by an organization, the audit will always be available to management and those responsible for ordering it.

86. With data in transit, which of the following will be the *MOST* major concern in order for a DLP solution to properly work?

    A. Scalability

    B. Encryption

    C. Redundancy

    D. Integrity

    B. In order for a DLP solution to work with data in transit, first and foremost it has to be able to read the data as it is transmitted. Typically, this will be done by having the DLP system unencrypt and then re-encrypt packets as they pass through it. This enables the point-to-point encryption to still be in place, but also allows the DLP system to do its inspection and processing of data in a secure manner.

    A is incorrect because scalability is a concern all around with any system or technology, but is not a specific concern with data in transit like encryption is, which can make an entire system ineffective if not done correctly. If a system is not scaling and is making processing very slow, at a minimum it would be a performance issue and would not result in the exposing of data or bypassing of policies.

C is incorrect because redundancy is not a major factor in ensuring that a DLP system properly protects data. Although a lack of redundancy can lead to problems with availability or speed, it will not expose sensitive or protected data in the event of an outage.

D is incorrect because integrity is not a major concern with a DLP solution. The focus is on ensuring that only authorized parties are able to access the data, as well as how it is accessed, because confidentiality is paramount. Also, because connections are typically encrypted, integrity will be assured through the use of trusted keys to read and access the data upon receipt.

87. Which of the following, if important to the cloud customer or required by regulation, is something that must be addressed by a contract, versus an SLA, to ensure compliance?

    A. Certifications

    B. Availability

    C. Incident management

    D. Elasticity

A. Certifications, based on industry and independent standards, are a primary means for a data center to ensure certain security controls and operational best practices are followed by a cloud provider. Certifications provide both the standards and best practices required for specific types of data or the classification of it, as well as requirements for regular audits and remediation for any deficiencies found from the audits. If certifications are required or desired, they must be documented and agreed to as part of the contract. Many cloud providers maintain a number of certifications by default to serve the needs of their customers, or the vast majority of their customers. Because a cloud provider is likely serving a large number of customers, it is unlikely that they will be willing to obtain any additional certifications required by specific cloud customers and will instead only offer the ones they have already obtained and maintain. Even if a cloud provider does currently have a certification that is desired or required by the cloud customer, it should still appear in the contract as a requirement to ensure the continued maintenance of the certification by the cloud provider.

B is incorrect because availability is an operational issue that would be addressed by SLA requirements instead of the contract.

C is incorrect because incident management, including its timing and process, is an operational issue that would be covered by the SLA and not the contract. The contract may require that an incident management process exist with the cloud provider, but the exact details and specific requirements of it would be contained within the SLA.

D is incorrect because elasticity would also be an operational issue covered by the SLA and not contained within the contract, with the exception of the contract possibly requiring the capability in general at a high level. The SLA would contain the exact requirements for elasticity and how it is to be implemented and controlled.

88. Which of the following aspects of the physical environment is considered an external redundancy issue?

    A. Generators

    B. Cooling chillers

    C. Power distribution units

    D. Storage systems

A. Generators are considered an external redundancy issue because they are outside the interior of the data center; they work on the incoming power feeds and their availability. They do not serve a redundancy capacity for power once it has entered within the data center itself, and they are independent of the data center.

B is incorrect because cooling chillers are contained within the interior of the data center and operate on systems within it. Although in some instances there may be external coolers that pump in cold air from the outside, in general they are considered internal.

C is incorrect because power distribution units (PDUs) are internal to the data center and provide power directly to the racks, actual systems, and other internal components of the data center. They receive power from the outside and operate on the interior, and as such, are an internal redundancy issue.

D is incorrect because storage systems are part of the actual systems and operations of the data center, and by definition are an internal redundancy issue. They are contained within the racks or on the floor of the actual data center, and they receive inputs of power and network after they pass into the data center and have gone through their own internal redundancy capabilities. Therefore, storage systems are near the end of the chain and are solely internal to the data center.

89. Which of the following methods is often used to obscure data from production systems for use in test or development environments?

    A. Tokenization

    B. Encryption

    C. Masking

    D. Classification

C. Masking involves replacing sensitive data fields with opaque and randomized values. It is particularly used for preparing production data for test or development environments, where the data is needed in the same format, but having connections to real users or sensitive data is not important. Unlike tokenization, masking does not have the ability to map the data back to the original values, which is why it is typically used for testing in nonproduction environments.

A is incorrect because tokenization involves replacing sensitive fields with opaque values while preserving the mappings back to the original data. It is a tactic typically used in live systems to protect sensitive data and retain the real mappings on another system. By using tokenization with test data, you are still exposing potential security risks in less secure environments because the mapping back to the original values is possible. Therefore, masking is more appropriate.

B is incorrect because encryption would not be used to prepare data for testing in nonproduction systems. It would be used for the transport or protection of data in a nonproduction environment in some cases, but once the data is there and loaded into the environment, encryption would not provide any protection and will still result in having sensitive or production data in a test or development environment.

D is incorrect because classification is the determining of security controls and categories for data and the degree of protection required. It would not play a role in the loading of production data into a nonproduction environment.

90. As part of an audit, systems and processes are tested to evaluate whether they are in compliance with regulatory or organizational policy requirements. What is the official term for determining any discrepancies between the real and desired states?

   A. Audit findings

   B. Gap analysis

   C. Audit deficiency

   D. Compliance analysis

B. A gap analysis is an official report on the differences and inconsistencies between the intended or required configurations and operations of a system or application and the reality of what is actually in place and in effect.

A is incorrect because *audit findings* is a common term used for the gap analysis by many in the industry, but it is not the official term used as part of the auditing process.

C is incorrect because *audit deficiency* is not a term used to refer to the concepts within a gap analysis.

D is incorrect because *compliance analysis* is not a term used to refer to what is officially known as gap analysis, nor is it a term used to refer to anything within the IT industry.

91. In a cloud environment, apart from confidentiality, what is the *MOST* important factor to consider with a key management system?

    A. Integrity

    B. Nonrepudiation

    C. Availability

    D. Archiving

C. Cloud-based systems and applications are heavily dependent on encryption for virtually all communications and storage systems. The confidentiality and protection of the keys are the most important factors in providing the security of data within the system. Beyond confidentiality, the availability of the key management system is vital for any applications and access to work in order to make data available. If the key management system becomes unavailable, it is impossible to access systems or their data, effectively shutting down all operations until access to the key management system can be restored.

A is incorrect because encryption is not designed or intended to provide integrity of systems or data. As such, confidentiality and availability of the key management system are the most important factors. However, integrity does come into play some with the key management system because any altering or corruption of keys will also render them useless, which is what makes backups and redundancy imperative as well.

B is incorrect because the important factor for encryption is having the correct set of keys. If you are in possession of the correct working keys, it is assumed that you have obtained them from an appropriate known source, because they would have been used to encrypt the data or communication initially. Thus, nonrepudiation is automatically provided because you can verify the keys are correct and from the correct source if you can successfully use them to decrypt the encrypted data.

D is incorrect because archiving is not an important factor in key management systems. Keys are only good as long as they are used to encrypt data or communications, and the long-term archiving of keys would be unnecessary if they are not currently used. There would be no reason to keep keys in archive format like there is for logs and other important data within systems and applications.

92. Which of the following top security threats involves attempting to send invalid commands to an application in an attempt to get the application to execute the code?

    A. Cross-site scripting

    B. Injection

    C. Insecure direct object references

    D. Cross-site request forgery

B. Injection involves sending invalid commands through input fields in an application with the intent of getting the application to execute the code and thus bypass many security controls that are in place. If an application does not properly validate input fields to ensure that they are in the correct format and do not contain extraneous code or commands, the application may expose data or configuration information to a malicious actor.

A is incorrect because cross-site scripting involves attempts to have the user's client or browser execute commands against a site. Because it is executed against the client side or browser, it is not a direct attempt to inject commands into the application. It is intended to have the user's browser access the application with their own credentials and bypass common security tactics such as same-origin policies.

C is incorrect because insecure direct object references involve the exposure of internal information or configurations that appear within the code and are viewable on the client side. This can include directory structures, filenames, configuration items, information about service accounts or credentials, or any other type of information that should not be exposed outside of the actual system hosting the application or services.

D is incorrect because cross-site forgery requests involve having a trusted client of an application or trusted user send unauthorized commands under their own credentials. They essentially involve leveraging a valid, trusted user's session and credentials to attack a site or application.

93. Which of the key aspects of security is concerned with ensuring information and data is in its intended format and has not been altered?

   A. Integrity

   B. Confidentiality

   C. Availability

   D. Privacy

A. Integrity is the main security principle concerned with data being in its intended form and accurate. This allows the data to be considered trustworthy throughout its entire lifecycle, ensuring that it has not been altered in an unauthorized manner or by an unauthorized party.

B is incorrect because confidentiality is concerned with ensuring that no one but authorized users are able to access or read data. It is not concerned with the content of the data in regard to the editing or manipulation of it.

C is incorrect because availability is the main security principle concerned with data being available to authorized parties as needed and in the form needed. It is not focused on the content of the data or the protection of it from unauthorized altering.

> **D** is incorrect because privacy is concerned with the confidentiality of personal data and ensuring that it is not viewed or accessed by anyone unauthorized to do so. Akin to confidentiality, privacy is not focused on the editing or manipulation of data.

94. Which of the following has user training as a primary means of combating and mitigating its success against a cloud application?

    A. Data breaches

    B. Account hijacking

    C. Advanced persistent threats

    D. Malicious insiders

> **C.** Advanced persistent threats involve a malicious actor establishing a presence within a system or application, with the goal of accessing information or resources over an extended period of time while avoiding detection. Some of the primary ways of establishing such a presence are through attacks such as phishing, infected USB devices, and social engineering attempts to get users to execute code on a system. One of the most effective ways to combat many of these types of attacks is through user education to avoid their successful execution and entry into a system. This should be coupled with other technological countermeasures as well.
>
> **A** is incorrect because data breaches are active exploits done by attackers that require policy and technological solutions to prevent. Overall, user training will not be an effective countermeasure for data breaches, with the exception of those that occur as a result of advanced persistent threats.
>
> **B** is incorrect because account hijacking is a major threat in which malicious actors are able to obtain credentials to access a system. Although training can be used to mitigate account hijacking, technological countermeasures are also very effective against it (unlike with advanced persistent threats). Countermeasures such as the use of multifactor authentication systems can effectively eliminate the hijacking of account credentials for accessing a system.
>
> **D** is incorrect because user training will not be an effective tool against malicious insiders. By nature, malicious insiders have decided to use their legitimate access for unauthorized purposes; therefore, training efforts will not be an effective mitigation.

95. You have been tasked with developing a list of requirements for cabling design in a new data center as well as ensuring that any designs developed by the networking team meet standards. Which standard should you consult?

    A. IDCA

    B. BICSI

C. Uptime Institute

D. NFPA

B. The Building Industry Consulting Service International (BICSI) issues standards and certifications related to complex cabling of data systems. The standards are focused on cabling setups and designs, but also include specifications on power, energy efficiency, and setup and configuration of hot and cold aisles within a data center.

A is incorrect because the International Datacenter Authority (IDCA) establishes standards for all aspects of data center design. While it does include some guidance on cabling design and implementation as part of its Infinity Paradigm, it is just one small section of their overall guidelines and not a focus of them. BICSI is a far more focused and comprehensive set of standards specific to cabling design.

C is incorrect because the Uptime Institute is focused on data center tiers and topologies. It establishes a paradigm of four tiers, with each tier building in more redundancy and reliable systems than the previous tier. It focuses on redundancy and reliability of all aspects of data centers and data center operations, as well as provides testing protocols for ensuring compliance with standards.

D is incorrect because the National Fire Protection Association (NFPA) issues guidelines for fire protection for any type of building or facility, not just data centers. Specific to a data center, the standards provide guidance for electrical wiring and emergency procedures for all systems within a data center.

96. Which network protocol is essential for allowing automation and orchestration within a cloud environment?

   A. DNSSEC

   B. DHCP

   C. IPsec

   D. VLANs

B. The Dynamic Host Configuration Protocol (DHCP) is designed to automatically provide an IP address and other crucial network information to hosts on a network, as well as to provide for the centralized management of their network presence. This differs from the traditional static approach where a host would have specific configuration entered into it, which would need to be changed individually and directly on the host if the need ever arose. With a cloud environment, where systems auto-scale and are dynamically optimized and moved around constantly, the static method would never work. With DHCP, it is trivial for new hosts to be enabled as well as for hosts to be moved between physical hardware programmatically and the network information to be easily updated and changed as necessary.

A is incorrect because DNSSEC is a protocol for ensuring the integrity of DNS resolutions and their validation back to an authoritative host. It does not offer any capabilities for providing network configuration information to hosts or assisting with the automation or orchestration of a dynamic environment.

C is incorrect because IPsec is a protocol that works along with IP communications and encrypts each packet of a session. It is used for point-to-point communications security and would not play any role in the automation or orchestration of systems within a cloud environment.

D is incorrect because VLANs are virtual network segments used to isolate devices by application, purpose, or environment; they assist with providing access controls and restrictions based on networking. While they are crucial to making a cloud environment work with security practices and regulatory requirements, VLANs are not essential or a part of the automation and orchestration of cloud services.

97. Which of the following tools has the ability to analyze incoming traffic for patterns and content and take appropriate actions based on them before the traffic reaches the actual applications?

   A. XML accelerator

   B. XML firewall

   C. Web application firewall

   D. Firewall

C. A web application firewall (WAF) is typically an appliance that inspects HTTP traffic before it hits an application server and has the ability to apply a set of filters and rules to it. A WAF will typically be used to detect and block XSS and injection attempts before they hit the actual application, but it also has the ability to detect and manipulate almost anything that is found in an HTTP communication stream. A WAF can also be used to block specific traffic based on originating IP address, type of request, or virtually any other aspect of the request.

A is incorrect because an XML accelerator is intended to process XML traffic and data packages before they reach an application server. This allows a highly optimized appliance to offload substantial processing requirements and load from application servers, and it allows for faster and more efficient processing of requests and data.

B is incorrect because an XML firewall serves the purpose of inspecting incoming XML traffic and applying security policies and processing to determine if it is legitimate and should be allowed to reach the application servers. While it serves a similar functionality to a WAF, it is focused solely on the processing of XML data and not on general processing of HTTP requests and communications.

D is incorrect because firewalls are network appliances and work solely on network layer traffic, applying rules based on ports, protocols, and IP source and destinations. Firewalls are not capable of inspecting packets at the application layer or applying rules to such packets.

98. The ISO/IEC 27018 standard focuses on privacy in cloud computing and consists of five main principles. Which of the following is *NOT* one of the principles established in the standard?

    A. Communication

    B. Consent

    C. Yearly audit

    D. Penalties for privacy violations

    D. ISO/IEC in general are standards based on IT policies and best practices. They are done at a higher level, so they are flexible for a variety of diverse systems and requirements, and they serve as a strong framework for implementing regulatory or organizational policies and requirements. As such, they do not articulate or cover potential penalties, either civil or criminal, that could be triggered in the event of privacy policy violations. Penalties can differ widely from jurisdiction to jurisdiction, and the applicable regulations in each jurisdiction would be where any potential penalties are covered.

    A is incorrect because communication to individuals about the use and storage of their personal information is a crucial component of the standard. Many regulatory requirements specifically articulate communication and transparency to their customers about their personal data and privacy, and it has been incorporated as a key component in most of the best practices systems as well.

    B is incorrect because consent to use or store private and personal information is also a key component of the standard as well as many regulatory systems. While it is imperative to properly communicate and inform users and customers as to which of their data you will use, collect, or keep, it is also imperative to get their informed consent to do so under most regulatory systems.

    C is incorrect because, as with any regulation or standard practice, the main mechanism for the validation and compliance enforcement is through the audit process.

99. Which of the following concepts of cloud computing necessitates the logical separation of systems that would normally be done by physical separation in a traditional data center?

    A. Resource pooling

    B. Multitenancy

C. Elasticity

D. Measured service

B. Multitenancy is the concept of having multiple customers sharing the same physical infrastructure and systems. With a traditional data center model, different customers use their own dedicated and segregated physical hardware, typically within their own cages and with totally separate networking cabling and hardware as well. With a cloud deployment, all customers share the same physical hardware, thus requiring the use of logical segregation to ensure security.

A is incorrect because resource pooling does not deal with the segregation or isolation of resources and access without a shared environment. Resource pooling is the aggregation and allocation of compute resources across all customers.

C is incorrect because elasticity refers to the ability of a system to scale up or down based on current demands, and to ensure that at any given point a system or application has the exact resources it needs. This is done to eliminate having an excess or deficit of resources at any time, and so that customers are paying for exactly what they need and are consuming.

D is incorrect because measured service refers to the concept within cloud computing where the cloud customer only pays for those services they use. It does not relate to any technical capabilities or the segregation of services within the environment.

100. Which common threat is mitigated by the use of DNSSEC?

A. Spoofing

B. Snooping

C. XSS

D. DDoS

A. DNSSEC is explicitly designed to prove the validity and authenticity of DNS lookups from their authoritative host. It is intended to eliminate the possibility of rogue DNS servers intercepting lookup requests from devices or clients and inserting incorrect IP address resolutions in an attempt to direct traffic away from the legitimate destination. DNSSEC works by applying digital keys to the authoritative DNS host and then signing lookup and resolution requests when sending them back to the requestor. With the ability to authenticate those keys back to the authoritative host, trust is established that the DNS resolutions are correct and from the proper authority, and not inserted by a rouge or malicious host. DNSSEC ensures the integrity of DNS resolutions, but not the confidentiality or availability of them. It also is intended to work without requiring additional lookups when making the initial DNS request, instead sending back all required information from a single query.

B is incorrect because DNSSEC is only designed to ensure the integrity of DNS resolutions; it will not provide any encryption or protection for the confidentiality of data communications or connections. Once the DNS lookup has been completed and the results validated by the requestor, the role of DNSSEC ends, and another technology such as TLS or IPsec would need to be leveraged to ensure confidentiality and prevent the snooping of communications and data transfers.

C is incorrect because cross-site scripting is a potential application and client vulnerability, and the lookup and integrity of DNS resolutions that DNSSEC is intended to provide would not be a factor or tool used to mitigate or prevent it.

D is incorrect because distributed denial-of-service (DDoS) attacks are threats to a system or application in the area of availability. DNSSEC is just intended to mitigate against integrity attacks and threats, so it would be of no use in the mitigation against a DDoS attack.

About the CD-ROM

The CD-ROM included with this book comes complete with Total Tester customizable practice exam software with more than 300 practice exam questions and a secured PDF copy of the book.

System Requirements

The software requires Windows Vista or higher and 30MB of hard disk space for full installation, in addition to a current or prior major release of Chrome, Firefox, Internet Explorer, or Safari. To run, the screen resolution must be set to 1024 × 768 or higher. The secured book PDF requires Adobe Acrobat, Adobe Reader, or Adobe Digital Editions to view.

Installing and Running Total Tester Premium Practice Exam Software

From the main screen you may install the Total Tester by clicking the Total Tester Practice Exams button. This will begin the installation process and place an icon on your desktop and in your Start menu. To run Total Tester, navigate to Start | (All) Programs | Total Seminars, or double-click the icon on your desktop.

To uninstall the Total Tester software, go to Start | Control Panel | Programs And Features, and then select the Total Tester program. Select Remove, and Windows will completely uninstall the software.

Total Tester Premium Practice Exam Software

Total Tester provides you with a simulation of the CCSP exam. Exams can be taken in Practice Mode, Exam Mode, or Custom Mode. Practice Mode provides an assistance window with hints, references to the book, explanations of the correct and incorrect answers, and the option to check your answer as you take the test. Exam Mode provides a simulation of the actual exam. The number of questions, the types of questions, and the time allowed are intended to be an accurate representation of the exam environment.

Custom Mode allows you to create custom exams from selected domains or chapters, and you can further customize the number of questions and time allowed.

To take a test, launch the program and select CCSP from the Installed Question Packs list. You can then select Practice Mode, Exam Mode, or Custom Mode. All exams provide an overall grade and a grade broken down by domain.

Secured Book PDF

The entire contents of the book are provided in secured PDF format on the CD-ROM. This file is viewable on your computer and many portable devices.

- **To view the PDF on a computer**, Adobe Acrobat, Adobe Reader, or Adobe Digital Editions is required. A link to Adobe's website, where you can download and install Adobe Reader, has been included on the CD-ROM.

 NOTE For more information on Adobe Reader and to check for the most recent version of the software, visit Adobe's website at www.adobe.com and search for the free Adobe Reader or look for Adobe Reader on the product page. Adobe Digital Editions can also be downloaded from the Adobe website.

- **To view the book PDF on a portable device**, copy the PDF file to your computer from the CD-ROM and then copy the file to your portable device using a USB or other connection. Adobe offers a mobile version of Adobe Reader, the Adobe Reader mobile app, which currently supports iOS and Android. For customers using Adobe Digital Editions and an iPad, you may have to download and install a separate reader program on your device. The Adobe website has a list of recommended applications, and McGraw-Hill Education recommends the Bluefire Reader.

Technical Support

For questions regarding the Total Tester software or operation of the CD-ROM, visit **www.totalsem.com** or e-mail **support@totalsem.com**.

For questions regarding the secured book PDF, visit **http://mhp.softwareassist.com** or e-mail **techsolutions@mhedu.com**.

For questions regarding book content, e-mail **hep_customer-service@mheducation .com**. For customers outside the United States, e-mail **international_cs@mheducation .com**.

ALE (annualized loss expectancy)   The value derived by multiplying the single loss expectancy (SLE) by the annualized rate of occurrence (ARO). Thus, ALE = SLE × ARO.

application programming interface (API)   A set of functions, routines, tools, or protocols for building applications. An API allows for interaction between systems and applications that can be leveraged by developers as building blocks for their applications and data access through a common method, without custom coding for each integration.

ARO (annualized rate of occurrence)   An estimated number of the times a threat will successfully exploit a given vulnerability over the course of a single year.

auditability   The ability to properly capture, analyze, and report on any and all events that happen within a system or application, such as data access and modification, user actions and processes, controls and compliance, and regulatory and contractual compliance.

authentication   The process of evaluating credentials presented by a user, application, or service to prove its identity as compared to values already known and verified by the authentication system.

authorization   The process of granting or denying access to a system, network, or application after successful authentication has been performed, based on approved criteria set by policy or regulation.

backdoor   A means or method of accessing a system or application while bypassing the typical and required authentication and authorization methods. Backdoors can be unauthorized methods that are discovered by malicious actors to get into a system, or they can be methods that are purposefully employed by developers or support staff to access systems for maintenance or other support activities (although this is not recommended, because such backdoors can also be leveraged for malicious reasons). Backdoors can be created by either developers or hackers.

baseline   A baseline is part of the change management process, which establishes an agreed-upon standard configuration and the attributes that comprise it, and forms the basis for managing change from that point forward.

Big Data   Refers to the collection, processing, and analysis of data sets that are so large that traditional data processing and analysis tools are inadequate to properly handle them. The concept of "Big Data" is often applied in regard to predictive analysis and user analytics of data sets rather than referring to a specific size of the data involved.

Bring Your Own Device (BYOD) The practice of allowing employees of an organization to use their own computers, phones, tablets, or other electronic resources to access official computing resources, rather than using provided and supported devices.

business continuity The capability of an organization to continue the operation of systems or applications at a determined level after an incident or a disruption of service.

business continuity management A process that is designed to identify risks, threats, and vulnerabilities that could disrupt or impact services, with the intent on determining mitigation strategies and response processes should they occur.

business continuity plan A developed and tested document, containing information from stakeholders and staff, for the continuation of operations and services in the event of a disruption or incident.

business impact analysis (BIA) A structured methodology to identify and evaluate the possible risks and threats that operations or services could be impacted by, as well as the possible or likely extent of impact and disruption.

chain of custody The formal documentation showing the chronological control and disposition of data or evidence, either physical or electronic. This documentation includes creation, all changes of possession, and final disposition. It is absolutely essential to maintain the integrity of evidence and admissibility in legal proceedings.

change advisory board (CAB) A group that assists the change team and change management process by evaluating, prioritizing, and approving change requests.

change manager An individual in a role with the change management process that ensures the overall change process is properly executed. This person also directly handles low-level tasks related to the change process.

cloud application An application that is never installed on a local server or desktop but is instead accessed via a network or the Internet. A cloud application merges the functionality of a local application with the accessibility of a web-based application.

Cloud Application Management for Platforms (CAMP) Within a PaaS implementation, CAMP serves as the framework and specification for managing platform services, encompassing a RESTful protocol for managing services; the model for describing and documenting the components that comprise the platform; and the language describing the overall platform and its components and services, as well as metadata about it.

cloud auditor An auditor that is specifically responsible for conducting audits of cloud systems and cloud applications. The cloud auditor is responsible for assessing the effectiveness of the cloud service and identifying control deficiencies between the cloud customer and the cloud provider, as well as the cloud broker if one is used.

cloud backup The process of using a cloud-based backup system, with files and data being sent over the network to a public or private cloud provider for backup, rather than running traditional backup systems within a data center.

cloud backup service provider A public or private cloud services organization that offers backup services to either the public or organizational clients, either on a free basis or using various costing models based on either amount of data or number of systems.

cloud backup solutions Services that run within a public or private cloud offering backup solutions, either through client-based software that does automatic or scheduled backups or through manual backups initiated by a user or system.

cloud computing A model for enabling ubiquitous, convenient, on-demand network access to a shared pool of configurable computer resources (for example, networks, servers, storage, applications, and services) that can be rapidly provisioned and released with minimal management effort or service provider interaction. This cloud model is composed of five essential characteristics, three service models, and four deployment models.

cloud computing reseller An organization that sells and offers cloud services, and possibly cloud support services, to various organizations and works as a middleman between the cloud customer and cloud provider.

Cloud Controls Matrix (CCM) A formally published guide by the Cloud Security Alliance that enables cloud customers to evaluate a prospective cloud provider in regard to their security posture. It also allows a cloud provider to structure their security approach.

cloud customer An organization or individual that utilizes and consumes resources and services from a cloud provider. This can be in the form of free public services and systems or private and fee-based applications or solutions.

cloud data portability The ability to move data between cloud providers.

cloud database A database that is installed in a cloud environment and accessed via the network or the Internet by a user or application. By the database being installed in a cloud environment instead of a typical server environment, elasticity, scalability, and high availability can be achieved and maximized.

cloud deployment model How cloud computing is delivered through a set of particular configurations and features of virtual resources. The cloud deployment models are public, private, hybrid, and community.

cloud enablement The creation of a public cloud environment through the offering of services or infrastructure.

cloud management The oversight and operations management of a cloud environment by the cloud service provider, whether it is a public or private cloud environment.

cloud migration The process of moving services, systems, applications, or data from a traditional data-center hosting model into a cloud environment.

cloud OS (operating system)   Typically used to denote an operating system in a Platform as a Service (PaaS) implementation and signify the implementation within a could environment.

cloud provider   A service provider that makes storage or software applications available via the Internet or private networks to customers. Since they are offered as a service, the platform and underlying software, as well as operations and security systems, are maintained by the provider and abstracted from the customers.

cloud provisioning   The process of allocating cloud resources from the cloud provider to the cloud customers based on specific requests and requirements of the customers as far as the number of virtual machines and their specific computing resources.

Cloud Security Alliance (CSA)   The most prominent and well-known organization to raise awareness of best practices for security within a cloud environment.

cloud server hosting   The hosting and location of servers within a virtualized cloud environment, rather than the virtual or physical hosting that's done in a traditional data center.

cloud service   Capabilities offered via a cloud provider and accessible via a client.

cloud service broker   A partner that servers as an intermediary between a cloud service customer and cloud service provider.

cloud service category   A group of cloud services that have a common set of features or qualities.

cloud service partner   One that holds a relationship with either a cloud service provider or a cloud service customer to assist with cloud services and their delivery.

cloud service user   One that interacts with and consumes services offered by a cloud service provider.

cloud testing   The testing of systems, services, or applications by leveraging cloud platforms and resources to simulate the size and scale of real-world traffic and users.

Common Criteria   A set of international guidelines and specifications for the evaluation of IT security resources to ensure they meet an agreed-upon set of security standards, specifically focused on government computing and security needs and requirements. The Common Criteria for Information Technology Security Evaluation is formalized as an international standard in ISO/IEC 15408.

community cloud   A cloud infrastructure provisioned for exclusive use by a specific community of consumers from organizations that have shared concerns (for example, mission, security requirements, policy, or compliance considerations). It may be owned, managed, and operated by one or more of the organizations in the community, a third party, or some combination of these, and it may exist on or off premises.

configuration management Establishing a controlled means of consistency throughout a system's lifecycle, based on its requirements and technical specifications, to properly ensure configuration controls, performance standards, and design requirements.

cross-site scripting (XSS) A very common type of security vulnerability found with web applications, where an attacker can inject client-side scripts into web pages that are then viewed and executed by other users. The goal of XSS from an attacker's perspective is to bypass the security controls of an application such as an access control with a same-origin policy.

data at rest (DAR) Data that resides on a system in persistent storage, such as disks, tapes, databases, or any other type of storage device.

data in transit (DIT) Data that flows over a networked connection, either through public unsecured networks or internal protected corporate networks.

data in use (DIU) Data within a system or application that is currently being processed or is in use, either through the computing resources or residing in memory.

data loss prevention (DLP) An overall strategy and process for ensuring that users cannot send sensitive or protected information outside of networks or systems that are secured and protected. This can be related to the intentional attempt by users to transfer such information, but it also applies to preventing the accidental sending or leakage of data.

data portability The ability to easily move data from one system to another without having to re-enter it.

denial-of-service (DoS) attack An attempt to make computing resources or a network unavailable to its intended users by denying legitimate traffic access totally or by degrading performance to unacceptable levels.

direct identifiers Information that specifically applies to a unique individual, such as name, address, phone number, e-mail address, or unique identifying numbers or codes.

Distributed Resource Scheduler (DRS) A utility from VMware that balances computing demands and available resources within the virtualized environment.

dynamic application security testing (DAST) The testing of an application while it is in an operational state with currently running systems, applications, and networks.

dynamic optimization (DO) The process of moving and reallocating virtual machines and resources within a cluster environment to maintain optimal performance with balanced and distributed resource utilization.

eDiscovery The process for a criminal or civil legal case where electronic data is determined, located, and secured to be used as evidence.

encryption The process of encoding and securing data so that only authorized parties in possession of the correct information, credentials, or keys can access it.

enterprise application An application that runs on a large and distributed scale and is deemed mission critical to a company or organization.

enterprise cloud backup A cloud-based backup and recovery service that is related to and similar to those offered for personal use, but scaled and focused on large-scale and organizational-level services.

Eucalyptus Free and open source software for utilizing Amazon Web Services (AWS) to build public and private cloud offerings. The use of the word "eucalyptus" is intended as an acronym for Elastic Utility Computing Architecture for Linking Your Programs to Useful Systems.

event An action or situation that is recognized by software that then causes some action or response by the software to be taken.

Federal Rules of Civil Procedure (FRCP) The set of rules and procedures that govern civil legal proceedings in the United States federal courts to provide uniformity and efficiency in resolving legal matters and proceedings.

Federal Rules of Evidence (FRE) The set of rules that apply to United States federal courts for collecting evidence in a uniform and official manner.

federation A group of IT service providers that interoperate based on an agreed-upon set of standards and operations.

FIPS 140-2 A security standard published by the United States federal government that pertains to the accreditation of cryptographic modules.

firewall A part of a computing network provided by either hardware or software implementations that controls which network connections are allowed to be made in regard to origin, destination, and ports, while blocking all other inbound or outbound connections.

HIDS (host intrusion detection system) A host-based intrusion detection system that monitors the internal resources of a system for malicious attempts, as well as potentially packet inspection and network monitoring.

host A computer that is connected to a network and provides computing services to either users or other hosts on the network.

hybrid cloud A cloud infrastructure that's a composition of two or more distinct cloud infrastructures (private, community, or public) that remain unique entities but are bound together by standardized or proprietary technology that enables data and application portability (for example, cloud bursting for load balancing between clouds).

hypervisor A virtual machine manager that allows and enables multiple virtual hosts to reside on the same physical host.

identity provider (IdP)   A system responsible for determining the authenticity of a user or system, providing assurance to a service that the identity is valid and known, and possibly providing additional information about the identity of the user or system to the service provider requesting it.

IDS (intrusion detection system)   A device, appliance, or software implementation that monitors servers, systems, or networks for malicious activities.

incident   An event that could potentially cause a disruption to an organization's systems, services, or applications.

indirect identifiers   Information about an entity that cannot be used solely to identify that entity uniquely, but can be used in combination to potentially do so. Examples include place of birth, race, employment history, and educational history.

information rights management (IRM)   A subset of digital rights management that is focused on protecting sensitive information from unauthorized exposure or use.

Infrastructure as a Service (IaaS)   The capability provided to a consumer to provision processing, storage, networks, and other fundamental computing resources in order to deploy and run arbitrary software, including operating systems and applications. The consumer does not manage or control the underlying cloud infrastructure but has control over operating systems, storage, and deployed applications—and possibly limited control of select networking components such as host firewalls.

interoperability   The ease and ability to reuse components of a system or application regardless of underlying system design and provider.

IPS (intrusion prevention system)   A network-based appliance or software that examines network traffic for known exploits, or attempts to use exploits, and actively stops them or blocks attempts.

ISO/IEC 27001 and 27001:2013   A formal specification for information security management systems that provides, through completion of a formal audit, certification from an accredited body for compliance. ISO/IEC 27001:2013 is the latest revision.

IT Infrastructure Library (ITIL)   A collection of papers and concepts that lays out a vision for an IT Service Management (ITSM) framework for IT services and user support.

jurisdiction   The authority to exert regulatory and legal control over a defined area of responsibility. Jurisdictions can overlap between the local, state/province, and national levels.

Key Management Service (KMS)   A system or service that manages keys used for encryption within a system or application that is separate from the actual host systems. The KMS will typical generate, secure, and validate keys.

key performance indicator (KPI)   A metric that provides a quantitative value that can be used to evaluate how effectively key business requirements are being met.

malware   A broad term that encompasses software, scripts, content, and executable code that takes the form of viruses, Trojan horses, ransomware, spyware, and other malicious programs that intend to steal information or computing resources.

managed service provider   A provider of IT services where the technology, software, and operations are determined and managed away from the customer or user.

mean time between failures (MTBF)   A measure, typically in hours, of what the average time between failures is for a hardware component to determine its reliability.

mean time to repair (MTTR)   A measure for hardware components of the typical or average time to repair and recover after a failure.

measured service   Cloud services that are delivered and billed for in a metered way.

metadata   Data that gives additional or descriptive information about other data. This can be in the form of structural data that pertains to how the information is stored and represented, or descriptive data that contains information about the actual content of the data.

mobile cloud storage   Cloud-based storage, typically used for mobile devices such as tablets, phones, and laptops, that enables the user to access their data from any network location and across multiple devices in a uniform way.

multitenancy   Having multiple customers and applications running within the same environment but in a way that they are isolated from each other and not visible to each other, while still sharing the same resources.

NIDS (network intrusion detection system)   A network-based device placed at strategic places on a network to monitor and analyze all network traffic traversing the subnet and comparing it against signatures for known vulnerabilities and attacks.

NIST SP 800-53   Titled "Security and Privacy Controls for Federal Information Systems and Organizations," NIST SP 800-53 provides a set of security controls for all systems under the United States federal government, with the exception of systems dedicated to national security.

nonrepudiation   The ability to confirm the origin or authenticity of data to a high degree of certainty.

object storage   A storage method used with IaaS where data elements are managed as objects rather than in hierarchical storage with a file system and directory structure.

on-demand self-service   The ability for a cloud customer to provision services in an automatic manner, when needed, with minimal involvement from the cloud provider.

Open Group Architecture Framework, The (TOGOF)   An open enterprise architecture model that is intended to be a high-level approach that design teams can use to optimize success, efficiency, and returns throughout a system's lifecycle.

operational level agreement (OLA)   An official ITIL term that relates to a specialized service level agreement (SLA) pertaining to internal parties of an organization, rather than between a customer and provider.

overwriting   The process of securely removing data from a system by writing blocks of random or opaque data on storage media to destroy any previous data and make it unrecoverable.

pen (penetration) testing   The process of testing systems and applications for vulnerabilities and weaknesses by employing the same tools and strategies as malicious actors. Any exploits discovered can then be proactively addressed by the organization before a malicious actor can discover them.

Platform as a Service (PaaS)   The capability provided to the customer to deploy onto the cloud infrastructure any consumer-created or acquired applications written using programming languages, libraries, services, and tools supported by the provider. The customer does not manage or control the underlying cloud infrastructure, including the network, servers, operating systems, and storage, but has control over the deployed applications and possibly configuration settings for the application-hosting environment.

portability   The ability for a system or application to seamlessly and easily move between different cloud providers.

privacy level agreement (PLA)   A declaration published by the cloud service provider documenting their approach to data privacy. The cloud service provider implements and maintains the PLA for systems hosted with them.

private cloud   A cloud infrastructure provisioned for exclusive use by a single organization comprising multiple consumers (for example, business units). It may be owned, managed, and operated by the organization, a third party, or some combination thereof, and it may exist on or off premises.

protected health information (PHI)   A special designation of data under United States law that encompasses any health-related data that can be tied to an individual, including health status, healthcare service sought or provided, or any payment related to healthcare.

public cloud   A cloud infrastructure provisioned for open use by the general public. It may be owned, managed, and operated by a business, academic organization, or governmental organization, or some combination thereof. It exists on the premises of the cloud provider.

recovery point objective (RPO)   A duration of time in the past that an organization is willing to revert to in order to restore lost data or services following an interruption.

recovery time objective (RTO)   A defined maximum time duration for which an organization can accept the loss of data or services following an interruption.

relying party   A system or application that provides access to secure data through the use of an identity provider.

Representational State Transfer (REST)   A system for designing and implementing networked applications by utilizing a stateless, cacheable, client-server protocol, almost always via HTTP.

request for change (RFC)   A key component of the change management process that involves a formal documented change request, including what change is needed, why it is needed, the urgency of the change, and the impact if the change is not made.

resource pooling   The aggregation and allocation of resources from the cloud provider to serve the cloud customers.

reversibility   The ability of a cloud customer to recover all data and applications from a cloud provider and completely remove all data from the cloud provider's environment.

runtime application self-protection (RASP)   Security technology and systems integrated into a system or application that enables it to detect and prevent attacks in real time.

sandboxing   The segregation and isolation of information or processes from others within the same system or application, typically for security concerns.

service   A computing system or application that processes data.

service level agreement (SLA)   A document agreed upon between a customer and a service provider that defines and maps out minimum performance standards for a variety of contract requirements. An SLA typically includes minimum standards for processes, uptime, availability, security, auditing, reporting, customer service, and potentially many other requirements.

service provider (SP)   An organization that provides IT services and applications to other organizations in a sourced manner.

Sherwood Applied Business Security Architecture (SABSA)   SABSA is a proven methodology for developing business-driven, risk- and opportunity-focused security architectures, at both the enterprise and solutions level, that traceably support business objectives. It is widely used for information assurance architectures and risk management frameworks, as well as to align and seamlessly integrate security and risk management into IT architecture methods and frameworks. SABSA is composed of a series of integrated frameworks, models, methods, and processes, and can be used independently or as a holistic integrated enterprise solution.

Simple Object Access Protocol (SOAP)   A messaging protocol that is operating system agnostic and used to communicate with other systems through HTTP and XML.

SLE (single loss expectancy)   The monetary value assigned to the occurrence of a single instance of risk or exploit to an IT service, application, or system.

SOA (Service-Oriented Architecture)   A system of providing IT applications and data service to other components through communications protocols over a network, independent of any particular technology, system, provider, or implementation.

SOC 1/SOC 2/SOC 3   Audit and accounting reports, focused on an organization's controls, that are employed when providing secure services to users.

Software as a Service (SaaS)   The capability provided to the customer to use the provider's applications running on a cloud infrastructure. The applications are accessible from various client devices through either a thin client interface, such as a web browser (for example, web-based email), or a program interface. The consumer does not manage or control the underlying cloud infrastructure, including the network, servers, operating systems, storage, and even individual application capabilities, with the possible exception of limited user-specific application settings.

software-defined networking (SDN)   An approach to separate the network configurations for the control plane and the data plane. This allows an abstraction for network administrators to configure and control those aspects of the network important to modern systems and applications without having to get involved with the actual mechanisms for forwarding network traffic.

SQL injection   A method used by malicious actors to insert SQL statements into a data-driven application in various input fields, attempting to get the application to access arbitrary code and return the results to the attacker. This could include attempts to access a full database or protected data within it, or to modify or delete data.

static application security testing (SAST)   Security testing of applications by an analysis of source code, binaries, and configurations. This is done by testers who have in-depth knowledge of systems and applications, and is performed in a nonrunning state.

tenant   One or more cloud customers who share access to a pool of resources.

tokenization   The process of replacing and substituting secured or sensitive data in a data set with an abstract or opaque value that has no use outside of the application.

Trojan   An attempt to trick a user or administrator into executing an attack by disguising the true intention of a program or application.

trust zones   A security concept of separating systems and data into different levels or zones and applying security methods and practices to each zone, based on the requirements of that particular group of systems. In many instances, zones of a higher degree of trust may access those with a lower degree, but not vice versa.

underpinning contract (UC)   A contract negotiated and agreed upon between an organization and an external service provider or vendor.

vertical cloud computing   The optimization of cloud computing resources for a particular stack or vertical, such as a specific type of application or system, or by a particular industry sector or need.

virtual host or virtual machine   A computing environment that is a software implementation running on a host system versus a physical hardware environment.

VM-based rootkit (VMBR)   A type of rootkit that is installed in a virtualized environment between the underlying host system and the virtual machine. It is then executed and used when the virtual machine is started. A VM-based rootkit is very difficult to detect in an environment, but also very difficult to successfully implement.

volume storage   A more typical or standard file system used with IaaS that provides a virtual partition or hard disk to a virtual machine and can be used as a traditional hard drive would be, with a file system, folders, and file organization methods.

web application firewall (WAF)   An appliance or software plug-in that parses and filters HTTP traffic from a browser or client, and applies a set of rules before the traffic is allowed to proceed to the actual application server.

web portal   A web-based application that provides tools, reporting, and visibility for a user into multiple systems. In a cloud environment, a web portal provides metrics and service capabilities to add or expand for the customer to consume.

XML appliance   An appliance that is implemented within a network to secure and manage XML traffic. It is particularly used within a cloud environment to help integrate cloud-based systems with those still residing in traditional data centers.

INDEX